D1020742

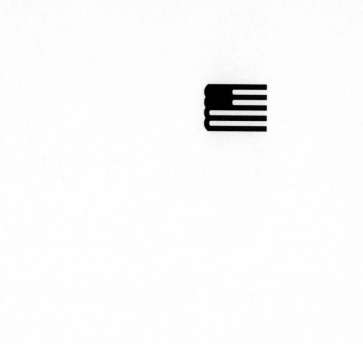

BATTLE

FOR

OUR MINDS

Western Elites and the Terror Threat

MICHAEL WIDLANSKI

THRESHOLD EDITIONS

NEW YORK   LONDON   TORONTO   SYDNEY   NEW DELHI

Threshold Editions
A Division of Simon & Schuster, Inc.
1230 Avenue of the Americas
New York, NY 10020

Copyright © 2012 by Michael Widlanski

All rights reserved, including the right to reproduce this book or portions thereof in any form whatsoever. For information, address Threshold Editions Subsidiary Rights Department, 1230 Avenue of the Americas, New York, NY 10020.

First Threshold Editions hardcover edition March 2012

THRESHOLD EDITIONS and colophon are trademarks of Simon & Schuster, Inc.

For information about special discounts for bulk purchases, please contact Simon & Schuster Special Sales at 1-866-506-1949 or business@simonandschuster.com.

The Simon & Schuster Speakers Bureau can bring authors to your live event. For more information or to book an event, contact the Simon & Schuster Speakers Bureau at 1-866-248-3049 or visit our website at www.simonspeakers.com.

Designed by Ruth Lee-Mui

Manufactured in the United States of America

1   3   5   7   9   10   8   6   4   2

Library of Congress Cataloging-in-Publication Data

Widlanski, Michael.
Battle for our minds : How western elites undermine the fight against terror / Michael Widlanski.
p. cm.
1. Terrorism—Psychological aspects. 2. Terrorism and mass media. 3. Intelligence service.
4. Terrorism—United States—Psychological aspects. 5. Terrorism and mass media—United States.
6. Intelligence service—United States. I. Title.
HV6431.W517 2012
363.3250973—dc23
2011027974
ISBN 978-1-4516-5903-0
ISBN 978-1-4516-5905-4 (ebook)

CONTENTS

INTRODUCTION

Osama bin-Laden's much-deserved death came much too late.

If bin-Laden had been killed or arrested in 1994, 1996, or 1998, many lives would have been saved. His Al-Qaeda terror network would *not* have become a symbol, a banner, and a clarion call for anti-Western terror. Cutting off the head of the terror snake is what is called "the decapitation option." It is a good option, but decapitation delayed is often decapitation denied. Before his death, bin-Laden spawned more snakes and passed on his poisonous mission to others.

After the major terror attacks of September 11, 2001—what we call 9/11—it was probably too late to stop the inspirational success of Al-Qaeda. Had bin-Laden been killed in Tora Bora, Afghanistan, in November 2001, it might still have been possible to suppress part of the poison bin-Laden unleashed. Sadly, this did not happen.

This does not mean that killing bin-Laden was mere headline hunting. The U.S. military and President Barack Obama deserve to be commended for their actions. Killing bin-Laden was necessary, morally and strategically, but it is not enough. This one successful anti-terror operation does not wipe away all the errors, inefficiency, and lack of imagination shown for years in the West's effort to counter terrorism.

Inspire is the Al-Qaeda online magazine in English, used to enlist more terrorists. The name *Inspire* shows Osama bin-Laden's long-term purpose. He did not expect to defeat the United States, Britain, and "corrupt" pro-Western Arab regimes all by himself.

Bin-Laden wanted to inspire copycat killers. Al-Qaeda and its imitators have carried out many major attacks since 9/11—from London and Madrid to Mumbai, Bali, and Sinai. Scores of smaller attacks or abortive major attacks were aimed at Paris; London; Los Angeles; New York's Times Square; Fort Hood, Texas; Little Rock, Arkansas; Washington, D.C.; Chicago; and Detroit.[1] FBI director Robert Mueller told Congress in September 2009 that terror plots had come to consume his daily schedule: "I do not remember a time when these types of loose networks were not a part of my morning briefing."[2]

We simply do not know how many more new terror groups and lone-wolf terrorists there might be, nor how many sleeper cells Al-Qaeda has pumped into the pipeline. Already we have seen disturbing changes. The 9/11 mass murderers were all Saudi or Egyptians: Muslim Arabs from the heart of the Arab-Islamic world. But since 9/11 the terrorists have been reinforced by second-generation Muslims born in the United States or Britain, such as Major Nidal Malik Hasan, who killed thirteen in Fort Hood. In addition, many non-Muslims have enlisted and converted to radical Islamic ideology inside mosques, the army, or even jails, an example being Richard Reid, the British "shoe bomber."

This adds a new factor of "homegrown terror" to the previous terror equation, making it more complex, more difficult, and more dangerous than before 9/11. Yet many Western elites—academia, government officials, and media—have slid back to the pre-9/11 complacency. "Like all fads, this one too shall pass," observed one expert, heaping scorn on recent congressional hearings examining Islamic radicalization in the United States.[3] Such comments minimize the threat from Arab-Islamic terror. Several Obama administration officials, for example, prefer to warn about "overreaction," anti-Islamic hate crimes, and "hysteria," even though no such phenomena exist.[4] Indeed, President Obama has said he would rather absorb another terror attack than overreact to terror: "We can absorb a terrorist attack. We'll do everything we can to prevent it, but even a 9/11, even the biggest attack ever . . . we absorbed it and we are stronger."[5]

Careful not to "overreact" to the terror threat, President Obama is unwilling or unable to utter certain terms: "radical Islam," "Islamic terror," "Arab terror," or "Islamic extremism." Obama and his advisors evade or minimize Arab-Islamic terror acts as if they were part of a Harry Potter fantasy novel, where the evil force is "He Who Shall Not Be Named." They are not alone. A leading U.S. newspaper asserts that the Islamic bombers merely got lucky on 9/11, but *those* terrorists have been succeeded by a new generation of inept bunglers who are no real threat.[6]

Sadly, terror today is not a mere flight of fantasy. This book describes the fight against terrorism as a battle of the mind that requires awareness and intelligence. This book cites the names of officials, media pundits, and academics who have hindered the battle against Arab-Islamic terror—and who continue to obstruct this battle. This book explains why and how the media-government-academia discourse on terror seriously cripples our ability to fight Arab-Islamic terror, because if we cannot name or describe our fear, we cannot overcome it. If we cannot name or describe our terrorist enemies, we cannot hope to defeat them.

Yes, Osama bin-Laden has been killed, but a real threat still lives, and it long since moved beyond Al-Qaeda to inhabit larger sections of the population. Evidence at several congressional hearings indicates that many mosques and Islamic "charity" institutions in the United States have been radicalized—as happened earlier in Islamic communities in Britain and France. Still, the Obama administration has acted and spoken as if the danger of terror has been exaggerated. Faced with terror attacks and abortive plots, President Obama, counterterror chief John Brennan, Secretary of Homeland Security Janet Napolitano, and others speak of "man-made disasters," or "the actions of a lone gunman."

Obama and like-minded elites in the media, academia, and think tanks scoff at thoughts of "Islamic extremism" or "Islamic terror." They prefer not even to say those words. When pressed, they say the danger of terror, and the battle with terror, must be confined only to Al-Qaeda, as if one group, one leader, is the whole problem. This is a narrow approach based on wishful thinking and lack of imagination: those are the worst enemies of good analysis and proper readiness. The biggest factor in America's lack of readiness on September 11, 2001, was a lack of imagination, according to the National Commission on Terrorist Attacks

Upon the United States, known as the 9/11 Commission. It said the U.S. government lacked the kind of imagination and questioning intelligence to stop terror. This book explains how those errors took root and how they have returned in even greater force. This book explains how to correct these errors of the mind, because defeating terror is primarily a battle of the mind.

Sadly, key people and institutions in Western media, academia, and government/intelligence—the elites—were dangerously myopic or willfully blind regarding critical facets of Arab-Islamic terror. This book uncovers how the elites aided terror by their action and inaction.

I use the term *elites* gingerly, but I do not really have a better shorthand term[7] for the influential institutions and people who have misread or minimized Arab-Islamic terror for at least two decades leading up to the major attacks of September 11, 2001, in America and thereafter: assaults and abortive terror strikes in London, Madrid, Mumbai, and elsewhere. We dare not treat terrorists like a minor irritation, a swarm of pesky gnats swirling in the summer heat—an annoyance that will pass.

These are lessons I first learned as a student in Egypt. I relearned them as a war correspondent in Lebanon, as a reporter and researcher in Syria and Jordan, and still later as a strategic planner in Israel. After my fellowship in Cairo, I researched the *gema'at Islamiyya*—"the Islamic groups," as they were known—men who fiercely opposed Anwar Sadat's policy of making peace with Israel. This led to a full-page article in the *Jerusalem Post* in early 1980 describing the threat to Sadat from the *gema'at*: radicalized Islamists inspired by the Pan-Islamic fervor of earlier extremists known as the Muslim Brotherhood. The *Post* editor knew my background as a former local reporter for the *New York Times,* but he also knew his paper was read by many diplomats. So he was a bit skittish about the article, perhaps because of its sensitive content. Discussing dangers to Sadat was not so popular in those heady days of Egyptian-Israeli entente. The editor softened my words, but eighteen months later Sadat was murdered by terrorists from the same Pan-Islamic background I described.

Those same *gema'at* were descendants of the Muslim Brotherhood, spawning men like the blind Egyptian sheikh Omar Abdul-Rahman, the leader of the cell that attacked the World Trade Center in 1993, as well as Ayman Zawahiri, the radicalized Egyptian physician who, with Osama bin-Laden, formed the Al-Qaeda monster that erased the World Trade Center and three thousand lives on September 11, 2001.

Threats of terror and political violence should be taken seriously. Too often Western officials, journalists, and academics downplay such threats with a shrug and the comment "Oh, they're just talking" or "Don't take everything they say seriously." Ignoring threats is one fault of these three elites—academia, media, and government/intelligence officials. Worse, often they ignore or minimize terror acts.

For example, in the United States, the pattern of willful ignorance and misdirection by media-academia-government elites continued even after the 1993 attack on New York's World Trade Center. The Western press, supposedly the watchdog of Western society, went to sleep. In academia, leading professors such as Edward Said of Columbia and John Esposito of Georgetown declared that Arab-Islamic terror was a myth.

The terror wave included major Arab-Islamic attacks and abortive attacks on Western diplomats, businesses, and soldiers in Africa, South America, the United States, and the Persian Gulf. Yet important U.S. intelligence officials said these were merely isolated incidents, "lone gunmen," and the equivalent of random lightning strikes. Just before 9/11, Paul Pillar, a leading counterterror official at both the Central Intelligence Agency and the Department of State, wrote that fear of terror was overblown. Death by drowning and lightning were more dangerous to Americans.[8] I also discuss the qualifications of CIA director George Tenet and Michael Scheuer of the CIA's "bin-Laden" unit, whose seeming lack of historical and linguistic knowledge of the Arab world is positively dumbfounding.

This book examines how each of the three elites responded to the rising terror tsunami, showing how academia, the media, and even governmental intelligence agencies actually became accomplices, witting or unwitting, with terrorists. The book examines the role of media personalities such as the *New York Times* publisher Arthur O. Sulzberger Jr. and *Times* journalists Thomas Friedman, John Kifner, James Bennet (now of the *Atlantic*), and Maureen Dowd, as well as Robert Fisk of the *Times* of London and the *Independent*. Broadcast journalists and executives such as Christiane Amanpour, Peter Arnett, and Eason Jordan of CNN and the late Roone Arledge and Peter Jennings of ABC are also examined.

Each elite had a role in shaping how we think about the terror threat, and the way we think about terror, in turn, is part of the key to defeating terror. We need to know how *they* think, what motivates them. We need to assess the role of radical Islam, nationalistic ideologies, and tribalism in Arab-Islamic terror.

The book also summarizes several counterterror approaches in small country-study sections, detailing what has worked and failed in several places around the world: Britain, France, Germany, India, Spain, Russia, Israel, and South America. A chapter on conclusions discusses briefly some of the generally proposed approaches to fighting terror from state and nonstate actors. Above all, this book stresses that the West *can* defeat Arab-Islamic terror.

Defeating terrorists requires imagining without pretending. To win the war on terror, we cannot let terrorists gain control of our minds. We need to study and investigate patterns of behavior—ours and theirs—and to learn.

We must not fool ourselves that there is only a small group of terrorists and that the problem is over when an Arafat dies, a Saddam is executed, a Hizballah or Hamas leader is liquidated, or even a bin-Laden is killed.

We are dealing with a movement that, like some germs, has mutated and replicated itself in different locations. We have to imagine where, how, and why terrorists plan to strike. We must not pretend that we really do not have a problem. Nor should we simply call them "madmen," because there is a definite method to their madness.

Our English word *genie* comes from the Arabic word *jinn,* which is the same linguistic root for the Arabic term meaning "crazy" or "mad." Every Arab child who has read or heard folk tales from *The 1001 Arabian Nights* knows that anyone who is "crazy" or demonic like a genie can still achieve great goals. That was Osama bin-Laden's message. It has captured many more hearts and minds than some of us care to admit.

So, how do we fight terrorism?

The answer is imagination. What kills terrorists is imagination—our imagination.

Imagination, however, was scarce in the days leading up to 9/11. That is the central conclusion of the biggest investigation into the greatest terror assault in modern history. The U.S. inquiry commission found that three thousand people were murdered because U.S. officials lacked the imagination, not the equipment, to defeat the terrorists. "Across the government, there were failures of imagination, policy, capabilities and management. The most important failure was imagination. We do not believe leaders understood the gravity of the threat."[9]

The 9/11 Commission Report, though flawed and often unimaginative itself (due to political infighting), still conveyed one bedrock truth: beating terrorism requires imagination.

Imagination is strong anti-terror medicine because terror warfare targets the human mind, and terror is a product of the human mind. For democratic societies, fighting terrorists requires more mental toughness, mental flexibility, and creativity than fighting conventional wars that stress physical resources and strength. This is not a new insight. It's an old truth that our leaders and our pundits have been ignoring.

> A new specter is haunting the world. . . . It is a new barbarism, a new form of warfare waged by small groups against neutrals or innocent bystanders as often as against actual foes. It is fought primarily not to win territory or even to cause destruction, but to command attention and to instill fear. . . .[10]

The good news is that we have or can develop the mental qualities to defeat terrorists.

Terrorism is not a plague decreed by God, but a disease created by man. Terrorists are not tornadoes or earthquakes. Many terror acts can be foreseen. Terrorists can be controlled and ultimately defeated by people of good and strong will, if we face the threat without blinking and without political blinders. The question is, are we willing to strip the veil of political correctness and factual inaccuracy used to mask the threat of Arab-Islamic terror, the most prevalent form of terrorism today?

Terror literally means fear, seizing someone's mind. Terrorists want to get into our heads. Their primary goal is not seizing territory, usually a classic goal of war. The *goal* of the terrorist is control of the mind, while the *methods* of the terrorist also rely on the mind: intelligence, communication, and manipulating opinion.

That is why this book confronts terror on the battlefield of the mind, and on this battlefield the West has been defeating itself. The *New York Times* said the 9/11 attacks came "out of the blue."[11] Nothing could be further from the truth.

Arab-Islamic terrorists had been attacking the West for a decade. They tried to destroy New York's World Trade Center in 1993. They had actually bragged, in mosques in New York and New Jersey, about their plans. Their followers continue to brag about their plans, as they demonstrate in Paris, Amsterdam, and London.

New York and Washington, the symbols of American and Western power and influence, had been specially selected by the 9/11 bombers because of that symbolic importance: the financial center of lower Manhattan along with the political-military center of the White House and the Pentagon.[12] These two cities were also symbols of Western lethargy, where key governmental and nongovernmental elites had been working hard to ignore evidence piling up on their very doorstep. When an Islamic terrorist murdered a rabbi in a New York hotel in 1989, officials blamed "a lone gunman," though the assassin's home was full of maps and plans to destroy buildings and landmarks around New York, suggesting something much bigger.

There are also landmarks in the statements and actions of terrorists and tyrants. Terrorists and tyrants have a common trait. When they threaten, they mean it.

Hannah Arendt said it fifty years ago: "would-be totalitarian rulers usually start their careers by boasting of their past crimes and carefully outlining their future ones."[13]

The best way to allow terrorists and tyrants to succeed is to say "they don't really mean it" or "we don't have anything to worry about." That is exactly what many Western intelligence agencies, media, and academic figures said before the great Arab-Islamic terror assault on the United States in 2001.[14] They were wrong then and many of them are repeating the same deadly mistake today.

Just weeks before 9/11, the *New York Times* featured a former CIA and State Department expert who said that Westerners were "bedeviled by fantasies about terrorism" and by a false "impression that extremist Islamic groups cause most terrorism."[15] One think tank journal said in a typical tone of reassurance: "The United States may be overrating the threat of terrorism which remains a weapon of the weak."[16] In other words: don't worry, be happy, and show empathy for the weak.

Professors in America and Europe assured us Arab-Islamic terror was not a real threat, but a myth created by alarmists: a phony "green menace" akin to bogus "red scares" of the 1950s.[17] Sadly, the menace was no myth, and the very real threat has actually spread like a mutating virus, changing form and developing its own new defense mechanisms. The changing threat now comes from homegrown Arab-Islamic terror-ists inspired by the 9/11 attack. France's top counterterror official said in mid-September 2010 that the terror threat to his country had reached its greatest level.[18]

Around the ninth anniversary of the 9/11 attack, the Eiffel Tower and the main Metro station in Paris were evacuated for fear of terror. Two weeks later, security officials in Britain, Germany, and France revealed they had stopped an Islamic terror plot aimed at European cities. They said the plot was similar to the massive Islamist attack on Mumbai, India, in 2008 in which at least 174 people died.[19] European officials know how easily terrorists move across national borders on the European continent. Arab-Islamic terrorists have already intervened in election campaigns in Spain, Germany, France, and Austria, trying to change the results with threats and attacks. This has prompted some countries to reach out for extra help, as when Germany signed an anti-terror agreement with India.[20] Indeed, Spain, Britain, and India have all suffered post-9/11 terror strikes by Islamic terrorists—the main source of terror in the world today.

Before 9/11, the West failed to address the radical Islamic terror threat adequately. There was a Western smugness after the fall of the Berlin Wall. Some saw the end of all dictators and the triumph of Western liberalism: "not just the end of the Cold War, or the passing of a particular period of postwar history, but the end of history as such . . . and the universalization of Western liberal democracy as the final form of human government."[21] Even *after* 9/11, one prominent scholar described a world where "peace, democracy, and free markets . . . had attained the same status as literacy: widespread although not universal, dominant, unchallenged."[22]

Yes, the age of great despots—Hitler, Mao, Stalin—appeared to have passed, but many smaller-scale dictators[23] have emerged. They have ambitious goals and are willing to employ terrorists. Indeed, the danger from twenty-first-century terrorists seems to equal, if not outpace, the danger from twentieth-century tyrants. Their totalitarian impulses are similar. We in the West need to know that terrorists, like tyrants, at least initially do not hide their intentions. They brag and strut. Later they try to hide themselves, their methods, and their weapons from us. We, however, cannot afford to try to hide from terrorists or from the facts. We must face them.

President Barack Obama, leader of the United States, epitomizes part of the hope and part of the problem. Communication, as this book shows, is at the heart of the battle against terror, and Obama is a great communicator. He chooses his words carefully. Obama studiously avoids certain terms: "radical Islam," "Islamic terror," "Arab terror," or "Islamic extremism." Addressing the Islamic world in a 2009 speech at Cairo University, he did not mention terrorism even once. Obama referred to "violent extremism," not mentioning jihad or Islam.[24] His secretary for homeland security, Janet Napolitano, has referred to "man-made disasters," not "terrorism," though she has recently changed her tone a bit.[25] Obama's top advisor on terrorism, John O. Brennan, tortuously defines *jihad* as a spiritual struggle, rather than "holy war," the common meaning in Arabic for *jihad*.[26]

Obama and his staff avoid any talk of war as far as terrorism is concerned. They want to "disrupt and dismantle" terrorist groups, not "destroy" them. This language suggests fighting an economic monopoly or an illegal cartel, not combat against an implacable enemy. Obama is a lawyer and former law school instructor. He and Attorney General Eric Holder treat terrorists as criminals—a legal matter, not a strategic problem. This approach affects their view of how captured terrorists should be interrogated and judged—in regular civilian trials, rather than in special tribunals, such as the West used for the mass murderers of World War II.

When one uses or avoids the word *war,* there are important implications. When one speaks of "war," one implies the need to marshal tremendous resources and energy for a supreme national effort. Obama is interested in something that is a lot more limited. He is not alone.[27] Many politicians, journalists, and strategic experts believe America and the West have overreacted to Arab-Islamic terror, and they repudiate the term "war on terror" for many other reasons, among them:

- *Terror* or *terrorism* seems hard to define.
- Terror is a tactic, not an enemy, and terrorists are really just criminals.
- *War* implies facing an enemy, a state, to be defeated by military means, while terrorists such as Al-Qaeda, Hizballah, Hamas, etc., are nonstate actors.

On the surface, these comments contain some partial truths, but taken together they imply a set of big lies used to avoid an uncomfortably harsh reality. We already have enough definitions of terrorists and terrorism. The State Department, the Defense Department, and many other U.S. agencies each has its own definition of terror. So do the various agencies of Britain, France, and Germany. We must stop defining terror and start fighting terror. We do not need to codify definitions or to placate the idiot who claimed "one man's terrorist is another man's freedom fighter." When hijackers fly a plane into a building or put bombs on buses or trains inside a democratic country governed by law, *that* is terror. Terrorists define themselves.

Terrorists are criminals, but they are also much more than that. They rob, they forge, they abduct, they assault, and they kill, but they do all of these things to attain a far-reaching political goal. Their goal is not to make a fortune, but to change or overturn a society. Even without employing nuclear terror—which *is* a real threat—today's terrorists have tremendous resources at their disposal. "Conventional weapons" such as small knives and small amounts of explosives can become levers used to destroy buildings with tens of thousands of people. Chemical or biological poisons may be used in ways that are as effective as attacks by hostile states in the twentieth or nineteenth centuries. A twenty-first-century "blitzkrieg" no longer requires armies of tanks or jets, warships, and muskets, just a few resourceful terrorists.

Abortive terror strikes at Los Angeles International Airport in 2000 and at an oil refinery just north of Tel Aviv in 2002 show the potential for disaster—as do the successful terror attacks in New York, Washington, London, Madrid, and Tokyo. We almost invite terrorists by offering easy access to our most vulnerable targets. As Philip Bobbitt has observed, we live in a global society of porous international borders between "market states" with highly complicated and highly vulnerable infrastructures.[28] Terrorists have the means and the will to gut whole sections of a city or cripple a democratically elected government as effectively as a hostile state can. Stopping them demands tremendous efforts—in intelligence and manpower—usually reserved for war. It also requires recognizing that most contemporary terrorists are Muslim extremists.

Barack Obama's view of Islam comes through the prism of his boyhood years—age six to ten—in Indonesia. Candidate Obama spoke about his views of Islam, radical and benign, during a long interview in July 2008 with Fareed Zakaria of CNN. Obama said the way to fight "Islamic extremism" was by (1) removing social and economic causes of that extremism, (2) stopping Western vilification of Islam, and (3) tempering Westerners' air of superiority toward Muslims. "We have to engage the Islamic world rather than just vilifying it."[29] President Obama's top advisors on terror have copied both the style and the content of his views on Islam and terrorism—none more so than Brennan, his principal advisor on counterterrorism:

"For more than three decades, I have had the tremendous fortune to travel the world and as part of that experience to learn about the goodness and beauty of Islam," observed Brennan in remarks in a security forum at New York University. "Like the president during his childhood years in Jakarta, I came to see Islam, not how it is often misrepresented but for what it is—practiced every day by well over a billion Muslims worldwide—a faith of peace and tolerance and great diversity."[30]

Obama and Brennan both stressed their view that Islam has been "vilified" and "misrepresented," and they highlighted their experience with Islam in Indonesia. This is unfortunate, because Indonesia, though the most populous Muslim country, has never been a generator of Islamic thinking. Arabia—and the Arabic-speaking community we call the "Arab world"—have been and remain the heart of Islam. The history of that community was written in Mecca and Medina, Damascus and Cairo, Baghdad and Jerusalem, but not Jakarta. It was written in Arabic, the language of Muhammad, the man Muslims call *al-Rasul*, the messenger, who spoke, as the Quran describes: *fi lisanin 'arabiyyin mubinin*—"in a clear Arabic tongue."

To understand Islam, one has to appreciate its formative years and its formative Arab nature and narrative. To comprehend Islam as a force in the world, one must recognize that Muhammad was not just a preacher but a general who led many battles to expand the territory of Islam— offensive battles, offensive holy war: *jihad*.

This is difficult for Barack Obama because he is also a product of his education at Columbia, Harvard, and the neighborhoods of Chicago. This is a politically correct education that stresses that Islam is *the* Third World religion,[31] and that Arabs and Muslims have been victimized by the West. In this milieu, Islam is not just "the religion of peace," but "jihad" is explained as an ideological struggle. When Muslims actually physically fight, that conflict is treated as an unavoidable defensive war that is euphemistically labeled "the little jihad." Actually, the Quran does not include custom-made jihads in convenient sizes.

Several times, when Obama and his staff have witnessed Arab-Islamic terror attacks, their instinctive reaction is *not* to react and to try *not* to see Islamic elements. When an Arab-Islamic terrorist murdered thirteen people at the Fort Hood military base in November 2009, Obama called it "a horrific outburst of violence,"[32] not terror. The Obama administration spent days trying to minimize the Arab-Islamic aspect of the attack by Palestinian-born Nidal Malik Hasan, who shouted "Allahu Akbar!"[33] as he shot his army colleagues. Similarly, when a Nigerian man, Umar Farouk Abdulmutallab, tried to blow up a plane over Detroit on Christmas Day, 2009, Obama, vacationing in Hawaii, did not react for three days. When he finally did comment, the president referred to the Nigerian terrorist as "an isolated extremist," though there is strong evidence that Obama already knew that the terrorist had ties to Arab-Islamic terror groups in Yemen.

Barack Obama did not invent this "see-no-terror-speak-no-terror" approach. He merely adopted it and expanded it. The politically correct and nonjudgmental appraisal of Arab-Islamic terror began to dominate Western media and university campuses in the 1970s and 1980s— Obama's college years at Columbia. In many ways Obama is but a faithful reader of the *New York Times,* the "newspaper of record," which fastidiously ignored signs of growing Arab-Islamic terror on its own doorstep. Obama seems to have been a good student of Edward Said. Said was the Columbia professor who scoffed at the idea of Arab-Islamic terror and who set the tone for much of Western analysis of the Middle Eastern affairs in the final part of the twentieth century.[34]

So, President Obama and his staff did not invent this approach, but they raised it to a new level. The Obama administration framed counterterrorism as a narrow struggle against the organization known as Al-Qaeda. This is a huge mistake about a small organization. Osama bin-Laden and Ayman Zawahiri, the leaders of what we call Al-Qaeda, never expected to fight a war by themselves, but rather to inspire others to pick up their banner. That is why isolating them as *the* terrorists is a bit like isolating the leaves on one branch of one tree, rather than looking at the storm Al-Qaeda deliberately unleashed in the whole forest.

Minimizing terror or flinching at terror did not begin in the United States or with Obama. Germany, France, and other European countries made deals with Arab terrorists in the early 1970s, even after the Palestine Liberation Organization attack on the Munich Olympics in 1972. Recently Britain released the man convicted of blowing up a Pan-Am plane flying over Scotland, murdering 270 people.[35] In the United States, the flaccid so-called anti-terror policies have roots in the administrations of Presidents Richard Nixon, Jimmy Carter, and even Ronald Reagan, as well as the media and academic communities of their times. Nixon, Carter, and Reagan spoke strongly about never negotiating with terrorists. Then they tried to make deals with them. Presidents Bill Clinton and George W. Bush spoke of Islam as "a religion of peace" even after the Islamic terror attacks during their administrations: the first World Trade Center attack in March 1993 and the catastrophe of September 11, 2001.

One understands why Presidents Bush and Clinton did this. Western democracies encourage freedom of religion. Muslims are respected citizens of Britain, France, Germany, Israel, the United States, and many other countries. Most Muslims have no ties to terror. The West, as Obama recently said, "is not at war with Islam,"[36] and Muslims are also victims of terror. Confronting Arab-Islamic terror challenges Western democratic societies as well as Arab-Islamic governments—such as Egypt and Saudi Arabia. These two countries were the "suppliers" of the 9/11 terrorists, and their countries' regimes sometimes used or encouraged terror against their opponents, only to find themselves attacked by those terrorists and their imitators.[37]

Threats by terrorists and tyrants are not merely rhetorical rants, and their initial attacks, which may first seem amateurish or primitive, can quickly escalate to something far worse. You can often spot shallow terror "experts" when they describe a terror attack as "amateurish" or "primitive." That is how some U.S. government experts described the first attack on the World Trade Center in 1993. If the second WTC attack, on 9/11, had turned out differently, that is undoubtedly how they would have described the simple and crude box cutters smuggled aboard the hijacked planes and turned into weapons that eventually murdered three thousand people.

"Experts" in the U.S. intelligence community, such as the head of the CIA's "bin-Laden unit," totally misinterpreted the motive for the attack. They tied it solely to U.S. policies in the Middle East.[38] Actually, the 9/11 attacks were a classic example of how the propaganda of the mouth could move to "the propaganda of the deed"[39]—a symbolic act or set of actions designed to stun enemies and to recruit new soldiers.

9/11 and the other post-millennium terror assaults began as a battle of the mind on the campuses of America. No campus was more important than Columbia University, the home of the "Great Books" curriculum, as well as the greatest university in New York. "Columbia" was a synonym for America, replacing "Kings College," the name by which the venerable school was known before America's revolution. Traditionally Columbia students were expected to master the heart of Western political thought and humanities—from the Bible, Plato, and Aristotle to Montaigne, Hobbes, and John Locke. Student radicals assailed these books and authors as little more than "dead white males." Led by the "Students for a Democratic Society" (SDS), they attacked Columbia's principles and seized its buildings in a massive wave of student riots in 1968, with smaller waves in 1970 and 1972. Like students who proclaimed the "Free Speech Movement" at the University of California at Berkeley, they did not seek free speech or democracy, but wanted to impose a political, economic, and educational agenda on U.S. universities. They were forced to give up the buildings, but they left a legacy. One Columbia professor, Edward Said, completed the radical conquest, becoming the new king of Kings College as he abducted American academia.

Crowned America's premier academic intellectual by Columbia itself and by New York's top newspapers and journals, Professor Said single-mindedly razed Western standards of scholarship on the Middle East. His suave sabotage of the mind laid the foundation for the lack of preparation and lack of imagination that allowed the postmillennial terror.

1

TERROR AND ACADEMIA: SABOTAGING THE WESTERN MIND

Why was the West so surprised by terrorism on September 11, 2001?

After 9/11, some focused on two men who spent a lot of time in Washington, D.C.: Bill Clinton and George W. Bush, leaders who might have been more vigilant.[1] Yet the real answers begin not in Washington but in New York, with two men who hated each other but had more in common than is widely known: Professor Edward Said of Columbia University and Rabbi Meir Kahane.

Both were controversial men who dissembled and even lied about their public and private lives, and their paths vectored with Arab-Islamic terror in several telling ways. Professor Said, one of America's most influential intellectuals, probably deserves more credit than anyone for the West's being unready for terror. Rabbi Kahane founded the extremist Jewish Defense League (JDL), advocating vigilante defense of Jews in dangerous New York neighborhoods. Later he moved to Israel, adopting such ultraright-wing political positions (such as the forced expulsion of Arabs from Israel) that he was banned from running in Israeli elections. Returning to the United States for a visit, Kahane was murdered by a member of the same terror group involved in attacking the World Trade Center. So Kahane's lasting claim to fame was that he was probably the first person

killed by an Arab-Islamic terrorist on U.S. soil—more than a decade before 9/11. But no one in law enforcement paid attention to the evidence,
partly because they so disliked Kahane.

Edward Said was seen as an oracle on the Middle East, even though
English and comparative literature were his official fields of inquiry. The
New York Times wrote that his book *Orientalism* "made its presence felt in
most disciplines and is credited with generating totally new approaches in
such traditional fields as anthropology, comparative literature, history, and
political science."[2]

Said often worked alongside or in tandem with Professor Noam
Chomsky, a linguistics scholar at the Massachusetts Institute of Technology. Said and Chomsky helped establish schools of thought known as
postcolonial theory and antihegemonic theory. Both men distinguished
themselves as intellectuals with an attitude: anticolonial, anti-Zionist,
anti-American. They became almost cult figures in academia. For thirty
years their work was cited on more university reading lists than any other
contemporary academics.[3]

Generations of social scientists, journalists, and government/intel-
ligence officials—trained in history, anthropology, political science, and
sociology—were intellectually nurtured on the doctrines of Said and
Chomsky. But Said in particular had a lasting impact on the way academics view themselves and their role.

In midlife, Said belatedly affirmed his own identity as a Palestinian
Arab "refugee," and he became a militant Palestinian political activist and
member of the supreme body of the Palestine Liberation Organization
(PLO) known as the Palestine National Congress (PNC). In fact, Said
served as the academic voice of PLO leader Yasser Arafat (often writing Arafat's major speeches and representing him diplomatically), but
they quarreled after Arafat signed agreements with Israel in 1993. Said
was called "the professor of terror" by his detractors—a title he actually
flaunted.[4]

Like Edward Said, Rabbi Kahane sought a bigger pulpit—but not
in synagogue. Kahane's charisma brought him thousands of Jewish followers, and he moved beyond defense and vigilantism. The JDL strongly
protested the repression of Soviet Jews, winning the JDL many headlines
and animosity from mainline Jewish organizations. JDL harassed Soviet

diplomats and artists—such as the Bolshoi Ballet—in an effort to high-light the plight of Soviet Jews. One protest led to the death of Iris Kones, the secretary of artistic impresario Sol Hurok, who had brought the Russian artists to America.[5] Beyond the headlines, Kahane had hidden an "extracurricular," un-Jewish aspect of himself unknown to his followers. This side surfaced only many years later.[6]

When Kahane moved to Israel, he said he wanted to protect Israeli Jews against Arabs. Polls showed, however, that most Israelis felt they did not need Kahane's help. Kahane won a small following and left a small impact in Israel,[7] and the way he died in the Diaspora ironically might have made a more important contribution than any facet of his life if U.S. authorities had seriously investigated his murder.

THE RABBI AND THE TERROR SHEIKH

Kahane was shot dead on November 5, 1990, in a crowded New York hotel by El-Sayyid Nosair, a gaunt Egyptian Islamic fanatic who had moved to New Jersey. Nosair was a close follower of Sheikh Omar Abdul-Rahman, a blind cleric who led an Egyptian terror group that murdered Egypt's president Anwar Sadat in 1981.

After Kahane's murder, "investigators uncovered a wealth of evidence in Nosair's home and work locker that indicated the existence of a nascent jihad army," remarked Andrew McCarthy, a former U.S. prosecutor.[8] However, the Federal Bureau of Investigation—the FBI—did not study the man who murdered Kahane and who was part of the blind sheikh's inner circle. No one looked at his friends too hard. He was said to have "acted alone." Yet, in Nosair's apartment, police found sixteen boxes of bomb manuals, sensitive U.S. Army cables and documents, and pictures and maps of New York landmarks. These materials included teletypes from the U.S. Joint Chiefs of Staff and detailed photographs of bridges, the Statue of Liberty, and the WTC towers—as well as copious notes in Arabic.[9] These documents were confiscated by the FBI. They went unread and untranslated for years.[10] They were not introduced at Nosair's trial, and he was acquitted of Kahane's murder but found guilty of illegal possession of a firearm—a judicial fiasco. It took six more years for Nosair to be convicted as a co-conspirator in the larger Arab-Islamic terror conspiracy—three years after the first attack on the World Trade Center in 1993.[11]

Sheikh Omar set up a broad terror network in New Jersey and Brooklyn, recruiting men and money. He indoctrinated those who came to his mosque in Jersey City, which had a spectacular view of New York Harbor and the World Trade Center. The blind sheikh's ability to enter the United States and thrive in target-rich New York shows that U.S. officials were far blinder. Especially blind was the State Department, which issued Sheikh Omar a visa, and what was then the Immigration and Nationalization Service, which failed to deport him despite obvious fraud in his documents. But it was the FBI that really botched several clues to his terror plans, such as not hearing attack instructions the sheikh gave Nosair over open telephone lines.

"The blind sheikh may as well have been speaking in Martian as Arabic, since there were so few Middle East language specialists available to the FBI, much less to the local police," recalled author Lawrence Wright.[12] In short, the U.S. government—CIA, FBI, National Security Agency—and the New York City Police Department (NYPD) were clueless and toothless in their counterterror preparations. But were the terrorists just as feckless?

Quite the reverse is true: rather than the U.S penetrating Sheikh Omar's terror organization (a precursor of Al-Qaeda), Sheikh Omar actually succeeded in getting one of his own agents to penetrate the U.S. intelligence community and the U.S. Army at the highest levels. Former Egyptian major Ali Muhammad (his name is often written as "Mohammed") became a briefer on intelligence matters at the U.S. Army Special Warfare School at Fort Bragg, North Carolina. Muhammad trained at least forty "country teams." Muhammad used his time well: materials he photocopied became parts of the Al-Qaeda training manual. Later, he even personally trained Osama bin-Laden's bodyguards. He also carried out surveillance for Al-Qaeda's attacks in 1998 on the U.S. embassies in Africa, in which two hundred people died and four thousand were wounded.[13]

Terrorist Ali Muhammad did not even hide his Islamist tendencies when working for the United States. In fact, U.S. Army and intelligence officials were solicitous and respectful of his idiosyncrasies and special needs. (Years later, this pattern of behavior was repeated in the case of another army major, Nidal Malik Hasan, who murdered thirteen people at Fort Hood, Texas, in November 2009.)[14] Surprisingly, even years after 9/11, some U.S. officials—who failed to stop the plots by Sheikh Omar and bin-Laden—treated the early Al-Qaeda/jihad attacks in the 1990s as "amateurish."[15]

Sheikh Omar Abdul-Rahman was later convicted in the first attack on New York's World Trade Center in 1993, when a truck bomb exploded in the building's basement. Six people were killed and a thousand wounded when the explosion opened a hole 150 feet wide and five stories deep. However, the buildings did not collapse, and the false sense of security inside the U.S. intelligence and law enforcement community remained intact. The CIA did not even set up a unit specializing in Al-Qaeda until 1996. Meanwhile, the FBI mistakenly believed that all the terrorists who executed the assault had been captured. The FBI and police actually released from custody the man who had made the bomb, Abdul-Rahman Yasin, even though his body had been scarred by some of the chemicals and there was bomb residue on his trousers.

Yasin was a very interesting fish who was caught and then released casually by U.S. officials. Although he was born in Indiana, he had been raised in Iraq, returning to the United States only six months before the 1993 attack. Like the man who planned the attack, Ramzi Yousef, Yasin traveled on an Iraqi passport. Yet no red lights or alarms went off in the offices of the FBI, CIA, or local law enforcement.

"The FBI questioned Yasin twice," according to journalist Stephen Hayes. "He disclaimed any significant role in the bombing and appeared cooperative, providing many details of the plot," wrote Hayes. "So they let him go. In fact, FBI agents even drove him home after the interviews."[16]

Within two weeks of the first World Trade Center attack, bomb maker Yasin flew to Amman, Jordan, entered the Iraqi embassy, and got a new Iraqi passport under the name Abdul-Rahman S. Taher and made his way to Saddam Hussein's Iraq. Perhaps it is only coincidence but the date of the first World Trade Center bombing—February 26, 1993—was the second anniversary of Saddam's public surrender in the Iraq-Kuwait war of 1991, when the Iraqi dictator promised not to invade Kuwait again. Iraq tried to make a kind of plea bargain agreement in connection with the 1993 World Trade Center attack. It offered to trade Yasin back to the United States for questioning in return for a U.S. statement that Iraq was not responsible for the attack. The United States refused.[17]

Federal prosecutors' own court memorandum on the 1993 WTC conspiracy is like an indictment of the government's own inaction and negligence leading up to 9/11: "The crimes and acts alleged in the indictment are not random, disconnected acts of unthinking brutality. They are, instead, all parts of the same very real battle the defendants and their co-conspirators saw—and still see—themselves fighting. The attack on Rabbi Kahane did not occur in a vacuum. It was instead a small, albeit brutal step in a terrorist campaign that comprehended not only assassinations of individuals but the mass destruction of political, social, and economic assets of the 'infidel' West, of which the United States was deemed the leader."[18]

How did this happen? How, even after Kahane's murder in 1990 and after the WTC attack in 1993, did the United States not wake up to the danger of Arab-Islamic terror?

ARAB-ISLAMIC TERROR: LOST IN TRANSLATION?

One factor was that "the FBI, as late as 1998, had only two Arabic speakers who could translate documents written in Arabic."[19] FBI director Robert Mueller later claimed that after 9/11, the FBI had learned its lesson: "We have hired nearly 300 new counterterrorism translators specializing in Middle Eastern languages."[20] The documents tied Nosair, Kahane's murderer, to an extremist Arab-Islamic plot to strike at the United States, specifically targets on the East Coast: the United Nations, bridges and tunnels, and the FBI's New York headquarters. Federal officials and local New York politicians blocked serious investigation by the NYPD's strong anti-terror unit, which had its own language specialists.

New York City's leader in this critical period was David Dinkins, its first black mayor. He was a relatively bland official in almost every way. He was a shy and somewhat diffident man sandwiched between the terms of the colorful and controversial figures Ed Koch and Rudy Giuliani. Both Koch and especially Giuliani were atypical New York politicians who almost never shied away from a fight even when charged with unfairly picking on a particular community. Dinkins, however, was always whispering in the ears of the police to be "sensitive" to charges of being too harsh. This message radiated downward. As Heather MacDonald of the Manhattan Institute found, "NYPD veterans are still haunted by their truncated investigation of Rabbi Meir Kahane's 1990 assassination, which could have picked up early warning signs of the 1993 World Trade Center bombing."[21]

The FBI pushed the NYPD off this case and others, testified Edward T. Norris, Baltimore police commissioner and former NYPD deputy commissioner of operations, to a congressional inquiry in October 2001. This meant the FBI and other federal agencies (which were unfocused and unprepared) did not exploit NYPD's home-court advantage and its talented, experienced staff. Worse, future inquiries were relayed to the U.S. Department of Justice, run by Janet Reno, where preventing terror took a backseat to preventing charges of racial profiling and preventing file sharing between FBI and CIA.

Why were the links between Nosair and Sheikh Omar not investigated?

The simple answer is that U.S. government officials did not want a politically inconvenient and politically incorrect investigation. Lack of interest even more than lack of translators stopped the follow-up that might have prevented further terror. Officials buried the evidence as they dismissed the possibility that the Kahane murder might have been more than the act of a lone gunman. Local and federal officials did not want a lengthy investigation of an Arab/Muslim conspiracy that might pit one New York minority against another.[22] Why transfer the Arab-Israeli conflict to the streets of New York? Why dredge up rumors of Islamic extremism and talk of "jihad," especially in the case of an unsavory victim like the "racist" Kahane?

SABOTAGING THE INVESTIGATION:
POLITICAL CORRECTNESS VS. FACTUAL ACCURACY

The man most responsible for this mind-set was Professor Edward W. Said, who died on a September day in New York, two years after the 9/11 attacks he helped make possible. Said did not plant bombs or hijack planes; he hijacked much of the intellectual community, particularly inside the United States, paralyzing its critical faculties. His magnum opus,

Orientalism, published in 1978, lambasted virtually all Western experts on Islam and the Arab world as arrogant racists serving as agents of Western imperialism. Said's judgment was that "political imperialism governs an entire field of study, imagination, and scholarly institutions."[23]

When Said died, the *New York Times,* which had promoted his career, wrote in a front-page obituary that his book *Orientalism* "established Mr. Said as a figure of enormous influence in American and European universities, a hero to many, especially younger faculty and graduate students on the left for whom *Orientalism* was a kind of intellectual credo, the founding document of the field that came to be called post-colonial studies."[24] But Said's influence extended far outside academia.

After the success of *Orientalism,* any Western scholar, journalist, or government official who looked closely and critically at any Arab-Islamic group or phenomenon was no longer a scholar, a journalist, or an official. Instead he or she became "a racist" or "an imperialist." The views of such a Westerner *had* to be dismissed out of hand.

Overly scrutinizing Arab-looking men at airports was ruled out as discriminatory and prejudicial. At least two airline company presidents testified that the U.S. government fined airlines using any procedure that suggested "profiling," even though, statistically and historically, young Arab men were much more likely to be hijackers of airplanes. The 9/11 Commission skirts this factor in its report, likely because one or more of its members was involved in the "anti-profiling" policy.

Yet, one member of the commission, John Lehman, a former secretary of the navy, discovered that such an "anti-profile" policy existed, as shown by the following exchange with Secretary of State Condoleezza Rice:

LEHMAN: Thank you. Were you aware—and it disturbs me a bit, and again, let me shift to the continuity issues here.

Were you aware that it was the policy of the Justice Department—and I'd like you to comment as to whether these continuities are still in place—before I go to Justice, were you aware that it was the policy and I believe remains the policy today to fine airlines if they have more than two young Arab males in secondary questioning because that's discriminatory?

RICE: No, I have to say that the kind of inside arrangements for the FAA are not really in my . . .

Lehman later explained why he asked Rice about "secondary questioning": "We had testimony a couple of months ago from the past president of United, and current president of American Airlines that kind of shocked us all. They said under oath that indeed the Department of Transportation continued to fine any airline that was caught having more than two people of the same ethnic persuasion in a secondary line for questioning, including and especially, two Arabs."[25] The "anti-profiling" rule had a critical impact, thought Lehman.

"We're spending nine-tenths of the money we have on people who have 99/100ths of one percent of the likelihood of being terrorists, because we want to be politically correct. It's crazy."[26] Lehman explained he was not favoring racial profiling, but he opposed any rigid government policy or quota against overscreening certain groups. Such a rigid policy was an example of entrenched "political correctness," he averred.

> No one approves of racial profiling, that is not the issue. The fact is that Norwegian women are not, and 85-year-old women with aluminum walkers are not, the source of the terrorist threat. The fact is that our enemy is the violent Islamic extremism and the overwhelming number of people that one need [sic] to worry about are young Arab males, and to ask them a couple of extra questions seems to me to be common sense, yet if an airline does that in numbers that are more than proportionate to their number in particular line, then they get fined and that is why you see so many blue haired old ladies and people that are clearly not of Middle Eastern extraction being hauled out in such numbers because otherwise they get fined.

Paying attention to young Arabs in airport waiting lines was not the only policy stigmatized as racist. Those who perceptively detected a "return of Islam," those who warned of a growing "Islamic rage," or those who marked a trend to authoritarianism in Islamic communities—as did Professor Bernard Lewis or Professor Elie Kedourie—were attacked by Professor Said.[27]

"Lewis's polemical, not scholarly, purpose is to show, here and elsewhere that Islam is an anti-Semitic ideology, not merely a religion," declared Said.[28] Yet it was Lewis, not Said, who studied Islam, while it was
Said, not Lewis, who viewed the world through a polemical prism rather
than a scholar's lens.

Edward Said heaped insults, while Bernard Lewis, like other Orientalists, had amassed historical, cultural, and religious evidence—showing,
for example, that Islam *had* political attributes and a political ideology or
agenda.[29] For the next twenty-five years, Said escalated his anti-Lewis
tirades, and his approach was far more important than a personal vendetta.
When the *New York Times* assayed the Iranian Revolution of 1978–79,
Said scoffed at the idea that Iran would be worse off under Khomeini than
under the shah. Said assailed *Times* foreign affairs columnist Flora Lewis
for relying on Bernard Lewis (no relation to the columnist), Kedourie,
and other Orientalists whose historical and linguistic knowledge easily
surpassed his:

> At the end of the year during which Iran "fell" the *Times* turned to Islam
> at last. On December 11 full two pages were devoted to a symposium
> entitled "The Explosion in the Moslem World." . . . Doubts about what
> "we" were to think about Islam were cleared up when, on the last four
> days of 1979, the *Times* published a series of four long articles by Flora
> Lewis, all attempting seriously to deal with Islam in crisis ("Upsurge in
> Islam," December 28, 29, 30, 31). . . .
>
> Too frequently her authorities were Orientalists who have made
> known their general view: Elie Kedourie, who in late 1979 did a study
> of the Islamic revolution purporting to show that it was equivalent to
> Marxism-Leninism, was quoted as saying that "the disorder of the East
> is deep and endemic," and Bernard Lewis (not a relative of Flora Lewis)
> pronounced on "the end of free speculation and research" in the Islamic
> world, presumably as a result of Islam's "static" as well as "determinist,
> occasionalist, and authoritarian" theology. One could not be expected to
> get a coherent view of Islam after reading Flora Lewis, whose scurrying
> about in sources and unfamiliarity with the subject give her readers a
> sense of a scavenger hunt. . . .[30]

Apparently Said did not know that the *Times* was much closer to his own views than he imagined. The *Times* had rejected a learned op-ed article by Bernard Lewis a year earlier based on Lewis's study of Khomeini's writings. Lewis had tried to warn the *Times* and President Jimmy Carter that Khomeini was not a democratic reformer: "It became perfectly clear who he was and what his aims were. And that all of this talk at the time about [him] being a step forward and a move toward greater freedom was absolute nonsense," asserted Lewis. "*The New York Times* wouldn't touch it. They said 'We don't think this would interest our readers.'"[31]

Edward Said set a frame of reference that became *the* frame of reference for the discussion of the Middle East. His Mideast was not bordered by Morocco on the Atlantic and Iraq and Iran on the Gulf. Said's Mideast was not a geographical or cultural map but a tightly charted ideological and polemical frame. His Mideast began and ended by asserting that Arab and Islamic society had been wronged by America, Britain, France, and Israel—and nowhere more so than the "atrocities" inflicted on Palestine's Arabs. For Said the Middle East *was* the Arabs, even though there are many non-Arab communities in the Middle East (Kurds, Berbers, Armenians, etc.). Non-Arabs and non-Muslims were forgotten by Said's anticolonialist narrative. When Arabs and Muslims conquered others, that was somehow *not* imperialistic.

For Edward Said, the West was synonymous with aggression, colonialism, and imperialism. The entire non-Western world was equated with "Islam," as shown by his book—*Covering Islam: How the Media and the Experts Determine How We See the Rest of the World*.[32] The heart of colonialism and the core of the "conflict in the Middle East" was "The Palestinian Question" or, as Said called it, "The Question of Palestine"— the title of the book Said wrote right after *Orientalism*. Palestinian Arabs became *the* focus for trendy anticolonialism[33] and *the* frame for intellectually addressing Mideast matters, though Palestinian affairs had nothing to do with most conflicts in the Middle East: Algeria versus Morocco, Iran versus Iraq, Iraq versus Kuwait, Iran versus the Saudis, Libya-Egypt, Syria-Jordan, Syria-Iraq, Shiite-Sunni, and so on.

Despite myriad local conflicts and tribal wars, the West's chattering class began to equate "the problems in the Middle East" first with "the

Arab-Israeli Conflict," then with "the Israeli-Palestinian Conflict," and most recently as "the Palestine Conflict." Western elites adopted this fashion trend. The trendsetter was Edward Said.

Strangely, Western academics, officials, and journalists were swept up by the "centrality" of the Palestinian conflict to all Middle Eastern matters—*pace* Edward Said—exactly when most Arabs showed that "the Palestinian matter" (*al-qadiyya-al-felastiniyya*) was passé.[34] Scholars Fouad Ajami, A. I. Dawisha, Richard Dekmejian, and others documented twenty to thirty years ago that Palestinian and Pan-Arab themes lost their resonance among Arabs.[35] Said's ideas gained their greatest currency in the West just as Arabs disdained them as anachronistic and irrelevant. After Said's proselytizing, it was hard to find a Western diplomat or CIA official who did not cite "the Palestinian question" or "American aid for Israel" when gauging motives for Arab-Islamic terror attacks in Africa or Argentina, India or Iraq.

Behind such views, there was no solid research—neither by Said nor by his followers, merely a stark political agenda. Said revealed his motives after Israel and Egypt signed a peace treaty in 1979. He prayed the Palestinian–Islamic–Third World issue would become the centerpiece of regional and global foment and violence aimed at the United States, Israel, and others who supported the peace treaty:

> As for the region itself, what are the important actualities? In the first place, there is now the possibility that for the first time since 1967 a genuinely popular Arab nationalist response might develop to the United States and to its allies in the treaty, and that portends a wave of extraordinary upheaval in the area. The Palestinian issue, as I suggested earlier, has become far more than an irredentist question; it has turned into the symbolical nexus of nearly every Arab, Islamic, and Third World popular (in the literal sense of that word) issue in the area.[36]

Arab rage, declared Said, was a natural response to Western colonial aggression. Like cement, this view hardened into the conceptual mold of journalists, scholars, diplomats, and intelligence analysts for years to come. After 9/11, Britain's 7/7, Spain's train bombings, and India's Mumbai massacres, Said's argument—unsupported by fact or history—was revived.

Said did not create this frame of reference instantly or by himself, but he was its most successful promoter. He refined the idea.

Quickly supporting Arab causes was no longer the domain of the traditional "Arabist" or "Arab lobby"—oil companies like Aramco, Western officials who saw Arab oil as a strategic asset, or British and American Arabists who had spent lifetimes among the Arabs, some as Christian missionaries or aid workers.[37] Said legitimized this perspective and took it away from the largely rightist business and old-boy diplomatic community, bringing it into the more liberal, leftist academic community. His books gave it academic cachet, but he did not operate in a vacuum. Said was lifted high by a massive wave of oil, specifically a fourfold rise in oil prices in 1973–75, partly the result of a well-planned oil embargo. Oil powered Palestinian Arab public relations, as the Arab League recognized the PLO as *the* representative of the Palestinian people.[38] The League's twenty-plus members threw money and clout behind the "Palestinian idea" at the United Nations and in academia, arranging a hero's welcome in New York for terrorist Yasser Arafat.

Petroleum producers such as Saudi Arabia, Iran, Libya, and Kuwait began investing in universities, from Columbia, Harvard, Georgetown, and Yale on America's East Coast to colleges in Florida, California, and Texas. They also invested in British schools such as Oxford, Cambridge, University College of London, and the London School of Economics along with France's Sorbonne. Oil fueled academic endowments, often with ideological stipulations. Petroleum by-products now included professors.

The University of Newcastle, for example, got Saudi money and hired the creative and popular Denis MacEoin to teach on Islam but removed him after he gave a course on Sufism, a field disdained by the Saudis.[39] The London School of Economics (LSE) gave a lesson in economics, lining its pockets with money from Libyan despot Muammar Qadhafi, asking him to address the entire student body by video link. Qadhafi's son, Saif-al-Islam, sought respectability, and he acquired a doctorate from the London School of Economics under questionable circumstances. He funneled more than a million dollars from the Qadhafi family foundation to LSE, getting the much-desired doctorate whose authenticity was challenged amid charges of alleged plagiarism. Saif-al-Islam (the name means

"Sword of Islam") subsequently led his father's brutal repression of dissidents.[40] British universities were thirsty for oil funds. Their campuses, not surprisingly, became hotbeds for radicalism and terror.

> For many years it has been clear that British university campuses are breeding grounds of Islamic extremism. Omar Sheikh was radicalised in the 1990s while studying at the London School of Economics (LSE). In 2002 he was responsible for the murder of the *Wall Street Journal* reporter Daniel Pearl. The following year two undergraduates just across the road from LSE, at King's College London, went to Israel to become suicide bombers in a bar in Tel Aviv.[41]

Oil money from states with links to terror flowed into UK universities, changing curricula and academic standards. These included Saudi Arabia, whose leaders were close to the Bin-Laden family and to extremist Wahhabi ideology, and Iran, the world's greatest terror state. King Fahd of Saudi Arabia gave twenty million pounds to Oxford in 2008. Saudi prince Alwaleed gave eight million pounds each to Cambridge University and the University of Edinburgh. Iran donated to Durham University, where its cultural attaché addressed students "on the very day the Tehran government announced the executions of two young men involved in protests against the regime."[42] Was anyone concerned?

"The British model is not in open crisis at present but its vulnerability already had been exposed in recent years by the rise in extremism among young and apparently well-integrated second generation immigrants," said Spanish diplomat Fidel Sendagorta. "Nothing illustrates these dangers better than the fact that British universities have become the leading recruiting centres for radical organizations, ahead of jails and mosques in run-down districts."[43] Russia charged that the London School of Economics was a recruiting center for Islamists who joined Chechen fighters.[44] Sweden's first Islamic suicide bomber, Taimour Abdulwahab al-Abdaly, was radicalized at the University of Luton (later renamed the University of Bedfordshire), graduating in 2004. Calling on Muslims to "take matters into their own hands," he began preaching at the nearby Luton Islamic Centre in 2007.[45]

Many British universities ignored the dangers. LSE's directors belittled critics of their approach until the 2011 Libyan insurrection raised issues that forced the resignation of LSE's director, Howard Davies. LSE faculty, students, and other observers asked whether money transfers from Qadhafi were part of a pattern of money influencing academic standards. U.S. universities have tried at least to seem a bit more sensitive. Harvard University returned a $2.5-million gift from the United Arab Emirates in 2004 because the UAE had supported a think tank linked to anti-Jewish incitement. That same year, Columbia University, also the recipient of much Arab money, faced complaints from students who said the on-campus and in-class atmosphere had become highly antagonistic to Israel and to Jews, especially in its Middle East languages and studies programs. Students made a documentary film on the subject, attracting public attention. Columbia President Lee Bollinger agreed to a limited inquiry of charges by students that some professors bullied them in class, in effect forcing them to exhibit pro-Arab and anti-Israeli views. Ultimately, no professors were disciplined. Some students felt the inquiry was a whitewash, allowing the promotion of one controversial professor, much of whose academic writings revolved around the previous work of Edward Said. About this time, when I visited the place where I had gotten three degrees a generation earlier, I could not help but notice that department offices and corridors were often festooned with virulently anti-Israeli messages in a manner that would have been deemed very partisan and very unprofessional during my years at Columbia.

Three years later, in 2007, Columbia allowed Iranian president Mahmoud Ahmadinejad to speak on campus. It was a bold decision, perhaps a foolish one: welcoming a leader who has repeatedly justified (and perhaps planned) attacks on Americans, who has consistently called for (and perhaps planned) Israel's destruction, and who has also repeatedly denied the Holocaust. After many Columbia alumni and New York news media reacted angrily to the decision, Columbia President Lee Bollinger issued a written statement denouncing Ahmadinajad's positions, but still allowed him to use Columbia as a platform. Bollinger also introduced Ahmadinajad's speech, and said there was evidence the Iranian president was a "cruel and petty dictator." Yet, allowing Ahmadinajad to speak, Bollinger said, was proof of the finest side of academic freedom, adding "This is America at its best."[46]

Meanwhile, from Canada to California a pro-Islamist and even pro-terror atmosphere now dominates many campuses, where there now are regular Islamic solidarity rallies, "Palestine Day," or "Boycott Israel" protests.[47] At the University of California at Irvine and at Georgetown University in Washington, Michael Oren, a highly acclaimed and bestselling historian, was shouted down by Islamic militants. Oren, who holds advanced degrees from Princeton and Columbia, could barely speak. At the University of California at San Diego, conservative writer David Horowitz was assailed by mask-wearing pro-Hamas students with signs that said "God Bless Hitler." When Horowitz confronted one student, she admitted wanting to see all Israelis killed.[48] Even with a police escort, Benjamin Netanyahu (then Israel's former prime minister) had to cancel an appearance in 2002 at Concordia University in Montreal due to Muslim student violence. On American, Canadian, and European campuses, a strong anti-Israel and anti-U.S. atmosphere took hold, while strident Arab nationalism and Islamism were de rigueur. The father of this intellectual heritage was Edward Said.

SAIDISM: PREVENTING THE PREVENTION OF TERROR

For a quarter-century, Said lampooned and lanced American patriotism and Zionism. He and his ideological disciples compared those who warned of Arab-Islamic extremism or terror with those far-right extremists in an earlier era who spoke of a "red menace" or a "yellow peril." Professor Fawaz Gerges, a frequent guest on America's radio and TV news talk shows, scoffed at comments by Yitzhak Rabin and Shimon Peres comparing the radical Islamic threat to the threat of communism and Nazism. "The threat of terrorism has spawned a big industry, and has struck fear and horror in the American psyche," asserted Gerges.[49] People who warned of Arab-Islamic terror were alarmists at best and racists at worse, declared the Saidists, and their thoughts were embraced by the media, which even made jokes about the idea of an Arab threat: "The Red Menace Is Gone, But Here Is Islam."[50]

Said laid the foundations for Gerges, John Esposito of Georgetown, and Fred Halliday of the London School of Economics to speak of "the myth of confrontation" between radical Islam and the West.[51] British campuses became hothouses for Islamic extremists known as Al-Muhajiroun.

Places such as LSE and University College of London (UCL) were the intellectual incubators of one of the murderers of Western reporter Daniel Pearl as well as the "Christmas Day Bomber," who tried to detonate an airplane over Detroit on December 25, 2009.[52] Arab-Islamic terror was not a myth in 2001 or 2009, and London, it seems, was not that far from Detroit, nor, in some ways, from Washington.

On the eve of 9/11, Esposito, an intelligence advisor to the Clinton White House, warned against concentrating on Osama bin-Laden:

"Focusing on Usama bin-Laden risks catapulting one of the many sources of terrorism to center stage, distorting both the diverse international sources and the relevance of one man."[53] Esposito was not just another academic. He was head of the Middle East Studies Association and a program director at Georgetown's School of Foreign Service, where many future U.S. diplomats and CIA agents are trained. Esposito asked whether "the Islamic Threat" was "myth or reality."[54] His mythical book went through four printings from its first edition just before the first World Trade Center attack (1993) until the second attack on 9/11.[55]

Thousands had to die to force Esposito to revamp the marketing of his views on the "myth" of Arab-Islamic terror, in his next book, *Unholy War: Terror in the Name of Islam*. In it Esposito peddled the quaint notion that until Al-Qaeda attacked America, Osama bin-Laden, Ayatollah Khomeini, and other "activists," "radicals," and "extremists" (not terrorists or despots) confined their "focus and impact . . . to the local and regional level" in ways "both violent and non violent."[56] One must pinch oneself to recall that Esposito was describing a time when Arab-Islamic terrorists had already executed a quantum leap from the local to the global. Well before 9/11, Iran exported terror to Lebanon and South America via Hizballah, the Iranian-financed "party of God." It had already killed hundreds of French soldiers and U.S. marines on peacekeeping duties in Lebanon, while Al-Qaeda had killed hundreds when it struck at several Western targets in Africa and the Gulf.[57]

Esposito's insipid description of Islamic "radicals" as "both violent and nonviolent" more aptly describes radical vegetarians or irate animal lovers, and not killer-states and groups that have carried out lethal bomb attacks, killing hundreds of people in Scotland, Germany, Arabia, Israel Argentina, Lebanon, and various parts of Africa:

In some sense, bin-Laden and al-Qaeda represent a watershed for contemporary Islamic radicalism. Although in the past the Ayatollah Khomeini and other major Islamic activist leaders had called for a broader
Islamic revolution, both violent and nonviolent, the focus and impact of
most extremist movements from North Africa to Southeast Asia had
been at the local or regional level.[58]

FROM COLUMBIA TO TIMES SQUARE TO
THE WORLD TRADE CENTER

This kind of fuzzy focus analysis of Mideast terrorism could not have
taken root without the seminal contribution of Edward Said. After the
1993 World Trade Center attack, the *New York Times* made an unusual
gesture to an academic author—giving Said several pages in its prestigious
weekend magazine for an article titled "The Phony Islamic Threat."[59]
With alacrity, Said steered inquiry *away* from Islamic terror.

Other academics followed, lest they be branded "anti-Arab," "Orien-
talist," "imperialist," "a tool of Israel," or a "racist." Leaders of the Middle
East Studies Association (MESA), such as Esposito, sought out Arab
state funding for their programs, even from Qadhafi's Libya. Columbia
University's Middle East Institute sought, received, and initially did not
disclose money from the United Arab Emirates to fund an "Edward Said
Chair" in Middle East studies. Columbia also gave Said its highest title—
"University Professor"—a rank then held by only three men.

On September 11, 2002, the first anniversary of the 9/11 attacks,
MESA convened the First World Congress for Middle Eastern Studies
(WOCMES) and gave the first "WOCMES Award for Outstanding
Contributions to Middle Eastern Studies" to Edward Said, who had lo-
botomized Middle East studies. It was a stunningly symbolic and intuitive
gesture—an award on 9/11 for the man who helped bring about 9/11.

MESA's actions and those of Columbia were truly unusual. It was like
the academy granting knighthood, a lordship, followed by sainthood to a
living saint.

Given Said's obvious clout in academia, it is not surprising that his
views were enshrined from coast to coast and across the oceans. Key institutions marginalized discussion of Arab-Islamic terror in the two decades
leading up to the 9/11 terror attacks. Researching "Arab terror" or "Islamic

terror" was considered bad form. In keeping with Said's criticisms, one could only mention the term diffidently, usually by equating "Arab terror" to "Jewish terror" and "Christian terror" or "Western terror." This approach typified books and journalistic products ranging from *The Age of Sacred Terror* (by two Clinton administration officials) to CNN's award-winning program *God's Warriors* by Christiane Amanpour.

"In retrospect, the new elite in Middle Eastern studies had failed to ask the right questions, at the right times, about Islamism. They underestimated its impact in the 1980s; they misrepresented its role in the early 1990s; and they glossed over its growing potential for terrorism against America in the late 1990s,"[60] observed Martin Kramer, an American-born former director of the Dayan Center at Tel Aviv University. Kramer criticized the new generation of Mideast studies teachers for avoiding the hard truths in the lead-up to the Arab-Islamic terror assault on the West. Said's thinking bestrode the three interrelated elites that share much responsibility for the terrible success of the 9/11 attacks: academia, the media, and government.

One measure of Said's impact is that after the first fatal attack on the World Trade Center in February 1993, Columbia's Middle East Institute (MEI) convened a conference, not to ponder terror, but to pander to it. Richard Bulliet, then head of MEI, did not focus on the attack but rather the alleged persecution of the attackers, who murdered six people and wounded more than a thousand. Rather than face terror on his doorstep, Bulliet discovered "a new anti-Semitism against Muslims," driven by "the propensities of the non-elite news media to over-publicize, hype, and sell hostility to Islam."[61] Bulliet's sense of proportion seemed unmoved by the fact that the 1993 attack left a crater 150 feet wide and five stories deep and was meant, like 9/11, to destroy New York's two biggest buildings, killing as many people as possible.

The idea was to use a rented van packed with explosives and cyanide to destroy the base of the buildings. A respected U.S. anti-terror expert has noted: "Had they not made a minor error in the placement of the bomb, the FBI estimates, some 50,000 people would have died."[62] Ramzi Yousef, who planned the attack, later told interrogators he wanted to knock one tower into the other, killing all 250,000 people who worked in or visited the World Trade Center each day.

This means the attack in 1993 could have been between ten to nearly a hundred times more deadly than the attack of September 11, 2001.

One should recall that those attacking the WTC in 1993 might not even have been caught had not one of the terrorists returned to the rental agency to collect a refund (pretending the rented van had been stolen). Months after the 1993 bombing, Columbia's Bulliet expanded warnings against "alarmist" Islamophobes: "We at some point are going to reach a threshold where people no longer need evidence to believe a generic terrorist threat from religious Muslim fanatics."[63] His words proved eerily prophetic in a reverse way. On March 1, 1994, another Arab-Islamic terrorist struck at a major landmark in New York City—the historic Brooklyn Bridge. Again U.S. officials ignored the glaring signs of terror planning and organization inside New York's Muslim community. Perhaps displaying a rare case of bureaucratic humor, they called it a case of "road rage."

Rashid Baz, a Lebanese gunman armed with a machine gun, a shotgun, and two handguns, ambushed a motorcade of religious Jews, followers of the Lubavitch Hasidic sect, as they were crossing the Brooklyn Bridge. A pale, sixteen-year-old yeshiva student, Ari Halberstam, was killed, and fourteen others were wounded, several shot in the head. Witnesses say Baz was incited to his attack by the murder of twenty-nine Palestinian Arabs praying in a West Bank mosque a few days earlier, and by sermons on the West Bank attack he heard at the Islamic Society of Bay Ridge and another sermon at Brooklyn College. The Bay Ridge sermonizer reportedly declared Jews were "racist and fascist as bad as the Nazis" [sic].[64] Several years later, another imam emerged at the same Bay Ridge mosque: Sheikh Reda Shata, an Egyptian-born and Saudi-trained speaker who has saluted Arab suicide bombers. Sheikh Shata lionized the leaders of the Hamas terror network, calling its slain leader "a fallen lion." He has preached that Muhammad was the perfect human being, and that anyone who raises doubts about Muhammad or criticizes him is a "predator" or an "animal." No charges were ever filed against any of the Brooklyn sermonizers, and a decade after the Brooklyn Bridge attack, Sheikh Shata was extolled as a moderate in a big Pulitzer Prize–winning series in the *New York Times*.[65]

Baz was convicted of murder and fourteen counts of attempted murder, and sentenced to 141 years in jail. Two Jordanian men who helped

Baz prepare the weapons and car for the bridge assault went unpunished, though they owned an arsenal of illegal weapons and combat gear. In a plea agreement, they got suspended sentences. U.S. authorities buried the "hate-crime" element of the crime and stopped investigations into a wider terror conspiracy. Officials refused to classify the event as terror until six years had passed.[66] A year later, New York governor George Pataki said a more rigorous investigation might have succeeded "in alerting Americans to the dangers of terrorism and in pursuing all possible leads to their conclusions."[67] Such an investigation might have resulted had there been more rigorous press coverage, but the New York Times, for example, continued to minimize or marginalize terror events in its own backyard, such as the attempted Times Square bombing in 2010, and the capture of two men who planned to bomb the Empire State Building in 2011.[68]

BOMBERS ON CAMPUS AND THE MILLENNIUM

Most Americans condemned the attacks of September 11, 2001. However, academics, as one report showed, seemed preoccupied with America's guilt:

> In the wake of the September 11 terrorist attacks, Americans across the country responded with anger, patriotism, and support of military intervention. The polls have been nearly unanimous—92% in favor of military force even if casualties occur—and citizens have rallied behind the President wholeheartedly. Not so in academe. Even as many institutions enhanced security and many students exhibited American flags, professors across the country sponsored teach-ins that typically ranged from moral equivocation to explicit condemnations of America. While America's elected officials from both parties and media commentators from across the spectrum condemned the attacks and followed the President in calling evil by its rightful name, many faculty demurred. Some refused to make judgments. Many invoked tolerance and diversity as antidotes to evil. Some even pointed accusatory fingers, not at the terrorists, but at America itself.[69]

Academia's response to the World Trade Center attacks of 1993 and 2001 owes much to Edward Said, Noam Chomsky, John Esposito, and other prominent professors who set the tone at America's most prestigious universities. However, terrorists got more than a welcoming atmosphere on campus. Recruiters and fund-raisers for Arab-Islamic terror got academic and economic sanctuary in several institutions in the 1980s and 1990s.

THE FLORIDA TERROR NETWORK

In the 1980s, Arab-Islamic terrorists began clustering around a computer scientist with a gift for networking. Born in Kuwait to Palestinian parents, the balding and bespectacled Sami al-Arian built links for Hamas and Islamic Jihad, two sisters spawned by the Muslim Brotherhood movement in Egypt, where Arian lived for thirty years. At his new home at University of South Florida (USF), Arian worked under the cover of the Islamic Association of Palestine,[70] the Islamic Concern Project, and the World and Islam Study Enterprise. These groups bespoke "concern" and "study," but they spewed hatred, collected money for suicide bombers, and set up conferences, periodicals,[71] and mosque sermons calling for jihad.

"The formula was simple," observes counterterror expert Steve Emerson: "use the laws, freedoms, and loopholes of the most liberal nation on earth to help finance and direct one of the violent international terror groups in the world."[72] Arian worked with Ramadan Abdullah Shallah, an adjunct professor at USF. In 1991, Arian and Shallah brought a mutual friend to teach in Florida: Basheer Nafi. In 2003, Nafi, who had lived in Britain, was charged by the U.S government with being the head of Islamic Jihad in Britain.[73] In 1995, Shallah left Florida, emerging in Syria as head of Palestinian Islamic Jihad, setting off a U.S. investigation of Arian and his activities.[74] Critics wondered how a major university could "have ties to a terrorist front organization for nearly 5 years without it raising the eyebrows" of officials.[75]

Another terrorist on the U.S. campus scene was Musa Abu Marzook. He had strong monetary and organizational links with Arian and Shallah while studying engineering (the favorite degree among terrorists) at Columbia State University in Louisiana. Marzook did not hide his Hamas ties as he raised money for it and other groups.[76] Khalid Sheikh Mohammed, who built bombs for the 1993 WTC attack, got his engineering skills at North Carolina A&T University. Regarding these men, anti-terror expert and criminologist Harvey Kushner asks two questions:

- "How much damage to America did they all do over twenty years?"
- "How much of the secret terror network was overlooked" because questioners were "frightened by political correctness"?[77]

There is no clear answer, but those who scrutinized Arian, Marzook, or their colleagues were branded racists or Arab-bashers due to the academic climate established by Edward Said.

KNOWLEDGE=POWER, IGNORANCE=TERROR

Edward Said felt that Western knowledge of the Middle East was aimed at controlling everything in the Middle East. "To have such knowledge of such a thing," averred Said, "is to dominate it."[78] "Orientalism" was a system to strengthen the West at the expense of the East.[79] Assailing Orientalism, Said hoped to weaken the West and strengthen the East. Events show how well he succeeded.

Said demonized the discipline of Orientalism and its practitioners as Arab-bashers or Islam-haters, but he did not stop there. He linked all Orientalists—historians, philologists, political scientists, and so forth—with Jean-Léon Gerome, whose painting *The Snake Charmer* festoons the cover of *Orientalism*.[80] It shows a nude boy with a large serpent wrapped around him. This was not just a chance symbolic representation for Said. He explicitly asserted that Orientalists had a sexually demeaning outlook on Arabs and Muslims, leering at them while planning to rape them: "Arab society is represented in almost completely negative and generally passive terms, to be ravished and won by the Orientalist hero. We can assume that such a representation is a way of dealing with the great variety and potency of Arab diversity, whose source is, if not intellectual and social, then sexual and biological."[81]

Had these passages not come from a renowned Ivy League professor, we might assume they emanated from a movie caricature in *Dr. Strangelove* fulminating about dark plots to sap people of their "precious bodily fluids."[82]

EDWARD SAID AND THE BIAS AGAINST AREA STUDIES

One of the best ways to develop good Western counterterror intelligence is "area studies"—something Edward Said strongly opposed. Area studies stresses careful attention to language, culture, and religion. Instead Said promoted a Marxian approach in economics, sociology, and politics[83] (an approach still evident in CIA analysis and from other officials). Said's Marxian view could explode as a Marxist rant if Said was provoked by events like the Israeli-Palestinian treaty of 1993, which, Said told British and Arab audiences, was really a Zionist-capitalist plot:

> With its well developed institutions, close relations with the US and ag-gressive economy, Israel will in effect incorporate the territories econom-ically, keeping them in a state of permanent dependency. Then Israel will turn to the wider Arab world, using the political benefits of the Palestin-ian agreement as a springboard to break into Arab markets, which it will also exploit and is likely to dominate. Framing all this is the US, the only global power, whose idea of the New World Order is based on economic domination by a few giant corporations and pauperisation if necessary for many of the lesser peoples (even those in metropolitan countries).[84]

Said was baptized as an Anglican and raised as an Episcopalian, but his religion was radical politics. His writings show little affinity for literary Arabic and Islam. He scoffed at those scholars—Westerners or Arabs—who paid attention to language and religion. To him they were insular, even racist. However, it was exactly those area specialists who were most sensitive to societal changes, especially changes with an Islamic compo-nent. Conversely, the pseudoscientific, antiseptic, and antireligious Marx-ian approach of Said blinded Western policy makers and scholars to the massive religious upheaval in Iran and, subsequently, in other parts of the Arab-Islamic world.

Middle Eastern scholars such as Ali Dessouki and Richard Dekme-jian have spoken of the relative inability of Western social scientists (or the Western-schooled Arab social scientists) to perceive the Islamic resur-gence of the 1970s until it exploded in the Iranian Revolution. Dekmejian said this "conceptual myopia" meant Western Middle East specialists were "unprepared to consider the potency of religion as a revolutionary force," constantly seeing an "inevitable" secularization of regional politics along Western models.[85] By the 1980s, Islam was resurgent, and, as Des-souki wrote, "Islam appears both as an apology for the status quo and as a regime-challenging ideology."[86] However, critically studying the political impact of Islam was a taboo subject in Said's book—and subsequently in much of Western academe.

FAILURE TO PRODUCE WESTERN ARABISTS

Under Said's inspiration, Middle East studies departments at U.S. universities came to be bastions of anti-Western propaganda. Schools that once gave the CIA and other intelligence agencies talented manpower now pretty much dried up as providers of "talent." Earlier, many of these departments had produced Western-born scholars who were role models for American students whose native language was English but who could read and speak in several of the important Mideast languages: Arabic, Hebrew, Persian, and Turkish. Instead the departments became dominated by people born in the Arab-Islamic world, and worse, by a faculty ideologically committed to the undemocratic regimes of the Arab-Islamic world.[87]

Being a Muslim or an Arab did not grant a scholar or dissident immunity from an attack by Edward Said if the scholar was critical of Arab politics or culture.

Said was especially snide and venomous when describing Arab academics with whom he disagreed, such as Fouad Ajami and E. Shouby:

> Ajami is a Lebanese Shiite educated in the U.S. who first made his name as a pro-Palestinian commentator. By the mid-1980s, he had become a professor at Johns Hopkins and a fervent anti-Arab nationalist ideologue, who was quickly adopted by the right-wing Zionist lobby (he now works for people like Martin Peretz and Mort Zuckerman) and groups like the Council on Foreign Relations. . . . The author of two or three ill-informed and tendentious books, he has become influential because as a "native informant" he can harangue TV viewers with his venom while demoting the Arabs to the status of sub-human creatures whose world and actuality doesn't matter to anyone.[88]

Such Arab-born scholars, Said hinted, were corrupt traitors. Iraqi author Kanan Makiya, who chronicled Saddam Hussein's brutality, was condemned. Meanwhile, Said often forgave or praised Saddam and other dictators. The United States attacked Saddam in 1991 and 2003, proclaimed

Said, not because Saddam invaded Kuwait, not because he invaded Iran, not because he might have invaded Saudi Arabia, not because of his atomic weapons program, not because he murdered thousands of his own citizens with poison gas and other means, not because he threatened "to incinerate half of Israel," but *only* "because of its [Iraq's] potential for anti-Israel troublemaking."[89]

When Said described Saddam Hussein, one felt he was talking about a poorly understood, underprivileged teenager whose only crime was to take a neighbor's car for a joyride without permission: "Saddam's Iraq was targeted for military and political termination, quite irrespective of its history, its complicated society, its internal dynamics and contradictions."[90]

For Edward Said, the burial pits of Saddam's mass-murder victims were really craters from U.S. bombs. The suffering of Iraqis was always caused by American sanctions, by Israel, or by the Iranian ayatollahs: "The claim that Iraq gassed its own citizens has often been repeated. At best, and according to U.S. official sources, this has sometimes seemed uncertain, depending not on truth or principle, but on the policy of the moment. There is at least one War College report, done while Iraq was a U.S. ally, which claims that the gassings of the Kurds in Halabja was [*sic*] done by Iran."[91] Said never provided his readers with a source for this baseless claim.

TERROR'S DEBT TO ACADEMIA

Edward Said's intellectual bequest remains *Orientalism* the book, and Orientalism the ideology, which has stifled Western inquiry into the Arab-Islamic sphere. It spurred an intellectual climactic change in academia, media, and government—the three institutions most responsible for the West's being unprepared to face Arab-Islamic terrorism. It enshrined lack of curiosity and imagination as the right posture for students of the Middle East. When the 9/11 Commission criticized lack of imagination, it could have thanked Edward Said.

Edward Said's intellectual heritage was essentially a struggle against curiosity, opposing Western curiosity of the Arab East and also Arab curiosity of the West. He saw Western curiosity as part of imperialism. He saw Arab curiosity as sycophancy or fellow-traveling with the imperialists.

Perhaps the best verdict on Said's work and the work of his disciples was offered by the great Saul Bellow's fictional character Mr. Sammler, who asks, "You wondered whether this Western culture could survive. . . . Or whether the worst enemies of civilization might not prove to be its petted intellectuals who attacked it at its weakest moments. . . ."[92]

Edward Said prepared the way for academics, the press, and government to overlook Arab-Islamic terror in attacks in New York in 1989, 1993, and 1994. Much of the same pattern has returned after New York's 9/11, Madrid's 3/11, and London's 7/7. The American press has bent over backward not to divulge Islamic angles in terror incidents as disparate as the Washington, D.C., area sniper killings and the Los Angeles airport shooting in 2003, while the U.S. government and the U.S. Army tried to conceal the Arab-Islamic elements in the Fort Hood murders of 2009. In Britain, where there is a growing Muslim population, Parliament passed the Racial and Religious Hatred Act in 2006, largely at the behest of the Muslim community, over the objections of artists and civil libertarians. In short, a Western reporter or official alluding to Islamic motivations or Arab nationalist feelings in a terror case will likely face accusations of anti-Muslim and anti-Arab bias: a victory for Edward Said's life's work.

When Osama bin-Laden's terrorists crashed their hijacked airplanes into the heart of New York and Washington on September 11, 2001, Western leaders were astounded. Perhaps they had only been hypnotized into a kind of sleepwalking through events by Edward Said and his ilk— and their followers. The *New York Times* staff wrote a book that claimed the attacks were "out of the blue." Nothing could be further from the truth.

2

TERROR AND THE PRESS:
THE DEVIL'S BARGAIN

Terrorists need oxygen to survive and thrive, and their oxygen is media attention. Without the smooth caress of the press, terrorist groups die a lonely death. Without the press, terrorists lose their political and psychological influence, forfeiting ways to recruit new members or gain sympathy from fellow travelers and latent supporters.

This means terrorists and journalists need each other. Each side needs access and name recognition. Terrorists need notoriety and headlines. Reporters need headlines, airtime, and bylines. Sadly, some journalists, including leaders in print and broadcast journalism, made a devil's bargain with terrorists. Based on my research and my own firsthand experience in the Middle East—Egypt, Jordan, Syria, Israel, and Lebanon—I will describe how some award-winning journalists—from the *New York Times* and the *Times* of London and from ABC to CNN—have actually aided terrorists. Some reporters, editors, and producers have helped terrorists by being careless or lazy. Some have skipped over incriminating details about terrorists. Some have carefully covered up terror events. So, let us examine the symbiotic link between terrorists and journalists.

PULITZER PRIZES AND THE PROPAGANDA OF THE DEED

A century before Osama bin-Laden and Yasser Arafat, European terrorists saw the value of "the propaganda of the deed"—a terror act that galvanizes people to a cause. "Seen in this perspective, the journalist and the television camera are the terrorists' best friends," observes Walter Laqueur, because "the success of a terrorist campaign depends decisively on the amount of publicity it receives."[1]

This was true even in the 1970s, when dramatic hijackings propelled the Palestinian movement to prominence. Yet these words are also an apt way to describe the attacks of Al-Qaeda, whose symbolic assaults are meant to inspire more attacks by like-minded people. Starting with the Palestinian pioneers of modern Arab-Islamic terror, exploiting the media changed the terror equation forever. It is no longer just about capturing a quick headline and gaining short-term fame. Today hijacking the media is at the heart of terror doctrine and tactics. This is true especially in protracted conflicts such as the current battle against Arab-Islamic terror, but terrorists can enslave the media even in a short war. Two recent wars show how.

A Harvard study on the Hizballah-Israel war of 2006 showed how the media became "a weapon of modern warfare." It described how "an open society" (Israel) was "victimized by its own openness," while a closed terror organization (Hizballah) manipulated "the daily message of journalism and propaganda."[2] Israel, whose citizens and territory were attacked, was charged with atrocities, particularly with bombing a defenseless Lebanese village called Qana. The charge was based on doctored "evidence" fed to reporters led around by the terrorists, but this was enough to stall the Israeli advance into Hizballah-held southern Lebanon.[3] Hizballah had invaded Israel to kill and kidnap several Israeli soldiers, also murdering many civilians, and it emerged from the war physically battered but politically strengthened as Lebanon's main political and military force.

In 2008, the United Nations enslaved itself to the media manipulation carried out by another terror group, Hamas, which had attacked Israel mercilessly with hundreds of rockets even after Israel withdrew all its forces and population from Gaza a year earlier. After many rocket attacks on its cities, Israel moved into Gaza to uproot the terrorists' rockets, mortars, and arms depots. The Hamas terrorists rushed to their favorite media outlets with reports of Israeli atrocities. Freedom-loving regimes such as Libya and Sudan demanded a United Nations investigation of war crimes.[4] The result was a UN media-driven "human rights report" based on Hamas-supplied accounts. Portions of the report were eventually recanted by its own principal author. Still, the UN report crippled Israel's terror-fighting abilities for three years.[5] Israeli leaders feared that using force would brand them as war criminals. There will likely not be wide media reexamination of these terrorist-manipulated events. When the media (or diplomats) have been played for fools by terrorists, they usually do not admit it, and the press rarely cleans up its own mess.

Terrorists are trained to claim, if captured, that they have been abused and tortured. Seized Al-Qaeda manuals and the U.S. experience with the scandals of the Abu Ghraib prison in Iraq and Guantánamo prison in Cuba prove this.[6] Events prove press coverage can have an immediate impact on the battlefield and in the war against terrorists. When *Newsweek* reported in 2005 that U.S. interrogators deliberately desecrated a copy of the Quran as a way of breaking Muslim prisoners, riots erupted in Afghanistan and Pakistan. At least fifteen people died. Investigations failed to turn up even one such case. *Newsweek* eventually retracted its charge.[7] Did anyone notice?

Charges of widespread U.S.-led torture at both prisons filled the airwaves and the front pages for many months in 2004 and 2005. The *New Yorker* magazine and CBS News vied for the honor of showing the most suggestive photographs of alleged torture. However, intense investigations of the charges of atrocities at both prisons showed that torture of suspected terrorists was *not* U.S. policy. "Waterboarding"—simulated fake drowning—was used in only three cases of the most extreme Al-Qaeda terrorists believed to have information about ongoing terrorist plots. Investigations of torture at Abu Ghraib and Guantánamo turned up much more limited abuses, often involving the debasement of prisoners, such as forcing them to strip naked just to embarrass them. There were three serious convictions and sentences for Abu Ghraib violations, but the scale of the abuses was exaggerated by the Western media.[8]

LEVELING THE ODDS ON THE HIGH-TECH BATTLEFIELD

With media coverage—and even media sympathy—a relatively primitive terror group or a nonadvanced state supporter of terror can humble the most technologically advanced countries. Even "primitive" terrorists can ride piggyback on the West's own media technology, using the media to gain "strategic reach" and "even the odds."

When gangs in old, rough-and-tumble New York assailed a lone person at night, they got surprised, sometimes, by a victim carrying a gun. Humorist Damon Runyon called this "the Old Equalizer"—a weapon that changes the odds. Today's media have become the New Equalizer. They hold a weapon that, when handled well, can equalize the odds against a superior opponent, even a superpower.

The media are powerful. Even decades ago, when there was a coup in a distant country, one knew who the victors were when they took over the local radio station. Today, Al-Qaeda's "cavemen" do not need their own broadcast station. After all, they can borrow Al Jazeera, CBS, France 2, or CNN whenever they want, even as they scamper from one hideout cave to another. Furthermore, these "cavemen" with their "primitive weapons" know more about us and our information societies than we know about them, because as one expert on the Arab media observed, "the flow of information is overwhelmingly one way, from West to East."[9] Even seemingly defeated terrorist groups such as Al-Qaeda/Taliban in Afghanistan[10] or Yasser Arafat's Fatah[11] in the West Bank or the isolated and beleaguered Hamas in Gaza can recoup losses. They can snatch victory from the jaws of defeat. Good media strategies reframe the terms of debate. Countries attacked by terror—the United States, Britain, India, Israel—find that they must defend themselves against charges of abusing the human rights of terrorists or of harming civilians whom terrorists used as "human shields."

This trend did not occur overnight, but the changes now seem sudden. The questions changed. "How did terrorists successfully attack America?" and "How did they manage to attack London/Madrid/Mumbai?" became "How do America and its Western allies treat Al-Qaeda prisoners?" "Is Israeli force disproportionate?" "Are people being tortured?" "Are holy books being ripped?"

Under media barrage, viewers and readers are *not* being asked how or why Islamic terrorists want to destroy downtown New York, Madrid, or London. They are not asked why and how Fatah, Hamas, and Hizballah attack Israeli cities with suicide bombers and rockets (even after Israeli territorial withdrawals) or why Lashkar-e-Taiba murdered about 170 people in bloody terror assaults on Mumbai in 2008. Instead, TV viewers, radio listeners, and newspaper readers dwell on the premise that it is some policy of the country attacked that makes terrorists hate them so. Western media have come to prefer to ask some questions, avoiding others—perhaps inadvertently aiding the terror groups. Meanwhile, the terrorists have exploited cameras and manipulated microphones to hold a conversation, on their own terms, with the citizens of the attacked countries, especially their intellectuals and attentive publics. This helps them stymie anti-terror policy while raising recruits.

TERROR AND THE MEDIA: MONEY AND STATUS

Even wealthy terrorists, such as the late Osama bin-Laden, need to advertise in order to survive, to raise money, and to obtain followers.[12] In turn, the media work hard to cooperate with terrorists. They often create and promote a terrorist mystique as part of a search for a new story and a new cast of characters.[13] Some journalists lower their ethical standards to appeal to terrorists as celebrities, lobbing them soft questions, offering them an open platform for their views—a kind of blank check.

"I wanted to let you know personally that I would obviously be very interested in also sitting down with you for an interview," implored Katie Couric, then-host of NBC's *Today* show, in 1999. She was writing to Ted Kaczynski, the "Unabomber" who made sixteen letter bombs, killing three people and wounding twenty-three others. "It would give you a chance to explain your experiences to our huge audience and also the opportunity to share your views and concerns, which I know you've long wanted to."[14]

Peter Jennings was America's most-watched TV news host for many years. In several tender interviews of Yasser Arafat, Jennings sweetly called him by the avuncular nickname "Abu Ammar."[15] Jennings was probably not so affectionate with any Western leader, but he and other broadcasters tended to shower attention and softball questions on terrorists in ways quite different from their hardheaded approach to presidents and prime ministers. "In 2000, for example, CBS News and NBC News broadcast significantly more stories mentioning bin-Laden than segments referring to Great Britain's Tony Blair and Germany's chancellor, Gerhard Schroeder."[16]

Terrorist groups need to maintain a reputation. They often create an event not from a deep ideology but from the need to gain attention, to keep active in order to stay noticed. Arab-Islamic terrorists in particular are conscious of the need periodically to create a *hadtha* ("event" in Arabic) or an *'amaliyya* ("operation") to prove they exist, to signal policy changes, to enlist new members, and to raise money locally or abroad.

Arafat's Fatah organization staged a May 1980 attack on Jews praying at the Tomb of the Patriarchs in Hebron for tactical reasons.[17] Six people were murdered to show that Arafat's organization was alive and kicking and that it had not ceded its leadership role to the increasingly popular local West Bank mayors.[18] Similarly, the Hamas organization executed a chain of mass-murder bombings in February and March 1996 after Israel killed Hamas's primary bomb maker and strategist, Yihya Ayyash. Many researchers who have studied Al-Qaeda believe that Ayman Zawahiri changed his strategic approach and moved closer to Osama bin-Laden and his more incendiary anti-American purview in 1998. Zawahiri switched focus to the "Far Enemy" from the "Near Enemy"—after failing to attract followers in his own Egypt-oriented jihad organization, which had assassinated President Anwar Sadat.[19]

Not all the things terrorists do, of course, are scripted and choreographed for the media. Parts of their activities—how they transfer money globally, for example—are concealed. Still, many terror goals require media attention. Some terror groups try to "take credit" for attacks committed by other terror organizations because they hope to gain airtime or money or new recruits. However, one must remember that terrorists are not the only ones who seek publicity for their work. Indeed, some of the initial media goals of terrorists are similar to those of politicians and journalists:

- *Access*—getting prominent headlines and airtime
- *Name recognition*—getting one's name or organizational "brand" readily known
- *Setting the agenda*—gaining power to frame issues and set the terms of debate

Journalists and politicians will do a lot to gain access, name recognition, and the ability to set the agenda, but terrorists will do *almost anything* for these goals. It is more than a matter of degree. It is a matter of means, not just ends. The terrorists are more like dictators or authoritarian rulers in their willingness to use any means to control the media and their product. For example, murdering reporters or threatening murder was standard operating procedure for Hitler, Stalin, and Saddam. Even autocrats of less tyrannical stature such as Vladimir Putin or Hugo Chávez use force or threat of force to control the media. Murder and press intimidation are regular tools in the media policy of Hizballah, Hamas, and PLO/Fatah.

JOURNALISTS, AUTOCRATS, AND TERRORISTS: SYMBIOSIS AND SEDUCTION

Knowing how journalists face these dangers is critical to understanding the nature of modern tyranny and modern terror, because the way journalists discuss terrorism affects terrorism itself. As veteran newsman Walter Cronkite observed, "Journalists from time immemorial have affected the course of events by asking judicious questions and conducting timely interviews."[20] Journalists who avoid asking tough questions or who avoid or skew coverage also alter the course of events. "News, if unreported, has no impact. It might as well have not happened at all."[21]

This happened in Nazi Germany. William Shirer, the historian of Nazism, was a CBS reporter in Germany when Hitler's regime spent great energy to control press coverage. Shirer recalled how the Nazis threatened to expel him for explaining that on the eve of the 1936 Berlin Olympics, the Germans had only *temporarily* relaxed some anti-Semitic persecutions, removing a few anti-Jewish street signs for the short term.[22] Other reporters were not as brave. Some even sympathized with Hitler and the Nazis.

"In mid-March 1933 Frederick Birchall, who was then serving as *The New York Times* Berlin bureau chief, was in the United States. In a nationally broadcast CBS radio speech he denied that Hitler was a dictator. He described him as a 'bachelor and a vegetarian and he neither drinks nor smokes.'"[23] Shirer saw how reporters, even if they started out anti-Nazi, could slowly be taken in by Nazi media manipulation and the "deadly conformity" of the local press.[24] The enforced pack mentality of the local press slowly infected the foreign press. Reporters were cut off from news sources among the population and forced to read heavily censored local "news" that reinforced the propaganda of the dictatorship. Shirer confessed that "a steady diet over the years of falsifications and distortions made a certain impression on one's mind and often misled it."[25] Reporters were squeezed by their own employers. Louis Lochner of the Associated Press admitted that AP told him not to report things that would get him thrown out of the country.[26] Others feared arrest or that their dissident sources might be sent to concentration camps.[27] Some gave in to fears of physical attacks. Direct threats, sly intimidations, or seductive offers (e.g., interviews with top Nazis) swayed some reporters. Even those appalled at Nazi policies found reasons to mute their comments or to hold back on reporting all the facts.

This kind of atmosphere is not unique to Nazi Germany. It repeats itself at other times and in other locales—from Moscow to Beirut, and from South America to Africa. Despotic regimes and terrorist groups control a journalist's environment. They create situations in which reporters skip over truths that can be painful to the regime and even more painful to the reporter. *New York Times* reporter Walter Duranty won a Pulitzer Prize for coverage of the Soviet Union in 1932, while hiding Soviet-induced food famines and persecutions in which five million to twenty million people died.[28] Writing to his editors in New York in 1932, Duranty said that other reporters wrote "big scare" stories and "malignant propaganda" against the Soviets while "to the best of my knowledge there is no famine anywhere."[29] This was a huge cover-up of the forced collectivization of private farms in the Ukraine and the Caucasus. Stalin's forces deliberately starved hundreds of thousands of farmers known as *kulaks,* but Duranty reported Soviet bumper crops. *Times* editors began to have grave doubts about his coverage, but kept him in Moscow because sending a new reporter was nearly impossible. Similar rationales occurred in Hitler's Berlin and the PLO's Beirut.

Duranty also concealed Stalin's outrages at show trials where hundreds were condemned to death. As historian Robert Conquest wrote, "Walter Duranty of the *New York Times* spoke Russian, had been in Russia for years, and knew some of the accusers. For years he had built a disgraceful career on consciously misleading an important section of American opinion."[30]

Whitman Bassow, a Russian studies scholar who became *Newsweek*'s bureau chief in Moscow, said the Russians used blackmail to curtail Western reporting of the famine. Bassow especially criticized Duranty, citing other reporters' beliefs that Duranty made special deals with the

Soviet leaders—special treatment in return for good coverage. "Walter Duranty's coverage of the famine was consistent with much of his reporting from the Soviet Union," writes Bassow, "slanting stories to fit his own vision of men and events."[31] A similar dynamic will be shown in the work of award-winning reporters based in Beirut and Baghdad fifty years later.

Stalin's press policy and the media strategy of many terrorist organizations are akin to Hitler's press policy as Shirer described it: "to talk peace, to prepare secretly for war and to proceed with enough caution in foreign policy and clandestine rearmament to avoid any preventive military action."[32]

To understand this interplay between terrorists, authoritarian rulers, and journalists, we must look behind the scenes at the inner workings of the Western media.

WITHOUT FEAR OR FAVOR:
THE *NEW YORK TIMES* AND THE CLASSIC ETHOS

For most of the twentieth century, the single most important news medium was the *New York Times*. Its editors, reporters, and publisher were wooed by statesmen, presidents, and royalty. On the morning of 9/11, early in the new century, the *Times* was still very important, probably the one news source consulted or referenced first by other media. About seven o'clock every evening, the New York Times News Service sends its articles to more than five hundred newspapers in the United States (in which there are only about one thousand daily newspapers).[33] Moreover, the New York Times Company owns fifteen local newspapers and half a dozen broadcast stations of its own, including the *Boston Globe*. Many broadcasters and newspapers around the world were also subscribers of the *Times*' news service. On September 11, 2001, "the Gray Lady"—as the *Times* was known—had passed her 150th birthday, but the lady still had great influence.

With the advent of the Internet, the *Times* became more of an international paper. People who worked for "the Paper" did not think of themselves as employees but as "*Times*men" and "*Times*women." They had a sense of mission, though they often joked about it, to carry out the quest of the paper's modern founder, Adolph Ochs, to be the best newspaper anywhere. Ochs, eldest son of a German Jewish immigrant family, had made the *Times* an information-gathering behemoth whose sources and resources rivaled many government agencies. One story is illustrative.

TO LEAK AND HOW TO LEAK—THAT IS THE QUESTION

President Franklin Roosevelt, Secretary of State Cordell Hull, Undersecretary Edward Stettinius, and British foreign minister Lord Halifax were irate when *Times* reporter James "Scotty" Reston obtained the position papers of the world powers conferring on post–World War II security arrangements. The talks culminated in the creation of the United Nations, but Stettinius and Halifax warned the *Times* that if Reston kept revealing their thoughts, the talks would collapse. The Soviets suspected Western trickery. Delegations probed themselves and each other—and the *Times*—to discover the source of the leak of the material that ultimately won Reston a Pulitzer Prize. Lord Halifax, Reston's friend, was not the source of the story, but he cut off all meetings with Reston. "I'm not going to keep your friendship at the expense of the American Secretary of State."[34]

In 1961, President John Kennedy begged the *Times* not to publish its discovery of his planned Bay of Pigs invasion of Cuba. The *Times* acceded. When the plan turned into a disaster, Kennedy chided the *Times* for not warning him off the whole project. Sometimes, U.S. presidents, such as Dwight Eisenhower, did not even have to ask the *Times* not to publish sensitive national security material. The *Times*, for example, had discovered the secret of American U-2 reconnaissance flights over the Soviet Union, which were crucial to U.S. intelligence efforts to monitor Soviet military activities. The *Times* didn't write a word, until one of the planes was shot down.

On the other hand, Kennedy grew angry when the *Times* military correspondent, Hanson Baldwin, published exclusive information that showed in detail how well the United States had monitored Soviet missile development. This was not just a monumental military leak but also a political embarrassment. Kennedy, a hawkish Democrat, had campaigned for office partly on the claim of an "American missile gap." The *Times* article showed not only that the United States had a vast superiority in missiles but also that it might consider a "first strike" to eliminate Soviet missiles.

As Kennedy's secret tapes show, Kennedy was outraged. The FBI wire-tapped the *Times* correspondent and tried to intimidate him into revealing his sources.[35] However, this was not just because of the personal pique of Kennedy. He and his advisors were really afraid that the leak would damage American abilities to monitor the Soviet missile program.

Such a clash between journalistic ethics and other democratic principles of governance was not unique, but the drama was not always played out in an institutional setting. Silver-haired Murray Schumach, the acknowledged dean of local *Times* reporters, was a kind of legend, the epitome of unruffled elegance, sitting in the front row of the city room. Known as the reporter's reporter, it was a mystery why he was not part of the *Times* elite—the foreign correspondents in thirty-odd capitals and war zones around the world.

One day I worked up the courage to ask Murray, and he told me why. He *had* been a foreign correspondent, covering the war in Korea, and he had developed a story on secret contacts between the United States, North Korea, and China that might lead to a truce. The U.S. military asked him not to write the story that might have aborted the secret truce talks, leading to a longer war and more deaths. "I didn't ask my editors. I just made a decision. But afterwards, I decided that I never wanted to be in that position again, and so I asked never to go overseas again."

This event shows the deep sense of mission, patriotism, and conscience in one man, but he was not alone. Many at the *Times* asked themselves tough questions in their quest to be good journalists and decent people. Next to Schumach sat Peter Kihss, a legend for his ability, his modesty, and decency. Kihss was reportedly the only one in New York City who read the budget every year. It was a huge book, weighing several pounds, and city officials always feared what Kihss might find hidden inside.

"The Vacuum Cleaner," they called him, because he sucked up even the most minor facts that otherwise fell into the cracks. He was the antithesis of the brash and cynical reporter. Kihss was a quiet man, always slightly bent in his tweedy jackets but insanely upright, even naïve, in his pursuit of stories, often giving his interviewees a chance to recant a self-incriminating remark.

"I always look into things and hope the people we're talking to did not do what we thought they had,"[36] he once told a colleague. Kihss wrote slowly and somewhat painfully, weighing every word. He knew just how much weight the *Times* carried. An unintentionally incorrect or slightly distorted comment might end someone's career or life. An accurate story, a penetrating account, could be just as deadly.

In the back rows of the newsroom sat the young reporters. One was Michael T. Kaufman. In 1971 he wrote a penetrating exposé of Rabbi Meir Kahane. He found that the rabbi had had an extramarital affair with a non-Jewish woman. After being jilted, she killed herself. Kaufman discovered Kahane had also masqueraded as a non-Jew, using the name Michael King.[37] The rabbi asked the reporter not to ruin his life, the lives of his elderly parents, his wife, and children. Kaufman detested Kahane's views but he downplayed the intimate information that might have ended Kahane's career very early. Thirty years later, after a Kahane follower, Dr. Baruch Goldstein, murdered twenty-eight Palestinian Arabs in Hebron, the reporter wondered whether he had made a mistake.

> Had I written more boldly, would the rabbi's credibility with his follow-ers have lessened? Would young men like the then 19-year-old Baruch Goldstein have freed themselves from the rabbi's spell? Was that my job, to bring the rabbi down? I do not know. Over the years I have asked a number of rabbis about it. Some said that setting out to destroy a repu-tation by revealing secrets of a private life is tantamount to murder. But I am more impressed by those who told me that showing mercy to the cruel is wrong and sinful.[38]

THE MARK OF THE *TIMES*: SENSE OF MISSION AND SENSE OF SELF

Schumach, Kihss, and Kaufman were the soul of an earlier *Times*: men and women with a sense of mission, conscience, and conscientiousness. By the 1980s, the *Times*, like Western journalism in general, had changed. Foreign correspondents and columnists of earlier eras had a sense of his-tory and spoke several languages. They aggressively probed societies and governments: Henry Kamm, Flora Lewis, and Cyrus Sulzberger, for ex-ample. Kamm, who spoke many languages, was the *Times'* roving foreign correspondent. An energetic man who looked twenty years younger than he really was, Kamm could journey at a moment's notice to any trouble spot on the planet. A ruddy road warrior with wavy blond hair and a winning smile, he bragged how he had been thrown out of more countries than any other *Times*man, probably more than any other reporter in the world. Kamm got into the toughest spot, Stalinist Albania, where he wrote a story before being expelled. Such energy was not unique. Correspondent and columnist Flora Lewis was famous for her tenacity. She once reportedly ran after an evasive statesman even while eight months pregnant.

Still, the *Times* occasionally let its sense of self undo its sense of duty, even in foreign affairs, particularly if the affairs had a German or Jewish component. Like many German Jews, Ochs was proud of the achievements of Jews, and he was opposed to discrimination against Jews. But he also wanted Jews to blend in with America. The *Times* always had a Christmas tree in its lobby, never a menorah to mark Chanukah, the Jewish holiday. The *Times* had an annual charity drive—the Neediest Cases— keyed to Christmas. And in public statements, Ochs was sure to mention the Sermon on the Mount as well as the Ten Commandments.

Ochs did not want the *New York Times* to be called "the Jewish Newspaper." He lowered its Jewish profile, even in its hiring.[39] During the 1930s, "it was often said of *The Times . . .* that it was 'owned by Jews and edited by Catholics for Protestants.'"[40] Ochs and son-in-law Arthur Hays Sulzberger gave many jobs on the paper to family members. However, they worked hard to lower the profile of Jewish reporters at the *Times*—not giving them prominent out-of-town assignments that rated big bylines.

Ochs and successor Arthur H. Sulzberger blocked or limited *Times* reports that would have shed an early light on Hitler's persecution of the Jews in Germany. That was a central conclusion of Richard Shepard, a reporter and editor at the *Times* who wrote *The Paper's Papers*—an examination and review of the *Times'* personal and private archives. In 1931, Jewish groups assailed the *Times* for not reporting anti-Semitic attacks in Berlin. In 1932, as Hitler's power grew, Ochs opposed anti-Nazi efforts that accentuated the Jewish plight: "I feel a strictly Jewish crusade will do more harm than good. I believe the condemnation of Germany should be universal, embracing all creeds and races, who believe in 'liberty, equality and fraternity.'"[41]

This "universal" or "politically correct" stance about Jewish victims is something the *Times* displays, at other times and in other locales, in its treatment of terror acts by terror groups that single out Jews. For example, in 1993 the *Times* largely hid the Jewish angle in the first World Trade Center attack. One of the terrorists in that attack, Abdul-Rahman Yasin,[42] said he and his colleagues first wanted to attack neighborhoods in Brooklyn where there were many Jews. They switched their plan to the World Trade Center because "the majority of the people who work in the World Trade Center are Jews."[43] The headline and the body of the article hide or downplay this Jewish element: "Suspect in 1993 Bombing Says Trade Center Wasn't First Target." The headline tells us what the target wasn't, not what it was.

Just as the *Times* downplays the Jewish identity of victims or potential targets, it tends to hide the Islamic and Arab side of terrorists. An article on the conviction of Ramzi Yousef and two comrades for his "Bojinka Plot"—the plan to explode twelve airliners in midflight—ignores the Arab or Islamic identity of the plotters and their Islamist ideology.[44] As the *Times* consistently blurs the focus to remove, reduce, or veil victims who are Jews, it underreports or overlooks acts by Fatah in Jerusalem, Hamas in Tel Aviv, and Al-Qaeda in India (where Jewish sites were selected).

FROM THE HOLOCAUST TO COVERAGE OF TERROR IN ISRAEL

Attacks by Arab-Islamic terror groups—Fatah, Hamas, Al-Qaeda, Hizballah—are minimized, covered by nonstaffers, tucked away in remote parts of the newspaper, or explained or reported in indirect language and the passive voice.[45] This recalls the way the *Times* reportage largely sidestepped the mass murder of Jews in the Holocaust, treating it, as researcher Laurel Leff asserts, as "a minor footnote."[46]

The *Times* family was more embarrassed by Jews than motivated to try to save them, as Leff, herself a former reporter, observes. Cyrus Sulzberger, nephew of the publisher and the *Times'* top roving correspondent, was all too typical. Sulzberger "did not evidence much interest in the fate of the Jews in the countries he covered, even though he was stationed in the most critical regions at the most critical periods: Austria in 1938 as Germany annexed the country; the Balkans in 1940 and the first half of 1941 as savage pogroms broke out in Rumania; the Soviet Union in the second half of 1941 and the beginning of 1942 as mobile killing squads roamed through eastern Poland and the Baltic states; and eventually in the Middle East in 1943 and 1944 as Palestine became the last place of refuge for Europe's surviving Jews."[47]

Ochs's successor as publisher, Arthur Hays Sulzberger, was so acutely sensitive about his own Jewish background that he prohibited using certain words in the *Times*. Sulzberger "was vehemently against collective phrases such as *the Jewish people* and launched a campaign to roust them from *The Times*. He instructed editors to substitute expressions like *people of the Jewish faith* or simply *Jews*."[48]

The *Times'* awful Holocaust coverage—or rather its cover-up—was finally acknowledged in the *Times* only in 2001 by former executive editor Max Frankel. He described "the staggering, staining failure of the *New York Times* to depict Hitler's methodical extermination of the Jews of Europe as a horror beyond all other horrors in World War II."

In 1941, six years after Sulzberger succeeded Ochs, a former U.S. president gave the *Times* a scoop on a silver platter. Herbert Hoover, who was active in refugee relief, sent publisher Sulzberger exclusive and sensitive data on the plight of Jews in Nazi-controlled Poland. It was one of the earliest descriptions of Nazi efforts to exterminate Jews. It did not make the *Times'* front page. It was buried on page 11.[49] Even after six million Jews died, the *Times* had trouble finding ink for a Jewish link. "The front-page story on the liberation of Dachau never mentioned the word *Jew*."[50]

FROM BEIRUT TO 9/11: VEILING VICTIMS

Today, the *Times* calls terrorists "militants" or "extremists"—a journalistic and linguistic atrocity now adopted by other news organizations. It avoids calling Arab-Islamic terrorists Arabs or Muslims. Just as the *Times* was a pioneer in good journalism, it became a pioneer in bad journalism well before 9/11: its veiled coverage of the 1993 Arab-Islamic terror attack on New York and its muted and stilted reporting of Palestinian hijackings, suicide bombers, and media manipulation of terror consistently hide or understate important facts and details.

In May 2009, the NYPD arrested four men who plotted simultaneous attacks on two Bronx synagogues and a New York air guard base north of the city.[51] One must read the *Times* articles very carefully to find any mention of the fact that all four men were Muslims who wanted contact with a terror group from Pakistan—Jaish-e-Muhammad. The lead defendant converted to Islam in prison, but the *Times* did not use that as a reason to investigate why prisons produce Islamic terrorists.[52]

After thirteen people were shot dead at Fort Hood, Texas, the *Times* ran several stories about traumatic stress among returning U.S. soldiers.[53] The articles hinted that Major Dr. Nidal Malik Hasan "broke" under stress of being assigned overseas, but, of course, Hasan was never in combat and had never been overseas. The men and women who *had* been overseas did *not* murder their fellow soldiers. The *Times* confused the issue in order to humanize an Islamic terrorist. It published an especially long op-ed that blamed Hasan's actions on the war on terror: "Seeing the Fort Hood shooting as an act of Islamist terrorism is the first step toward seeing how misguided a hawkish approach to fighting terrorism has been."[54] The *Times* also relayed Hasan's complaints that he was not being allowed to pray properly.

Washington Post columnist Charles Krauthammer noticed one more egregious example of this kind of *Times* terror coverage: "A week after the first (1993) World Trade Center attack, the *New York Times* ran the following front-page headline about the arrest of one Mohammed Salameh: 'Jersey City Man Is Charged in Bombing of Trade Center.'" This prompted Krauthammer to say: "Ah yes, those Jersey men—so resentful of New York, so prone to violence."[55]

FOCUSING ON COUNTERTERROR TACTICS RATHER THAN TERROR

One way the *Times* betrayed its journalistic duty was by not reporting or by underreporting many terror atrocities of the late twentieth and early twenty-first centuries, and not explaining their significance. For the *Times*, the main story was how a democratic country—Israel or the United States—sought out and pursued the terrorists, how it treated them, how it interrogated them. It ran many human interest stories on alleged victims of American or Israeli firepower. On this the *Times* was attentive to every detail, assigning its own staff reporters, giving the stories prominence. Terror attacks—Americans killed by anthrax or blown up on the USS *Cole*, and Israelis killed by bombs or snipers—were often ignored. Sometimes these events were covered by small wire-service reports buried under a lingerie advertisement on page 19.

The *Times* had a strange and blasé attitude toward Arab terror in the

1970s and 1980s. Russ Braley, a reporter for the *New York Daily News*, recalled the friendly relationship between *Times* correspondent Eric Pace and George Habash, head of the Popular Front for the Liberation of Palestine (PFLP), a Marxist, Syrian-oriented member of the PLO. In June 1970, the *Times* featured an admiring profile of Habash by Pace, calling him a leader "fast becoming the voice of the new Arab revolution."[56] A month later, the *New York Times Magazine* ran a large feature by Pace on "The Violent Men of Amman," describing them as "commandos." This was when the PLO was taking over Jordan's major cities, murdering Western diplomats, and directing traffic in Jordan's capital, Amman. Morris Draper, a U.S. diplomat, was abducted—then released a day later—by the PLO in June 1970. Another U.S. diplomat, Major Robert Perry, a Yale graduate and fluent speaker of Arabic, was shot dead at his front door by the terrorists. PLO leaders bragged about declaring an independent state in northern Jordan, but Arafat and Habash came close to their real vision of seizing all of Jordan with the help of Syria. George Habash, allied with Arafat and Syria, said victory over Israel first required taking Jordan.[57] King Hussein, who survived three assassination attempts in mid-1970, stopped restraining himself when PLO groups hijacked five planes in three days in September 1970. One plane was blown up in Cairo. Four were hijacked to Jordan, where three were blown up on September 12, 1970—a media extravaganza.[58]

This thuggish behavior reemerged in Lebanon a few years later. The PLO-Fatah set up a state within a state from Beirut south to the Israeli border. It was known as "Fatah-land." Western reporters in Beirut did not exert themselves explaining how Lebanon had ceased to be a real country, how the PLO made it a kind of zombie state where terror was the rule. Beirut reporters rarely asked the five W's and the H of reporting: who, what, when, where, why, and how. Why, when, and how had Lebanon become a terrorist haven? What did this mean for Lebanon itself, its citizens, and its neighbors Israel and Syria? Who was pulling the strings and what were the benefits?

Lebanon should have been a reporter's delight—exotic and accessible. Reporters could lead a good life while always finding a good story. There were great human angles for news or features. In the off hours, with the mountains, the sea, and the restaurants, there was no shortage of something to do. Like Israel, Lebanon was both strange and familiar, Oriental yet Western—a mélange of religious and ethnic groups. Going to Israel was a plum assignment, but reporters rarely fought to go to Lebanon.

"The only word I know in Arabic is 'sniper,'" Jim Markham, the *Times'* Beirut bureau chief, confided to me during a short visit to Israel in 1980.[59] It was an honest and revealing remark from one of the best reporters at the *Times*. Other reporters were less honest, not willing to admit they were working in a place where they were targets of Palestinian terror groups and their Syrian overlords, who used media manipulation techniques— many copied from the Nazis or directly learned from the Soviet KGB.

FROM HITLER AND THE KGB TO ABU MAZEN AND ABU SHARIF

Mahmoud Abbas, who succeeded Yasser Arafat as Fatah and PLO leader, studied in Moscow at the KGB's Patrice Lumumba University. This is where Third World leaders were tutored in leadership and disinformation techniques.[60] Abbas wrote a doctoral thesis titled in Arabic "Al-Wajh al-Aakher: Al-'Alaqat al-Sirriyya Bayn al-Naziyya wa-al-Qiyada al-Sihyuniyya" (The Other Face: The Secret Ties Between Nazism and the Zionist Leadership). In it, Abbas largely denies the Holocaust occurred, or at least says its proportions were exaggerated. The book was once widely sold in the Arab world. Today it is hard to find. Western media and diplomats call Abbas a "moderate," and the official Palestinian websites do not show the book in their biographies of Abbas. The current PLO leader is widely known to the media by the affectionate *kunya* or nickname Abu Mazen (father of Mazen).[61]

Some reporters covering the PLO in Lebanon, Gaza, and the West Bank laugh at the idea that Arafat, Abbas, and associates were sharp media operators with a preplanned media strategy. They blithely wave off the PLO's tremendous media successes at the UN in 1975 ("Zionism is racism" resolution) and in Lebanon in 1982 (when Western media swallowed casualty figures produced by Arafat's brother Fathi, who ran the Palestinian Red Crescent). Some reporters do not appreciate fully the success of the 1987–89 Palestinian-Israeli war of attrition known as the Intifada, nor the 2000–2001 "Al-Aqsa Intifada."[62] Robert Fisk, then of the London *Times*, referred to Arafat's "tiresome, ramshackle and hopelessly inefficient publicity organization."[63] This is either poor analysis or willful ignorance. The well-oiled

PLO media machine did a good job in Jordan, Lebanon, and the West Bank. Media gaffes were typical only in Arafat's last years (2002–2004), when health problems (subcranial bleeding and Parkinson's disease) damaged his appearance and judgment. Israeli-imposed isolation probably sparked some of the wild ranting in interviews—as when he thumped his chest and told CNN's Christiane Amanpour, "I am General Arafat."[64]

This conduct was not always the case. Throughout his career, Arafat was a smooth and often ruthless media player. The man who wrote a petition in blood to get into Egyptian newspapers in the 1950s was the man who planned hijackings in the 1960s and who plotted the takeover of the Munich Olympics in 1972.[65] All along, Arafat had backup plans and phony names for straw-man organizations. He liked wiggle room if things went bad. Arafat was a slippery, lizard-like creature who cold-bloodedly committed the worst crimes and then hid under two rocks we may call "creative ambiguity" and "plausible deniability." The groups Black September, Tanzim, and Al-Aqsa Martyrs Brigade were all run and paid for by Arafat, but the names allowed him to claim to the West that he was really moderate and hated terror, while at the same time telling Arab audiences how much he supported *shahada*—martyrdom.

PLO documents show that Arafat, Abbas, and media aide Bassam Abu Sharif always tried to sway the press with threats, money, or other means.[66] Abu Sharif suggested to Arafat that they duplicate in Ramallah the kind of press control that the PLO had enjoyed at the Commodore Hotel in Beirut. Abu Sharif and Abbas were chosen in the 1980s and 1990s to be the PLO's voices to the West, especially the media. This media fixation began with systematic media training and doctrine in the 1970s.

"Courses in political propaganda were taught by the PLO to their own elite. A chief concern of the Organization was the need to impress its will on its own 'masses.'"[67] Jillian Becker cites a lecture by Dr. Farid Sa'd to the PLO's planning center on December 27, 1977, where, she notes, Sa'd showed that he had studied Nazi propaganda techniques as a basis for the PLO's own theory and methods.

> The basic premise from which non-intellectual propaganda springs is that the vast majority of the masses is in a state of passivity which renders it incapable of fully understanding any doctrine, and Hitler used

to compare it with a female, meaning by this comparison of his that it is paralyzed in its will, and easily succumbs. Therefore very rarely does non-intellectual political propaganda resort to a detailed explanation. It is content to use stimulations in a systematic way to create the desired response.[68]

Unlike reporters sent to Moscow or Paris, most Western news media did not make their staffers learn the local language—Arabic—before going to Beirut. This made reporters lean on "easy" sources: other reporters, French- or English-speaking officials and diplomats. It also made them dependent on local "fixers" the PLO controlled.[69]

Getting a working proficiency in Arabic usually took longer than most reporters wanted to stay in Beirut. And not wanting to stay in Beirut was understandable.

> Beirut wasn't always a place journalists feared. Once a city of glittering, sun-drenched elegance, it was a prize assignment for Western journalists. But in the last ten years, Beirut has become a danger zone. Journalists have been threatened, shot, kidnapped, run out of town and bludgeoned to death. In a city ruled by anarchy and terror, they are inviting targets for Arab governments and groups that feel maligned by their reporting . . .
>
> The nightmare became omnipresent in 1980, when Syrian President Hafez al-Assad launched a campaign of terror against journalists who wrote about political unrest in his country. In the summer of 1980, Reuters Beirut bureau chief Bernd Debusmann was critically wounded by Syrian gunmen, and *Le Figaro* and the BBC moved their offices from Beirut to Nicosia, Cyprus, after Western intelligence agencies confirmed reports that their correspondents were on a Syrian hit list.[70]

JOURNALISTS IN DENIAL

German-born Reuters Beirut bureau chief Bernd Debusmann was trying to track down a story about dissidents inside Syria. As he and his wife left a dinner party in Beirut, two men with silencers jumped out of a car and fired five shots into his body. Miraculously he lived and was flown out of the country for treatment, but the story on which he was working was killed. Reuters was happy to bury the whole affair by claiming that there was "no known cause" for the attack.

The man who hosted the dinner party knew the cause. British radio correspondent Tim Llewellyn also fled Beirut a few months later after he, too, was threatened by Syria. His employer, the British Broadcasting Corporation (BBC), moved its offices to Cyprus. German reporter Robert Pfeffer, who investigated cooperation between Arab terror organizations and the German Baader-Meinhof group, was assassinated in 1979. ABC's Sean Toolan was murdered in July 1981, his body left on a Beirut street right after ABC ran a documentary, *The Unholy War,* tying the PLO to the KGB. Toolan's journalistic colleagues John Kifner of the *New York Times* and Robert Fisk of the London *Times* claimed Toolan had angered a jealous husband.[71] That was convenient. It required no more inquiry or professional courtesy by fellow reporters: typical Beirut journalism. Typical of Beirut justice, no murderer was ever caught.

Neither Fisk, the *Times'* Thomas Friedman, nor any of the other Western journalists reported that Arafat's Fatah organization had captured and imprisoned author-journalist Ken Timmerman, keeping him in a West Beirut underground dungeon for three weeks. Timmerman said his colleagues simply did not want to report the story.[72]

Fisk was among reporters who minimized the full extent of Syrian, PLO, and later Hizballah intimidation of Lebanon-based journalists. "The only Western journalist in Beirut whose death could be attributed without a shadow of doubt to Palestinian gunmen was Robert Pfeffer," averred Fisk. This statement is very misleading.

In Lebanon, it is very hard to know anything beyond a shadow of a doubt. Fisk attributes some violence to Syria alone, even though terror attacks and assassinations that benefited Syria, such as the bombing of the U.S. Embassy, also involved cooperation and execution from other groups such as the PLO and Hizballah.

Fisk ruled out the deaths of Larry Buchman (ABC) and Edouard Saab (*Le Monde* and *L'Orient–Le Jour)* as an accidental plane crash in Jordan and a random sniping, respectively. He attributes solely to Syria the murder of Salim al-Lawzi, editor of *al-Hawadith* (Events), an Arabic newspaper published in London, who in March 1980 made a short and final visit to Lebanon.[73] Fisk's downplaying of Syrian and PLO murder of journalists also flies in the face of his own comments that he was so terrified about being kidnapped or assassinated in Lebanon in 1986 that he could barely leave the house. "There were days in 1986 when I was myself so frightened of being kidnapped that I would drive to work in west Beirut at 90 mph or stay closeted at home for fear that I too would be taken to join my friend [reporter Terry Anderson, kidnapped in 1985] in his torment."[74]

Fisk typifies the journalists who came to Lebanon, intoning the goals of the PLO while cursing everything Israeli. Fisk cites Edward Said's *The Question of Palestine* as obligatory reading for those who want to understand Lebanon. His political view is encapsulated by his own citation of Noam Chomsky: "as long as the United States remains committed to an Israeli Sparta as a strategic asset . . . the prospects are for further tragedy: repression, terrorism, war, and possibly even a conflict that will engage the superpowers. . . ."[75] These two academic authorities—Edward Said and Noam Chomsky—both visited Hizballah in Lebanon: Said threw rocks across the border at Israel; Chomsky posed with Hizballah leader Sheikh Hassan Nasserallah.

Under the careful nurturing of the PLO or Hizballah, other reporters also came, by degree, to identify with the terrorists. For many reporters it was second nature to blame Israel for Lebanon's problems while not looking too hard at the actions of the PLO or Syria—or instead even making excuses for them. There was no serious examination of the fact that the PLO and Syria in Lebanon often used a good-cop, bad-cop routine to intimidate journalists. The PLO pretended to be a provider of services—from translation and transportation to spiritual guidance and food—at the Commodore Hotel in Beirut. It was an efficient and successful operation, but some reporters, such as Fisk, painted them otherwise. Fisk turned the PLO terrorists, who ran a state within a state, into underdogs, a "rag tag army of a few hundred gunmen."[76] The PLO was not ragtag, but in fact well equipped. It had well over 20,000 men,[77] and about 1,000 of them were killed in the 1982 war, along with 370 Syrian soldiers killed and 1,000 wounded. About 6,000 PLO "gunmen" were captured by Israel, and they were not merely "gunmen." They had many mortars, rockets, and SAM missiles. Israeli military historian Chaim Herzog, who once served as head of Israel Defense Forces (IDF) intelligence, wrote:

As Israel gradually took control of the territory in southern Lebanon and mopped up the PLO centres, a vast network of stores of weapons, ammunition dumps and military supplies was revealed throughout the entire area. It was estimated that sufficient small arms were revealed to equip five infantry brigades, and that some 100 trucks a day for over a period of a month would be required to remove what had been discovered. Huge underground stores tunneled into the mountains were discovered, in addition to major dumps located in the cellars beneath large civilian apartment buildings.[78]

Fisk's figure of "a few hundred gunmen" is ridiculous. About 8,000 PLO fighters were evacuated from Beirut after Israel besieged the Lebanese capital. Authors Ze'ev Schiff and Ehud Yaari chronicled the war in detail: "over the course of twelve days a total of 14,398 Palestinian and Syrian fighters, including 664 women and children, were evacuated from Beirut; 8,144 left by sea, and 6,254 Syrian soldiers and members of the Palestinian Liberation Army left overland on the Beirut-Damascus Highway."[79]

Fisk's misreporting is not surprising. At the start of his book on Lebanon, he admits taking pointers from the analyses of Palestinian activist Said and antihegemonic linguistics professor Chomsky. "The most powerful analysis of the period is contained in Noam Chomsky's *The Fateful Triangle: The United States, Israel and the Palestinians*, a book of great detail"[80]—and even greater anger. In this respect, Fisk is not alone. Even the CIA cites Chomsky as a source on the combat in Lebanon for its NationMaster encyclopedia.[81] But Fisk goes further.

Fisk regularly uses examples from the Holocaust or Nazi atrocities as analogies to and metaphors for Israeli actions and policies, comparing the Sabra and Chatilla massacre to the Nazi destruction of the Czech town of Lidice.[82] He often likens Israel to an armed juggernaut loosing Nazi-like blitzkriegs without care for innocent lives. He does not mention that the PLO, Hizballah, or Hamas—Israel's main foes—usually hide behind civilians, while deliberately putting missiles in apartment buildings.

Worse, Fisk puts forward events and statistics to suit his purpose: "The civilians in Lebanon died, in their thousands, because the Israelis bombed their homes, repeatedly and from a great height over a period of weeks."[83] Yet I traveled widely in southern Lebanon in June–September 1982, and only a few buildings in Tyre and Sidon, south Lebanon's two big towns, were damaged. Fisk's reporting of "thousands" killed is wrong. Reporters traveling with the Israeli army in those first two or three weeks of fighting told me of seeing Israeli jets flying low and darting in between some of these buildings. They also reported soldiers being greeted by Lebanese throwing rice as a sign of welcoming their eviction of the PLO. Fisk, Kifner, Friedman, et al.—the Beirut-based reporters enjoying PLO press services at the Commodore Hotel in Beirut—did not cover the story.

I only got into Lebanon in the third week of June 1982, when the initial ardor of the welcome for the Israelis had already worn off. Yet the local population—Shiites, Christians, and Druze—still greeted Israeli soldiers in a friendly manner. Fisk did not report this turn of events until March 2, 1983—almost a year after the war broke out.

In his book, Fisk again ignores this reality, which evokes an entire period. He claims the Sabra-Chatilla massacre was the moral equivalent of Auschwitz and that Israeli soldiers knew what was happening but turned a blind eye and a deaf ear to the cries of the Palestinians being murdered there.[84] These charges cannot be substantiated. They were rejected by an Israeli inquiry commission headed by Supreme Court justices. Unlike the U.S. 9/11 Commission's approach to U.S. officials, the Israeli inquiry took a very tough line with Israel's leaders. It censured defense minister Ariel Sharon and Israeli army chief of staff Lieutenant General Rafael Eytan.[85]

Just months before the 1982 war, the Israeli government charged that Beirut's press was controlled by Syrian/Palestinian intimidation. *Time* magazine acknowledged the atmosphere of fear, noting that "Britain's *Guardian* has even described the atmosphere in Beirut as 'censorship by terrorism.'" ABC News president Roone Arledge, whose reporter had been murdered, called the charges "utter nonsense."[86]

Publicly, reporters and news organizations pretended they had nothing to fear from Syria or Palestinian terror groups. Privately, they spoke differently. Kifner, the *Times* Beirut bureau chief in 1980–81, claimed in an article at the time that reporters saw the PLO "more as a protector of journalists than as an intimidator." Friedman, who succeeded Kifner, preferred, several years later, well after leaving Beirut, to quote a different passage: "As my colleague John Kifner once wrote, reporters in Beirut carried their fear with them just like their notebooks and pens."[87]

This is not the kind of admission Friedman or Kifner would have made publicly while working in Beirut. Reporters there liked to pretend they could freely report on Syria or the PLO, when in fact they could not. Reporters censored their work when discussing Syria and Arafat's PLO. No one rushed to report on the way Syria milked Lebanon's vast smuggling industry (from cars and washing machines to alcoholic drinks). Nor did the Beirut correspondents pursue the burgeoning trade in heroin and cocaine in the Syrian-controlled Bekaa Valley in eastern Lebanon. Drugs were the reason Syrian troops liked serving in Lebanon. Drug traders gave General Ghazi Kanaan, the Syrian commander, a "tip" every year, in addition to other profits: a gold bar.

Western reporters would outdo each other in 1982 in writing about atrocities—real and alleged—committed by Israel and its Christian allies. They mostly skipped three stories of major massacres of Syrian citizens by Syria's regime in June 1980 (Tadmor Prison), February 1981 (the first Hama massacre), and April 1982 (the second Hama massacre).[88] Edward Cody of the *Washington Post* delicately chided his colleagues in 1981 when he commented on the late and partial way they had relayed (or usually not relayed) news of the first Syrian government massacre of several hundred Muslim Brother dissidents in Hama: "In an atmosphere created by the wounding of Reuters correspondent Berndt Debusmann, shot in the back by a gunman . . . the Hama reports have not been widely published from the area."[89]

Being a reporter for the powerful *New York Times* did not make you bulletproof. Yet many correspondents often liked to look tougher than they really were. Some, like Kifner and Friedman, liked to act as if they were bulletproof. Kifner, for example, prided himself on being a tough, streetwise reporter (to this day his speaker's bureau touts the six wars he has covered). This tough war reporter illuminated the dark side of Beirut in 1980 by not writing about it. Kifner concealed the fact that he and several colleagues were abducted for twenty hours by a Palestinian terror group. Kifner, his *Times* colleague Bill Farrell, and three others were driving south of Beirut to check out a rumor that Israel had landed forces near Damour, the Christian town that had been destroyed by the Palestinians. They were stopped at a roadblock by PLO forces, thrown into tiny jail cells, and periodically stripped and interrogated. From their separate cells, they heard several short bursts of bullets from time to time, and feared the sound was the execution of one or more of their colleagues. After fifteen hours they were taken to PLO offices for a bite to eat and profuse apologies. They promised each other not to write about the affair. That likely would have been the end of the incident, but the story spread among *Times* correspondents. It then reached Ze'ev Chafets, then head of Israel's press office, who jumped at the chance to embarrass the *Times* for hiding how its reporters covered up for terrorists.[90]

Chafets grew up in the tough inner city of Detroit and was as streetwise as anyone at the *Times*. He lodged official and public charges with the *Times'* Jerusalem bureau chief, David K. Shipler, knowing Shipler would not be able to avoid the story, which would thus force the *Times* and Kifner to recount the Palestinian kidnapping of journalists. When Kifner's belated account appeared, elements of the story were missing in the *Times* article, though a full story appeared in the *Times'* news service. Perhaps it was just an oversight or a glitch, but it also seemed like more *Times* self-censorship.

To curb the damage, *Times* editors told Kifner to write an account of the abduction. Kifner agreed, but attached conditions. He did not want to anger any of the Palestinian groups. In the pre-Internet era, articles from the *Times* would not be read in Beirut by anyone unless the article also appeared in the *International Herald Tribune,* which was published in Europe and flown to Beirut within a day. Kifner insisted his article *not* be published in the *Tribune.* He marked his copy "no IHT," but someone in the *Times'* New York headquarters made a monumental goof, and the article appeared in the *Tribune*—and in Beirut. When Kifner saw the article, he sped to Beirut's airport without stopping to pack a suitcase, and took the very first plane out of the country, afraid for his life. For weeks the *Times* dispatched discreet but powerful signals to placate Arab terrorists. It sent Cairo bureau chief Henry Tanner to meet Arab officials and Palestinian leaders in Cairo, Riyadh, and Damascus to arrange a "safe conduct" for Kifner to Beirut. When *Times* editors were sure Kifner would not be attacked, he returned to "covering" Beirut.

About this time, the *Times* asked Tom Friedman, already in Beirut at United Press International, to join the *Times*. Friedman went to New York for several months, returning to replace Kifner as bureau chief in April 1982, only weeks before the 1982 Lebanon war between Israel and the

PLO. Like Kifner, Friedman often soft-pedaled the realities of working in Beirut. Friedman visited Israel in September 1982, and I escorted him during some of his research on the Israeli side of the Sabra massacre story. I asked him about PLO pressure on reporters in Beirut, but Friedman waved it off.[91]

"When I write about Arafat, it's like when I write about [Israeli prime minister Menachem] Begin. If they don't like what I say, so they won't talk to me for a week." I didn't believe Friedman then, and I don't believe him now. As Friedman himself wrote long after leaving Beirut, "Any reporter who tells you he wasn't intimidated or affected by this environment is either crazy or a liar."[92]

TERROR ANALYSIS:
THE DANGERS OF INTERPOLATION AND EXTRAPOLATION

Friedman's comments were revealing. He was hiding the truth about the risks of vexing Arafat and displaying bad analysis. One could not compare the attitudes toward the press held by Arafat and Begin in 1982. Arafat was a terrorist who killed his critics, while Begin was an elected leader who did not murder his critics.[93]

Reporters are a bit like intelligence analysts who have to reach conclusions with limited data. This sometimes requires a reporter or an intelligence analyst to gauge a problem when knowing some, but not all, the angles: that is *extrapolation*. That is okay if you are honest about what you know and what you do not know. Where reporters go wrong is when they *interpolate*—introducing extraneous data without knowing its provenance, or, worse, introducing data that they know is bogus.

In Beirut, reporters interpolated, because reporters in Beirut were always afraid. This became clear during several visits in 1982–84, including visits to the *Times* bureau and the "watering hole" of the Western press—the Commodore Hotel in Sunni Muslim–oriented West Beirut. Before the Lebanon war of 1982, I had worked as a reporter-researcher for the *New York Times*, first at Columbia University, and later in Jerusalem in 1980–81, until I was drafted into the Israeli army. In the army I was given a job as a writer and producer at Israeli Army radio, but the 1982 war in Lebanon gave me a chance to monitor Arab radio broadcasts and then to do real field reporting. I traveled widely around Lebanon as a reporter for IDF Radio, known in Hebrew as Galei Tzahal. I made trips to Tyre, Sidon, and Damour, all south of Beirut, to Aleiy and Bahamdun in the mountains to the east overlooking the city, and even to Jbail, well up the coast toward Tripoli and Lebanon's northern border with Syria. I was not only seeking news and features, but also hoping to see how my colleagues in Lebanon worked. Occasionally I took off my uniform (and my Uzi submachine gun and Sony tape-recorder) because the IDF uniform could scare away interviewees, including Western newsmen. One of these was William Farrell, former bureau chief in Jerusalem for the *Times*, now based in Cairo. During the 1982 war, Farrell went to Lebanon to reinforce the *Times'* regular coverage. Bill Farrell was a gregarious Irishman from Brooklyn who wrote beautifully and who told great jokes, sometimes seasoned with words in Yiddish that he learned from his wife, Linda, or from friends in the neighborhood. We were well acquainted, but when he saw me in Beirut wearing an Israeli uniform, he turned white as chalk. He backed away from me as if I had the plague. It was clear he was afraid of being seen with an Israeli, and he knew that he and other reporters were being watched.

A Scandinavian reporter told me that the Syrians and the PLO each had their own way of intimidating reporters. Right after the Scandinavian reporter wrote something unflattering about Yasser Arafat, he was brought to Arafat's office at three in the morning for a short chat. "It was their way of saying to me, 'We know where you live, and we can get to you whenever we want, and no one will interfere.'"

Rather than talk to reporters, I talked to the men and women in the street, using my knowledge of Arabic and French. At times I did interviews at the Galerie Semaan checkpoint between Muslim West Beirut and Christian East Beirut. I found that I could get some interesting stories speaking to people in their own tongue. For example, in a conversation in late June 1982 in a church overlooking Beirut's harbor, members of the Maronite Christian Phalange militia—known in Arabic as *al-Kata'ib*—confided in me that they hoped to get a chance to exact revenge on the Palestinians for their massacres of Christians during the 1975–76 Lebanese civil war. Most of my Hebrew-speaking Israeli colleagues at IDF Radio thought this was just *kalaam fadi*—empty talk—a bluff by Maronite gunslingers who did nothing but chatter. Most Israeli soldiers thought of the Phalange soldiers as *hayalei shokolad*—Hebrew for "chocolate soldiers"—expected to melt under the first sign of pressure. Though I believed the Phalange men were not real fighters, I thought their threat was real, because their thirst for revenge was real. There had been numerous massacres in Lebanon in the previous decade, and the Maronite Christians had suffered their share.

When I got a weekend pass from combat coverage, I went back to Jerusalem and sought out and warned one of Israel's top cabinet ministers. Yosef Burg, a rotund, bespectacled politician, was also a trained psychologist and rabbi. I looked for him at his synagogue, Heichal Shlomo, and he invited me to his home and listened to me for a few minutes. I told him Israel was perfectly justified in trying to destroy or curtail PLO terror, but the longer the IDF stayed in Lebanon, the greater the chance that the Maronites would try to execute their revenge while hiding behind Israel's skirts. Burg was one of Israel's most experienced and respected politicians, a recognized scholar as well as Israel's chief negotiator in autonomy talks with Egypt. He was very courteous, but he apparently forgot or discounted what I said.

A few months later, the Maronites carried out their threat: murdering about three hundred Palestinians—mostly women and children—at the Sabra and Chatilla refugee camps in southern Beirut. The massacre was revenge not only for earlier massacres of Christians but for the murder of Lebanese president-elect Bashir Gemayel, the leader of the Phalange. A huge car bomb killed Gemayel on September 14, 1982, murdering seventy other people and leaving a hole about a block wide. It was a classic Syrian operation. The Palestinians were Syrian allies, and Israel sent its tanks into Palestinian-controlled West Beirut to clamp a lid on the violence.

The bombing proved that Syrian and Palestinian forces were still active in Beirut even after the public pullout of Syrian forces and most PLO fighters two weeks earlier. Israel was reluctant to send its own men into the dangerous and uncharted streets of Muslim West Beirut. It was a recipe for disaster. Either the troops would overreact or underreact due to lack of preparation. Israel's army is largely composed of reserve soldiers (computer technicians and clerks, for example). Most were unschooled in Arabic, unfamiliar with the Beirut urban terrain, and untrained in crowd control and police methods. So Israel relied on its Arabic-speaking allies, the Phalange militia, which knew Beirut. But this choice, while understandable, was disastrous.

The Phalange was not really a close or natural ally of Israel. Its founder, Pierre Gemayel, was a protofascist, but its enmity toward Syria and the PLO convinced Israeli leaders it could be trusted. They were dead wrong. Some Phalange leaders later became pro-Syrian in their outlook.[94] One was Elie Hobeika, the Phalange commander who led the attacks in Sabra and Chatilla, murdering mostly women, children, and old men—people who could not run away fast enough.

Reporters in Beirut adopted a facile and false storyline that Israel had directed the massacre, and that another Israeli ally, the South Lebanese Army (SLA), was part of the atrocity. The SLA was a ragtag unit. It had many different religious groups—Greek Orthodox (and other smaller Christian sects), Druze, and even Shiites. It was led by ex-Lebanese army major Saad Haddad, a short and gruff southern native who was the antithesis of high-living French-speaking Maronites who bronzed themselves on the beaches of Junyeh, north of Beirut. Haddad and the SLA were (figuratively and literally) miles away from Beirut. Haddad's SLA operated in the villages of Kleia and Marjuyyn, in sight of the Israeli border. SLA rarely ventured north, not even to the coastal towns of Tyre and Sidon, let alone fifty miles farther to Lebanon's capital.

Anyone who knew anything about the cultural and religious divisions in Lebanon would have waved off the idea that Haddad's units had been active inside Beirut—not because of the various Muslims, but because the Maronites likely would have resisted violations of their turf. Still, most of the PLO-vetted press corps embraced this preposterous "story" as if it were an undeniable fact—among them Robert Fisk of the London *Times* and Thomas Friedman of the *New York Times*.

Friedman was apparently vacationing outside the country when Syrian agents blew up an entire city block of Beirut to assassinate Bashir Gemayel. Friedman was still outside Lebanon when angry Phalange gunmen invaded the Sabra and Chatilla areas to carry out a massacre. He returned to Beirut "to play catch-up," hurriedly trying to recoup the story. *Times* editors in New York realized this might be *the* story of the year, a good bet for a Pulitzer Prize. Within a short time, Friedman had "all" the facts and composed an indictment like which he had never written about a Palestinian or Syrian massacre during his time in Beirut.

The *Times'* front-page headline was rather tame. But Friedman's account was not. It had all the drama and the clarity of a good crime novel, stressing two points:

- Israel's Christian allies murdered innocent Palestinians.
- Israel was believed to have been involved and to have cooperated in the murder.[95]

Friedman's long account was noteworthy for what it stressed and what it ignored. It quoted Amin Gemayel, brother of the slain president-elect, denying any involvement by the Phalange militia, but it did not offer any direct comments from Israelis or from Major Haddad of the SLA. It did quote unnamed diplomats as calling Israeli denials "disingenuous," a term better applied to Friedman's reporting. It is interesting to mark where Friedman employs the terms "all," "evidence," and "clear" in his story.

> Lebanese Army troops and civil defense volunteers moved into the Shatila refugee camp today to establish order and remove the mounds of rotting corpses, the evidence of a mass killing of Palestinian men, women and children by Lebanese Christian militiamen.
>
> The grisly task of clearing out the bodies from a camp still reeking with death took place as new information emerged about the extent of the massacre of Palestinian civilians and the role played by Israeli forces in the events of the last four days.
>
> (In Jerusalem, the Israeli authorities said they knew in advance that the Phalangists were planning to enter the camps, but never imagined that a massacre would occur.) [This paragraph, written based on reporting by the *Times* bureau in Jerusalem, turned out to be accurate.]
>
> It is still not known how many people were gunned down in the Shatila camp and the adjacent Sabra camp or killed in exchanges of fire with Christian militiamen. A Western diplomat who toured Shatila early this morning managed to count 106 bodies. . . .
>
> It is also clear that the events in Shatila and Sabra took place within

the view of one of the main Israeli observation posts in west Beirut, and the Christian militiamen entered the area of the camps and left the area of the camps by passing through Israeli lines.

Also there was no indication, witnesses said, that Israeli forces made any concerted effort to interdict the operations of the Christian militiamen, who rested between forays into the refugee camps side-by-side with Israeli troops.

The makeup of the Christian militia force that went into the camps remains unclear. All reports indicate that members of Maj. Saad Haddad's Israeli-armed and trained militia were on the scene, but it was not known if they joined the Phalangists who went in. Also, it was not known whether the Phalangist militiamen who did go in after arriving from east Beirut had done so on orders from the Phalangist Party or were a breakaway group. . . .

Israel's surprise at the outcome, the diplomats said, seems disingenuous given the history of Christian-Palestinian relations in Lebanon and the importance placed on the issue during the negotiations. . . .

Far down in the story, there is a parenthetical mention of Lebanon's long history of massacres between competing Lebanese groups, but Friedman really did not give context or show trends and numbers.

There is a highly trained group of Phalangist soldiers, known as the Damuri Brigade, which has been in Damur, just south of Beirut, ever since the Israelis took the town. The brigade is made up of many of the sons of Christian families massacred by Palestinians in Damur in February 1976 in retaliation for the Christian massacre of Palestinian civilians at the Tel Zaatar refugee camp. The Damuri Brigade has long vowed to be at the forefront of any effort to rid Lebanon of Palestinians and there are some here who believe that its members may have been the Phalangists who took part, wearing Phalangist uniforms.

As for the others, the evidence points to their being members of the Christian militia of Major Haddad. All of the residents and doctors in the camps spoken to by reporters said that Haddad men, in their uniforms, and Phalangists joined in the operation. Officials here said that it appears that the Israelis have sought to place blame solely on the

Phalangists since Major Haddad's militia is virtually integrated into the Israeli Army and operates entirely under its command.

Part of the Friedman story featured a subheadline—"Israelis Wanted Areas 'Purified.'" The text strongly suggested this "purification" was aimed at Palestinian civilians rather than suspected strongpoints of hidden Palestinian forces. Friedman quoted at length a Norwegian doctor claiming Major Haddad and his men invaded a hospital and separated five hundred Palestinian civilians hiding there from the rest of the hospital population.[96] Haddad and his men then marched the five hundred Palestinian civilians toward Sabra, where we are led to believe they met a tragic fate. This narrative itself recalls Nazi "separations" of Jews from local populations in Europe in World War II: "The foreign staff members were put in one area and the Palestinian staff and refugees in another. The Palestinian civilians, estimated by the doctors to have been between 500 and 600 people, were marched off at gunpoint down the mainstreet of Shatila."

Friedman's reliance on the testimony of Beirut hospital workers is problematic at best. At worst, it is dishonest. Lebanon's health system was closely tied to the PLO. Friedman had to know this. Arafat's own brother, Fathi Arafat, ran the Palestinian Red Crescent in Lebanon. After the 1982 war, the PLO continued to exploit hospitals and health officials for propaganda and for terror operations—this time in Gaza and the West Bank. During the 1987–89 "Intifada," Palestinian health officials falsely reported Israeli use of "dum-dum bullets" or other internationally banned weapons.[97]

After writing his major article on the massacre, Friedman went to Israel to question Israeli officials, before writing a retrospective examination titled, THE BEIRUT MASSACRE: THE FOUR DAYS.[98] This article, which ran on September 26, 1982, was better balanced and researched than the original hurried article. It toned down atrocity claims and putative massacre figures, but kept the general thrust, adding some errors in fact and analysis. Its most honest part was admitting that the investigation "left many unanswered questions." It also said "the full truth may never be known."

The opening paragraph read: "The massacre of more than 300 Palestinian and Lebanese men, women and children at the Shatila refugee camp by Christian militiamen has left many unanswered questions."

Nevertheless, Friedman continued to promote the idea that the massacre had been carried out by the South Lebanese Army of Major Saad Haddad. He did so despite two factors:

- The circumstantial "evidence" against Haddad was flimsy and from prejudiced, largely unnamed Palestinian sources who hated Haddad.
- There was a firm denial from Haddad, which Friedman heard directly from Haddad. Friedman chose *not* to cite his own interview, preferring a quotation from Robert Fisk of the London *Times*.

Since I was at the Friedman-Haddad interview[99] and understand the nature of the "evidence," I will describe both. Friedman, who had been relatively restrained in his coverage of a terror group (PLO), was quite aggressive in pursuing that group's foes (Israel and Haddad's SLA). Here are relevant parts of Friedman's reconstruction:

> But the Phalangists were not the only Christian militiamen moving out of the airport Thursday afternoon. There is also a sizable body of circumstantial evidence suggesting that members of the militia of Maj. Saad Haddad, armed and trained by Israel, were also at the airport and may also have moved up to the staging area, despite Israeli denials that they were involved in any way in the slayings.
>
> The evidence includes interviews with Lebanese soldiers who were on duty in the traffic circle, and had been on duty there since Sept. 3. They said they saw Haddad militiamen there, dressed in uniforms readily distinguishable from those of the Phalangist militiamen. They also said the Haddad men were noticeable because they lacked the Phalangist insignia on the left breast pocket reading "Lebanese Forces."
>
> Further, scores of survivors from the camps said in interviews that some of the militiamen spoke with southern Lebanese accents and addressed one another by such names as Ali, and Abbas. Both are Shiite Moslem names. Roughly half of Major Haddad's 6,000-member militia members are Shiites from the south.[100]
>
> Finally, Major Haddad said in an interview with The Times of London that some of his men "may have been serving with other forces in Beirut" when the massacre in the camps occurred.

It seems clear that there were militiamen for Major Haddad's group in the strike force that entered the camps on Thursday afternoon.

What is not clear is whether the Haddad militiamen could have reached the camps—far from their normal area of operations in the south along the Israeli border—without the knowledge or active cooperation of the Israelis.

At the least, the circumstantial evidence indicates that some members of the Haddad militia passed through Israeli lines in an apparent effort to join up with the Phalangists going into the Palestinian camps. . . .

In summary, the Israelis do not appear to have found, nor do there appear to have been, 2,000 P.L.O. guerrillas who remained behind in West Beirut. Clearly there were some, but the weight of the evidence suggests that the number was in the low hundreds at most.

Friedman never explained why it was so unlikely that PLO fighters who lived in Beirut could use the tumult of the Gemayel assassination to slip across neighborhood lines in Beirut by going one or two miles, while it was a near certainty that Haddad's country bumpkin militiamen, who were strangers in Beirut, could easily cross forty or fifty miles and join up and blend right in with the somewhat hostile urban-based Phalange militia.

THE ARAB WORLD OF TOM FRIEDMAN

Friedman reputedly knows Arabic but he did not say a single word to Haddad in Arabic.[101] Haddad, a short, simple man, had very clumsy English. Maybe Friedman felt ill at ease questioning in Arabic or maybe he wanted to keep Haddad off balance. Still, his interview technique was like a prosecutor cross-examining a defendant in a murder trial.[102] Friedman would ask a question and cut short Haddad's halting English, within a few words of the start of each sentence.[103] Haddad said he went to Beirut to pay a traditional condolence call at the Gemayel home after the murder of Maronite leader Bashir Gemayel. He denied he or his forces were at Sabra or Chatilla.

Friedman built his claim that Haddad's forces were at Sabra on the "fact" that "witnesses" said they heard the names Ali and Abbas. Friedman calls these Shiite names. This is said to "prove" the presence of Haddad's

forces, which included Shiites.[104] This is not just highly speculative journalism. It shows cultural illiteracy and historic imbecility.

Abbas is a perfectly good Sunni Muslim name, used even by PLO
leader Mahmoud Abbas (Fatah/PLO chairman) and Abu Abbas (hijacker
of the cruise ship *Achille Lauro*). Abbas was progenitor of a Sunni Islamic
empire: the Abbasid Caliphate. Anyone who has not heard of the Abbasid
Caliphate should not be a reporter in Lebanon.

Ali is a common Shiite name, but it is also used by Sunni Muslims in
Egypt and elsewhere.[105] "Name evidence" is nonsense, but it was a big part
of the storyline earning Friedman a Pulitzer Prize and establishing his
reputation as an "expert" in Middle Eastern affairs.

Years later, as a *Times* columnist, Friedman continued prosecuting
Israel or those suspected of being pro-Israel, while acting like a defense
attorney for Arab regimes or groups involved in or suspected of terror. His
view was not so much pro-Palestinian as it was Philistine—superficial and
unsupported by facts. Arabism without Arabic, Muslims without Islam,
triangulating Mideast tribes without understanding tribalism.

Shortly after 9/11, Friedman journeyed to Saudi Arabia to write
about a supposed "Saudi peace plan." This was part of a well-funded Saudi
effort to curb damage to the Saudi image caused by Osama bin-Laden
and the other Saudi-based and educated terrorists. Rather than writing
how the Saudi royal house had helped bin-Laden and consistently con-
founded U.S. terror investigations,[106] Friedman bragged about being taken
to dinner at Prince Abdullah's Arabian horse farm. There they hatched a
bold Mideast peace plan. It supposedly guaranteed full Arab recognition
of and peace with Israel in return for a total Israeli withdrawal to the pre-
1967 frontier lines. The Saudi image makeover, right after 9/11, damp-
ened criticism of the corrupt and extremist Saudi royal house. It converted
the oppressive Wahhabi regime into "peacemakers."

As with other Tom Friedman discoveries, the truth arrived late for
dinner. The Saudis subsequently made clear that their idea of "peace" also
meant allowing all Palestinians to enter Israel as returning refugees or
original residents—effectively destroying Israel.[107] Friedman did not mind
being a Saudi defense attorney, swearing Prince Abdullah was *the* most
uncorrupt Saudi leader. He periodically returned to brag about his trip
for dinner at then prince (now king) Abdullah's horse farm.[108] Even with

firm evidence that the Saudi leaders still spend millions of dollars, euros, and riyals sending their poisonously anti-Christian, anti-Jewish, and anti-Western teachings throughout the world, Friedman still nods to Mecca.

In 2010–11, Friedman was blind and deaf to seismic strategic changes in the region. Turkey, a modern Islamic state that had been a reliable NATO ally of the United States and Britain, and an anti-terror partner for Israel, sank into an Islamist morass, swayed partly by Saudi aid money and Saudi-funded textbooks in its education system. Its Islamic government turned terror-friendly, virulently anti-Israeli, anti-American, and pro-Syrian. It helped launch an "aid flotilla" aimed at breaking Israel's arms blockade on the Hamas terror regime in Gaza.[109] Friedman breathlessly told his readers what wonderful people the Turkish leaders were and how excited he was to have been there and to watch the Turkish chief rabbi hold hands with a Turkish Muslim cleric at a memorial ceremony of a terror attack on a Turkish synagogue. He admired Turkey's Islamist regime and its peacemaking efforts, without mentioning its approval of anti-Semitic films on Turkish television or its support for Hamas. "The strategic situation has never been more opportune—the Arabs are scared of the Iranians, the Saudi peace plan is still on the table, and the Palestinians are beginning to act rationally. But we lack the leadership to help us make a real change."[110]

Presumably, Friedman meant the kind of leadership of President Barack Obama, who *had* made a real change by spurring the PLO to undo twenty years of talks. It now refused even to talk directly with Israel. Obama was the first president who demanded more of Israel than the Palestinians had.[111] That was the leadership Friedman craved. Obama's first foreign trip was a bold journey to Turkey that emboldened militancy by Islamist Turkish leader Recep Erdogan. That was the leadership Friedman applauded. Friedman did not really "speak truth to power." He preferred to cheerlead, perched on the cutting edge of the current conventional wisdom.

From this lofty perch, Friedman was an umpire at a tennis match, though not surveying a mere game. In his high chair, Friedman sees equal fault with "both sides"—even when discussing attacker and victim. He reduces Arab-Islamic hostility to the West to superficial sentimentality, and he boils down the Arab-Israeli conflict to a purely territorial affair soluble by total Israeli withdrawal. The Arabs will make peace when Israel pulls back "from every inch of the West Bank and Arab districts of East Jerusalem, as it has from Gaza."[112] Friedman never admits that his territorial analysis has been dead wrong, literally, in Gaza and in Lebanon. Israel's unilateral pullbacks from Lebanon and Gaza produced more terror deaths and no peace. What if the core of the Arab-Israeli conflict is *not* a land dispute, but revolves around religion and culture—Arab-Islamic religion and culture? What if, in a parallel way, Arab-Islamic hostility to the West, and anti-Western terror, are also not really about Americans in Iraq and Englishmen in Afghanistan? What if the terror and the hostility are tied to religion, culture, and Arab-Islamic self-image: dangerous uncharted terrain where Friedman rarely treads without being armed with an arsenal of proven platitudes. When Nidal Malik Hasan murdered his U.S. Army colleagues in Fort Hood, the closest Friedman came to assessing real motives was that "Major Hasan was just another angry jihadist spurred to action by 'The Narrative.'"[113]

Such shallow and shoddy journalism bespeaks an ailing profession neglecting the underlying issues of Arab-Islamic terror. It is a profession that largely ignored the terror-media nexus in the three final decades of the twentieth century and the first decade of the twenty-first.

Arab-Islamic terror did not begin with Osama bin-Laden. Palestinian leaders Yasser Arafat, George Habash, and Mahmoud Abbas were pioneers in developing modern terror tactics and doctrine. Arafat in particular used the media as a basic part of his warfare and strategy: everything from hijacking to layered messages to different audiences. Bin-Laden and Ayman Zawahiri of Al-Qaeda and Hassan Nasserallah of Hizballah pushed the terroristic use of media still further, particularly video and Internet. They perfected the symbolic attack on Western power centers.[114]

Arafat, the media pioneer, and his lieutenants were coached in media methods and disinformation techniques by the KGB. Two of the most famous were Bassam Abu Sharif and Mahmoud Abbas, who specialized in handling contacts with press as well as with Israelis and Jews in general. They created the image of the "PLO moderate" interested in peace while never letting go of the rifle. Abbas was so successful in cultivating this moderate image that Israelis almost always called him by his *kunya*—nickname—Abu Mazen (father of Mazen). This avuncular and affectionate name is quite incongruous when used by adversaries. It would be like Winston Churchill calling Joseph Stalin "Uncle Joe" or John Kennedy calling Nikita Khrushchev "Nikita Sergeivich." Not many diplomats or reporters noted that Abbas got a "doctorate" from the KGB's Patrice Lumumba University for "research" on the "secret ties" between Zionism and Nazism. Arafat, Abbas, and Company were the new face of terror warfare.

3

CNN:
CERTAINLY NOT NEWS

The second half of the twentieth century saw new kinds of war, which brought the media into the battlefield in dramatic new ways. Some of this was the result of technological advancements—regular jet travel, miniature phones, cameras, and such. Some of the media entry was the result of the policies of those making war. Small states and organizations defeated large powers—not with brute force, but with media power—by making the war effort unpopular inside the large democratic states. This was a confusing process for the democracies as they found their own media used as a weapon against them. It led to questions, as Gil Merom observes: "How do insurgents win small wars against democracies in spite of their military inferiority?" and "How do democracies lose such wars in spite of their military superiority?"[1] States that had won world wars could not win small conflicts: in the first half of the twentieth century, Western democracies dominated the Near East and Far East, defeated Nazi Germany, and contained the Soviets. The twentieth century was "the American Century" because America led the free world to victory in two world wars and in a long battle against communism.[2] But the new era demonstrated the limits of power—it was an era, as Merom observes, "when democracies are inclined to fail in protracted wars."[3]

Guerrilla wars, wars of terror, and protracted conflicts in Algeria, Ireland, Lebanon, and Vietnam showed how small states and small organizations could confound Western power. The small guys overcame modern
democracies like the United States, Britain, France, and Israel by using
Western media and *Western* intellectuals to undermine Western military
power. France retired from Algeria, even though it had largely defeated
the FLN. A critical mass of intellectuals and the press had turned against
the war effort, convincing General Charles de Gaulle to leave. U.S. president Lyndon Johnson resigned himself to leave Vietnam after CBS News
anchorman Walter Cronkite turned against the war: "If I've lost Walter,
I've lost the country," said Johnson, announcing he would not run for reelection.

Exploiting the media became part of the central calculus of those
fighting against superior forces and technology. It was no accident Yasser
Arafat often recalled the lessons of Algeria in the 1950s and Vietnam in
the 1960s. They were models for his media policy from 1970 through the
turn of the millennium. But they were not his only models.

Arafat was born and raised in Egypt. He studied how Egyptian
president Gamal Abdul-Nasser used the media, employing powerful
state radio transmitters, Egyptian newspapers, and the influential Egyptian film industry to destroy opponents. The most powerful weapon was
the clear-channel radio broadcast *Sawt al-'Arab*—Voice of the Arabs.
It reached from Morocco to Iraq, and Abdul-Nasser used it to spark
Pan-Arab coups in Jordan and Lebanon in mid-1958, coups that were
stymied by British and U.S. interventions. Even when the attempts failed,
Abdul-Nasser was still the predominant Arab-Islamic leader of his day.
He could frame issues and fan Arab foment at will. He was less successful in mobilizing international public opinion against Israel, which
was still seen as a kind of underdog facing the combined might of the
Arab world.

PROPAGANDISTS AND PARACHUTISTS

Arafat closely studied the successes and failures of Abdul-Nasser. He also
studied the "Great Mufti"—Haj Amin al-Husseini, a distant relative who
was the dominant Arab media personality in the British mandate over the
Palestinian trust territory from 1920 to 1948. More than any other Third

World leader, Arafat was constantly conscious of using the media as a tool and as a weapon, both among his own Arabic-speaking audience and among non-Arabic-speaking Western audiences. Yasser Arafat became the undisputed head of the PLO through his masterful exploitation of the "Battle of Karameh" in March 1968. Israeli forces attacked his bases inside Jordan, inflicting a heavy toll but suffering their own losses, too.[4] It was a major propaganda victory for Arafat, especially after the Arab military debacle of 1967.

Skillfully using Arab oil money and political clout, Arafat became not just a Palestinian and Arab symbol but a larger symbol for developing countries and areas that had been ruled by the West. With his sharp media instincts Arafat realized the potential power of television. He and Mahmoud Abbas perfected the use of the claimed "atrocity" to turn the tables on more powerful opponents, such as Israel. Instinctively, the methods developed in the 1982 war in Lebanon and the Palestinian-Israeli fighting of 1987–89—commonly called the Intifada—were widely mimicked. For example, after the United States struck back at Syria for aiding several attacks on Americans,[5] some Western reporters were led by the nose to chronicle the putatively wanton destruction of Lebanese towns and villages. One noted case was a CBS reporter standing in front of part of the town of Aleiy in the Shouf Mountains overlooking Beirut, declaiming: "this is what the guns of the battleship *New Jersey* have done to this town." The only problem was that the report was wrong. Parts of Aleiy had been destroyed in earlier fighting between rival Lebanese factions. Similarly, many reporters and photographers used the backdrop of the coastal town of Damour (destroyed years earlier in Palestinian-Maronite fighting) in order to claim widespread Israeli destruction of southern Lebanon in 1982.

Palestinian and Syrian propagandists have used this tactic many times in Lebanon, the West Bank, and Gaza on "parachutists": the reportorial reinforcements who flew in to cover breaking stories such as the Lebanon war or the Intifada. The newcomers are often the willing consumers and purveyors of propaganda by Arab-Islamic terror groups or their state sponsors. Successful strategies in media management and war are often copied, and so other Arab and Islamic leaders and groups—from Hamas in Gaza and Hizballah in Lebanon to Saddam Hussein in the Gulf—have copied the Palestinian script, adding their own special touches. A generation later, in his analysis of the 2006 Lebanon war (Israel-Hizballah), Anthony Cordesman summarized the problem well: "Civilians and battles of propaganda and perception are the natural equivalent of armor in asymmetric warfare. Israel, the United States, and all powers that rely on the legitimacy of the ways they use force must get used to the fact that opponents will steadily improve their ability to use civilians to hide, to deter attack, to exploit the political impact of strikes, and to exaggerate damage and killings."[6]

THE INTIFADA, BREAKING NEWS SYNDROME, AND THE CNN EFFECT

The Palestinian-Israeli war of attrition of 1987–89 was named the Intifada. It was a mostly spontaneous series of events that became a choreographed script for media combat and strategic success.[7] When Western media adopted the Arabic term *intifada*, this was a victory for the Palestinians. Though the Intifada often involved violence and sometimes even terror, Western reporters called it an *intifada*, giving it an exotic ring. They branded it as a special kind of "uprising" or protest movement.[8]

"For the first time, the Palestinians have taken their destiny in their own hands," asserted Yitzhak Rabin in early 1988.[9] Rabin, then Israel's defense minister, saw that young Palestinians had found a formula for success: mass protests, low-tech riots, and attacks that embarrassed and weakened Israel politically more than actually inflicting major casualties on Israeli forces.

Western reporters know cameras energize events. Protests at the local school board or worker strikes at a factory are inflamed when cameras are present. This dynamic accelerates more quickly in Arab-Islamic societies that are authoritarian pressure cookers. Current Arab political foment shows it. When the lid pops off previously managed media and protest in repressed societies, revolutionary events can occur.

In Arab-Islamic society, public protest and cameras are a combustible mixture. That is why regimes in Jordan and Egypt, for example, have always tried to prevent protests and cameras even on mundane issues such as state subsidies for the price of bread.[10] In a flash, the issue is not the price of bread, but the leader's head.[11] With the advent of CNN, this escalation process increased markedly.[12] CNN's global network provided near-immediate gratification and feedback, a kind of "media loop" as demonstrators and rioters paused to watch themselves on television:

> During the overthrow of the shah in Iran, for example, activities in the country would come to a virtual halt during the BBC newscasts so that people could find out what was happening in other parts of their country. The same true during the initial phases of the Intifada. The BBC, VOA, Radio Monte Carlo were the prime sources of information to the Palestinians about what was happening in their own backyard. During the Intifada, however, a new element was added. The arrival of fax machines not only enabled the Palestinians with access to the machines to receive orders from abroad, they enabled Palestinian leaders to find out in real time the impact the rioting was having on others around the world. . . . It is impossible to underestimate the effect this feedback mechanism had on local Palestinians.[13]

"By the 1980's, satellites were getting more powerful and therefore required increasingly smaller reception dishes, a situation that enabled average citizens to buy dishes and receive transmission from direct broadcast satellites (DBSs)," observes communications professor Mark Alleyne. "Global news seemed to be no longer a hierarchical, mediated structure dominated by international news agencies.

"CNN came to symbolize for many the coming of a 'global village.'"[14] This reflected changes both in media technology and media policy, epitomized by Ted Turner, who founded CNN in 1980 with the idea of attracting a global audience. *Time* magazine "was so impressed that it made . . . Turner, its 'Man of the Year' for 1991."[15] Turner's style and views colored CNN's coverage. It was global-oriented, solicitous of Third World feelings, and often implicitly critical of his own government and country, the United States. Turner said the Vietnam War had changed his view of America and world politics.[16] His skeptical, even cynical view of U.S. power was on display during the Persian Gulf standoff involving Iraq, Kuwait, and the United States in 1990–91, when CNN's twenty-four-hour news format made it a natural outlet for war coverage.

"It was a CNN war, and we all knew it," comments Howard Kurtz, the media reporter for the *Washington Post*. "The story was changing by the hour and we came out only once a day."[17]

CNN: BETWEEN IRAQ AND A HARD PLACE

Saddam Hussein was a rapacious tyrant with fifty-five armored divisions—the largest army in the Arab world in 1980. He portrayed himself as the underdog, as the defender of the Arab world against the "Persian threat" as he unleashed an unprovoked attack on an Iran just weakened by its own Islamic revolution. Eight years and a million casualties later, Saddam barely survived the adventure. With the help of the United States and some Gulf countries, including Kuwait, Saddam narrowly escaped defeat at the hands of the highly motivated followers of the ayatollahs. Saddam settled for a bloody draw with Iran, but his appetite was not yet sated. Scarcely catching his breath, Saddam then turned on Kuwait, seizing its territory, claiming it had always been part of Iraq. When the West came to Kuwait's defense, Saddam, the secular Baathist socialist who burned mosques by the dozens, portrayed himself as a defender of Islam against "Western crusaders." Saddam emblazoned the Arabic phrase *Allahu Akbar*—God is Great—on all Iraqi flags. To add emphasis, he fired missiles at Israel, which had nothing to do with the war in Kuwait. After preying on his neighbors, after using poison gas against Iran and his own citizens, and after untold chapters of torture and executions of his own political opponents, Saddam faced the daunting challenge of trying to improve his image.

Fortunately for him, a new media player had recently entered the arena: CNN. As Saddam and others supplied the wars, CNN supplied the coverage, eager to grasp a dynamic storyline. Against the background of plumes of smoke or the sound of gunfire, its reporters, wearing safari shirts and flak jackets, used the nearest roof in Baghdad, Beirut, or Jerusalem to intone their reports.

Officially, CNN stood for Cable News Network, but it could have stood for "Creating News Now." When it opened in 1980, CNN stressed speed, highlighting the "when" factor in the news rather than the "how" or the "why," which were more complex and took more time. "Breaking news" was the watchword. CNN moved fast but not always carefully enough. It also struggled to find material to fill a twenty-four-hour window of news.

Its first "scoop" was breaking from a commercial in order to show live footage of Jimmy Carter in the hospital room of Vernon Jordan, the civil rights leader wounded by a would-be assassin. When there was a war or a global thirst for a special news story—like a flood or earthquake—CNN's market share rose fast. It thrived on the 1982 Lebanon war as well as the Intifada of 1987–89. The PLO in Lebanon and the United Intifada Command in the West Bank and Gaza understood the camera's power and its needs. TV craved pictures, dynamic pictures. Palestinians often staged events—even gory murders—for the cameras, especially for CNN. For instance, CNN got a tip that Arab militants were going to kill the *mukhtar* (headman) of the West Bank town of Qabatya. CNN's local field crew was led to the spot where the man was burned on a makeshift stake—just for the cameras.[18] It was not clear if he was dead before being burned for the audience at home.

Israel's top West Bank commander was Major General Amram Mitzna, a bearded idealist who was liked by his men but badly prepared for this new kind of war. He specialized in using armored columns, was trained for leading tanks in battle, not media. His men grabbed the CNN film—a colossal media blunder. Israel missed a chance to let the Palestinians show the cruel underside of the Intifada. Mitzna and his Israeli civilian superiors made many more mistakes of this kind over the next two years.[19]

Scheduling a live murder for CNN was a rare Palestinian media mistake that Israel rushed to correct. Palestinian Arabs were eager to show the world that theirs was a spontaneous uprising against "occupation," involving minimal bloodshed and almost no weapons from their side. The Arabs called this *al-silah al-abyaad*: the white weapon—a reference to clean weapons like the rocks used by David against Goliath. Here they were clearly not attacking Goliath, but murdering one of their own, even if they called him a traitor who had helped Israel. Over the next three years, the Arabs in the West Bank and Gaza killed more than a thousand of their brothers and sisters (usually in late-night murders or extralegal executions).[20]

General Mitzna believed CNN's film would distress Arabs who worked with Israel. But these Arabs already were distressed. Palestinian Arab society was going through an internal upheaval. The Intifada was a generational struggle for leadership as much as it was about fighting Israel. The self-immolating reign of terror unleashed by the Intifada was not easily reported, because it meant getting dangerously close to it.

LYNCHING THE PRESS

The second Palestinian-Israeli war of attrition (2000–2004) is known as "the Second Intifada" or "the Al-Aqsa Intifada." When it began, two Israeli reserve soldiers made a wrong turn on the road to Jerusalem, stumbling into the West Bank town of Ramallah. It was easy to make such a mistake.[21] Such errors were not usually deadly, because Israel and the Palestinian Authority had been cooperating. But on October 12, 2000, it was a fatal error for Yossi Avrahami, father to three small children, and Vadim Norzich, just married four days earlier. Both were drivers in their army units, and they were unarmed. An angry crowd encircled them, and they were dragged to a Palestinian police station. The police were unable or unwilling to protect them. The crowd pushed in the doors and murdered the Israeli reservists in a bloody lynching, burning and mutilating their bodies. One body was thrown out a window, after one of the lynchers, Aziz Salha, dipped his hands in the blood and held his red-stained hands aloft to the cheers of the crowd below.

Several Western cameramen were afraid to take pictures. Some who dared were beaten or threatened. BBC photographer Marc Seager tried to take pictures and was nearly killed for it. Seager said he was getting into a taxi on the main road of Ramallah when a throng of shouting Palestinian Arabs came down the hill from the town's police station, dragging something behind them.

"I saw that it was a body, a man they were dragging by the feet. The lower part of his body was on fire and the upper part had been shot at, and the head beaten so badly that it was a pulp, like red jelly." Seager said he reached for his camera but was beaten in the face. One Palestinian pointed at him, yelling, "No picture, no picture!" while another hit him, shouting, "Give me your film!"[22]

Only one film crew managed to record the event and keep its film—a private television channel in Italy. Many stations in Europe and the Arab world did not air the pictures, or they preferred to show only the briefest images. But enough outlets broadcast enough images to vitiate the Arab motif of "David fighting Goliath."

The pictures angered the Palestinians—Arafat's official Palestinian Authority and the man in the street. Both took their anger out on visiting journalists, especially Italians. A correspondent for a rival station, RAI (Italian State Television), took out an advertisement in the Arabic newspaper *Al-Hayat al-Jadeeda* identifying Mediaset as the photographers. He promised *his* station would never do anything to harm the Palestinian cause. "We thank you for your trust, and you can be sure that this is not our way of acting. We do not (will not) do such a thing."[23]

The pictures were an important lesson in media warfare: pictures could also embarrass terrorists. Perhaps for the first time, Israeli military planners had new ideas about the place of cameras on the battlefield. In April 2002, when Israeli forces stormed the Fatah suicide bomb squad headquarters in Jenin, Israeli commandos were outfitted with cameras on their helmets or backpacks. These pictures disproved later Palestinian contentions of an Israeli massacre of innocent civilians.

ATROCITY PICTURES VS. COUNTERTERRORISM

What looked like a cold-blooded murder of a twelve-year-old Arab boy in September 2000 was one of the main factors in sparking the Second Intifada. Dramatic scenes of the purported event were captured on film by Palestinian photographer Talal Abu Rahma, a Palestinian Arab stringer (part-time worker) employed by CNN and French television channel France 2. He accused Israeli forces of shooting twelve-year-old Muhammad al-Dura in fighting in Gaza and letting him bleed to death in his father's arms as they both sought refuge behind a barrel from what appeared to be a crossfire between Israelis and Palestinians.[24]

"The image of a boy shot dead in his helpless father's arms during an Israeli confrontation with Palestinians has become the Pietà of the Arab world," remarked the *Atlantic*. The scene eerily recalled Michelangelo's famous sculpture, the *Pietà*: a slain Jesus in the lap of mother Mary.[25] *Atlantic*'s national correspondent, James Fallows, revisited the shooting of the twelve-year-old. He listed a series of oddities and unanswered questions that arose from another twelve to fifteen seconds of film that were never broadcast—among them that the boy seemed to shield his eyes from the sun after he was supposedly dead:

> Why is there no footage of the boy after he was shot? Why does he appear to move in his father's lap, and to clasp a hand over his eyes after he is supposedly dead? Why is one Palestinian policeman wearing a Secret Service–style earpiece in one ear? Why is another Palestinian man shown waving his arms and yelling at others, as if "directing" a dramatic scene? Why does the funeral appear—based on the length of shadows—to have occurred before the apparent time of the shooting? Why is there no blood on the father's shirt just after they are shot? Why did a voice that seems to be that of the France 2 cameraman yell, in Arabic, "The boy is dead" before he had been hit? Why do ambulances appear instantly for seemingly everyone else and not for al-Dura?

The supposed "killing" of Muhammad al-Dura was originally depicted on sixty seconds of film by Abu Rahma, the Palestinian stringer who vouched for the film's authenticity. The film was aired with the commentary of France 2 correspondent Charles Enderlin on the first day of the Second Intifada. It was an emotional transfusion for the violence. The funeral of "Muhammad"[26] was also filmed and broadcast around the world, and he became a poster boy for the anti-Israel combat.

Boston University professor Richard Landes, a medievalist who studied in France, got interested in the event. Landes's investigation led to harsh conclusions:

> On 30 September 2000, Charles Enderlin, the Jerusalem-based head of the Middle East Bureau of the French television station France 2, presented sixty seconds of footage of what he described as the killing of a twelve-year-old Palestinian boy named Muhammad al-Dura targeted by Israeli soldiers. Enderlin claimed that he had additional film material of the boy's "death throes" that was too shocking to be shown. The selectively presented photo material, accompanied by the accusation of deliberate murder of a defenseless Palestinian boy, led to mass demonstrations against Israel and the Jews in the Western world. It also contributed to

riots by Arabs in Israel in October 2000. It furthermore opened the door
to the mainstreaming of comparison of Israelis to Nazis.[27]

For the Palestinians, the saga of al-Dura was an overnight sensation. For
the Israelis, the boy's seeming death was a cruel and unfathomable act. It
also felt like Israel was reliving the old blood libel: charges that Jews murdered Gentile children.[28]

"The Ballad of Muhammad al-Dura" was one of a series of songs that
became famous in the Arab world in October–November 2000. At least
three different versions of the song were produced by Egyptian singers,
appearing as a choir. Films of the song in various versions were telecast
regularly throughout the Arab world, and especially on the state television of the Palestine Broadcasting Corporation (PBC). The PBC was the
official broadcast arm of the Palestinian Authority. It had been given its
transmitters by Israel as part of agreements in 1993 and 1994[29] between
the two sides. Arafat and his PBC did not hesitate to use these transmitters to incite young children to emulate Muhammad, who, the song said,
had held rocks in his little hands.[30] Meanwhile, Israel's army and civilian
leaders awoke to the likelihood of fraud in the al-Dura episode only after
several days of Israeli apologies. It was too embarrassing for Israel's leaders to admit that they, too, had been hoodwinked by a media hoax. That is
why the Israeli government never formally joined the effort by independent media experts and scientists to uncover the truth.

One of the other lessons of the al-Dura hoax was that local Arab
journalists—stringers—could create "events" that shaped world affairs. Israeli security officials then subsequently discovered that some Arab stringers were determined Palestinian political activists. A few were actual or
suspected agents of terror. For example, the Israelis denied press credential
to Khaled Zighari, a photographer for CBS and Reuters. He unsuccess-
fully appealed the case to an Israeli court, where Israeli officials proved he
had ties to a terror group. Some of the Arab stringers were or are actually
quite proud of their organizational links, bragging about them on Arabic
websites like amin.org or even at public gatherings. Fayad Abu Shamala
told a Hamas rally in Gaza that "journalists and the media [are] waging a
campaign shoulder to shoulder with the Palestinian people."[31]

ATROCITY STORIES AS WAR STOPPERS

While the al-Dura case showed how an atrocity story could inflame passions, it's also true that an atrocity story can actually stop a war against terrorists. Hizballah renewed rocket fire on Israel in early 1996. Shimon Peres had just become the caretaker successor to murdered prime minister Yitzhak Rabin, pending elections. Peres ordered the IDF to stop the Hizballah attacks. The operation was code-named "Grapes of Wrath." Yet it ended far worse than "sour grapes" for Israel, which was sure it had the tools to stop Hizballah's attacks on Israeli civilians. Israel had developed its own state-of-the-art pilotless drones and other devices allowing the IDF to locate and suppress rocket fire within seconds. The response was almost automatic, and that is exactly what Hizballah wanted. Hizballah had placed the rocket launchers in a UN school in the village of Qana. Israel's effort to stop rocket fire on Israeli villages ended with the deaths of more than one hundred civilians, attested the Red Crescent organization. Israel faced world condemnation and did not have the time to explain that the Red Crescent (the Muslim equivalent of the Red Cross) often served as a propaganda arm for terror groups such as Hizballah and Arafat's PLO. How many people had died was not clear, but they had definitely become the human shields of Hizballah. A study by the Shorenstein Center on the Press, Politics and Public Policy at Harvard's Kennedy School of Government found that the Western press had been duped by Hizballah.

Nevertheless, Prime Minister Peres stopped the Israeli operation. Hostile mortar and rocket fire at Israel continued, while Israel only responded in a perfunctory manner to Hizballah's attacks on Israeli civilians. In mid-2006, Hizballah staged a daring land attack into Israel, killing several soldiers and abducting two others.[32] Israel launched a large operation to push the entrenched Iranian-trained terror group out of its underground bunkers on the border. However, once again charges of an "Israeli atrocity"—in the same village of Qana—halted the anti-terror drive. And again using the Red Crescent as a foil, Hizballah claimed fifty-six civilians were killed by an Israeli air attack. Bloody bodies were displayed on television—by the same officials who were working in 1996. Israeli generals stuttered that they had not attacked the village on the day in question. Arab leaders who tacitly backed Israel's decision to roll back the Iranian-armed and Iranian-trained Hizballah were now embarrassed. Pictures of dead Lebanese Arabs filled Arab TV screens. Prime Minister Ehud Olmert halted Israel's land operation, surrendering to the propaganda.

Later review and investigation by the UN, Human Rights Watch, and other groups (who originally accepted Hizballah's version of events) showed Hizballah manipulated the press and "evidence" of an "atrocity." The supposed death toll was artificially more than doubled. Moreover, many bodies—discolored from previous internment or storage—had been dug up and transferred to the site to make a case for an Israeli atrocity.[33]

The final results of the battle on the ground and the parallel battle for headlines and airwaves were revealing: Hizballah suffered great damage to its combat force, but its propaganda victory allowed it to recoup its physical losses. Hizballah retained its presence in southern Lebanon. Maybe as many as six hundred of its estimated thousand-man frontline squads died, but it could train and draft more men. It still had some fortified tunnel complexes, and it rebuilt what was lost. Most important, Hizballah, Iran's terror vanguard, got credibility. It was rearming while Israel was again retreating.

THE INTIFADA: ERASABLE EPISODES VS. MADE-FOR-MEDIA EVENTS

For Palestinian terror groups and television journalists, the Intifada was a coming-of-age. "Many media events during the Intifada were created not to provide new and important information"—as in a press conference—"but purely to provide the images needed by imagespeak," observed correspondent Jim Lederman.[34] He described how Gaza youths put on daily firebombing displays around sunset near Shifa Hospital for the sake of Western reporters. These made-for-media events became the rule, not the exception, in the Arab-Israeli conflict. They were designed by terrorist groups such as Fatah, Hamas, and Hizballah, sometimes with the connivance of news organizations. The technique of creating news, especially the phony atrocity story, was studied and adopted by state sponsors of terror such as Saddam's Iraq and Assad's Syria.

THE SPIRIT OF CNN

The spirit of CNN's operations in the Palestinian arena, and later in Baghdad, was executive producer Robert Wiener, who flaunted his dislike of the U.S. government, of Israel, and even of Judaism.[35] From his first day in CNN's Jerusalem offices at Capital Studios, Wiener literally left his mark. He removed all the mezuzahs, the Jewish signposts affixed to doorways in most Israeli homes and offices. Wiener, who is Jewish himself, had to know how offensive his act was even to nonreligious Israelis. It was like publicly stripping crucifixes in Rome or writing graffiti on a mosque in Cairo. Perhaps Wiener meant these and other acts to ingratiate CNN with both the PLO and Saddam. But that is certainly not the sole explanation. In his book, Wiener defends Saddam and his regime, while insulting three U.S. presidents:

> Baghdad came under major attack three times following the war—in 1992 (for allegedly not cooperating with the UN), in 1993 (after Clinton concluded Iraq tried to wack [sic] Pappy Bush during a visit to Kuwait), and in 1998 after the Clinton administration warned UNSCOM to pack its bags since the cruise missiles were going to fly again. As this book goes to press, Baby Bush, like his father and Clinton before him has called for the removal of Saddam Hussein—even if it means the United States will act on its own and defy the wishes of the United Nations, the European Community, the Arab League, and anyone who thinks it insane to send 250,000 Americans to fight a war with no logical endgame in sight.[36]

It is worth examining Wiener's technique:

- He guards Saddam's constitutional rights, stressing he was "allegedly not cooperating with the UN." Wiener *knew* Saddam never cooperated with the UN, but certainly undercut the UN "Food for Peace" plan, bribing many UN officials.
- He treats trying to kill George H. W. Bush in Kuwait dissmissively, even though the plot—involving at least thirty people—was proven and prevented. Wiener jokes about someone wanting "to wack" [sic] a former president, whom he has caricatured with the title "Pappy Bush."

- He ignores the fact that both George H. W. Bush and George W. Bush did indeed consult the UN, European allies, etc., before both wars in Iraq.

Wiener also knew Saddam regularly hampered efforts by UNSCOM (the UN special commission for nuclear inspections in Iraq), because there was much evidence, before both wars, of Iraqi nuclear activity, including the discovery in London's Heathrow Airport of Iraqi-bound nuclear trigger devices known as krytons.[37] Wiener seems less driven by a desire to tell the truth than by a desire to get a good show, to push his own ideological agenda, and to humiliate those with whom he disagreed: damn the facts—full speed ahead.

THE INDUSTRY STANDARD:
CNN'S TIES TO DESPOTS AND TERRORISTS

Wiener reveals deep ethical and professional transgressions in CNN's war coverage in Iraq in his book and subsequent movie. His disclosures are partial, in both senses of the word: incomplete and stilted. He is obviously not telling the full story of CNN's violations of the truth and journalistic ethics. Yet he mentions how CNN ignored some of Saddam's atrocities while giving his regime access and favorable treatment. Details of the professional sins by Wiener and other CNN figures emerged later, after discoveries of improper conduct carried out by CNN reporter Peter Arnett and admissions by CNN news director Eason Jordan. Arnett and Jordan confessed, only belatedly and partially, how CNN surrendered to intimidation by Saddam and his sons.

"I knew that CNN could not report that Saddam Hussein's eldest son, Uday, told me in 1995 that he intended to assassinate two of his brothers-in-law who had defected and also the man giving them asylum, King Hussein of Jordan," news director Jordan admitted in a *Times* op-ed article—eight years later. "If we had gone with the story, I was sure he would have responded by killing the Iraqi translator who was the only other participant in the meeting."[38] This is a convenient and self-serving confession: it says CNN *had* to deceive the public in order to save lives.

Jordan uses this story as the symbolic opening of his account of twelve years of CNN cover-ups in Iraq, where he traveled to supervise the coverage of Wiener, Arnett, and other CNN personnel. Yet, six months before writing his op-ed "confession" for the *Times*, he told a New York radio station that CNN would rather get thrown out of Iraq than surrender to threats:

> **BOB GARFIELD**: Back in '91 CNN and Peter Arnett in particular were heavily criticized, mostly by civilians, for reporting from within Baghdad during the U.S. attack in ways that they'd consider to be utter propaganda and to—out of context and not reflecting the overall reality of Saddam Hussein's regime. Have you analyzed what you can get access to without appearing to be just a propaganda tool for Saddam?
>
> **EASON JORDAN**: Well absolutely. I mean we work very hard to report forthrightly, to report fairly and to report accurately and if we ever determine we cannot do that, then we would not want to be there; but we do think that some light is better than no light whatsoever. I think that the world, the American people will be shortchanged if foreign journalists are kicked out, because even in Peter Arnett's case there were things that he reported on—and this is a long time ago now—but things he reported on that I don't think would have been reported at all had he not been there. We feel committed to our Baghdad presence. We've had a bureau there for 12 years with occasional interruptions when we've been thrown out, but we're not there to please the Iraqi government—we're not there to displease the Iraqi government—we're just there to do our job.[39]

In addition to proof that Jordan, Wiener, and Arnett did not tell the full story in their later "confessions," we also know from other CNN sources that the belated admissions by Jordan and Wiener are but a fraction of their deceptions.

Peter Collins, who worked as a reporter for CNN in Iraq, wrote about what CNN asked him to do and why this made him leave CNN. The cable news network had been blandishing Iraqi officials. It even brought in network president Tom Johnson in an effort to negotiate a journalistic coup—an exclusive interview with Saddam:

The day after one such meeting, I was on the roof of the Ministry of Information, preparing for my first "live shot" on CNN. A producer came up and handed me a sheet of paper with handwritten notes. "Tom Johnson wants you to read this on camera," he said. I glanced at the paper. It was an item-by-item summary of points made by Information Minister Latif Jassim in an interview that morning with Mr. Johnson and Mr. Jordan.

The list was so long that there was no time during the live shot to provide context. I read the information minister's points verbatim. Moments later, I was downstairs in the newsroom on the first floor of the Information Ministry. Mr. Johnson approached, having seen my performance on a TV monitor. "You were a bit flat there, Peter," he said. Again, I was astonished. The president of CNN was telling me I seemed less-than-enthusiastic reading Saddam Hussein's propaganda.[40]

The level of CNN collaboration with Saddam reached beyond the puffery of the political arena and into the military sphere. Collins described how CNN cooperated with Iraqi claims of an American war atrocity: that the United States had murdered innocent Iraqi farmers with sophisticated armor-piercing bombs known as CBUs.

I was CNN's reporter on a trip organized by the Ministry of Information to the northern city of Mosul. "Minders" from the ministry accompanied two busloads of news people to an open, plowed field outside Mosul. The purpose was to show us that American warplanes were bombing "innocent Iraqi farmers." Bits of American ordnance were scattered on the field. One large piece was marked "CBU." I recognized it as the canister for a Cluster Bomb Unit, a weapon effective against troops in the open, or against "thin-skinned" armor. I was puzzled. Why would U.S. aircraft launch CBUs against what appeared to be an open field? Was it really to kill "innocent Iraqi farmers"? The minders showed us no victims, no witnesses. I looked around. About 2000 yards distant on a ridgeline, two radar dishes were just visible against the sky. The ground was freshly plowed. Now, I understood. The radars were probably linked to Soviet-made SA-6 surface-to-air missiles mounted on tracks, armored vehicles, parked in the field at some distance from the dishes to keep them safe. After the bombing, the Iraqis had removed the missile launchers and had plowed the field to cover the tracks. On the way back to Baghdad, I explained to other reporters what I thought had happened, and wrote a report that was broadcast on CNN that night. The next day, Brent Sadler, CNN's chief reporter at the time in Baghdad (he is now in northern Iraq), came up to me in a hallway of the al Rasheed Hotel. He had been pushing for the interview with Saddam and had urged Mr. Johnson and Mr. Jordan to come to Baghdad to help seal the deal. "Petah," he said to me in his English accent, "you know we're trying to get an interview with Saddam. That piece last night was not helpful."

Jordan relates a few more atrocities by Saddam's regime that were never relayed to the global CNN audience. Why not? Why were they being publicized now? His answer is both pathetic and inadequate: "I felt awful having these stories bottled up inside me. Now that Saddam Hussein's regime is gone, I suspect we will hear many, many more gut-wrenching tales from Iraqis about the decades of torment. At last, these stories can be told freely."[41] In other words, CNN admitted part of its Iraq cover-ups only after Saddam was powerless and no longer of use as a news source.

Now that Saddam is no longer primed for a series of CNN exclusive stories, does not the public have a right to a full account of CNN cover-ups aiding Iraq's dictator? Franklin Foer of the *New Republic* interviewed Eason Jordan and Peter Arnett in October 2002 about CNN's coverage, and he felt he was deceived by Jordan:

> Would that this were an outbreak of honesty, however belated. But it isn't. If it were, Mr. Jordan wouldn't be portraying CNN as Saddam's victim. He'd be apologizing for its cooperation with Iraq's erstwhile information ministry—and admitting that CNN policy hinders truthful coverage of dictatorships. For CNN, the highest prize is "access," to score live camera feeds from a story's epicenter. Dictatorships understand this hunger, and also that it provides blackmail opportunities. In exchange for CNN bureaus, dictatorships require adherence to their own

rules of reportage. They create conditions where CNN—and other U.S. media—can do little more than toe the regime's line.[42]

Peter Arnett, a native of New Zealand, came to CNN after making his mark in Vietnam at the Associated Press in the 1960s, earning a Pulitzer Prize in 1966. After eighteen years at CNN, Arnett became its man in Baghdad in the 1990–91 war. One Arnett report stressed Iraqi claims that the United States had bombed a factory that made powdered baby formula, not chemical or biological weapons as the United States claimed.[43]

Was this true? Arnett confessed to Foer that he and his CNN colleagues sometimes made trade-offs for access. "There's a quid pro quo for being there," Arnett told Foer. "You go in and they control what you do. . . . So you have no option other than to report the opinion of the government of Iraq." Foer remarked that the CNN Baghdad office was located in the same building as the Iraqi Ministry of Information—a fact that signified "more than just a physical reality."[44]

Neither Arnett, Jordan, Wiener, nor anyone else at CNN wanted to report how Saddam intimidated the Western press and diplomatic corps. One example was when Saddam's men dumped the body of Farzad Bazoft on the steps of the British embassy on March 15, 1990. Bazoft, an Iranian-born British reporter who worked for the *Observer*, had been investigating a major explosion at an Iraqi arms factory in which seven hundred people reportedly died. He took soil samples at the site. Saddam arrested him, charged him with being a British and Israeli spy, and hanged him at the Abu Ghraib prison.

CNN apparently ignored the story on which Bazoft was working, as well as ignoring Bazoft's arrest and execution, but the 1997 CNN Almanac mentioned the event in its "this day in history" seven years later.

Arnett's work was tarnished still more by a scandalous CNN report about "Operation Tailwind" in 1998, which claimed that the United States had used sarin nerve gas against members of its own forces. Arnett and CNN said the United States had killed American soldiers who had deserted from the U.S. forces in Vietnam and run away to Laos. Under great pressure and thousands of letters from angry American veterans,

CNN recanted the report and fired those who were its producers. In his defense, Arnett said he had only read the text on the air, but had not prepared the report itself. After a while, he left CNN. He later worked for MSNBC covering the 2003 war in Iraq.

We are left with more questions than CNN answered. Why would CNN and Arnett have done the nerve gas story in the first place? The Tailwind story may be at least plausible for anyone who recalls how the U.S. military sometimes did despicable things, like using its own men to test the effects of drugs or radiation. But these events—like the Tailwind charges—happened long ago. Why did the network that specializes in breaking news go after a twenty-year-old story?

Perhaps the answer is that the story has symbolic value. It hints the United States is no better than Saddam: he gassed his own people, and the United States gassed its own troops. This may explain CNN's motive, but what of Arnett? What happened to Arnett in the later part of his career is puzzling and dismaying. Arnett earned his reputation as a hard-nosed field reporter. He was known as a reporter who covered the war from the rice paddies. He had a reputation for working hard and pursuing stories even in dangerous situations, such as reporting Soviet repression of dissidents in the 1980s. One profile of him observed: "He was thrown out of Indonesia by one government in 1962 (many believe him the inspiration for the film "The Year of Living Dangerously") and beaten up in Moscow by another in 1987."[45]

Arnett explained his job was not to pick favorites in war, but to report the truth about all sides. This was the classical view of the good reporters in Vietnam who felt the U.S. command often misled or lied outright. The daily U.S. Army press briefing in Saigon was derisively called "the Five O'clock Follies."[46] This journalistic distrust, even cynicism, combined with the dramatic early victories of the communist Tet Offensive of 1968 to hand the communists a psychological victory, and drove the United States from Vietnam. Tet was a psychological victory, a virtual victory that ensured a real triumph. Ultimately, the Tet offensive was pushed back, but North Vietnam and the Vietcong won the war inside the mind of America, not in the rice paddies.

"Tet is now generally recognized as a Communist defeat," observed Henry Kissinger, years later.[47] *Washington Post* reporter Don Oberdorfer agrees: "the Vietcong guerrillas ceased to be an effective military force."[48] Both suggest reporters made an error in analysis that drove perceptions the U.S. war effort had failed. The lesson: a small authoritarian foe—Vietcong or PLO or Hizballah or Al-Qaeda—can defeat a larger, technologically adept democratic foe by winning the battle of the mind. This is exactly what several Arab-Islamic leaders have said.[49]

CNN's Iraq coverage was not like reporters' tough coverage of Vietnam. The question about CNN is not about analysis but rather conduct. CNN's conduct during both wars in Iraq suggests it snuggled up to Saddam, censored damning material on him, and gave him access to the living rooms of the West. Such conduct recalls the *New York Times'* Walter Duranty hiding Stalin's crimes or Beirut's Western reporters playing softball with Syria and the PLO.

In the 2002 lead-up to the second Iraq war, Peter Arnett gave an anti-U.S. interview on Saddam's state TV. It was full of lies about the Iraqi public's support for Saddam and Saddam's graciousness to foreign reporters: "For 12 years I have been coming here and I've met unfailing courtesy and cooperation."[50]

COVERING AUTHORITARIANS AND TERRORISTS: THE UGLY REALITY

Terrorism is real news and a real danger. Reporting on terror from inside the belly of the beast is perilous work. Even the best reporters may falter under the pressure to produce stories while fending off threats to their lives from terror groups or despots. Reporters, photographers, editors, producers, and publishers need to strike a difficult balance. Journalists who lie to themselves will lie to the public and end up helping terrorists to win the battle of the mind that is the key to defeating terror.

Reporters have to be honest with themselves, because the public relies on them. The public needs to know the truth about the Arab-Islamic terrorists without the blinders of political correctness, especially when the beast of terror has moved inside Western countries themselves. Many media outlets have failed this test: masking murderers and veiling victims— before 9/11 and even afterward.

4

JOURNALISTS AS LAPDOGS

Sometimes a picture or a few words can capture the idiocy or evil of an era. An article in the *New York Times*—two months before the 9/11 attacks—captured the fatal combination of ignorance and arrogance among some U.S. counterterror elites:

> Judging from news reports and the portrayal of villains in our popular entertainment, Americans are bedeviled by fantasies about terrorism. They seem to believe that terrorism is the greatest threat to the United States and that it is becoming more widespread and lethal. They are likely to think that the United States is the most popular target of terrorists. And they almost certainly have the impression that extremist Islamic groups cause most terrorism. None of these beliefs are based in fact.[1]

JOURNALISM MASKS TERRORISM ON THE HOME FRONT

So began an opinion article in the *New York Times* shortly before 9/11. It claimed the threat of Islamic terror was not just exaggerated, but in fact a fantasy. It declared that the threat to the United States was overblown. The article was dead wrong on every major assertion. Yet this analysis—and not the analysis of people worried about Arab-Islamic terror—was on the breakfast tables and in boardrooms just before 9/11.

The *Times* opinion section rarely if ever hosts the opinion of Harvey Kushner, Daniel Pipes, or Steve Emerson, who have been warning about the rising danger of Arab-Islamic extremism and terror coming to America.[2] However, *their views,* and not the ones endorsed by the *Times,* have often been eerily prescient, as when Kushner's book *Terrorism in America,* published in 1998, showed a bull's-eye framing the World Trade Center. The book was also bitingly critical of academic textbooks that failed to mention the growing danger to the United States and other Western countries.[3] "I'm a firm believer that if we don't learn lessons from history, they repeat themselves," Professor Kushner observed, "especially when the terrorists are looking to repeat history."[4] These remarks appeared only in the Long Island edition of the *Times.* The names and views of Kushner, Pipes, and Emerson have not been seen in the regular news pages or the opinion pages of the *Times* because their views are decidedly critical of the foreign policy and security establishment, including views expressed and fostered by the *New York Times* itself. Even though Emerson, Kushner, and Pipes— and others like them—are critics, their views and expertise are crucial to helping Western institutions sensitize themselves to Arab-Islamic terror. Fortunately, their views are still sought by some of the very institutions they criticize, such as the law enforcement and security community. Kushner, for example, was a government witness in the first World Trade Center trial, and he has been a consultant of the FBI, though he has reproved it harshly.

America's greatest newspaper, the *New York Times,* evinces an inability to take criticism. It also abuses its special role to set the terms of debate, using the narrow purview of its opinion pages to inhibit discussion of the problem of Arab-Islamic terror. The *Times* helps set the agenda not just by its news pages but by its opinion section. It has kept the "alarmists" out of view, helping to put its readers to sleep. Sadly, the *Times* is not alone in this policy. Many important news media want to lower the news profile of Arab-Islamic terror in almost every way.

"Following the terrorist attacks on the World Trade Center and the Pentagon, Reuters was reported to have banned the use of the term *terrorism* in the context of the 9/11 incidents, and CNN was said to have discouraged its correspondents from using the t-word," according to Brigitte Nacos, a Columbia University professor who specializes in terror-media issues.[5] This same policy of not mentioning the term *terrorist* or *terrorism* has been favored by the *New York Times* and the British Broadcasting Corporation (BBC), among many others. Many of these same media, Nacos observes, spent the summer of 2001 presenting "the human face" of Palestinian suicide bombers who were attacking Israeli cities.[6]

CNN, the *Times,* and other media have extended this humanizing, humane, human interest treatment to Al-Qaeda and the latest generation of Arab-Islamic terrorists. They do this by overplaying mistreatment of captured terrorists as if they were like U.S. or British prisoners of war who were regularly tortured by Japanese or Nazi prison camp guards.

First, the truth is that mistreatment of Al-Qaeda prisoners—such as in Abu Ghraib—is the exception rather than the rule, and it certainly does not qualify as regularized torture. Similarly, the issue of waterboarding—an interrogation technique that has been relatively rarely used—is not like the Bataan Death March or the Nazis or Japanese using their prisoners as subjects for deadly experiments.

Second, nonuniformed terrorists are not entitled to the same treatment as uniformed soldiers. That is not my view. That is *statutory* international law, including the various Geneva Conventions. Yet, many in the media act as if a person who plans to blow up a building in New York is entitled to full legal protection. By the rules of war, such people may be summarily executed: this is true of anyone in Al-Qaeda, Hamas, Tanzim, Islamic Jihad, Hizballah, or Lashkar-e-Taiba, among others. They are non-uniformed combatants. They are terrorist in function. This means they do *not* have the legal rights of uniformed soldiers captured in combat.

Another way these Arab-Islamic terrorists are humanized by the media is when reporters try to show that the West is full of Christian and Jewish terrorists.[7] This approach was most recently demonstrated by Christiane Amanpour, the chief foreign correspondent of CNN, in her award-winning documentary, *God's Warriors.*[8] In the episode on Jews, Amanpour insinuates that all Jewish settlers in the West Bank and those supporting Jewish settlement are akin to terrorists. All strong Jewish nationalists—including Christian Zionists—are classified as extremists. In the section of the documentary called "God's Christian Warriors," the late Jerry Falwell and his Moral Majority organization are likened to terrorists, as are all evangelical Christians.

This is absolute nonsense, but it was award-winning nonsense: the series won several awards inside the journalism community.[9] Fortunately not everyone in that community is blind, deaf, and dumb.

"CNN should have called it what it was: a defense of Islamic fundamentalism and the worst type of moral relativism," declared MSNBC station manager Dan Abrams. He said CNN and Amanpour had engaged in the worst kind of advocacy journalism "rather than distinguish between Islamic terrorists who utilize fierce violence to achieve warped goals, and the merely fiercely religious or even just those who fiercely believe in the state of Israel, Christiane Amanpour avoided getting bogged down in objectivity."[10] A Christian commentator for Fox News, Father Jonathan Morris, said the CNN documentary was very dishonest. "There is a tremendous underlying bias about Christianity and Judaism."[11]

The Committee for Accuracy in Middle East Reporting in America (CAMERA), a pro-Israel media watchdog group, attacked the series, accusing it of "equating the extremely rare cases of religiously-inspired violence on the part of Christians and Jews with radical Islam's global, often state-supported, campaigns of mass killing."

Humanizing Arab-Islamic terrorists is the wrong angle for a human interest story. Clearly Al-Qaeda wants imitators. Favorable or humanizing coverage of terror may trigger copycats and cells of "homegrown" terrorists, especially from the "second generation" of Arab-Islamic immigrants in the United States, France, India, Great Britain, and Spain. "Americans are now learning what citizens of Indonesia, Saudi Arabia, Spain, the United Kingdom, and other foreign countries have long known: that some of our own can and will go to great lengths to kill their fellow citizens."[12]

RED-FLAG ISSUES VS. RED HERRINGS

Some American and British Muslims—many born in the United States and Britain—do indeed get involved with plots against their countries. Others aid the world jihad overseas, such as David C. Headley, a native of Chicago and the son of a Pakistani diplomat. Headley changed his original name, Daood Gilani, in 2006. He is accused of using his U.S. passport to funnel intelligence information and of being one of the main plotters in the Mumbai, India, terror assaults of 2008 in which more than 170 people died. He is also accused of aiding a plot in 2005 to kill a Danish cartoonist who drew cartoons critical of Islam and its prophet, Muhammad. Headley-Gilani was also arrested in 1997 for smuggling heroin. He allegedly worked as a double agent against the FBI and the U.S. Drug Enforcement Administration. This is quite a story, but it is hard to find facts about Headley-Gilani by reading the *New York Times* or watching CNN or other media standbys.[13] But the noncoverage of Headley is not unique.

Richard Reid, who converted to Islam in a British jail, tried to blow up an American Airlines jet flying between Paris and Miami on December 22, 2001, using explosives hidden in his shoe. It almost worked, but Reid was interrupted by passengers. Reid originally tried to carry out his attack from Israel, but Israeli security officials—who could not care less about political correctness—interviewed him at length and prevented him from getting on a flight from Tel Aviv. Another British man who trained with Reid in Pakistan in using similar explosives, Sajid Mohammed Badat, had second thoughts. But Badat never got rid of his bomb, keeping it under a bed at his parents' home in southwest Britain, where he was arrested. A British court sentenced him to thirteen years in jail. Several second-generation British Muslims used their non-Arab appearance and British-accented English to defer suspicions and to smuggle weapons while carrying out a bombing of a Tel Aviv nightclub in 2003.[14]

Several Somalis in Minneapolis were training to join the jihad abroad when arrested. Another, Shirwa Ahmed, became "the first American suicide bomber" on October 28, 2008, killing himself in Somalia's civil war "on behalf of the Islamist group al Shabaab, elements of which have links to al Qaeda in Pakistan."[15] Najibullah Zazi, an Afghan with U.S. resident status and Al-Qaeda explosives training, drove in September 2009 from Denver to New York, where Barack Obama was to speak at the UN and on Wall Street. Zazi was convicted of terror conspiracy.[16] One Al-Qaeda trainee planned to destroy the Brooklyn Bridge by cutting its cables. Few of these abortive terror plots have been widely reported or followed up in the mainstream U.S. press.

REPORTING ANTI-MUSLIM HATE CRIMES
RATHER THAN MUSLIM TERROR

Instead of warning about terror and investigating its dangers, many journalists have bent over backward to write favorably about Muslims and their communities, warning against "hate crimes" against Muslims. Yet statistics show a rise in crimes against Muslims only immediately after the 9/11 attacks. Anti-Muslim hate crimes accounted for nearly a quarter of the hate crimes that year. However, soon thereafter, crimes against Muslims in the United States declined consistently toward the pre-2001 levels.

Actually, the U.S. religious community that suffers the brunt of hate crimes is the Jewish community. American Jews suffer two-thirds of religious attacks annually. The FBI figures below illustrate the true picture, which has been distorted by Islamic lobbying groups such as the Council on American-Islamic Relations (CAIR).[17]

Despite the facts, some Muslim lobbyists and activist organizations have accused the U.S. government and the media of fanning hate crimes against Muslims. Some media, like the *New York Times*, embrace this view, and without checking the facts.[18] To placate the complainers, the U.S. government allowed some of these same Muslim groups access to the FBI, the U.S. armed forces, and the U.S. prison system, where they have vetted preachers and chaplains who turned out to be extremists themselves.

FBI HATE CRIMES IN THE UNITED STATES—BY RELIGIOUS BIAS

2009

71.9 percent were anti-Jewish   8.4 percent were anti-Islamic

2008

65.7 percent were anti-Jewish   7.7 percent were anti-Islamic

2007

69.2 percent anti-Jewish   8.7 percent were anti-Islamic

2006

64.3 percent were anti-Jewish   12.0 percent were anti-Islamic

2005

68.5 percent were anti-Jewish   11.1 percent were anti-Islamic

2004

67.8 percent were anti-Jewish   12.7 percent were anti-Islamic

2003

68.8 percent were anti-Jewish   11.5 percent were anti-Islamic

2002

65.9 percent were anti-Jewish   10.8 percent were anti-Islamic

2001

55.7 percent were anti-Jewish   27.2 percent were anti-Islamic

Media analyst William McGowan studied newspaper reporting on Muslim communities in the United States after 9/11. He found that even in the immediate aftermath of 9/11, American journalists, particularly the *New York Times,* provided "overly favorable coverage on the subject of Arab and Muslim Americans, who have become the object *du jour* of journalistic piety and skittishness."[19] McGowan focused on *Times* reporter Susan Sachs, who recounted how students of one Islamic madrassa "showed empathy" for those espousing hatred for America, their home. "Yet instead of seeing these sentiments as worrying examples of dual loyalty (in effect, no loyalty), Sachs tepidly described them as a sign of the 'strain' that immigrants and their children traditionally can feel 'between their adopted and native culture.'"[20]

McGowan's observations accurately capture the wishful thinking that reigned inside the establishment media in the United States—the *New York Times, Time, Newsweek,* NBC News, among others. He describes an NBC report in October 2001 that "declared Islam to be strictly 'a religion of peace,' veiling its more aggressive and violent side."

McGowan's verdict is harsh, but it is justified. His verdict would probably be still harsher if his book were written today, when the trauma of the terror attacks has worn off a bit. One would be hard-pressed to find a major establishment American media outlet that has done investigative articles on the role of mosques in New York, New Jersey, or Washington as centers for recruiting and fomenting terror since 9/11. One would not find such an article or an investigative television documentary *before* 9/11, but we would not find such a dearth of coverage of nativist terror, right-wing terror, anti-abortion terrorists, neo-Nazi sympathizers, and the like.[21] In contrast, McGowan shows that the *New York Times, Washington Post,* ABC News, and National Public Radio (NPR) soft-pedaled news of "the Lackawanna 6." These were six young Muslim American men—five of them native-born Americans—in the Buffalo, New York, suburb of Lackawanna who traveled to Afghanistan just before 9/11 for military training from Al-Qaeda, in anticipation of being "activated" as sleeper agents. One of the men even met bin-Laden himself. Some of the media, particularly NPR, insinuated that the accusations against the men, who were close to the Yemeni Arab immigrant community in Lackawanna, were some kind of plot by the administration of George W. Bush to justify the U.S. invasion of Iraq.[22] The *Times* preferred to highlight one Muslim chaplain who justified Muslims fighting Muslims hostile to the United States. It "neglected to bring the issue of Muslim servicemen's resistance to fighting fellow Muslims." This, McGowan said, was a deeply divisive issue in the U.S. military, and the prescience of his comment was shown by several incidents involving Muslim-Americans in the armed forces over the next seven years:

- On March 23, 2003, in a forward base in Kuwait during the invasion of Iraq, Hasan Karim Akbar of Los Angeles (born Mark Fidel Kools), an army sapper with the 101st Airborne Division, threw hand grenades into a tent and fired his rifle into the ensuing chaos, killing two officers. His death sentence is currently under appeal.
- In September 2004, National Guardsman and Muslim convert Ryan Anderson was convicted on five counts of attempting to aid a terrorist network, after he was caught in an Internet sting in which he tried to contact al-Qaeda operatives to disclose information on U.S. military vulnerabilities.[23]
- The Fort Dix plot: the FBI arrested six men on May 8, 2007, who were subsequently convicted of planning an attack against soldiers at Fort Dix, New Jersey.
- In June 2009, Abdulhakim Mujahid Muhammad, a convert to Islam, shot up the Little Rock, Arkansas, military recruiting center, murdering one soldier and wounding another.

The *New York Times*, the *Washington Post*, and most U.S. television networks except Fox have avoided the issue of radical Muslim preachers recruiting potential terrorists inside America's armed forces and its prison system. This is an issue of immense importance because both the military and the prisons are big sources of trained manpower for terrorists. There is also a significant "Black Muslim" population in prisons, which has already been tapped for terrorism.[24] This subject demands serious investigative reporting. The Western public has hardly received any.

Similarly, establishment media have usually not engaged in their own "enterprise journalism" by following up stories by others about radical Islamic penetration of U.S. and British armed forces and intelligence. A previously mentioned key example is the case of Ali Muhammad, an Al-Qaeda double-agent who advised the U.S. Army Special Warfare School at Fort Bragg, North Carolina. Muhammad, a former Egyptian army officer, personally trained Osama bin-Laden's bodyguards and personally scouted for Al-Qaeda's attacks in 1998 on the U.S. embassies in Africa.[25]

America's media were not shy about challenging the U.S. military over Vietnam or prosecution of wars in Iraq and Afghanistan, or treatment of suspected terrorists imprisoned at the U.S. base in Guantánamo, Cuba, but many media organizations were skittish about investigating the issue of divisiveness and even disloyalty in U.S. armed forces caused by radicalized Muslims—soldiers, chaplains, and officers.

FROM 9/11 TO FORT HOOD

This kind of reportorial reticence again appeared in the fuzzy coverage of the massacre at the Fort Hood army base in November 2009. U.S. Army Major Nidal Malik Hasan methodically shot and pursued people in the base dining room. When finally stopped, Hasan had murdered thirteen people and wounded about thirty others. As he shot, he yelled "*Allahu Akbar!*" ("God is Great!") in Arabic.

"We can't jump to conclusions now based on little snippets of information that come out," declared U.S. Army chief of staff General George Casey on CNN's show *State of the Union*.[26] General Casey beautifully illustrated the U.S. government's willful blindness to the spread of Arab-Islamic terrorism in its own ranks.[27] Casey's interviewers, in turn, barely pressed him on his incongruous remarks. CNN host John King hoped to elicit from the general a statement that Hasan was "acting alone."[28]

Three days after the Fort Hood massacre, Sunday interview shows[29] had to cover the story, but they made no mention of Hasan's radical Islamic transformation, nor his Palestinian background. Rather, Casey and his media hosts dwelt on how Muslim U.S. soldiers might be insulted if the murderer's Islamic motives were discussed openly: "And frankly, I am worried—not worried, but I'm concerned—that this increased speculation could cause a backlash against some of our Muslim soldiers," he told CNN. "And I've asked our army leaders to be on the lookout for that. It would be a shame—as great a tragedy as this was, it would be a shame if our diversity became a casualty as well."[30] Casey told NBC's *Meet the Press,* "Our diversity, not only in our army but in our country, is a strength. And as horrific as this tragedy was, if our diversity becomes a casualty, I think that's worse."[31]

Independent monitors of U.S. television networks found that the three main networks—ABC, CBS, and NBC—trod the politically correct path of President Barack Obama, who also urged Americans not to jump to conclusions. Under fierce attack for this attitude, Obama reversed his position a bit. So did the networks. "Until then," according to a report by newsbusters.org, "the broadcast networks had also downplayed his [Hasan's] Islamic connections. From Nov. 5 through Nov. 10, all three evening news programs only identified Hasan as a Muslim one-fourth of the time (14 times out of 48 reports). And out of those 14 times, seven included a defense of the Islamic religion and expressed concern about a 'possible backlash against Muslims in the military.' ABC reporter Bill Weir claimed that 'Muslims in uniform today face a challenge not seen since Japanese-Americans fought in World War II.'" This was a snide way to compare treatment of Muslim-Americans after 9/11 to U.S. governmental internment of thousands of Japanese Americans.[32]

The *New York Times,* the world's "newspaper of record," reported: "It is unclear what might have motivated Major Hasan, who is suspected of killing thirteen people. Senior military and law enforcement officials said they had tentatively dismissed the possibility that he was carrying out a terrorist plot. He seems to have been influenced by a mixture of political, religious, and psychological factors, the officials said."[33] The *Times* tried introducing uncertainty and pseudolegal "distance" into a clear-cut massacre committed at close range for political and religious reasons. The article mixed horrible reporting and bad writing: politically correct, factually inaccurate, journalistically callow, and grammatically gross. Hasan was "suspected of killing 13 people." This is idiocy. While it is common, for legal reasons, to use "alleged to" or "is charged with" or "is suspected of" in common criminal cases, this was not a common case, but mass murder committed in full public view. Hasan murdered his colleagues in public, at close range—thirteen of them. It was not a matter of suspicion.[34]

More troubling than this kid-gloves treatment of an Arab-Islamic terrorist is the fact that it is not an exception. It is standard operating procedure at the *Times*, the *Washington Post*, and other major Western news media who suddenly slip into indirect references, cloudy phrases, and passive descriptions when describing acts of terror committed by highly motivated Arab-Islamic terrorists. A *Washington Post* story says "Hasan's contacts with extremist imam Anwar al-Aulaqi began as religious queries but took on a more specific and concrete tone before he moved to Texas, where he allegedly unleashed the Nov. 5 attack that killed thirteen people and wounded nearly three dozen."[35] The cleric in question—whose name is sometimes written as Aulaqi and sometimes as Awlaki—has been very "specific and concrete" (to borrow the *Post*'s language) in instructions to various terror cells in the United States and Britain.

Elsewhere in the *Times* article, reporter Andrea Elliott tried to boost the image of Muslims in the military by asserting that Michael Monsoor, a member of the elite aquatic commando unit known as the Navy SEALs, died heroically pulling a comrade to safety. Later the *Times* issued a correction because Monsoor was *not* Muslim.[36] The *Times* also did not inform its readers that "the National Security Agency intercepted ten to twenty communications over the past year between Maj. Hasan and Anwar al-Awlaki, a Yemen-based cleric who knew three of the Sept. 11 hijackers"[37] and served as a spiritual advisor to the Lackawanna Six.[38]

POLITICALLY CORRECT, JOURNALISTICALLY SLACK

After 9/11, many questioned the performance of Western intelligence agencies, but they could just as easily have questioned the lack of perception and investigation on the part of the press. "As I watched the coverage of the attacks on the Pentagon and the World Trade Center," said media analyst Bernard Goldberg, "I wondered why I hadn't seen more stories on television news, long before these zealots flew their hijacked planes into American buildings, about the culture of anti-American hate that permeates so much of the Middle East—stories that might help explain how little Arab children can grow up to become fanatical suicide bombers."[39] The answer is that probing terror requires reporters or editors who can spot a story and will fight for it. Journalists then need the same traits often lacking in U.S. intelligence agencies:

- Imagination (to try to put oneself into the head of past, present, and future extremists, trying to envision their motivations and their environment)
- Courage (to confront a loaded topic and swim against politically correct currents, and the fortitude to enter a mosque, Islamic school, or community meeting)
- Education (to know what to seek but also to know some of the basics of Islamic religion and Middle Eastern politics)
- Work—lots of it

Since the days of Watergate and the Pentagon Papers, many people have come to believe that journalists are nearly all superheroes who "talk truth to power" in the face of all odds. One well-kept secret about working journalists is that many are unimaginative, gutless, and lazy. Even well-educated Western reporters often lack skills in foreign languages, alien cultures, and distant political systems. Many reporters are suckers for scams by terrorists and despots, relaying their propaganda to the public, legitimizing it, giving it credence. Western reporters once said Soviet dictator Yuri Andropov was a liberal who loved Western music and preferred drinking scotch to vodka.[40] Other reporters told us that Syria's Bashar Assad was a man of the future who "loved to go on the internet."[41] *Vogue* published a multipage spread on Assad's wife that airbrushed out any sign or mention of Assad's bloody rule. It was only days before Assad began killing hundreds of dissidents.[42] *Vogue* is albeit a fashion magazine, but we have seen this kind of "in-depth" and "well-informed" reporting before.

It is why we hear all the time about the "secular" Fatah versus the "fanatical Islamic" Hamas or the "moderate" PLO versus "the extremist" Hamas. Actually, the leaders of Fatah—Yasser Arafat, Khalil al-Wazir (nickname—Abu Jihad), and Salah Khalaf (nickname Abu Iyad)—were all part of the Muslim Brotherhood in Egypt in their youth. The Brotherhood, in turn, inspired the birth of Hamas. So the ideological backgrounds of Hamas and Fatah are not miles apart. Indeed, Arafat had very good relations with Sheikh Ahmad Yassin, founder of Hamas, and coordinated tactics against Israel with him—from the time of the Fatah leadership return to the West Bank and Gaza in 1993–94 and thereafter. There are even handwritten documents, captured by the Israeli police in 2002, that prove this.[43]

Unfortunately, reading and digesting evidence against terrorists takes time and work. The *New York Times* was willing to develop hundreds of thousands of dollars and hundred of man-hours to digest and analyze the Pentagon Papers in 1971.[44] Those documents cast doubt on the wisdom of many U.S. decisions in Vietnam. The attitude of the *Times* to important historical evidence was in my mind in early 2002, when I offered the *Times* an exclusive on scores of Palestinian terror documents seized at Orient House, the PLO's forward base in Jerusalem.[45]

The documents were a bombshell. They showed the personal direction and supervision of Arafat in murder operations. They proved that "moderate" Palestinian leaders like Faisal Husseini were involved in terror against Israel—even immediately following the signing of treaties with Israel in 1993–95. The documents spanned more than a decade. Some of them showed that the Second Intifada was not a spontaneous eruption of anger over Ariel Sharon's supposed defilement of the grounds of the Al-Aqsa Mosque,[46] but in fact a planned attack. There were many documents— Israel had confiscated over half a million—that were not just signed by Arafat, but included handwritten notations by him approving or changing the amounts of money to be paid to hired terrorists who stabbed, shot, and blew up Israelis. Signed letters showed cooperation between Arafat's Fatah and the more Islamic-oriented Hamas. This was incriminating evidence of the highest order, but *Times* Jerusalem bureau chief James Bennet did not want to meet me even to discuss the documents.

Where was James Reston—and his hunger for the UN/Bretton Woods papers—when I needed him? Where were the dedication and curiosity of reporters like Peter Kihss, Mike Kaufman, and Murray Schumach? Where was the ethos of the *Times* foreign correspondent? I could not imagine a serious journalist from the "newspaper of record" dismissing such a story without even a look.

The documents included photo ID cards for the Tanzim organization, which reporters claimed was a breakaway from Arafat's Fatah. The cards showed Tanzim was a nonuniformed army with military ranks inside Fatah. It proved Fatah and Tanzim had broken the Geneva Accords' prohibition of nonuniformed combat. The papers showed how Arafat promoted and paid members of the organizations. Numerous letters confirmed this: signed and dated letters between Arafat and Marwan Barghouti, the Tanzim leader later convicted of mass murder.

"We really don't have time," said Bennet, though, at the time, there were at least three other *Times* staff reporters reinforcing the *Times* Jerusalem bureau and Bennet's Intifada coverage. As a last recourse, I called a friend at the *Times* in New York who spoke to its new executive editor, Howell Raines, about the documents. Raines called Bennet, who grudgingly agreed to meet me. Bennet showed up a half hour late for the appointment in the *Times* office. When I saw that, I knew he was not going to do the story. Still, I showed him the Arabic documents and the English translations. Despite all the evidence, his response was "It's no smoking gun."

"For God's sake, it's a smoking pen," I answered. After all, for lawyers, judges, and historians, the best evidence is documentary evidence, especially if handwritten. It seemed Bennet would only be impressed with a video recording of Arafat murdering someone in front of a camera. This was not the same standard of evidence that Bennet and the *Times* applied to stories coming from the Palestinians. Bennet, who later left the *Times* to edit the *Atlantic*, was like other reporters who often accepted Arab testimony without corroboration on most issues—such as charges of atrocities. Yet he would not accept the most damning evidence[47] of the Palestinian leadership's direction of terror—at a time when it had signed treaties with Israel (the dovish governments of Yitzhak Rabin and Shimon Peres).

Later I saw one reason that Bennet and the *Times* would not want to use the exclusive material I had offered them. It seems they had staked out an analytical and political position defining Arafat as a peacemaker, as a moderate. *Times* editorials supported Arafat as a real alternative to Hamas, a man of his word, a hope for a better Middle East. Bennet appeared on television, testifying that Arafat was making strenuous efforts to stop suicide bombers, but "It would be very difficult for him to do that," said Bennet, suggesting that Arafat had very limited power over the Tanzim and Al-Aqsa Martyrs Brigades terrorists. However, Arafat's own records, offered exclusively to the *Times,* proved Arafat was the planner and paymaster of much of the terror.[48]

The whole episode[49] was proof, as Brigitte Nacos has observed, that few news organizations and reporters have the integrity and patience for documenting terror and for the "less-than-glamorous issues of terrorist prevention."[50] Some journalists even recall the ego-driven fictional reporter aboard the hijacked plane in the Bruce Willis action movie *Die Hard 2,* thinking of their careers and the boost from the "spectacular reality show" of a terrorist encounter.[51]

Governments—even democratically elected governments—make mistakes, especially in wartime. This is true in *every* kind of war, let alone a complicated terror war where there are unclear boundaries and human shields. World War II is often considered the most justified of all modern wars, but it produced a scathing and humorous *Catch-22,* depicting Allied bumbling. Today the catch is that many journalists think the idea is to catch any Western government any way you can. The Western journalist can always be a flag-waving patriot for a short period immediately following a terror attack and then return to the usual easy mode of fault-finding crusader against all-too-imperfect Western governments.

Reporters and analysts should not suspend their critical judgments for patriotism. Actually, patriotism requires constructive criticism of governments as well as a highly critical attitude to terrorists—who are not militants, not activists, but terrorists. That means evaluating the Western war effort. It also means being careful not to overdo critical and often carping investigative articles on government counterterror policy simply because it is easier and safer to write about the faults of a Western government than about the faults of a terror group. This means, as Walter Laqueur says, "The media cannot ignore terrorism," but it also means that "society would certainly be better off if the media were not driven by sensationalism."[52]

Terrorism is a disease that uses the communications media to spread and thrive. For terrorists like those in Al-Qaeda, violence is a symbolic act. For them, violence *is* communication. Journalists must not become part of the disease, because when a journalist does a bad job handling terror, then communication *is* violence.

"Without communication there can be no terrorism,"[53] but that does not mean we should censor our speech and our critical faculties, because without communication there is also no modern society, especially democratic society. For the reporter, the editor, and the publisher, the challenge is to bear witness—not false witness. The challenge is to be a fair and tough investigator for the sake of a democratic society, not for the sake of a big headline or a big rating or a big award.

John F. Burns, the chief foreign correspondent for the *New York Times*, deemed himself "the most closely watched and unfavored of all the correspondents" in Saddam Hussein's Iraq.[54] In a long oral history selection, he spoke eloquently about the challenges and fears of reporting on terror:

> Terror, totalitarian states, and their ways are nothing new to me, but I felt from the start that this was in a category by itself, with the possible exception in the present world of North Korea. I felt that that was the central truth that has to be told about this place. It was also the essential truth that was untold by the vast majority of correspondents here. Why? Because they judged that the only way they could keep themselves in play here was to pretend that it was okay.
>
> There were correspondents who thought it appropriate to seek the approbation of the people who governed their lives. This was the ministry of information, and particularly the director of the ministry. By taking him out for long candlelit dinners, plying him with sweet cakes, plying him with mobile phones at $600 each for members of his family, and giving bribes of thousands of dollars. Senior members of the information ministry took hundreds of thousands of dollars of bribes from these television correspondents who then behaved as if they were in Belgium. They never mentioned the function of minders. Never mentioned terror.[55]

"Being in the right place at the right time." For many journalists, a career, sometimes a lifetime itself, is made by fate: the opportunity to cover a major war, being on hand during a disaster, or discovering the threads of a political scandal.

Many aspiring journalists were indelibly affected by the experience of two young *Washington Post* reporters, Carl Bernstein and Bob Woodward, who chronicled the abuses of power by the administration of Richard Nixon: "Watergate." As important as Watergate was, the typical path to journalistic glory for most of the nineteenth and twentieth centuries was the war story. Winston Churchill himself attained public attention as a war correspondent covering the Boer War in Africa. Photojournalist Robert Capa eternalized war images from the European theater in World War II. Capa was even given a medal by Allied commander Dwight Eisenhower. Capa died during the Vietnam War, setting off a land mine. Homer Bigart (World War II and Korea), Ernie Pyle (World War II), Marguerite Higgins (World War II and Korea), broadcaster Edward R. Murrow (the Battle of Britain) were all made famous—or more famous—by war.

Being an experienced foreign correspondent, especially a war correspondent, lent a journalist an undefined aura that was really a certain kind of wisdom, maturity, and realization of the limits of one's own abilities and the fragility of life itself. Arthur Ochs Sulzberger, publisher of the *New York Times* from 1963 to 1992, had served in the U.S. Marines in the Pacific theater from 1944 to 1946, and again, as part of the Marine reserve, in the Korean War. Unfortunately, those who led the *New York Times* and CNN into the new millennium were not seasoned war reporters, nor veteran foreign correspondents. They were people who were *not* molded by the experience of World War II. Their personal views were *not* framed by ideological battles over "appeasement" or the Cold War. Their formative experiences were the struggle *against* war—particularly the Vietnam War and what they perceived as overbearing, corrupt, and even colonialist U.S. governments. After the 9/11 attacks they took a "nuanced" view of the attackers and their motives, and they scrutinized the "war on terror" as they would have searchingly probed a suggested return to Vietnam.

"The reason that the World Trade Center got hit is because there are a lot of people living in abject poverty out there who don't have any hope for a better life," declared CNN founder Ted Turner in a speech at Brown University.[56] It was less than six months after 9/11. Referring to the hijackers, he said, "I think they were brave at the very least."[57] Vietnam had transformed Turner's worldview. Vietnam also shaped the ideas of the young publisher of the *New York Times,* Arthur O. Sulzberger Jr., who had been an antiwar activist, getting arrested twice at antiwar demonstrations. After bailing his son out of jail, Sulzberger the father asked Sulzberger the son a question that brought a defiant response whose content foreshadowed future *Times* policies:

"If," asked the father, "a young American soldier comes upon a North Vietnamese soldier, which do you want to get shot?"

"I would want to see the American get shot," said the son. "It's the other guy's country. We shouldn't be there."[58]

Reporters and editors at the *Times* called him "Young Arthur," to distinguish the exhibitionist son from his modest father, who was well liked by *Times* staffers.[59] They referred to the senior Sulzberger by his affectionate childhood nickname, "Punch,"[60] while they derisively nicknamed the son "Pinch."

"Young Arthur" Sulzberger was forty-one years old when he became the publisher of the *Times* in 1992. The elder Sulzberger felt unsure about his son becoming publisher, partly due to his "hippy-like" behavior two decades earlier, including his "acting out" at family weddings by wearing outlandish costumes.

Young Arthur's first war as *Times* publisher was George W. Bush's "war on terror." It was a war that led to war in Afghanistan and then Iraq. One can imagine that the former antiwar protester had a Vietnam-era vision of falling dominoes and falling bodies trapped in a quagmire—the brave American rhetoric, in a Texas accent,[61] of Americans opposing tyranny giving way to a somber reality of bleeding Americans. Sulzberger thus urged his newspaper to probe the war from every angle—quickly.

"We're actually engaged, for the first time in my memory, in ongoing national debate as to whether or not this country should go to war," declared Sulzberger Jr. in a speech at the University of California at Berkeley, a school known for leading the academic protests against Vietnam. It was an apt backdrop for the *Times* publisher's remarks. He sensed the need to act with haste, lest America be drawn into another long war. He felt compelled to speak up quickly and loudly "in the ongoing national debate." Sulzberger explained that "those debates, at least in my experience, which is heavily-flavored by the Vietnam War experience—which was my growing up—those debates always seem to take place after Americans are already in combat, not before."[62] Sulzberger was not alone.

Only six days before the 9/11 attacks, the headstrong *Times* publisher had named a new top editor for the *Times*. Like his young publisher, Howell Raines was very opinionated, very sure of himself, but not very experienced or world-wise.[63] "The impetuous young Sulzberger, who liked to differentiate himself from his staid and gentle father, had been drawn—perhaps too drawn—to Raines," says former *Times* reporter David Margolick. Sulzberger "liked his liberal politics, his smarts, his schoolboy humor, his southern swagger, his chutzpah. The *Times* needed a good goosing, Sulzberger had felt, and Raines, who'd already put backbone and spleen into the *Times*'s oh-so-reasonable editorials, was the man to give it."[64] Unlike previous *Times* executive editors, Raines really had not had a career as a foreign correspondent, but only a long stint as editor of the *Times* editorial page. Like his publisher, he had strong views, weak experience, and a strong desire to make lots of changes at the paper. "Arthur Jr. had no interest in pledging measured reform. From the moment he became publisher, he was like a silversmith, noisily banging *The New York Times* into a shape that reflected his own values, beliefs, and personality."[65]

Opinion writers such as Maureen Dowd, Frank Rich, and Gail Collins were essentially an extension of Sulzberger-Raines. They used insults and low humor to excoriate the war effort and those who supported the war. Instead of illuminating serious questions about the war goals and order of priorities, they offered a lot of heat and little light. They endlessly flayed President Bush, Vice President Dick Cheney, and Secretary of Defense Donald Rumsfeld—using the kind of language that Punch Sulzberger, Adolph Ochs, and *their* editors would never have countenanced. For Dowd—a columnist who was a personal favorite of Sulzberger Jr.— Rumsfeld was "Rummy" or "the man who trashed two countries," and Cheney was "the Duke of Halliburton" and an "enviro-villain."[66] The "W" in George W. Bush, the forty-third U.S. president, stood for "wimp," affixing the same label that had been stuck on George H. W. Bush, the forty-first president. Being a "wimp"—*that* was the reason for the war, asseverated Dowd. Her sharp tongue was not matched by experience as a foreign correspondent or any national security training. *Times* columnist Dowd, who one might have thought had numerous degrees in psychology, many long years of experience in mental health practice, and hundreds of hours evaluating intelligence quotients and intelligence capabilities, gave a detailed diagnosis of the security staffs of both presidents, especially Bush 43.

> In the Bush family, the gravest insult is to be called a wimp. When *Newsweek* published its "Fighting the 'Wimp Factor'" cover about Bush senior when he was running for president in 1987, he was so angry he refused to talk to the magazine again until he had a meeting with the editors and the publisher, Katharine Graham. Mr. Bush even knew the precise number of times the word "wimp" appeared in the article. In his memoir, Bush Junior wrote: "My blood pressure still goes up when I remember the cover." The Bushes arranged their whole lives to put a veneer of Texas lock-'n'-load over Greenwich lockjaw. . . . You might think the United States would have an elevated debate before deciding to launch a major war against another country. But we've simply had a childish game of Chicken, with different factions sneering at one another: "You're a wimp!" "No, you're a wimp!"[67]

By not killing Saddam Hussein in 1991, Dowd said, the elder Bush had allowed the "wimp factor" to reemerge, but the younger Bush was a "macho" Texan and would change that. The son would prove to his father and his advisors that he would not make the same mistakes or get stuck with the same label. In her contribution to "elevated debate," Dowd said Bush 43 was nothing but an empty-headed fool trying to show his daddy, his daddy's friends, and the rest of the world that he was no wimp. Meanwhile, the younger Sulzberger, who had been *given* a newspaper by *his* daddy, and who had a career of trying to show off and defy *his* daddy—by getting arrested, wearing love beads and sandals to formal family weddings, even cross-dressing—enjoyed reading Dowd's glib "analysis," even though her columns were full of gossip and innuendo rather than solid research. "People [have] learned more about President Bush from Maureen's insights into what drove him as an individual . . . than they did from any of our reporters, who stuck more clearly to the nuts and bolts of the politics," declared Sulzberger Jr.[68]

This remark reveals the jejune, juvenile journalistic thinking inside the head of the world's most important media firm: Arthur Sulzberger Jr. esteemed his gossip columnist more than the research of his best reporters. Not surprisingly, many top reporters left the *Times* when serious investigations and hard news were often supplanted by weakly supported allegations on the news pages and gossip-infused insults on the opinion page.[69]

"A clique of conservative intellectuals," Dowd said, "are driving this war." It was a view reinforced by other *Times* columnists like Frank Rich and Paul Krugman, who conveniently forgot that the *Times* had criticized Bill Clinton in 1998 for allowing the degradation of UN inspections of Iraqi weapons. Indeed, the *Times* and its columnists and its news pages were uniting in loud denunciation of Bush's search for supposed weapons of mass destruction, claiming it was all a sham. But the *New York Times* itself had warned President Clinton and Congress three years earlier about those same weapons: "Even a few more weeks free of inspections might allow Mr. Hussein to revive construction of a biological, chemical, or nuclear weapon."[70]

Therefore, the contentions of the *Times*—via Dowd and others—that Bush was carrying out a right-wing conspiracy or a family feud against Saddam were simply not "analysis." It was more like a macabre cookbook. All supporters of Bush strategies were dehumanized, reduced—boiled down into bellicose ingredients in some witches' brew stirred by a conservative cabal of warmongering warlocks. It was all meant, Dowd said, to keep the West swimming in blood, instead of floating off to a peaceful era led by the United Nations and multilateral consultation.[71] The "neocon" cabal was led by Vice President Cheney, former assistant secretary of defense Richard Perle, and Undersecretary of Defense Paul Wolfowitz, whom Dowd called "Wolfie." Dowd cast her choicest epithets at Cheney and Perle (who, like Kristol, had no job in the Bush administration): "Darth Vader," the "Prince of Darkness," "Rogue Diva of Doom," and "Genghis Khan."

Bush's war, said Dowd, was *not* a response to a series of attacks by (or aided by) Al-Qaeda, Al-Qaeda-inspired groups, and state sponsors of terror (like Iran, Iraq, North Korea, and Syria). It was a prefabricated plot—oozing with testosterone—to "wrestle the world to the mat" (a reference to Rumsfeld's past as a collegiate wrestler). The neocons hatched their plot at a 1997 neocon conference, attested Dowd, and then they seized the chance and "installed it in President Bush's head."[72]

The conspiracy to fill Bush's empty head, described by Dowd, seemingly did *not* have anything to do with four airplanes and three thousand dead people in the worst terror attack in the world's history. It was *all* a political plot, and it was *not* connected to a decade of Al-Qaeda or Hizballah bombing Western embassies, hotels, and military installations on several continents. It was also totally divorced from evidence that Saddam was gathering or had gathered poison gas, biological agents, and uranium,[73] as well as giving documents and safe haven to members of Al-Qaeda or Islamic Jihad. It also had nothing to do with a series of anthrax attacks in the United States right after the September 11 terror assault. "Shortly after the hijackings, a series of anthrax attacks was carried out using the U.S. Postal Service as a delivery system. Between September 22 and November 21, unknown numbers of people were exposed to anthrax spores, resulting in twenty-two confirmed or suspected cases, and of those cases, five deaths."[74]

Of course it was legitimate for Dowd and other columnists to criticize Bush and his policy team harshly. Even conservative columnists, such as Charles Krauthammer, had raised doubts about the wisdom of trying to bring democracy to the Arab world. Other observers, including the author of this book, thought the Bush-Rumsfeld post-Iraq-invasion strategy was not well prepared. However, Dowd and her colleagues deliberately denied or avoided inconvenient facts showing Bush, Cheney, and Rumsfeld were right about some things:

- Saddam had aided people involved in the first World Trade Center attack, had used weapons of mass destruction (WMD) against Iran and his own people, had indeed kept up a program of developing WMD, had sought uranium for nuclear weapons, and had previously succeeded in hiding evidence of such actions.[75]
- After surging its forces and changing counterinsurgency tactics, America had succeeded in bringing a semblance of calm to most of Iraq, and it had succeeded in holding democratic elections in a country that had never had them.

- America, after some setbacks, had found many of the leaders of Al-Qaeda, had found and executed Saddam Hussein, and had successfully safeguarded the U.S. homeland for seven years after 9/11.

Dowd and other journalists were entitled, even obligated, to find mistakes in the Bush policies. But basic fairness and duty to one's profession meant that ad hominem insults should be avoided. Under previous editor-publisher teams, even the *Times* opinion sections—the editorial page and the op-ed page—observed a kind of restraint on national security issues and in personal criticism of the president of the United States, whether the president was Kennedy or Eisenhower. Sometimes the *Times* withheld publication of stories it felt might hurt national security.

This was not the policy of the millennial edition of the *New York Times*. It made a conscious decision to reveal U.S. operational intelligence techniques used to block post-9/11 terror attacks by Al-Qaeda and others. The *Times* made this decision despite several pleas from President Bush and the bipartisan leadership of Democrats and Republicans in Congress. The *Times* delayed publication for a year. On December 16, 2005, the *Times* went ahead as its reporter, James Risen, prepared to publish his own book on the subject. "Bush Lets U.S. Spy on Callers Without Courts" appeared ten days after President Bush invited *Times* publisher Arthur Sulzberger and editor Bill Keller to the White House Oval Office to ask the *Times* not to publish an article that, Bush said, would hurt America's counterterror efforts. The 3,300-word piece exposed an advanced and secret telephone surveillance program monitoring calls made from abroad into the U.S. It was a program that intelligence officials—not Bush or his political appointees—believed had already succeeded in stopping several attacks, something not mentioned in the article. Bush reportedly called the behavior "shameful," and he and other officials indicated the *Times* came to the White House already having decided to publish the material and reveal the program. National Security Agency director General Michael Hayden said that had the program been in place before 9/11, there is a good chance it might have prevented the attack.[76]

More important than the snide personal attacks and antiwar slant of the *Times* opinion sections was the slanting of the *Times* news pages in ways never seen before. The *Times* led a crusade against United States intelligence-gathering methods, publishing scores of articles on the Terrorist Surveillance Program (TSP), on the monitoring of bank transactions from suspicious overseas sites, on the monitoring of emails suspected as conduits of terror instructions, and, of course, on the interrogation techniques ranging from rendition to the now-infamous but rarely used and hardly deadly "water-boarding." The *Times* led Western journalists on a crusade that produced a few Pulitzer Prizes and some ruined careers in the intelligence and policy community, but many of the articles appeared partisan and politically motivated efforts best described as wild-goose chases:[77]

- Against supposed falsification of Western intelligence data concerning Saddam and his various programs to develop and use weapons of mass destruction.
- Against the torture of Al-Qaeda operatives as well as "innocent" people who just happened to be in Al-Qaeda camps.
- Against a Bush anti-terror policy that reportedly failed in every respect.

The problem with this view was that Saddam's WMD programs were not a figment of Bush's imagination, nor Cheney's. Indeed, some of the intelligence information came from other allied countries such as Britain, Germany, and Israel. The *New York Times,* the BBC, and CNN often deliberately tried to mislead on this point, pretending that Britain was opposed to war in Iraq or that Britain and other countries had not found damning evidence of WMD programs in Iraq.

The Sulzberger-Raines team patted itself on the back that its coverage of terror was nothing less than superb. Seven months after 9/11, the *New York Times* won seven Pulitzer Prizes, several for articles related to coverage of the aftermath of 9/11. But the awards hid a horrible reality:

- The *New York Times* had failed in pre-9/11 coverage of the threat of terror.
- There was something rotten inside the *New York Times* at the highest levels, something rotten about the way the *Times* had treated the terror issue itself, and the way it had led other media companies to follow its path.

The *New York Times* had not used its tremendous resources to investigate the background of rising Islamic terror in the 1990s, and it had not tried to unearth the ugly and emerging picture of a growing terror threat that lay partially hidden in government reports that usually went unread by the common man and woman. Almost as bad, post-9/11, the *Times* had embarked on a seeming effort to use its news pages to defeat the anti-terror policies of the democratically elected government of the United States. The *Times* appeared bent on showing that the American-led fight against Arab-Islamic terror was as bad morally as the 9/11 attacks themselves. It prominently featured articles claiming American torture of suspected Taliban in Afghanistan, American and allied torture of Al-Qaeda in the Guantánamo prison in Cuba, and tremendous abuse by America of eavesdropping against innocent people. These accounts were not totally wrong all the time, but they were terribly exaggerated most of the time, and they were often based on information that was partial—both incomplete and biased. Despite clear errors and bias, the reports were nevertheless prominently published and seemed designed to hem in American policy makers.

Twenty-one months after 9/11, the *New York Times* reporters and editors staged a coup against Executive Editor Howell Raines. It was a move unprecedented in *Times* history,[78] and it forced Sulzberger to remove Raines as editor against the publisher's own wishes. Sulzberger apparently never considered removing himself as publisher.

As for Sulzberger's favorite columnist, Maureen Dowd, there was a tiny change of tune and tone eight years after 9/11. Following two Arab-Islamic terror attacks in America—the fatal attack in Fort Hood and the near catastrophe over Detroit—Dowd castigated President Barack Obama for taking it all too nonchalantly. She said "he finally emerged to tell us some stuff we already knew." "We are under attack. There is evil in the world."[79]

It was astonishing to hear the *Times'* antiwar columnist sound like a devotee of Bush's war against the "Axis of Evil." What was the world coming to? Might this eventually lead to a more serious analytical and reportorial approach toward terror?

5

PROTECTING THE CIA AND BOOSTING BIN-LADEN

Flames from an act of terror are only the last part of a chain leading to that final, fatal explosion. To stop those flames and prevent those deaths, one must break the chain of events leading to that flash of fire and death.

Every fire has at least three ingredients: fuel, oxygen, and a source of heat. Remove one of those elements, and there is no fire. The fire of terror is similar but more complex: it requires terrorist fund-raising, recruitment of terrorists, and surveillance of and information on intended targets. It also requires an ideology and an indoctrination of terrorists, smuggling of material, and infiltration of terrorists. Each element is needed for that final burst of death. Stopping any one factor, or seriously curtailing several of them, can prevent the fire from igniting.

Pinpointing the weak link in the chain is what makes intelligence so important in fighting terror—more than it is in other forms of warfare.[1] Yet, for many years, the "counterterror intelligence" of Western countries— especially U.S. intelligence—was a living oxymoron, a cold fire producing more smoke than heat, and very little light.

This is particularly true of America's main intelligence service, the Central Intelligence Agency (CIA), whose motto is both very apt and something of a sad joke today. As one goes through the computerized turnstile scanners at CIA headquarters in Langley, Virginia, there it is, engraved in marble and taken from Christian scripture: "And ye shall know the truth, and the truth shall set you free" (John 8:32).

Sadly, the CIA and its sister agencies (the FBI and the former Immigration and Naturalization Service, or INS) were slaves to politically correct lies that shackled U.S. policy in fighting terror.

NOT CONNECTING THE DOTS AND NOT SPEAKING THE LANGUAGE

On the eve of the September 11, 2001, attacks on the United States, two leading members of the CIA exemplified the cold fire of U.S. intelligence: CIA director George Tenet and Michael Scheuer, head of the CIA's "bin-Laden unit" from 1996 through 1999. Neither had ever served as a field intelligence agent. Neither spoke Arabic. Apparently, they lacked any advanced education regarding the Arab-Islamic world. Their ignorance was nothing special in the top echelons of the CIA in the late 1990s—even in the "Counterterrorism Center." Of CTC's thirty agents, recounts one officer, "there were only two of us who spoke Middle Eastern languages."[2]

This was a far cry from the men and women who once formed the core of the CIA: the Office of Strategic Services (OSS). It was a World War II unit whose officers—field agents, researchers, and analysts—were "scholar spies." As Robin Winks, author of *Cloak and Gown*, writes:

> Those who worked in R&A [research and analysis] and in X-2 [counterintelligence] had a sense of place, for some largely from books, for others from knowing Italy, or England, or Istanbul as James Joyce knew Dublin: because they inhabited it with their mind, and their future, not merely with their body. They understood the function of trivia, of miscellaneous information, and understanding it could both remember an enormous range of data and assimilate that data into a coherent pattern that others might miss. They wanted to understand another society, often in order to understand their own; they tended to think that there truly was something called "national character," despite the possibility that such a belief would lead to stereotyping others, for they believed that Americans, or English, or Italians, or Russians tended—tended as a nation, as a collectivity, not invariably as individuals—to behave in a certain way given certain conditions. They were theoreticians of human

nature, with the human condition fragmented into that easy and admittedly at times misleading set of receptacles for collecting and analyzing data, the nation state.[3]

Tenet and Scheuer would not likely have been accepted in the OSS. So what made Tenet and Scheuer so special—one to head America's most important spy agency and the other to lead one of America's most important intelligence units?

Reviewing Tenet's biography, one searches for the special traits that made him, at age forty-four, the youngest CIA director in history. Tenet, a ruggedly good-looking man from a Greek immigrant family, was born across the river from the skyscrapers of Manhattan, in the working-class community of Flushing, Queens. He worked in his family's restaurant as a busboy. Tenet was deemed a good high school student, but he did not really exhibit signs of genius or originality in Georgetown University, where he got his bachelor of arts degree, nor at Columbia University's School of International Affairs, where he received a master's degree. He showed no special language aptitude (beyond the family's Greek heritage) nor outstanding analytical skills before landing several fairly low-level jobs in Washington. He worked for Bill Clinton's campaign, then as a staffer for Clinton's National Security Council, and later as a Democratic Party staffer on arms control matters and on the Senate Intelligence Committee.

It seems Tenet's greatest expertise was ingratiating himself to politicians —from senators and congressmen to presidents: from Democrat Bill Clinton to Republican George W. Bush. Politicians felt comfortable and unthreatened around Tenet, and so would terrorists, especially Osama bin-Laden.

After becoming CIA director, Tenet dragged his feet on CIA or Pentagon ideas that might have led to bin-Laden's death before 9/11 as well as in late 2001 or in 2002. Tenet vetoed the idea of using a missile-bearing drone aircraft to kill bin-Laden in 2002—a tactic used very successfully by Israel against the Islamic terrorists of Hamas. Tenet objected to the CIA using drones to kill terrorists because it was not in the CIA job description. His response to the idea was: "Over my dead body."[4]

Tenet's inability to adapt the CIA to the terror battlefield was overshadowed by his stupendous ability to adapt to changing political conditions. He worked harmoniously with President Bill Clinton and President

George W. Bush, even though Clinton and Bush had very different attitudes toward the role of intelligence. Bush, whose father had been a CIA director, insisted on full intelligence briefings almost every day, even when traveling. Clinton canceled his personal CIA briefings after only six months on the job, and he rarely followed up on the "PDB"—the President's Daily Briefing, a written briefing pack delivered to the White House. Clinton almost never spoke to his first CIA director, James Woolsey, barely meeting with him before naming him director in 1993. Woolsey later turned this state of affairs into a rueful comedy routine: "Woolsey loved to tell the story of the plane that crashed into the White House. 'They said it was just Woolsey trying to get an appointment with Clinton,' he said."[5]

President Clinton also barely spoke to or saw Louis Freeh, who, from September 1993 to June 2001, directed the FBI, the organization responsible for monitoring terror threats inside the United States (and investigating attacks overseas in which Americans were killed or wounded). Freeh says Clinton spoke to him only once during his last four years of office. This was when the FBI probed bombings by Al-Qaeda of two U.S. embassies in Africa, and three major attacks on Americans in Arabia: on the USS *Cole* in the port of Aden, Yemen, in 2000; on U.S. soldiers in Riyadh, Saudi Arabia, in 1995; and the colossal 1996 assault on the Khobar Towers residence used as U.S. military barracks in Saudi Arabia.

Turning Intelligence into Politics
Some of the great strain in the Clinton-Freeh relationship was probably due to Clinton's legal scandals and ongoing investigations carried out by FBI personnel.[6] However, it went beyond Clinton's distractions or his distaste for the FBI. As a matter of policy, the Clinton administration made the FBI the lead U.S. agency probing terror involving Americans, but it did so without seriously expanding FBI resources or giving the bureau strategic guidance. This hindered U.S. investigations of terror, effectively making terrorism a "law enforcement" problem. FBI agents and prosecutors were taught to handle terror legalistically, to make cases that could be brought to trial, and one did not want to taint evidence or raise other legal questions by sharing intelligence or evidence with the CIA. Clinton officials such as Attorney General Janet Reno and Deputy Attorney General Jamie Gorelick

(who would later sit on the 9/11 Commission) issued instructions limiting the information the FBI could share.[7] Former FBI director Freeh has charged that Clinton did not really help FBI terror investigations of two attacks on Americans in Saudi Arabia—in Riyadh in 1995 and in Dhahran (Khobar Towers) in 1996. Saudi Arabia prevented FBI investigators from touching evidence or even directly interviewing witnesses or suspects. Freeh said his agents only got some access after two years, after intercession by former president George H. W. Bush. The elder Bush had good ties to the Saudi royal family because of his defense of Kuwait and Saudi Arabia in the 1990 Iraq-Kuwait war.[8] Freeh says the Clinton administration in general was not aggressive in capturing anti-American terrorists or in preventing further anti-American terror. President Clinton and Sandy Berger, Clinton's second national security advisor, deny Freeh's charges. For its part, the 9/11 Commission does not exonerate Clinton, but says Freeh was not aggressive enough in assigning FBI agents to anti-terror duties. Clearly, Freeh's charges are meant also to hide his sins and FBI failures battling terror. The FBI botched many clues from 1989 to 2001, missing several chances to stop the 9/11 attacks. For example:

- The FBI badly mishandled evidence against the Arab-Islamic terror cell in New York and New Jersey, basically ignoring boxes of terror materials, mostly in Arabic, seized at the apartment of El-Sayyid Nosair, the man who murdered Rabbi Meir Kahane in 1990.
- An FBI informant, Abdusattar Shaikh, was the landlord of two of the nineteen hijackers on September 11, Khalid al-Mihdhar and Nawaf al-Hazmi.
- FBI center ignored a memo from Agent Kenneth Williams in its Phoenix branch, warning of unusually high numbers of Middle Eastern men enrolled in flight schools.
- Similarly, FBI headquarters refused to allow field officers to search the computer of Zacarias Moussaoui, "the twentieth hijacker," in which there were clear indications of the impending 9/11 attacks.[9]

Presidents George W. Bush and Bill Clinton, despite their different views and different characters, trusted George Tenet with the job of guarding America at a time of rising terror threats. The one consistent theme in

Tenet's remarkably unremarkable career is his ability to ride a desk like a surfboard, atop the choppy waves and through the political storms that buffet the intelligence community in Washington, D.C. These storms have become one of the most predictable and lamentable elements of Washington's weather since the abuses of power by President Richard Nixon in 1972. The Watergate scandal began when CIA-trained personnel burgled the Democratic Party campaign headquarters in the Watergate hotel and apartment complex for the benefit of President Nixon and his Republican Party. The scandal deepened when it was shown that Nixon's staff used intelligence techniques against political rivals. The outrage was natural and justified, but it ended up hurting the U.S. intelligence community's ability to defend America against terror.

Beginning in the 1970s, intelligence directors were chosen not for their proven ability to lead an espionage or data-gathering effort but for their proven ability not to upset politicians worried about intelligence chiefs who were too intelligent, too inquisitive, too power-hungry. No one wanted another J. Edgar Hoover, the legendary founder of the FBI. Hoover made the FBI an elite law enforcement agency but also amassed secret dossiers on politicians, antiwar protesters, and political activists such as Martin Luther King Jr. Hoover remained FBI director from 1935 until his death in 1972. Watergate reawakened the instinctive fears of elected leaders that the FBI and the CIA could use information-gathering skills to undermine democracy.

Fears that the CIA might become "an American Gestapo" were present even in the legislative deliberations of the 1947 National Security Act, which formed the CIA. The air of suspicion and political oversight deepened dramatically during the Nixon years, leading to an overreaction after the Watergate scandals.

"The CIA was being sacked like a conquered city," writes Tim Weiner, national security correspondent of the *New York Times*. "Congressional committees were combing through its files, the Senate focusing on covert action, the House homing in on failures of espionage and analysis."[10] A Senate committee headed by Senator Frank Church and a House committee led by Representative Otis Pike—as well as several commissions—published several itemized reports of all CIA assassinations over the years as well as detailed reports on all intelligence activities since its creation in 1947.

Although the names of agents and the specifics of methods were sometimes classified, foreign governments and terror groups likely found the reports excellent reading, as did many Americans worried by CIA excesses.

"Nearly every single secret—apart from the identification of sources and methods and current operations—of the CIA was revealed," said one British historian.[11] Weiner and others have written at length about the problems in the U.S. intelligence community throughout its history—difficulties resulting from an open society trying to run a series of clandestine intelligence services without succumbing to the ailments of nondemocratic countries. Authoritarian societies have few problems running intelligence services. But after the U.S. executive branch misused its intelligence services, it was only proper that the legislative branch would try to check abuses of power. So began a period of "intelligence oversight" by congressional panels that dominated and second-guessed U.S. intelligence decisions. It is natural in a democratic country sensitive to abuses by ambitious officials to make rules against one domestic law enforcement agency, the FBI, sharing information with another agency that collects information outside the country, the CIA. Bill Gertz, national security specialist of the *Washington Times*, strongly suggests that the rules, from Clinton's attorney general Janet Reno, may have prevented the prevention of 9/11. Several important leads (from the Philippines to Oklahoma) about hijacking plots were not passed along.[12] ABC reporter John Miller and author Michael Stone focus on a different set of critical leads (mostly in the New York area) that were not shared.[13] The American commission of inquiry into the 2001 terror attacks on the United States makes its own list.[14]

SINS OF OMISSION AND SINS OF THE COMMISSION

As a whole, the 9/11 Commission Report is not a document of penetrating analysis. It would be too extreme to call it a whitewash, but an examination of its findings shows an unusual effort at preserving a bipartisan façade of inquiry, while treading carefully through a minefield of professional incompetence and political cowardice.

"Composing a report that all commissioners could endorse carried costs," observed Ernest May, a Harvard University historian who served as the nonpartisan historical advisor to the 9/11 Commission.[15] May was an excellent choice to advise the commission. He spent a lifetime writing and researching the question of strategic surprise in diverse periods in history such as France facing Hitler in 1940 and the Kennedy administration facing the Cuban Missile Crisis in 1962.

"The report has weaknesses," May stressed. He explained why the commission found it difficult to fulfill the goal set by commission chairman and former New Jersey governor Thomas Kean "[to tell] future generations 'This is how it happened.'"[16] Simply put, the plague of partisanship and incompetence that beset America's intelligence community did not completely spare the commission that investigated 9/11. May quotes Kean:

> "If you want something to fail," he [Kean] explains, "you take a controversial topic and appoint five people from each party. You make sure they are appointed by the most partisan people from each party—the leaders of the party. And, just to be sure, let's ask the commission to finish the report during the most partisan period of time—the presidential election season."[17]

The report mentions *some*, but *certainly not all*, missed chances to stop the 9/11 attacks on New York and Washington, D.C., focusing briefly on a few "late leads."[18] The report summary lists nine "vulnerabilities in the plot" that might have been exploited by U.S. intelligence and enforcement agencies: for example, searching passengers, locking cockpit doors, and checking visa applications of the hijackers.[19] Did the United States need a high-level commission to discover this?

The commission also concluded that political leaders and security officials showed a "lack of imagination" in facing possible terror plots, but the commission report also shows little imagination. It shows a generally narrow historical focus on the danger of the Arab-Islamic terror threat to the West as it began to form itself in the 1990s. It shows a lack of imagination in examining in depth the failures of training and readiness of U.S. intelligence agencies—CIA, FBI, and National Security Agency (NSA). However, it shows a special lack of imagination and a reluctance to report harsh truths about policy makers.

Like the Israeli Commission of Inquiry into Israel's dramatic intelligence failure before the 1973 Arab-Israeli war,[20] America's 9/11

Commission Report largely skips over the responsibility of political leaders—presidents, senators, and members of the House of Representatives. Worse, perhaps, the 9/11 Report covers up a whole host of operational lapses and weaknesses in the American intelligence community. Indeed, outside the 9/11 Report, one of the major points of agreement in the various *nongovernmental* historical surveys of U.S. intelligence is that in the 1990s the CIA reached bottom just as America was under its most direct attack since World War II.

CIA director George Tenet owed his appointment to his political skills and his ties to Bill Clinton, in whose campaign he served. He was an administration arms control analyst, then a staff member, and later staff director for the Democratic Party on the Senate Intelligence Committee. In every way, Tenet was a committee man, and the committee unanimously approved Tenet's appointment as CIA director in 1997, despite a highly unusual protest letter from a large group of CIA field officers.[21]

"We are a group of officers who have served our nation in some hostile places," they said. "The operations directorate has been weakened more than at any time in its history," they asserted. "We deserve better. You deserve better than this."[22]

Two highly decorated CIA field officers stationed in the Middle East, Robert Baer and Gary Berntsen, have condemned the atmosphere of careerism that flourished under Tenet and his predecessor, John Deutch. "The CIA lost its way," Baer writes, and "was systematically destroyed by political correctness, by petty Beltway wars, by careerism, and much more."[23] Bill Clinton's national security advisor Anthony Lake actually tried to prosecute Baer, one of the CIA's best field officers, on charges of planning the assassination of Saddam Hussein in March 1995.[24] Lake himself was involved in several abortive—even scandalous—secret overtures to Iran, but Clinton later nominated Lake to head the CIA—only to withdraw the nomination under tremendous bipartisan criticism.[25]

Loss of Intelligence and Counterterror Ability

Amid the backstabbing at CIA headquarters, the CIA lost hundreds of its best field agents and analysts. Few people wanted to fill their shoes. "The nadir for the Clandestine Service (field agents) was in 1995, when only twenty-five trainees became new officers," the 9/11 Commission attests.[26] "The entire roster of case officers was reduced from 1,600 to 1,200, and there were only 400 collection management officers at American embassies to turn reports from case officers in cables back to Langley," reports an outside analyst.[27] "In 1998, the DCI was able to persuade the administration and the Congress to endorse a long-range rebuilding program. It takes five to seven years of training, language study, and experience to bring a recruit up to full performance."[28] This was too late to stop 9/11.

In the middle of this CIA personnel bloodletting, Bill Clinton wanted Lake, his own national security advisor (as well as a former advisor on security matters to Jimmy Carter), to lead the CIA. However, legislative opposition—even from Clinton's own Democratic Party—blocked this move. Clinton named John Deutch instead. In retrospect, it is not clear who would have been a more terrible choice.

On paper, Deutch seemed an excellent candidate—a distinguished chemistry professor from the Massachusetts Institute of Technology who had served one-year assignments at the Pentagon as a deputy defense secretary and undersecretary. But the chemistry professor, who liked the crisp salutes of the military, did not develop any chemistry with the more informal people at the CIA. Indeed, Deutch had horrible personal relations with almost everyone at the CIA, with meetings frequently ending in shouting matches. Deutch was also caught in vast security breaches that recall similar episodes of other Clinton advisors such as the document stealing by Sandy Berger and sloppy computer management by Martin Indyk. Deutch's breaches were investigated, but he was let off the hook without prosecution due to the intervention of his successor, George Tenet.[29] President Clinton gave Deutch a quick presidential pardon. The common ground between Lake, Deutch, and Tenet was a desire to direct a downsized CIA that did not create waves and that did not get sucked into scandals such as the Iran-Contra affair of the Ronald Reagan era.[30]

"Deutch laid down the law that recruitment of assets or spies with so-called human rights violations would require high-level approval," recounts author Ronald Kessler, who has studied the CIA and FBI closely. "Yet who else would know about terrorists and our enemies except those who were themselves involved in treachery? The message was clear: Stay away from informants who are not politically correct."[31]

James Woolsey, Clinton's first CIA director, berated the new regulations, known as "the Deutch Rules" or "the Torricelli Principles," for Representative Bob Torricelli of New Jersey.[32] "These rules make absolutely no sense with respect to terrorist groups because the only people who are in terrorist groups are people who want to be terrorists. That means they have a background in violence and human rights violations."[33]

Clinton's appointees Lake, Deutch, and Tenet were unlike Woolsey and quite unlike Reagan's CIA director, William Casey, who had himself been an experienced intelligence officer. Casey served as CIA director from 1981 to 1987. He was constantly looking for good agents and new sources of information. In contrast, Deutch worried that some sources might end up embarrassing the United States. His politically correct rules of agent enlistment thwarted the drafting of intelligence assets without constant vetting by CIA lawyers.[34] Creative, daring, and intellectually inquisitive field agents and desk officers were seen as a danger by Bill Clinton's staff. This was starkly different from the Reagan-Casey era. Author Bob Woodward says Casey "wanted 'unilateral' human assets—sources paid and controlled exclusively by the CIA, people less subject to the whims and fortunes of those in power."[35]

Casey did not want to rely on Middle Eastern governments for data or guidance, nor on data from Britain, France, Italy, and Saudi Arabia (which has figured in some U.S. policy mistakes in the last fifteen years). Tenet, however, had a special relationship with the Saudis, regularly briefing its U.S. ambassador, Prince Bandar. This was not the only difference in approach. Casey and Woolsey sought experienced officers. The later Clinton appointees did not think this was crucial.

Putting inexperienced desk officers in charge of sensitive anti-terror operations, former CIA field officer Berntsen writes, was "one of many things instituted by former Director Deutsch [sic] and his deputy and successor George Tenet that I felt undermined the Agency."[36] Tenet shared Clinton's desire for a smaller military and a smaller CIA, according to Berntsen: "Tenet seemed hell-bent on downsizing Operations and tying what was left of it in red tape."[37] Is it any wonder the CIA and FBI became more adept at the political battles inside Washington than in fighting terrorists? Political savvy and navigating political waters were much more crucial to an intelligence officer's career than having real intelligence.

"Intelligence" is more than just having data about a potential foe or current enemy. "Intelligence" means a probing inquisitiveness, a native intellect, and the "street smarts" we mistakenly call "common sense." This trait has become all too uncommon in government service. This is the kind of intelligence one seeks in an agent, in a good diplomat and a sharp foreign correspondent. Well before 9/11, agencies like the CIA became warehouses for human furniture: mediocre careerists and tired trumpeters playing the company tune. The CIA stopped welcoming talented non-conformists and area specialists like field agent Robert Baer. "Politics had seeped down to its lowest levels, in operations where I worked," avowed Baer, detailing how "political considerations" trumped operational findings and framed analytical results.[38]

POLITICIZING INTELLIGENCE AND NATIONAL SECURITY

Many have criticized George W. Bush's administration for its allegedly partisan use of intelligence data.[39] Yet, one of Bush's most important decisions—keeping George Tenet, a longtime Democrat, at the head of CIA—was hardly a partisan act. Indeed, even *after* 9/11, Tenet, a Democrat, kept his job. This may be because Bush did not want to seem to be undercutting the CIA in a period of crisis. As Thomas Powers observed, "in the days following the [9/11] attacks, Bush made a point of being photographed in earnest discussion with his chief advisers—Vice President Dick Cheney, National Security Adviser Condoleezza Rice, and George Tenet. The message appeared to be clear: the President is sticking with the agency and director he has got."[40] Bush may have kept Tenet for other reasons: he sometimes put friendship and personal loyalty ahead of competence.[41] Tenet ingratiated himself with Bush, briefing him personally during the 2000 presidential campaign and the subsequent transition period from the Clinton administration. Rarely has trust been so badly repaid on a personal, professional, and national level.

Several thousand deaths later, President Bush gave Tenet a medal—America's highest civilian award, the Presidential Medal of Freedom—and allowed him to continue leading America's intelligence community. For his part, Tenet and his top aides at the CIA did their best to undermine President Bush's policies.

Tenet invited Michael Scheuer to rejoin the CIA as his special advisor on Al-Qaeda from 2001 to 2005. Tenet encouraged Scheuer to write books that would attack Bush's policies. "As long as the book was being used to bash the president, they gave me carte blanche to talk to the media," declared Scheuer in an interview with the *Washington Post*.[42] This raises questions about Bush's decision to keep Tenet as CIA head, but it proves Bush was not motivated by partisan factors. The same cannot be said for Barack Obama, whose intelligence appointees have a decidedly partisan cast. Obama named Clinton's onetime chief of staff Leon Panetta (a former congressman with no intelligence experience) as CIA director, and lawyer and lobbyist Tom Donilon as his national security advisor after his first such advisor, General Jim Jones, could not get along with Obama's political crew.[43] Donilon, in contrast, worked with five Democratic presidents or candidates and was a consummate "political insider." U.S. military commanders and security officials, on the other hand, considered him a "dilettante."[44]

Tenet and Scheuer have written books offering their advice on terror and intelligence. Indeed, Scheuer got special permission—while still a CIA official—to write his views under the pseudonym "Anonymous." That Tenet allowed such an unusual deal with a working CIA agent suggests he liked what Scheuer was writing. Compare this light handling with the heavy censorship Tenet's CIA imposed on books written by highly decorated field agents Baer and Berntsen.

Tenet did not like books by talented, experienced, and successful men who denounced the agency's pack mentality. But Tenet's CIA liked how Scheuer undercut Bush policies. In his writings, Scheuer has several underlying themes. The loudest message is that the West caused Arab-Islamic terror by antagonizing Muslims. Remember, this is a man who has no Arabic expertise nor serious education about the comparative religions and political thought in the Middle East. Scheuer's ignorance is a glaring fault shared by other U.S. intelligence officials and think tankers (a point discussed in detail later).

The CIA's "bin-Laden unit" apparently paid no attention to the role of communication and ideology—Pan-Arab, Pan-Islamic, tribal themes—in the formation of states, movements, and even terror groups in the Arab-Islamic sphere. One strains to find discussion or even a reference in Scheuer's writings to the role of symbolic acts in Arab history, to the heritage and effect of charismatic leaders such as Gamal Abdul-Nasser of Egypt, Yasser Arafat, Saddam Hussein, and even Islam's prophet himself, Muhammad.[45] Scheuer pays little or no attention to the theory and practice of terrorist groups over the ages—such as the role of "the propaganda of the deed" terrorists use to reinforce oral and written messages. This "propaganda of the deed" means terrorists feel the need to act, to shoot, and not just to shout. Terrorists sometimes stage attacks in order to show that they are still active, to overcome internal strains, to recruit new members, to hold on to wavering ones, or to raise money. This is a crucial factor illustrated long ago by experts such as Walter Laqueur and J. Bowyer Bell, but Scheuer seems oblivious. "At times the whole strategy becomes the operational deed when this is all that is available—propaganda is achieved through operations, the Tsar assassinated or a symbol like the World Trade Center bombed."[46]

So, with no real examination of regional affairs, history of ideas, or terror theory, Scheuer leaves us with simple—or rather simplistic—explanations for Arab-Islamic terror: America and Israel are behind it all. It is not factually accurate, but at least—in the CIA, the State Department, and many universities—it is politically correct.

"America is being attacked because its foreign policies are perceived as attacks on Muslims and Islam, not because of its secular democratic society," writes Scheuer in the 2007 epilogue to his book.[47] This is exactly wrong, but Scheuer is entitled to his view, if he can make a case for it. However, he offers no real proof. Scheuer, who has not digested Al-Qaeda's message (even via translations), accuses everybody else of ignorance and wishful thinking. Indeed he sees wild prejudice against bin-Laden, whom Scheuer called a "mainstream"[48] Muslim: "These theories have shackled onto current U.S. leaders an almost pure ignorance of the Islamic world. Their ignorance-based policies toward the Muslim world are yielding rising numbers of American dead, totals that will increase until leaders in both parties start to see the world as it is, not as they imagine or want it to be."[49]

One tries hard to digest this: the CIA's top "expert" on Osama bin-Laden gets unprecedented permission from his intelligence agency to produce two books in which he accuses almost everyone else of not understanding Islam, not understanding bin-Laden, who Scheuer said is "mainstream" in his Islamic thinking.

MAINSTREAMING OSAMA BIN-LADEN

For hundreds of pages, this "expert" without any Arabic and without any field work at all in the Arabic-speaking areas of the Middle East accuses everyone in the policy community of "ignorance" and "hubris." Then this "expert" claims that the United States was wrong to invade Iraq because it is "the second holiest site in Islam."[50] *This* shows great ignorance, though there indeed were good arguments for not invading Iraq.[51]

To be clear: Islam's holiest site is the Black Stone in Mecca. It is to this site that Muslims make their pilgrimage, the haj. It is in this direction that Muslims pray daily—known in Arabic as the *qibla*. Islam's *second-*holiest site is the city of Medina,[52] originally known as Yathrib, which became the city in which Muhammad erected his mosque and his Islamic regime. There is no argument about this. None.

Within Sunni Islam (which constitutes more than 80 percent of the world's Muslims), this is as basic as 1 + 1 = 2. Anyone who takes a basic course in Islam learns this. One could make an argument that Jerusalem, which Muhammad originally chose as the direction of prayer (when he was actively courting Arabia's Jews for conversion), is the third-holiest site of Islam.[53] One might perhaps also mention Damascus, which was also the capital of Omayyad, the first caliphate, or Islamic state. Damascus was sometimes a pilgrimage site.

For Shiite Muslims, who represent less than 20 percent of the world's Muslims, the sites of Najaf and Karbala *inside* Iraq are holy sites, because they were places where Shiites were massacred for their beliefs. But Osama bin-Laden was not a Shiite, and neither is his Al-Qaeda organization. So, when the CIA's top "expert" on bin-Laden lectures us all—laymen and scholars—that we "just don't get it," it is a bit like an illiterate claiming that a Shakespeare poem has no rhyme or reason.

Scheuer's books—*Imperial Hubris* and *Through Our Enemies' Eyes*—are meant to open the eyes of the Western reader to the personality and ideology of the leaders of Al-Qaeda, but the two books skip over or gloss the ideological foundation of Al-Qaeda, which means "the base" in Arabic.

The ideological foundation of "the Base" is the thinking and writing of the Muslim Brotherhood, a group of Sunni Islamic extremists founded in Egypt in the first part of the last century.[54] The Brotherhood's message was critically important to the two organizational strands that would unite to form Al-Qaeda—bin-Laden and his followers from the Arabian Peninsula, and the Egyptian group of Ayman Zawahiri, who came from the Egyptian Jihad organization (which included blind Sheikh Omar Abdul-Rahman), which also assassinated Anwar Sadat in 1981 and carried out the first World Trade Center attack, in 1993.

Leading U.S. intelligence and policy-making officials have shown repeatedly how little they understand the ideological motivations and dialectical arguments of Arab-Islamic terrorists. Lieutenant General James Clapper, director of national intelligence, told Congress in February 2011 that the Muslim Brotherhood was an "umbrella" group that was "heterogeneous," "largely secular," nonviolent, and moderate—with "franchises" throughout the Middle East.[55] He was not accurately describing one of the most important and extremist organizations in the Arab-Islamic world. At the same hearing, CIA director Panetta assured the public that then Egyptian president Hosni Mubarak would resign by day's end. This did not happen, and it was based purely on "intelligence" Panetta gathered from a local radio report. Panetta's gaffe was only overshadowed by Clapper's incredibly uninformed comments on the Brotherhood, which were factually inaccurate in almost all respects. Under intense criticism and calls for Clapper's resignation, the Obama administration and Clapper each issued "clarifications." Other Obama administration officials have made similar comments. Indeed, many "experts" at the CIA and the State Department counterterrorism branches simply do not know much about Arab-Islamic thinking or culture.

The Brotherhood—known in Arabic as *Jamiat al-Ikhwan al-Muslimoun* —was founded by Hassan al-Banna in 1928, and its thinking was developed by Sayyid Qutb. Both were Egyptians. Al-Banna was assassinated by the secret police of King Farouk in 1949, and Qutb was executed by the pan-Arab regime of Gamal Abdul-Nasser in 1966. Each man was viewed as a threat to the government of Egypt of his time, and the underlying ideology of the Brotherhood is rightfully seen as threatening by many Arab regimes. The Brotherhood and its offshoots, such as Hamas, have shown periods of quiescence, but Western analysts who describe these organizations as relatively "moderate" are terribly off the mark, as are attempts to describe the "moderate wing" or "political wing" of the Brotherhood or of Hamas.[56]

After the United States announced killing Osama bin-Laden on May 1, 2011, Hamas leader Ismail Haniyeh stormed into the Hamas TV studio in Gaza to condemn the United States for murdering "a great Arab warrior." Haniyeh was so distraught at bin-Laden's death that he harangued the press for several minutes about the evil perpetrated by America against an upstanding Muslim.

"If this news is true," declared a red-faced Haniyeh, "then this means that it is part of the American policy based on the oppression and bloodshed in the Muslim and Arab world."[57]

Only a few days earlier, many Western officials and intelligence analysts had hailed Haniyeh, the Hamas "prime minister" in Gaza, for reaching a "unification" agreement with the "moderate" Palestinian leadership of the PLO and Fatah.[58] European leaders and staffers in the White House and State Department spoke aloud about welcoming and recognizing Hamas, the group that excelled in suicide terrorism.

Actually, real moderation and compromise are the last things one will find in the Muslim Brotherhood, Hamas, and like-minded organizations. These groups and their ideology are unbending, though they often exhibit what we might call "tactical patience"—perhaps in keeping with the Quranic comment *"Allah ma'a al-sabiriyyin"* (God is with the patient, if they will be but patient) (Quran, 2:153).

Aside from the Muslim Brotherhood, there are many extremist Islamist groups that developed in different geographic locales and amid diverse cultural and religious backgrounds (for example, Sunni versus Shiite, Indian subcontinent, Southeast Asia). Despite some differences, these movements share many qualities. Their common ground is summarized by the ethos of the Muslim Brothers—to cleanse the Arab-Islamic world of corruptive elements and to unite the world under Islam and Islamic law.

The Muslim Brothers also shared traits of other extremist Islamic groups over the past several hundred years, such as the Wahhabis in eighteenth- to twentieth-century Arabia, the Mahdists in nineteenth-century Sudan, and others. As Stephen Humphreys has perceived, these movements "overtly aimed at the forcible overthrow of societies and governments that they regarded as scandalously corrupt and heretical," preferring to replace them with regimes similar to that of Muhammad's original Islamic community in Medina.[59] So, the Muslim Brothers aimed their complaints at corrupt *Arab* societies and governments that had abandoned what they saw as the ethical foundations of Islam. They tried to assassinate Egyptian leader Abdul-Nasser in 1954, and they have tried to overthrow the Baathist regimes in Syria and Iraq at various times. Well before Al-Qaeda, Islamic-oriented groups were the dominant opposition force from Morocco on the Atlantic to Iraq and Iran on the Persian Gulf.

"By the late 1970's," as Ali Dessouki has observed, "Islamic resurgent movements constituted the major ideology of dissent in the Arab world regardless of the type of political system or its declared ideology."[60] These Islamist groups, it is important to understand, are more interested in the tone and color of their society rather than in the prerogatives of political leadership. The sheikhs are not running for office. As the French scholar of Islam Gilles Kepel has written, "the Brothers preached the unity of the faithful, placing special emphasis on personal morality."[61] For al-Banna and Qutb, Islam was an all-encompassing system, a way of life. First and foremost, they insisted that Muslims unite in observance of an Islamic way of life, casting aside Western corruptive influences.

Qutb was a gifted poet and newspaper editor who had been an activist of the Wafd nationalist party, and he had been a colleague and friend of Egyptian novelist Taha Husayn. The latter tried to moderate the antigovernment tendencies of his colleague, encouraging Qutb to visit America, which he did (1949–51), studying U.S. society closely. Qutb was disgusted by much of what he saw—loose sexual values, racism, materialism, disintegration of the family unit, financial corruption. During his time in America, Qutb published his epic work *Al-'Adalat al-Ijtima'iyyah fi al-Islam* (*Social Justice in Islam*).[62] Qutb set forth Islam as a socially conscious way of life that offers solutions better than those of Christianity, communism, capitalism, and Judaism. For Qutb, a good Muslim does not swim in luxury. Rather, he or she leads a frugal life, sharing income with the poor. Luxury, said Qutb, caused "atrophy of the senses."[63] Qutb revised the book several times, and the work was translated into many of the local languages spoken in non-Arab Muslim countries, among them Persian (Iran), Pashtu (Afghanistan), and Urdu (Pakistan). After returning from America, Qutb tried to work with the new revolutionary regime

of Abdul-Nasser, but the regime and the Brothers broke on several issues. Qutb was thrown in jail for years; there his views radicalized still
more. There can be no doubt that his political thinking was built around
his social and religious consciousness. His view grew darker and more
pessimistic with the years. Qutb came to see most Arab governments as
throwbacks to the pre-Islamic status of *jahiliyyah*: the total ignorance of
idolaters. As one translator of Qutb has written: "Sayyid Qutb decided
that Egypt, together with the rest of the contemporary Islamic world
was strictly comparable to pre-Islamic Arabia in its disregard for divine
precepts, and that its state could therefore rightly be designated by the . . .
term *jahiliyyah*."[64] Qutb essentially demanded a revolution inside the
Arab-Islamic world that would lead to "the replacement of *jahiliyyah* by
the Islamic order once the circumstances had matured."[65] This view of the
Muslim Brotherhood, its leaders, and its ideological descendants in Al-
Qaeda should not be news for Michael Scheuer or other supposedly serious students of Arab-Islamic terror groups. Scheuer claims to have read
and to respect the historical analyses of Bernard Lewis, particularly two of
his shortest recent books, *The Crisis of Islam* and *What Went Wrong*. Lewis
clearly identifies what irks and motivates radical Islamists:

> Their critique is, in the broadest sense, societal. The Islamic world, in
> their view, has taken a wrong turning. Its rulers call themselves Muslims
> and make a pretense of Islam, but they are in fact apostates who have
> abrogated the Holy Law and adopted foreign and infidel laws and cus-
> toms. The only solution, for them, is a return to the authentic Muslim
> way of life, and for this the removal of the apostate governments is an
> essential first step. Fundamentalists are anti-Western in the sense that
> they regard the West as the source of the evil that is corroding Muslim
> society, but their primary attack is directed against their own rulers and
> leaders. [66]

Lewis's perception here is not uniquely his own. Albert Bergesen has
written of Brotherhood ideologue Qutb: "His ideas have gone on and influenced generations of Islamist militants throughout the Muslim world."
Bergesen says Qutb's imprisonment and execution "increased the saliency
of his theories about jihadic politics against existing Arab regimes."[67] Has

Scheuer not read these observers of extreme Islamic movements, or has he simply not understood them?

Yes, al-Banna and Qutb also wanted to push foreigners out of the realm of Islam—Dar al-Islam—but the thrust of their ideology is inwardly aimed. This is an essential element of their thought. Scheuer is either ignorant or oblivious. Similarly ignorant, it seems, was his boss, CIA director George Tenet, who supported Scheuer.

The Brotherhood's seminal thinkers—al-Banna and Qutb—were critically influential in Islamist movements not only in Egypt and in Saudi Arabia, but also in Sudan, Morocco, and even in Shiite Iran. Scheuer refers to them very briefly and largely incorrectly in the 442 pages of *Through Our Enemies' Eyes* and basically ignores them in *Imperial Hubris*. He does not even get the names right. In *Through Our Enemies' Eyes*, Sayyid Qutb is called Mohammed Qutb.[68] This is like an "expert" on fascism writing a book and making references to Barney Mussolini. One expects this kind of sloppiness from a struggling junior high school student who does not really do his homework. This is not what we expect from a senior CIA official with a Ph.D. in British history from the University of Manitoba.

A major troubling element in Scheuer's analysis is his belief that hatred of Israel is a main motivating factor—if not *the* motivating factor—in Al-Qaeda attacks against the West. "To understand the perspective of the supporters of bin-Laden, we must accept that there are many Muslims in the world who believe that U.S. foreign policy is irretrievably biased in favor of Israel," declares Scheuer.[69] But if the ideology of Al-Qaeda is based on the ideology of the Muslim Brotherhood—which is directed primarily against corrupt Arab-Islamic regimes—then his theory has a lot of holes in its very foundation. After all, the Brotherhood was founded in 1928; Israel in 1948. In other words, Israel could not have been the cause of Arab-Islamist ennui, although it has certainly become a frequent excuse. Similarly, the radicalization of Sayyid Qutb—the Brotherhood's defining ideologue and a guide to other radical groups—took place during his American trip (1949–51) and during his later years in Egyptian jails. America was not deeply involved in the Arab world at the time, and American policies to Israel were hardly at their warmest during this period.

Scheuer's second main line of argument is that Osama bin-Laden is really a good Muslim. Osama—*pace* Scheuer—really did not want to hurt the West, especially America. The leader of Al-Qaeda, according to Scheuer, was driven to his actions by the actions of the West—particularly America—inside the Arab world. Parroting the anti-imperialist line of Edward Said,[70] Scheuer says Al-Qaeda's goal is getting the West out of the Arab East. If only the United States, Britain, Spain, France, and Germany would stop pushing Arabs around, then Al-Qaeda would call off its attacks and plans for more bloodshed. This is just nonsense.

A serious examination of the writings and speeches of the leaders of Al-Qaeda (bin-Laden, Zawahiri, Omar Abdul-Rahman, et al.) and their Muslim Brotherhood progenitors makes this clear. Much later writings and media appearances—particularly those aimed at a Western audience—try to mask Al-Qaeda's unremitting enmity to Western life, sometimes substituting an argument of Al-Qaeda acting "defensively" against Western aggression or Zionist expansionism.[71]

Yes, let us acknowledge that America, Britain, and France have carried out policies that anger Arabs. Some of the European powers in particular have been colonial powers in the Arab world. There are many Syrians and Egyptians who do not have fond memories of these policies, including a massacre of Arabs in Damascus in 1920 and foiling political independence in Egypt at least three times. But the United States, Britain, France, and Germany have also done a lot to protect Arab countries. They reversed Saddam Hussein's invasion of Kuwait in 1990–91. The United States in particular has actually forced Britain and France to withdraw some colonial interests (for example, Suez in 1956).

Obviously, Arab-Islamic terror organizations want Israel to disappear, and they would also love for non-Islamic America, France, Britain, Germany, China, Russia, and Japan to disappear, too—or to convert to their version of Islam. But they want something else first. They want Egypt, Arabia, Syria, Jordan, Iraq, and Morocco—among others—to stop being "apostate" or "renegade" Arab Muslim states. To them, a "heretical" regime run by Muslims is far worse than a Christian or Jewish society.

This internal Arab/Muslim "corruption" has nothing to do with Israel, which has been isolated and boycotted by Arab and Islamic countries for most of its modern history. On the other hand, the United States, Britain,

France, Japan, and so forth are countries that, by virtue of their economic and social ties with the Arab-Islamic world, can be seen to have had a corruptive influence on Arab-Islamic societies. This is a common theme of jihadist or *salafi* activists in Sunni parts of the Arab-Islamic world. It is also a theme of the revolutionary regime in Iran founded by Ayatollah Ruhollah Khomeini.

We can also go beyond these logical and historical proofs that the pseudo-anticolonialist argument of Scheuer (and Noam Chomsky and Edward Said) that "America made the Arabs angry by hurting Arabs and helping Israel" is unfounded. We can look to those who have examined the texts and appearances of bin-Laden, Zawahiri, and other leading influences in Al-Qaeda. One such source is *The Al-Qaeda Reader*, edited by Raymond Ibrahim, formerly of the Library of Congress: "This volume of translations, taken as a whole, proves once and for all that, despite the propaganda of al-Qaeda and its sympathizers, radical Islam's war with the West is not finite and limited to political grievances—real or imagined—but is existential, transcending time and space and deeply rooted in faith."[72]

A somewhat similar compendium of Al-Qaeda's video and online messages was compiled by a team of French academicians—Gilles Kepel, Jean-Pierre Milelli, and Pascale Ghazaleh. They reached a similar conclusion to Ibrahim:

> The very content of the pamphlets and tracts published electronically is another factor in the telescoping of time between the Middle Ages and today. These texts are full of references to the epic tales of the Prophet's [Muhammad's] companions and the history of the Arab caliphs—inexhaustible sources for a founding myth that seeks to edify by establishing the criteria by which to judge contemporary events and determine the principles of political action. In this literature, history is simply the infinite repetition of a single narrative: the arrival of the Prophet, the rise of Islam, the struggles to extend its dominion, and its expansion throughout the world. Each generation must apply itself anew to the task of this incomplete proselytism, taking up the original jihad to this end against a multifarious enemy that Al Qaeda's discourse reduces to the characteristics of the initial timeless enemy as stigmatized by the

classical authors: the unbeliever, the infidel (*kafr*) the apostate (*murtadd*), and so on.[73]

One cannot imagine that Michael Scheuer, the CIA's top bin-Laden analyst, did not receive the basic texts of Al-Qaeda. Did he ignore these texts or did he not understand their import—even in translation? After all, Scheuer thanks the Foreign Broadcast Information Service for helping him, though he cites the agency's name incorrectly: "I would like to salute, as I did in my first book, the officers of the Federal [*sic*] Broadcast Information Service (FBIS)."[74]

Sure, Scheuer is sloppy and uninformed, but is it possible he has such poor comprehension? One is left to assume that he blinds himself, that he committed the biggest sin for an analyst—substituting his own wishful thinking for cold analysis. Indeed, Scheuer's message is a hopeful one: Al-Qaeda and other radical Islamist groups can essentially be bought off by a change in American policy and rhetoric. One can almost hear him say, in the cadences of James Carville, "It's the West, stupid."[75]

But, of course, it's *not* the West, stupid. It's Westernization, stupid.

The Arab-Islamic extremists want to be as strong as the West, and they want to conquer the West, but they do not want their societies to be like the West.

That is the common ground between Al-Qaeda in the caves of Pakistan, Hamas in the refugee camps in Gaza, Hizballah in Lebanon, and the ayatollahs in Iran. The ghosts of Hassan al-Banna, Sayyid Qutb, and Ayatollah Khomeini agree on that. What is really amazing is that George Tenet and the CIA looked to Scheuer as their "go-to guy" on bin-Laden, and almost as amazing is that some serious counterterror experts and media outlets have vouched for Scheuer's professionalism.[76]

The CIA's decision to use Scheuer as its point man on Al-Qaeda takes on an even more bizarre quality when one contemplates the extreme personal mind-set of Scheuer himself. Lawrence Wright says Scheuer believed that FBI cooperation with his CIA unit was merely an attempt by the FBI to steal CIA data.[77] This does not begin to describe Scheuer's demons. One hesitates to make personal charges against Scheuer, but the evidence is so damning that one would be remiss to skip over the data.

When hiring a foreign correspondent, an ambassador, or an intelligence agent, one seeks competence and expertise—a specialist who can draw general lessons. One seeks an expert—someone who knows the local scene but who will not "go native" or suffer from "localitis"—identifying with the subject of research more than with one's own home, or one's duties. With Scheuer, America seems to have gotten the worst of both worlds—an intelligence agent who does not display intelligence in any sense, who does not really know the local scene, local culture, or local languages but who still over-identifies with the subject of his research: Osama bin-Laden.

How else can one explain America's "top expert" on America's most wanted terrorist comparing bin-Laden, the greatest mass murderer in American history, to some of the great figures of American history: Thomas Jefferson, Patrick Henry, and Thomas Paine.[78] "Thus bin-Laden and his reformer colleagues had claim to the right asserted by Jefferson, Henry, Paine, and their colleagues after they had exhausted all avenues of peaceful remonstrance."[79] Scheuer, who fancies himself a student of American history, also compares bin-Laden to John Brown, who led the antislavery raid in Harpers Ferry. A reader of Scheuer is consoled that he has, as yet, apparently not compared bin-Laden to Martin Luther King and Mohandas Gandhi.

"After reviewing what bin-Laden has said since first speaking to the Western media in late 1993, there appeared inescapably, for me, a stark contrast between what I considered to be bin-Laden's clear, calm, and carefully chosen words and the media's portrait of him as a more-or-less blood-crazed 'terrorist.'"[80]

It is perfectly correct, even necessary, to respect one's foes and enemies. This is what any boxing coach or martial arts teacher would say. It is quite another thing to avoid using the word *terrorist* to describe Osama bin-Laden. This specific rhetorical reticence, this reluctance to speak disparagingly of bin-Laden, reappears throughout Scheuer's writings. After all, Osama bin-Laden *was* a terrorist. Few people deserve the title more. Scheuer puts the term in quotation marks, which is exactly what many Arab-Islamic media do in their print and broadcast reports when discussing Western anger over "terrorist attacks."[81]

Compare this to the way Scheuer describes Arabs who, he says, helped Israel to stop Al-Qaeda from gaining a foothold in neighboring southern Lebanon. Scheuer disdainfully calls them "Palestinian turncoats."[82] This is not a passing thought, but a deeply felt issue with Scheuer. He prefers to call Israelis terrorists, not Hizballah, Hamas, or Al-Qaeda. In the introduction to *Through Our Enemies' Eyes,* Scheuer fully quotes the words of a very anti-Israeli British journalist, Robert Fisk: "The use of the word 'terrorist'—where Arabs who murder innocents are always called 'terrorists' whereas Israeli killers who slaughter 29 Palestinians in a Hebron Mosque or assassinate their prime minister, Yitzhak Rabin are called extremists—is only part of the problem."[83]

These are instructive psychological clues. These kinds of outbursts do not happen once or twice but rather many times in Scheuer's writings, his media appearances, and his Internet eructations. He seems to identify with bin-Laden with the almost-wide-eyed wonder of a new adept or acolyte. One recalls the case of newspaper heiress Patty Hearst, who was kidnapped in 1974 and came to identify with her terrorist abductors. The Hearst case came to be known as an example of Stockholm syndrome. Is Scheuer suffering from the same thing? One has to wonder whether Scheuer's mind has been hijacked by Osama bin-Laden. Bin-Laden apparently thought so. He applauded Scheuer, endorsing him in a message sent to the American people. "And if you would like to get to know some of the reasons for your losing of your war against us, then read the book of Michael Scheuer in this regard."[84]

It is interesting that Scheuer's books are advertised with blurbs citing bin-Laden as approving what Scheuer says about him and Al-Qaeda. Some people might mistakenly think that bin-Laden lauded Scheuer for his fine scholarship, but really, bin-Laden supported Scheuer in his video message for exactly the same reason that bin-Laden also supported the writings of Noam Chomsky: both men actually serve the interests and the propaganda of Al-Qaeda.[85]

To read and listen to Scheuer's words is to be assaulted by messages that do not seem to come from a U.S. intelligence official but from an adherent, a convert, a true believer in the propaganda of Arab-Islamic terrorists. Here are some examples:

- America's anti–bin-Laden policy (and bin-Laden's reprisals) result from insults and the proselytizing of evangelical Christians, as when Scheuer says, "clerical comments most U.S. citizens disregard are taken as threatening by Muslims . . ."[86]

- "Bin-Laden's description of Christians as rapacious Crusaders bent on converting or annihilating Muslims has the ring of historical truth— as noted, the Crusades are still a fresh memory and wound across the Islamic world—as is validated by CNN's real-time coverage of events that always seem to leave Muslims battered, bloodied, or dead at the hands of non-Muslims, particularly Christian and Jewish hands."[87]

- U.S. efforts to limit the options of Arab-Islamic terror groups are really aggressive and/or undemocratic infringements on all Muslims—as when the United States unjustifiably (in Scheuer's eyes) tries to ban the broadcasts of Hizballah television station Al-Manar, one of the most viciously anti-American and pro-terrorist outlets in the world. "Washington completed a self-defeating trifecta by listing the Lebanese Hizballah's al-Manar television network as a terrorist organization."[88]

If Scheuer knew Arabic or if he actually watched an hour of Al-Manar broadcasts, as this author has, he might speak differently. Hizballah's TV station regularly runs montage films depicting Jews eating human flesh and drinking the blood of Muslim and Christian children. It is a station that daily—every day—celebrates those who attack Americans, Europeans, Jews, and all non-Muslims. Compared to Al-Manar, Al Jazeera (even with the bin-Laden videos) is the Disney Channel.

In a CBS interview with Katie Couric in September 2007, Scheuer served as the amplifier for a newly released bin-Laden video. It is worth paying attention to the respectful tone of Scheuer, who virtually salutes bin-Laden for offering Americans the chance to convert to Islam as a way of forestalling further attacks on the United States:

COURIC: Michael Scheuer once headed up the CIA's bin-Laden unit and spent years tracking the terrorist. Well, apparently bin-Laden has been tracking him too. He's actually mentioned in the video. Michael is now a CBS News analyst.

Michael, there is no explicit threat in this video, but given the date of its release, prior to September 11th, is there some kind of threat involved in your view?

SCHEUER (CBS News terror analyst): I think there's a very clear threat, Katie, here that he's basically saying your policies remain the same, this is what got you into this mess that you're in and losing two wars and hurting your economy. And he says at one point we're going to continue this war against you until you stop these policies.

COURIC: But he does not get into specifics, does he?

SCHEUER: No, he doesn't. And what probably is the most important part of this threat is that bin-Laden goes into very, very much detail about offering Americans a chance to convert to Islam and thereby end the war between us. Bin-Laden is making sure that Muslims know that he offered us a chance to convert before he attacked us again.[89]

However, bin-Laden never stopped trying to launch further attacks on America. The "conversion option" is merely a posture. Scheuer has also written, perhaps wistfully, that he cannot understand why bin-Laden never attacked Israel.

"It has been a mystery to me as to why al Qaeda has so far refrained from attacking a specifically Jewish or Israeli target, especially because bin-Laden has long supported the Palestinians," writes Scheuer.[90]

Scheuer is wrong here, too. Al-Qaeda has tried to attack Israel several times. It has gained some traction inside the Sinai Desert, in Gaza, and in Lebanon. In general, it is the aggressive American/Western pursuit policy (despite all its faults) against Al-Qaeda and strong Israeli anti-terror policies around Israel's borders (with strong support from Jordan and middling support from Egypt) that have stymied Al-Qaeda efforts against U.S. and Israeli targets. It was not the goodwill of Osama bin-Laden.[91]

Like Chomsky, Scheuer has also arrived at an antiwar posture full of conspiracy theories, anti-American diatribes, and anti-Israel ranting.[92] Neither Chomsky nor Scheuer has any problem exaggerating Israel's "crimes" or calling any Israeli or any Israeli policy "terrorist."[93] However, in Scheuer's case, these presentations are tinged with broad hints of anti-Semitism. He refers to American citizens who support Israel as a "fifth column" and "enemies." Scheuer even invites attacks on them:

> There is indeed an identifiable fifth column of pro-Israel U.S. citizens—I have described them here and elsewhere as Israel-Firsters—who have consciously made Israel's survival and protection their first priority, and who see worth in America only to the extent that its resources and man-power can be exploited to protect and further the interests of Israel in its religious war-to-the-death with the Arabs. These are disloyal citizens in much the same sense that the Civil War's disloyal northern "Copper-heads" sought to help the Confederates destroy the Union. The Israel-Firsters help Israel suborn U.S. citizens to spy for Israel; they use their fortunes and political action organizations to buy U.S. politicians with campaign donations; and most of all they use their ready access to the media to disguise their own disloyalty by denigrating as anti-Semites or appeasers fellow citizens who dare to challenge them. The Israel-Firsters are unquestionably enemies of America's republican experiment and will have to be destroyed as the Copperheads were destroyed—by the people, after a full public debate, at the ballot box.[94]

If one really wants to know why it took the CIA so long to kill Osama bin-Laden, the answer begins with George Tenet and Michael Scheuer.

6

COUNTERTERROR INTELLIGENCE: OXYMORONIC OR JUST MORONIC?

Sigmund Freud said that every man is a genius when it comes to rationalization and self-deception. The great psychologist never met the CIA's Paul Pillar, but Pillar proves Freud's observation.

For more than a decade, Paul Pillar was a central fixture of the U.S. intelligence community.[1] Pillar's analysis showed spectacular errors in judgment for more than a decade, which Pillar later rationalized. Pillar's writings do display some academic depth and analytical nuance. Yet Pillar's analysis shares a vast common ground with the views of George Tenet and Michael Scheuer. Pillar understated the danger of Arab-Islamic terror, while promoting the path of talking rather than fighting, under almost all circumstances.[2] Pillar is a prolific writer who often sweeps disturbing facts under the carpet—such as Iran's direction of terror and atomic weapons building, or the continued PLO assaults, or the implacability of Islamic terrorists. "Only a fraction of Islamic terrorism today can be blamed even indirectly on Iran," Pillar said in a book on terror in late 2000.[3] He also scolded those who warned of terror only months before 9/11, claiming that the danger of terror was vastly overestimated, and, in fact, smaller than being struck by lightning.[4]

As for the Al-Qaeda and jihadist networks that attacked the World

Trade Center twice—once in 1993 and again in 2001—Pillar seemed to belittle them until they struck again. "Paul Pillar coined the phrase 'ad hoc terrorists' to describe Ramzi Yousef and the World Trade Center plotters."[5]

Years later, a petulant Paul Pillar was still angry that many of his critics reminded him how often his predictions turned out wrong.[6] "After any disaster, those who had been screaming that the sky is falling tend to get credit while those who had expressed a more temperate outlook tend to get criticized, regardless of whether the latter's analysis was better reasoned and more valid."[7]

In the 1990s, Paul Pillar was a top analyst at the U.S. State Department before moving to the CIA, where he held several high posts. Pillar was deputy head of the CIA's Counterterrorism Center, serving also as executive assistant to CIA director Tenet. He was the CIA's national intelligence officer for the Near East and South Asia from 2000 to 2005. Pillar was an author of the 2002 National Intelligence Estimate (NIE) saying that Iraq had weapons of mass destruction (WMD), and he was principal author of the late 2007 NIE that said Iran was *not* making nuclear weapons. The first NIE seemed to be far off the mark when U.S. soldiers in Iraq found little WMD,[8] while the 2007 NIE made the CIA the butt of jokes of Western intelligence services.

"We judge with high confidence that in fall 2003, Tehran halted its nuclear weapons program," declared the opening words of the NIE report crafted by Pillar. This was not a flip comment, but a missile carefully aimed at George W. Bush's policies. Pillar confirmed this in a 2007 radio interview shortly after the report was leaked.

"If the intelligence community is going to be criticized in many of the ways that it was in the Iraq case, then one should not be surprised that . . . the estimators might have shaped an estimate in a way that would take this military option off the table," Pillar averred. "A great deal of time and attention and negotiation typically goes into not just what the judgments are . . . but how they're arranged," Pillar said. "What's going to be in the first paragraph, even more so, what's going to be in the first sentence."[9]

The CIA picked Pillar to write the report knowing Pillar's views, because Pillar had attacked Bush's use of intelligence a year earlier in an article in *Foreign Affairs*, writing: "In the wake of the Iraq war, it has become clear that official intelligence analysis was not relied on in making even the most significant national security decisions, that intelligence was misused publicly to justify decisions already made, that damaging ill will developed between policymakers and intelligence officers, and that the intelligence community's own work was politicized."[10] Pillar and Tenet had to know this was not so, that they were smearing Bush. After all, Tenet had told Bush that the evidence of Iraqi weapons of mass destruction was "a slam dunk."

Pillar was right about politicization of the intelligence process, but it was coming from the CIA itself, which was committing a brazen rewrite of events to cover its own sorry record of intelligence gathering and mis-analysis. Worst of all, the CIA was basically whitewashing Iran as a terror threat and nuclear weapons proliferator.

CIA's Pillar-framed conclusions contradicted all previous CIA findings and the analysis of several other major Western intelligence services. At the time of the report, Pillar was considered a Middle East expert, though he did not speak any local languages, and had not served in the field. Indeed as reporter Steve Coll once wrote, "He was not an Arabist, but he had studied political Islam and the Middle East. He was a manager and an intellectual, an author of books and academic journal articles. From within the Counterterrorist Center he would emerge during the next six years as one of the CIA's most influential analysts."[11]

Pillar was influential indeed. He actively lobbied his views both in and out of government, writing for prestigious journals such as *Foreign Affairs* and the *National Interest,* and appearing on National Public Radio—even while working at the CIA or State. In think tanks in Washington and New York and at university seminars, he pushed the claim that Iran had abandoned its atomic weapons program. Within months of the 2007 NIE, the report was shaken by tremendous countervailing evidence, and the CIA had to recant Pillar's judgment. Yet the report served its apparent purpose: it blocked any effort to push for stronger sanctions or military action against Iran.

Pillar himself said in public and semipublic forums that his 2007 NIE was written in a way that precluded policy makers from using military options against Iran the way they had used the 2002 NIE as a basis for attacking Iraq. Essentially Pillar was acting like a referee who tries to make up for one bad call with an equally bad call in the other direction. But this was a classic example of two wrongs do not make a right, because the 2002 error, if an error, was an honest error, while the 2007 error was a politically skewed error that helped Iran.

The report came out when Iran was actively building a Hizballah army in southern Lebanon and working feverishly to arm and train elements of Hamas as well as Yasser Arafat's Fatah and PLO. Pillar, who had been a top analyst on the Middle East for years, had to realize the wider ramifications of his Middle East analysis.

The U.S. intelligence community's on-again, off-again assessment of Iranian intentions to make nuclear weapons is probably the most public example of its attempt to dictate policy to the Bush administration. If Bush had any plans to try to stop Iran militarily from making bombs, the 2007 NIE virtually erased any public legitimacy for such an effort. Coming after an already existing controversy over whether the Bush White House had or had not pushed for intelligence findings of weapons of mass destruction in Iraq, the new NIE also had a few other effects:

- It made the Bush administration look foolish, having been reprimanded by its own intelligence agency.
- It made the CIA look ridiculous for having contradicted itself without any serious factual underpinning, while several European intelligence agencies continued to cite Iran as actively seeking atomic weapons.
- It struck a severe blow to America's credibility as a great power.

It is worth comparing these events to a 1981 internal dispute between the Reagan administration and a U.S. intelligence agency. At that time, Secretary of State Alexander Haig gave a speech calling for the United States to step up vigilance against "a new enemy"—growing terrorist activity directed with the help of the Soviet Union.[12] CIA director William Casey had also taken a similar view, perhaps inspired by Claire Sperling's book about "terror networks."[13] Ron Spiers, director of the State Department's Bureau of Intelligence and Research (INR), accosted Haig and told him he had "overstated the case," because the Soviet Union had actually discouraged Palestinian groups from certain kinds of terror acts.

Interestingly, some other key officials in State and CIA—such as Ray S. Cline—publicly highlighted the Soviet role in terror well before Sperling's book. In a 1979 conference on terror, Cline wrote that he wanted "to put the information about the extraordinary surge of terrorist activity in the past 10 years into a strategic framework that makes sense," comparing the Soviets to carmakers who supplied the vehicle and the auto parts to Arab motorists-terrorists. Cline, himself a former director of INR and deputy director of CIA intelligence division, cited the Soviet KGB's role in persuading the Soviet Politburo to accept the PLO and to aid it.[14] Haig and Casey asked for studies on the subject, and the U.S. bureaucracy produced results that were, predictably, mixed. They showed an increase in terror activity but, at the time, not a clear-cut case of overweening Soviet control. Subsequent events were more clear-cut than U.S. government studies.

PLO documents captured by Israel in Beirut in 1982 and Soviet files released or discovered after the fall of Soviet communism in 1989–90[15] show that Cline, Sperling, and Haig were more correct than State's sanguine analysts. The USSR made a conscious decision to penetrate and guide Palestinian groups run by Arafat (Fatah), George Habash (the Marxist-oriented Popular Front for the Liberation of Palestine, or PFLP), and Abu Nidal.

Wadi Haddad, the deputy to George Habash, was recruited into the KGB in 1970. "Haddad devised a new strategy of aircraft hijacking and terrorist attacks on 'Zionist' targets in Europe which made front-page news across the world and attracted the favourable attention of the [KGB] Centre. 'To kill a Jew far from the battlefield,' he declared, 'has more effect than killing hundreds of Jews in battle.'"[16] So, it is clear the Soviets aided terror in promoting actual full-scale war against Israel.[17] The Soviets even helped Arab terror attacks against Western diplomats while securing diplomatic status and respectability for the PLO. As Christopher Andrew of Cambridge University notes: "The British Foreign Secretary, Lord Carrington, declared: 'The PLO as such is not a terrorist organization.' Arafat's success in driving a wedge between the United States and its European allies further enhanced the [KGB] Centre's interest in him."[18]

Former deputy CIA director Cline's well-documented 1984 book on the subject specified the Soviet direction of terrorist camps from North

Korea and Yemen to East Germany as well as the KGB "university" for Third World leaders in Moscow.[19] In fact, Soviet leaders and the PLO met in the Kremlin in November 1979 to coordinate aid and policy shortly after the Iranian seizure of the U.S. embassy in Tehran. A captured document illuminates the cynicism of both the PLO and the Soviets, who sent money and guidance to the PLO and to "anti-imperialist" forces in Iran while assuring the United States that the USSR saw the kidnapping of diplomats as improper:

"Therefore, we will not get involved in complicated discussion on the subject," Foreign Minister Andrei Gromyko told Arafat, adding, "and in no way are we going to protect the Americans in this matter. We think there are no differences of opinion between us in this matter, despite the difference in status between us—we as a state and you as a national liberation movement. This is quite satisfactory."[20]

There are two important points here:

- There were those in the U.S. State Department and intelligence community *then* who minimized the Soviet role and the idea of state sponsorship of terror.
- The rival interpretations were addressed *inside* the U.S. intelligence community, and they were not used as clubs by one side to beat the other or force policy.

CONNECTING DOTS AND AGENCIES:
CONCEPTUAL AND BUREAUCRATIC GRIDLOCK

One of the classic intelligence problems arises when intelligence officials adopt a narrow focus of research because of bureaucratic reasons ("that's not our department" or "that's not our job"). Another is the failure to interpret data or a situation correctly due to calcified conceptions that ignore the historical or cultural angle. Good intelligence often requires a narrow, concentrated field of vision. Sometimes it also requires looking at the big picture and using peripheral vision to pick up slight movements on the margins of the picture. This kind of problem is especially prevalent among CIA or State Department "experts" on the Middle East who are often "Arabists" without Arabic. Francis Fukuyama, who saw them up close, once remarked that they were "an elite within an elite, who has been more systematically wrong than any other area specialists in the diplomatic corps."[21]

To his credit, in a pre-9/11 book, former Clinton advisor Anthony Lake wrote about the organizational focus problem (which dovetails with Morton Halperin's bureaucratic model):

> There is a tendency within government to try to compartmentalize the problem and fit it into boxes. There are issue boxes: Proliferation. Traditional terrorism. Modern terrorism. Crime. Critical infrastructure security. There are jurisdictional boxes: International. National. State. Local. Government. Business. There are response boxes: Law enforcement. Diplomacy. Intelligence. Emergency management. Each involves a separate organization, ethos, and approach. As Pentagon spokesman Kenneth Bacon replied when asked about the response to the terrorist bombing of Khobar Towers, "This is the FBI's job. We don't ask the FBI to fly F-16's over Iraq and they don't ask us to take over their investigations."[22]

A year before the 9/11 attacks, Lake correctly summarized the fact that the old categories and conceptions did not match the new threats: "These boxes are distinct, discrete and disunited—but the threats they aim to address are just the opposite."[23]

Like the 9/11 Commission, Lake could have cited many more instances of one U.S. government agency saying "that's not our job" (for example, Tenet saying CIA's job was not to use missiles against bin-Laden) or one agency not sharing information with another. Secretary of Defense Donald Rumsfeld drastically expanded all aspects of defense intelligence gathering (Defense Intelligence Agency, the DIA) in 2002 after getting poor help and information from the CIA. The 9/11 Commission recounts only a fraction of many horror stories of the CIA and FBI not cooperating on intelligence leads that might have prevented the 9/11 terror attack.

The CIA and State's INR also face conceptual paralysis. Analysts like Michael Scheuer and Paul Pillar dismiss the idea of state-abetted terror in the "new" era of terror by Islamic groups. "That scenario is now invalid," says Scheuer. Anyone who sees the possibility of state sponsors of terror groups is "looking through a lens yellowed with age."[24] This must be a news flash for Iran and Syria, both of which still advise and nurture

Fatah, Hamas, Hizballah, and Islamic Jihad. To this day, Iran and Syria aid, abet, and execute terror—even against their own people. This simple fact does not stop Pillar from preaching friendship and partnership with them—even as they murdered hundreds of peaceful protesters in 2009 and 2011.[25]

"Something akin to a normal relationship with the Islamic Republic of Iran can be envisioned, notwithstanding all there still would be to dislike and distrust about it."[26] As Syria used tanks and snipers to kill its own citizens in 2011, he wrote, "There is underestimation of how much worthwhile business could be conducted with the incumbent regime, however distasteful it may be."[27]

Both Pillar and Scheuer have very feeble or myopically selective memories when it comes to the atrocities committed by Arab-Islamic terrorist states and groups, managing to find a silver lining even in the thundercloud of a tornado. For example, Scheuer for some reason does not mention the awesome Khobar Towers bombing in Saudi Arabia in 1994—where nineteen Americans were killed by a sophisticated fuel truck bomb whose explosive force was close to the total of all four fuel-rich planes that impacted on September 11, 2001. Strong evidence—forensics and testimony—shows that both Iran and Al-Qaeda were involved in the Khobar attack. Scheuer also does not mention Iran's hand in massive bombings of an Israeli embassy and Jewish community center in South America in the 1990s, roughly paralleling Al-Qaeda bombings of American embassies in Africa. Is there a pattern here?

A more discerning analyst would perceive how many terror organizations still get logistical, political, and financial assistance from state sponsors. Sometimes they get tipped off, as when Saudi Arabian and Pakistani officials have alerted or helped hide Al-Qaeda terrorists. Often, terrorists get sanctuary and the extraterritorial equivalent of "basing facilities." Hizballah, Hamas, and other terror groups have gotten such help from Syria and Iran. Indeed, Iran treats some terror groups as extensions of its national strategic reach—a reach that has included terror operations in South America.

CIA OR CYA: CLUELESS IN AMERICA OR
COVERING UP YOUR ASSESSMENTS

As these cases illustrate, bad personnel leads to bad intelligence services. This is especially true when the intelligence agency must deal with evolving terror groups, rather than long-standing armies, navies, and air forces. Large armies, huge stores of munitions, and such can sometimes be tracked and identified with mechanical means—spy planes, satellite photography, SIGINT (signals intelligence that tracks communications phone traffic and emails). America's National Security Agency handles most of the high-tech SIGINT, but there are several other American intelligence services that have their own analytical branches (such as the DIA), and some of whom also furnish technological assistance, such as the National Geospatial-Intelligence Service, based in St. Louis, which directs the mapmaking and surveying for the U.S. intelligence community.[28] This reliance on technology may help explain why the CIA gets only about 20 percent of the U.S. intelligence budget.

The United States has developed great technological means to detect, for example, transfers of nuclear material, movements in and out of missile silos or across borders. Some of the incredible high-tech surveillance routines we have seen in movies or on television shows (such as *24*) are actually part of the real world. But it is human intelligence—HUMINT—that can be crucial in war-peace situations, as two examples from the Middle East wars of 1967 and 1973 demonstrate. Before the 1967 war—known as the Six-Day War—Israel had an agent, Eli Cohen, inside the very top elite of the Syrian government. This helped produce the dramatic Israeli victory. Before the 1973 war—known as the Yom Kippur War or the October War—Israel got information very late from someone thought to be an agent inside the Egyptian government of Anwar Sadat. The result was strategic shock that cost nearly three thousand Israeli lives in three weeks.[29] Human intelligence is even more crucial in tracking small cells of terror organizations. Especially in the 1990s, some Western intelligence agencies—particularly the CIA—let the human intelligence component become degraded. This also happened in Israel. What was the reason?

Bad intelligence and weak anti-terror operations are what happens when heads of intelligence services attempt to curry favor with their political masters or with the political winds of the moment, promising great results with little investment. Politicians do not want to have to spend more money on training or placing agents. They hate it even more when an agent or a team of agents gets killed or arrested. When an intelligence chief tells the statesman or stateswoman "we don't really need agents behind enemy lines because we have electronic sensors doing the job," that chief gets a pat on the back in the short term, but a rude awakening in the long term. The United States has been surprised many times over the last fifteen years by terror and by developments in the Middle East. For example, the United States first discovered Saddam Hussein's various weapons programs after Saddam's two sons-in-law defected to the West before returning home to be tortured and executed by Saddam. Later, after the second Iraq war, the CIA was surprised by the apparent absence of WMD—weapons of mass destruction—but the truth is that we still do not know for sure what happened. There is some evidence that some of Saddam's weapons systems may have been sold and/or smuggled out of the country, perhaps to Syria, perhaps to Iran. We simply do not know, and Saddam had no more sons-in-law left to tell us.

Another example of such surprise found Israel astonished by the amount and types of fortifications as well as arms smuggled into southern Lebanon and the Gaza Strip over the last decade. Israel is one of the world's leaders in computer technology and fiber optics, yet none of its technological devices could replace the loss of human intelligence in Gaza, Lebanon, and the West Bank. Israel only began to regain its human intelligence abilities in the West Bank after a major military incursion in 2002.

Another still more insidious corruption of the intelligence process is when intelligence officials tell their civilian bosses the things they think they want to hear. Henry Kissinger, who knows about this state of affairs from the inside, observes: "What political leaders decide, intelligence services tend to seek to justify. Popular literature and films often depict the opposite—policymakers as the helpless tools of intelligence experts. In the real world, intelligence assessments more often follow than guide policy decisions."[30] What Kissinger says is usually the case. But not always.[31]

To read the 9/11 Commission Report or some of the briefings by U.S. "counterterror experts" is to get a crash course in American instrumentalism. The message: "We can get the job done if we work hard enough and have the right equipment." It is like hearing a football coach huddled with his players, calling for "better execution," "not missing signals," and "better teamwork," while pointing at a flow chart. However, preventing terror is not a game, and it is way beyond just equipment, execution, and desire.

This is not just an American problem. I once tried to show a few captured PLO-Hamas documents to the Jerusalem district commander of the Shin Bet, Israel's domestic intelligence agency, but he waved me aside.[32] "We don't really care about history," he said.[33] I thought it was important to show him that the PLO's Yasser Arafat and Hamas's Sheikh Yassin had been communicating on joint goals and strategies against Israel. Though political rivals, they were cooperating on attacks against Israel. To this day, many Israeli leaders—and even some officials in Israeli intelligence—believe that Israel's security will be safeguarded when Israel helps the PLO/Fatah forces regain the Gaza Strip from Hamas. A surprising number of these officials—not just the politicians, but even commanders of Israeli military intelligence—have little or no Arabic and very sparse historical training.

One of the advantages that European intelligence agencies and counterterror experts have over the United States is a greater sense of history and languages. Another advantage for the Europeans is basically growing up on a continent whose history is marinated in terror—anarchists, separatists, and social revolutionaries from Russia, Hungary, Italy, Austria, Spain, France, Ireland, and Germany, among others. Historians of terror such as Paul Wilkinson and Walter Laqueur are steeped in the material and can draw comparative lessons from various periods and different locales that are appropriate even for the postmillennial terror of Arab-Islamic extremists.

Wilkinson, for example, has shown that terrorists will almost always try to create a "defensive" narrative, showing that they were attacked or that they were responding to aggression or provocation. Variations of this message will be aimed at different target audiences: (1) people the organization is trying to recruit as agents or allies, and (2) potential victims who may be useful in reducing the will of the society being attacked.

European-born analysts such as Laqueur and Wilkinson are used to following highly variegated terror organizations (for example, Baader-Meinhof, Irish Republican Army, Basque separatists, Palestinian organizations, Japanese Red Army) that have more than occasionally joined forces or furnished aid to one another, sometimes with the aid of one or more state sponsors. One gets the somewhat surreal impression reading the work of some U.S. government analysts who seem to believe in static "sides" or "teams," perhaps like in baseball or football. A New York Yankee would not pitch a game or hit a home run for the Boston Red Sox, nor would a Miami Dolphin catch a touchdown pass from the Green Bay Packers. But terrorism is more than a game, and having a "scorecard" alone does not prepare the analyst for Sunni Muslims working with Shiite Muslims or Japanese or Irish terrorists working with Palestinian Arab terrorists. It is "hard for westerners, weaned on their own myth of unitary nationalism . . . to understand the multiple, layered identities so characteristic of the Arab world," as Palestinian political scientist Rashid Khalidi trenchantly observed.[34] Creative anti-terror thinking requires going beyond the scorecard, "thinking outside the box," recognizing a danger not by previous statistics or "terror organization rosters" but by an almost instinctive "feel" that comes from familiarity with a region or deep knowledge of history.

In the 1990s and at the start of the new century, these qualities were in short supply in the U.S. intelligence community. Analysts such as the CIA's Scheuer and Pillar or many at the State Department's INR seem sometimes to have had great problems wrapping their minds around the idea that terror makes strange bedfellows. But here are some examples:

- Iran and Iraq can be killing each other for eight or nine years (1980–88) but can then smuggle arms to each other when America seems to be threatening one of them (1990–91).
- Iraq and Syria can fight on-again, off-again physical or ideological battles, but they can smuggle arms and men to each other when America seems to be attacking (2002–2004).
- Hamas and Fatah—both Palestinian organizations (Sunni) with no ideological or religious connection to Iran—have both taken training, weapons, and money from the Shiite regime in Tehran, even though almost all Palestinians are Sunnis and even though neither Hamas nor Fatah has Shiite roots.

- Hamas and Fatah, though they have spent the last five years actually trying to kill each other, have cooperated (and are still cooperating) on attacks against Israel. They sometimes even use third and fourth parties such as the Palestinian Islamic Jihad, the Popular Front for the Liberation of Palestine, and even some agents of Al-Qaeda.
- Fatah (Sunni Palestinian) and Hizballah (pro-Iranian Shiite) apparently cooperated on the bombing of the U.S. embassy in Lebanon in 1983.
- Iran, Hizballah, and Al-Qaeda apparently cooperated in the 1996 bombing of U.S. military barracks in Khobar Towers in Dhahran, Saudi Arabia.

We will discuss some of these events in detail later and why certain U.S. intelligence analysts seem to skip over them.

Aside from failing in one's assignment, perhaps the worst intelligence or policy failure is the inability to admit failure or even that inadvertent mistakes were made. This trait is common in politicians but is unforgivable in intelligence agencies. One sign of politicization in an intelligence service is when top personnel cannot even acknowledge operational or conceptual errors. George Tenet is a classic example. His immediate post-9/11 testimony to Congress does not even use the word *failure*. This failure to admit error usually means failure to correct error.

Maimonides, the great Arabic-speaking Jewish sage, was a man of science and philosophy who lived on the edge of the realms of Islam and Christendom. Like other Jewish sages, he also served as an advisor to Arab rulers.[35] In one treatise he writes that people cannot reform or mend their ways without looking inward to see where they have sinned. Intelligence analysts and policy makers all make mistakes, but the real sin is in not being willing to examine oneself or to admit even the possibility of error. Conversely, making mistakes should not automatically be treated as a crime. Not every mistake requires the establishment of a congressional "truth commission."[36] Terror is worse than other crimes, but almost as bad is not learning from past events or from past mistakes in dealing with terror. Here the CIA's record is almost criminal.

PRESIDENTS AND THEIR INTELLIGENCE

To be fair to Tenet, Pillar, and even Scheuer, the CIA's institutional myopia to Arab terrorism grew out of the deep risk-averse mind-set of U.S. government institutions beginning in the post-Vietnam era of the 1970s. As presidential historian Timothy Naftali has observed, "The Nixon Administration would be the first in U.S. history to consider international terrorism a national problem."[37] The Nixon administration would also be seen as the U.S. administration that most exploited intelligence agencies—the CIA and FBI—against American citizens.

Amid a spate of Arab plane hijackings during his term, President Richard Nixon was actually the first president to set forth the supposed U.S. policy of making no concessions—a policy that he breached more than he observed.[38] But Nixon and his advisor Henry Kissinger often pressed *other* governments to make concessions to terrorists, such as asking Israel to release convicted terrorists from jail.

This White House attitude was actually built on the preexisting "Arabist" tendency in the U.S. State Department, NSC, and CIA of trying to placate "moderate" Arab governments, trying gently to get them to change policy or to isolate or suppress "hard-line" or "rejectionist" Arab terrorists, while trying to co-opt "moderate" terrorists. Most of the adherents of this Arabist approach usually did not know much Arabic or Arab political culture. They also did not really question whether this policy worked, even though it clearly did not work, nor did they question whether it was moral, even though sometimes it clearly was immoral. Here's one example:

Yasser Arafat's terrorists seized the U.S. embassy in Sudan and murdered three Western diplomats in early 1973, upon Arafat's direct orders, though they pretended they were from a supposedly independent group called Black September. America's response came from Harold Saunders, who had been a CIA official for thirteen years and recently come to the National Security Council's Middle East Desk. Many at the CIA believed Arafat could be an American intelligence asset. Saunders "proposed the strategy that Kissinger and Nixon ultimately approved: On the theory that any unilateral reaction by the United States would upset moderate Arab countries and kill any hope of Arab-Israeli negotiations, Saunders suggested quiet encouragement of the Arabs to deal with Black September. Nevertheless, Washington had known for years that the moderate

Arab states, such as Saudi Arabia and Kuwait, were funding Fatah, which controlled Black September."[39]

A few months later, Egypt and Syria attacked Israel in the October 1973 war: so much for moderation and the peace process. The CIA connection to Arafat apparently began in 1969 via CIA Beirut station chief Robert Ames—three years before the PLO carried out the Munich Olympics massacre: so much for intelligence and moderation. Supposedly it was worthwhile to keep the PLO link alive in exchange for information Arafat supplied on other terrorist groups. U.S. officials hid and classified evidence proving Arafat murdered Western diplomats (see below). The great intelligence Arafat gave the United States and the West is such a secret that nobody knows what it was.

At its outset, modern U.S. counterterrorism substituted wishful thinking and the frequent reported sightings of Arab and Islamic moderation for tough, cold analysis. This deeply ingrained institutional view grew under the administrations of Richard Nixon (1969–74), Gerald Ford (1974–76), and Jimmy Carter (1977–80). This view survived even the administration of Ronald Reagan, whose staff included many—from Secretaries Alexander Haig and George Shultz to advisors Robert Mac-Farlane, John Poindexter, and Oliver North—who tried to champion a tougher and larger counterterror profile for the United States. In the end, as historians Timothy Naftali and David Wills have observed, respectively, the Nixon and Reagan administrations often spoke loudly against terror while actually employing a soft stick to tickle at the problem. Wills notes that hostage situations seemed to paralyze Reagan's judgment and heighten emotional responses, producing hesitation: "Ronald Reagan came to the presidency vowing 'swift and effective retribution' against terrorists that attacked Americans. Contrary to this rhetoric, though, the administration rarely implemented any sort of action that could be construed as such."[40]

Beginning with Nixon, the bureaucracy developed a rationale to conceal —for over thirty years—the fact that Yasser Arafat, in 1973, ordered the execution of two U.S. diplomats and a Belgian diplomat at the U.S. embassy in Khartoum. The CIA and the State Department had a "smoking gun"—a recording of Arafat giving the order by telephone—but the tape of Arafat's execution order was one of America's most closely held secrets, because officials believed that Arafat was interested in peace and that he would prove an intelligence asset.

Similar arguments were used for not proceeding against Ali Hassan Salameh, known as "the Red Prince," who directed the PLO's massacre of eleven Israeli athletes at the 1972 Munich Olympics. Similar rationales were used for not acting against another terror group, the Palestine Liberation Front, which hijacked the *Achille Lauro* cruise ship in 1985, murdering Leon Klinghoffer, an elderly American in a wheelchair who was shot dead and then flung overboard into the Mediterranean Sea.[41] When the ship docked in Egypt, the government of Hosni Mubarak co-operated with the Palestinian terrorists and covered their escape. Mubarak hid the fact that a murder of an American had been committed, and then released the four terrorists.[42] Mubarak and his foreign minister, Esmat Abdel-Meguid, lied several times and in several different ways: no murder was committed, they claimed; when the murder was discovered, they said the men had already left Egypt; and when it was learned that they had not yet left Egypt, officials said their whereabouts were unknown. Egypt hid the fact that a group loyal to Arafat, who Egypt claimed was "moderate" and "peace loving," had committed piracy on the high seas and murdered a crippled, elderly U.S. citizen. When one of Reagan's security advisors suggested trying to ground the plane on which the terrorists were escaping, Secretary of Defense Caspar Weinberger and others opposed the move, following the usual stand-pat institutional prejudices.

YES, MR. SECRETARY

Many CIA officials, like those in the State Department and other agencies, often act as if they must tutor elected leaders and their appointees— presidents, cabinet members, senators, congressional representatives— slowly explaining what the world is really like. CIA Middle East intelligence officer Paul Pillar fits this description. Some of Pillar's public appearances have the quality of the British civil servant from the television comedy series *Yes, Minister* who pretends to be serving his cabinet minister while laughingly running the country behind the minister's back without heeding any of his instructions.[43]

Pillar became a kind of point man in the institutional defense of the CIA, making a side career of writing reviews of books critical of the CIA while extolling CIA successes. In a *Foreign Affairs* essay, he waved off all critical analysis by *New York Times* reporter Tim Weiner and Professor Amy Zegart of UCLA, both of whom have devoted years to studying the American intelligence community.

> The widespread public perception that the U.S. intelligence agencies chronically perform poorly has created a receptive audience for a slew of books and articles that both exploit and help to perpetuate misunderstandings. The most recent and most prominent specimen of this genre is Tim Weiner's *Legacy of Ashes*, which won the 2007 National Book Award for nonfiction—but probably would have been a better candidate in the category of fiction. His much-heralded history of the CIA is a selective and haphazard treatment of the agency's record. The book's heft and alleged grounding in historical legwork (Weiner says in his preface that he read "more than fifty thousand documents") have earned laudatory reviews. However, readers who know a little bit about the CIA and anything about historical research will not react so favorably to Weiner's work.[44]

Even though Weiner made a few historical errors, Pillar never applied similar critical treatment to some of the completely erroneous claims of some of his own colleagues. He never called the books by Scheuer and Tenet "fiction," while many of Pillar's claims—such as tremendous CIA intelligence successes in the Middle East—are half-truths or prevarications. Pillar's defense of the CIA rings hollow. He blithely conceals many CIA field and analytical failures, while claiming many "invisible" successes.[45] After sliming Weiner, Pillar attacks Zegart and the 9/11 Commission Report itself, claiming they are inaccurate and unfair. He's wrong on both counts.

Two years before 9/11, Zegart published a book, *Flawed by Design*, that showed how the organization of some of America's intelligence and military institutions was hurting policy implementation and intelligence. "When it comes to selecting, shaping, and implementing U.S. foreign policy, the devil often lies in the details of agency design," wrote Zegart.[46] Her words seem prescient when one reads the 9/11 Commission Report describing how various American agencies—CIA, FBI, NSA—did not have proper channels for sharing information that might have prevented the loss of three thousand lives and the ruination of many more.[47] Zegart made similar points in her second book, *Spying Blind*. When events proved Zegart correct, this too, for the CIA's Pillar, was an unpardonable offense: "Zegart confesses in her preface that she was researching the difficulties faced by U.S. government agencies attempting to adapt to new challenges when 9/11 suddenly supplied the perfect dramatic event to illustrate her argument. She has therefore tailored her depiction of the official reaction to 9/11 to fit her broad preexisting thesis."[48]

This is simply intolerable because Zegart got it right, while Pillar's analysis was consistently off:

- in 2000, when he said terror was exaggerated, and then there was terror.
- in 2002, when he said there was Iraqi WMD, and little was found.
- in 2004, when he said the United States would never succeed in reversing the declining situation in Iraq, and it did just that two years later.
- in 2006–2007, when he pushed a report claiming Iran had stopped pursuing nuclear weapons, only for the CIA to be forced to recant the report thereafter.
- in 2011, when he called for dealing with the Assad regime in Syria shortly before Assad butchered hundreds of his own citizens.

Pillar's conclusions and his petulant pique are not analytical but anal, not trenchant but tortuous, and above all, pedantic rather than precise—like so much of the CIA's post-9/11 writing. Defending the CIA's anti-terror record, Pillar's central thesis is that the U.S. intelligence community gave American policy makers a clear idea of the threat to the United States in 2000–2001, and therefore U.S. intelligence was actually a success:

> Furthermore, given that policymakers were fully aware of the jihadist threat and there is no reason to believe that strategic insights about al Qaeda were missing or incorrect (neither Zegart nor the commission provides any evidence to the contrary), then strategic intelligence must have done its job effectively. The missing piece was something very

different: tactical information about a specific plot—a common problem in counterterrorism.[49]

One has to reread the words and scratch one's head: If 9/11 was an example of how "strategic intelligence must have done its job effectively," what would be an example of strategic intelligence that did *not* do its job effectively? A radioactive "dirty bomb" in an American or European city? An anthrax attack?

There is a sense of self-satisfied smugness in Pillar's article rejecting all reproach of the CIA. It also infuses Pillar's book on terrorism, written one year before the attacks of September 11, 2001. Pillar assures us the ayatollahs in Iran are calming down and getting more mature with age, and we must not really worry about Hizballah terrorists and sleeper cells in many South American countries:

> Revolutionary fervor and the export of violence are most apparent in the early stages. With Iran, for example, much of Tehran's early efforts to foment similar Islamist revolutions in other states were based on the fear that the clerical regime would need to change its environment to survive—the same idea that, for the Bolsheviks, underlay Leon Trotsky's doctrine of "permanent revolution."[50]

One should alert the CIA's top Middle East intelligence officer that—with or without Trotsky—Iran's regime believes in exporting its revolution. Here are some clues:

- Iran rigged the 2009 "elections" and then mercilessly repressed internal dissent, leaving hundreds killed and wounded.
- It aided Syria and North Korea in establishing a nuclear reactor in Syria.
- It has helped aid, arm, and train Hamas and Hizballah terrorists.

Pillar wants us to believe that ayatollah-run Iran wants to become more "moderate" and that Western nations need to calm down and not overreact to terror. It should be noted that even other government experts such as Michael A. Sheehan—New York City's deputy police commissioner for counterterrorism—have basically agreed with his analysis. Sheehan also served a stint in the U.S. State Department, and he said after a spate of bombings in the early 1990s that Iran and Hizballah moderated their activities due to European and Arab diplomatic pressure. "We can see that after the Europeans and Saudis put political pressure on Iran and its Hezbollah surrogates, they stopped the killing."[51] Sheehan admits this Saudi view was essentially "a cynical equation" that states "okay, we know you killed those Jews and Americans" and that killing Americans and Israelis will be tolerated up to a point, especially in Israeli-controlled areas, but will not be abided when it begins to threaten Saudi and European interests.[52]

Sadly, Sheehan seems to accept the notion that, after 1996, Iran and Hizballah really became "establishment"—either as members of the world community or as part of the Lebanese political system. He calls them "bloody but restrained terrorists."[53] This discounts the possibility that Iran and Hizballah use *taqiyya*—the Islamic doctrine of deception, which authorizes and even encourages Muslims to pretend to be something they are not. The full meaning of *taqiyya* will be discussed in the chapter on ideologies. For now, it is enough to say that *taqiyya* is important for all Muslims, especially Shiites in Iran and Hizballah. When Pillar or Sheehan neglects this factor, they miss a big part of the picture.

In the last fifteen years, Iran and Hizballah have both used diplomatic initiatives to stall for time to build nuclear weapons in Iran or to establish two fortified army divisions and sophisticated tunnel networks in southern Lebanon. Sheehan also seems to think, as does Pillar, that those worried about Iran and other terror dangers may step over the edge and become alarmist exaggerators. Pillar, for example, in his 2000 book, regrets "the emotional content of discussions on terrorism." He reminds us "that fewer Americans die from it [terror] than drown in bathtubs (or are struck by lightning or—choose your own favorite comparison)."[54]

This is both extraordinarily unintelligent and spectacularly wrong. According to U.S. government statistics:

In the United States from 1980 through 1995, a total of 1318 deaths were attributed to lightning (average: 82 deaths per year {range: 53–100 deaths}). Of the 1318 persons who died, 1125 (85%) were male, and

896 (68%) were aged 15–44 years. The annual death rate from lightning was highest among persons aged 15–19 years (6 deaths per 10,000,000 population; crude rate: 3 per 10,000,000). The greatest number of deaths attributable to lightning occurred in Florida and Texas (145 and 91, respectively), but New Mexico, Arizona, Arkansas, and Mississippi had the highest rates (10.0, 9.0, 9.0, and 9.0, respectively).[55]

Anyone who even tries to compare lightning and terror is making light of terror. Such an "expert" really does not understand the societal impact of terror. Clearly, more people tend to die of other causes—natural and unnatural—than terrorism. Indeed, even during most modern wars involving Western democratic countries, more people died in automobile accidents than in combat.[56] Yet few would deny that, from a societal perspective, wars are more important than car crashes. Lightning-versus-war statistics hide the fact that terrorism rips societies apart, and that terrorism is *designed* to rip societies apart. From an economic perspective alone, the direct and indirect costs of the 9/11 attack were said to be as much as $2 trillion.[57] That is only one reason why the prevention of and response to terrorism in free societies should *not* be proportional to death statistics. Terrorists only need one "lucky attack"—one huge bolt of lightning—to change all the statistics forever.

Indeed, Pillar's 2000 book adds another comforting thought: "Most of the terrorism that has damaged U.S. interests is foreign, as are most of the significant terrorist threats that confront the United States today."[58] This is the same Pillar who, writing several years later in *Foreign Affairs*, would declare that U.S. intelligence officials had completely warned everyone of the upcoming jihadist danger. In the year before 9/11, his book was full of comforting thoughts such as the view that international terror had basically been defeated: "The frequency of international terrorist incidents worldwide, for example, was cut in half from its level during the mid-1980's to the rate that existed for most of the 1990's."[59] Furthermore, said Pillar, U.S. counterterror operations showed "measurable success [by] . . . the solving with remarkable speed of some of the most egregious terrorist crimes against the United States in the 1990's, including the bombings of the World Trade Center in New York in 1993, the Murrah Building in Oklahoma City in 1995, and the U.S. embassies in Nairobi and Dar es

Salaam in 1998."[60] Once again Pillar plays fast and loose with the truth and exhibits a very limited law enforcement/criminal perspective on counterterrorism: if you get a conviction, you close the case. The problem is that he skips over disturbing details such as the eerie similarity between the truck bomb terror approach of the 1993 World Trade Center attack and the 1995 Oklahoma attack. The latter was attributed exclusively to Timothy McVeigh, who was convicted and executed, but evidence unearthed by journalists in Oklahoma suggests that McVeigh had significant ties to Arab-Islamic terror.[61] This lead was never seriously pursued. Another disturbing detail that Pillar skips over is one of the most spectacular terror attacks of the period—the 1996 fuel truck bomb attack in eastern Saudi Arabia that murdered nineteen U.S. soldiers and wounded three hundred in Khobar Towers. The intense explosive impact—perhaps nine thousand gallons of fuel linked to sophisticated bombs—was equivalent to ten tons of TNT. The blast was so strong it was felt and heard across the Saudi border twenty miles away in Bahrain. (For purposes of comparison, the four airplanes used in the 9/11 attacks were estimated to be carrying eleven thousand gallons of fuel, but without the sophisticated bombs attached.) The CIA and FBI were basically unable to get past Saudi Arabian government obstacles to the American investigation. The Saudis refused to allow the Americans to ask questions of those Saudi citizens suspected in the attack. The Saudi minister of interior, Prince Nayef, personally snubbed FBI director Louis Freeh when the latter came to ask for cooperation.[62] The prince also released two Islamist leaders who were part of Al-Qaeda.

Pillar's soothing book is almost as comforting as the State Department's pre-9/11 report on global terrorism. The verdict there: "The Saudi Arabian Government, at all levels, continued to reaffirm its commitment to combating terrorism."[63] This is a truthful statement that is still an incredible lie. Everyone in the State Department had to know it was a lie. Why? Throughout the 1980s and the 1990s the Saudi regime thwarted attempts by American counterterror and law enforcement officials to obtain information or apprehend terrorists in past terror attacks (in which hundreds of people were killed) and, perhaps, in upcoming attacks (in which thousands died). They stifled FBI attempts to interview witnesses or collect evidence in murderous attacks on Americans in Riyadh in 1995 and in Dhahran (Khobar Towers) in 1996. The Saudis blocked U.S. efforts to capture the man who masterminded the 1983 truck bombing murder of 241 U.S. marines in Beirut: Imad Mughniyeh, the Hizballah master bomb maker. As Dore Gold writes:

> The first sign of how Saudi Arabia actually dealt with the terrorist challenge came in April 1995. The United States received information that a specific flight of Lebanon's national airline, Middle East Airlines, would carry Imad Mughniyeh of Hizballah. . . . The flight, from Khartoum to Beirut, was scheduled to make a stopover in Jeddah, Saudi Arabia. The FBI dispatched agents to arrest Mughniyeh; President Clinton's national security advisor, Anthony Lake, had coordinated the operation with the Saudi ambassador to Washington, Prince Bandar bin Sultan. At the last minute, however, the Saudi government blocked the Lebanese airliner from landing. Mughniyeh got away.[64] The Clinton administration strongly protested the incident; in his understated diplomatic way, Secretary of State Warren Christopher explained, "We expressed our concern that we had not had the cooperation we hoped to have."[65]

Rather than firmly responding to Saudi collusion with terror, the United States covered up. The State Department said: "The Government of Saudi Arabia continued to investigate the bombing in June 1996 of the Khubar Towers housing facility near Dhahran and to cooperate with the United States in its investigation of the incident." It took two and a half years for the Saudis to allow indirect questioning by the FBI of men arrested in connection with what was, in many ways, the most spectacular terror bombing until 9/11. Because of this smothered investigation, even the 9/11 Commission is unsure who was behind the Khobar attack.

Osama bin-Laden was congratulated for the attack, according to the commission. There are other indications of his involvement, including several statements and newspaper interviews in Arabic. Bin-Laden, who was well connected throughout Saudi Arabia and with its royal family, probably helped the attack. However, the Saudis captured several Saudi Shiites from the oil-rich eastern provinces of Saudi Arabia who were part of the attack and who belonged to the Saudi faction of Hizballah (somewhat similar to the Lebanese version). They said they were trained by members of the Iranian Revolutionary Guards. Yet Saudi officials did not pursue this avenue politically, preferring to "bury the hatchet" and keep things quiet with Iran.

We may never know the full truth behind the Khobar Towers attack, but the sophisticated weaponry and planning—advanced detonators, explosives, and blast funnels—indicate a state sponsor like Iran, which has also fashioned advanced explosives and bombs for use by Shiite groups attacking Americans in Iraq. There is a likelihood, then, that here we may have an example of a hybrid attack involving both Iran, a local Shiite terror organization, as well as bin-Laden. This kind of "hybrid model" is not typical of Middle Eastern terrorism, but it is more common than most Western intelligence officers or media pundits believe.

The truth is that Saudi officials' first instinct after a terror attack on their territory is to cover up the full details lest they embarrass and weaken the regime. This is the tendency of most Arab regimes, such as Egypt,[66] but the Saudis excel at it. Saudi Arabia covered up the full nature of the massive seizure of the Grand Mosque in Mecca in 1979, when hundreds were killed and wounded. It took two weeks—and tanks and artillery—for Saudi authorities to recapture the holiest site in Islam from a band of Saudi Islamists whose views resembled those of bin-Laden. The Saudi cover story, that it was only a small-scale incident, was swallowed by the CIA and U.S. diplomats.

"'In retrospect, the attack appears to have been the isolated act of a small group of religious fanatics,' concluded classified CIA intelligence memorandum entitled 'Saudi Arabia: The Mecca Incident in Perspective.'"[67] The mosque attack was carried out mostly by Saudi Sunni Muslims who felt the Saudi regime had become corrupted, but the group also included some foreigners, including at least several American-born converts to Islam. Those who survived the siege were quickly tried and executed without being interviewed by American personnel. The same thing happened to a group of Saudis convicted of exploding a car bomb in November 1995 outside a Saudi National Guard base where Americans were training Saudi forces. Five Americans were murdered, as well as two others. The four convicted men were executed on May 31, 1996. "The FBI had wanted to talk to the four before they were executed, but the Saudis said no," reports Robert Baer.[68] As Baer and Gold each note, the Saudi regime did not want the FBI or CIA checking clues that might lead inside the Saudi power structure itself. Therefore, it is both sad and laughable when a serious U.S. counterterror expert like Jessica Stern accepts at face value Saudi regime claims to have succeeded in reeducating and moderating die-hard Islamists. "Is it possible to deradicalize terrorists and their potential recruits? Saudi Arabia, a pioneer in rehabilitation efforts, claims that it is. Since 2004, more than 4,000 militants have gone through Saudi Arabia's programs, and the graduates have been reintegrated into mainstream society much more successfully than ordinary criminals."[69]

Too many American think tankers and U.S. officials accept Arab counterterror claims at face value. However, Arab state cover-ups make a mockery of U.S. counterterrorism policy, as shown by the U.S. anti-terror report four months before the Saudi and Egyptian agents of Al-Qaeda crashed planes into New York and Washington:

> The US Government has a long memory and will not simply expunge a terrorist's record because time has passed. The states that choose to harbor terrorists are like accomplices who provide shelter for criminals. They will be held accountable for their "guests'" actions. International terrorists should know, before they contemplate a crime, that they cannot hunker down in safehaven [sic] for a period of time and be absolved of their crimes.[70]

Paul Pillar, once the CIA's top analyst for the Middle East, seems to echo the pacific blandishments of Michael Scheuer, the CIA's ex-expert on bin-Laden. Pillar urges avoiding "absolute solutions"[71] to "eradicate" terror, suggesting "accommodation and finesse"—even negotiating, as set forth in Pillar's first book. Pillar has long thought that negotiating with terrorists, with Saddam's Iraq and the ayatollahs' Iran, is the best path. When U.S. leaders think differently, Pillar, even when sitting in the CIA, will publicly and privately try to undermine the policy of his government.

Pillar, like Scheuer and Tenet, has an idée fixe that terrorism is a manageable item in the loss column that can be carried over to the next financial quarter, as it were. It is not an absolute evil or an absolute problem, but a relative problem, to be solved incrementally. Therefore, "the United States should expect only incremental improvement in the state sponsor's behavior and should be willing to reward such improvements incrementally."[72] Western responses to terrorism, he believes, require a cost-benefit analysis of relative merits for appropriating national and international resources, and a compassionate estimation of the terror actor's own situation. Thus "in articulating which changes in terrorist related behavior it wants to see, the United States should stress measures that would be most feasible for the state sponsor to take."[73] Terror demands a modulated and negotiated response, says Pillar, if we can only believe and have patience in our pursuit of the negotiating process.

Even after a twenty-year record of directing and guiding terror, Iran is ripe for change, Pillar said in his 2000 book on terrorism: "Iran presents reasons for engagement *despite* continuing well-founded concerns about sponsorship of terrorism. There has been simply too much change in Iran—particularly an internal political evolution that has included the election of Mohammad Khatami as president in 1997 and a sweeping victory by reformists in parliamentary elections in early 2000—to let terrorism keep Iran-U.S. relations in a freezer." This was really wrong in 1999, and it is surreally wrong in 2009. Khatami, like all Iranian presidents since 1979, had been screened by the ayatollahs. There is an almost tragicomic quality to this claim of "reform in Iran." It is tragic because Pillar actually offers to serve up insurgent Iranian groups like the Mujahidin-e Khalq as a sacrifice to the ayatollahs.[74] It is comic because its "reform" talk recalls earlier Western episodes of hopeful pseudo-analysis, such as claims Yuri Andropov would reform the Soviet Union because, supposedly, he drank scotch rather than vodka. This analysis is not a result of serious regional research, because the CIA has not had anyone in Iran in thirty years. It is an outgrowth of Pillar's general view on ending conflict, as seen in his 1983 book, *Negotiating Peace*. This book has some of the faults typical of political science doctorates: it is heavy on statistics and categories of the econometric variety, but is much too short on real analysis and wisdom. One feels that Pillar, like many social scientists, needs to heed the warning of Albert Einstein and the example of Moses: "Not everything that counts can be counted," said Einstein, adding "not everything that can be counted counts."[75]

For his part, Moses, whenever he directed a census of the Children of Israel, did not just count by the numbers, but also by name, family, and tribe. This gave his statistics a certain provenance, a certain depth. In contradistinction, Pillar's book was largely written without reference to nonstate actors and hybrid terror actors who sometimes act independently but who often have state-terror sponsors.

After recently retiring, Pillar has again publicly attacked anyone who even thinks about using force against Iran—even after the Iranian regime's bloody repression of demonstrators and Iran's continued pursuit of atomic weapons. For a layman to believe this is naïve, but still perfectly legitimate. However, it is disturbing that an intelligence analyst would pursue the incredibly circular "logic" along with the supposed "facts" Pillar uses for his argument. Its false assumptions are:

- that there is *no* proof that Iran wants nuclear weapons. (But in fact, just look at the centrifuges and the hardened sites dispersed around Iran or just ask President Ahmadinejad or "Supreme Leader" Khamenei.)
- that there is *no* proof such weapons would make security matters worse. (Just ask Iran's neighbors: Kuwait and Oman westward to Jordan, Saudi Arabia, and Israel.)
- that talks or sanctions could persuade Iran to forgo nuclear weapons. (Just ask North Korea and the ghost of Saddam whether "sanctions" persuaded them.)
- that Israel's 1981 strike on Iraq's nuclear reactor did not really stop Iraq's bomb. (Documents captured in 1991 show otherwise.)

Pillar, who now teaches at Georgetown University, was asked by the *National Journal* to answer the following: "Iran and North Korea: Can They Be Deterred and Contained?" Pillar's answer shows his views are not disturbed by the facts:

> The assigned question is quite broad and diffuse, not least because the two countries concerned present much different challenges. Too much bad policy flows from throwing "rogue regimes" into a single, oversimplifying pot. One obvious difference is that North Korea already has nuclear weapons while Iran does not. Another difference is that the North Korean regime is far more mercurial, penurious, risk-acceptant, blatantly criminal, and vulnerable to implosion than the Iranian regime,

notwithstanding the most recent uncertainty and excitement in the streets of Tehran. Something akin to a normal relationship with the Islamic Republic of Iran can be envisioned, notwithstanding all there still would be to dislike and distrust about it. It is hard to envision anything that could be called normal in relations with the gang in Pyongyang.

Attractive alternatives to what the United States and its four principal partners (South Korea, Japan, China, and Russia) have been doing lately in confronting North Korea are not readily apparent. The North Koreans' latest nuclear test appears . . .

It is by no means a foregone conclusion that Iran will acquire nuclear weapons, or even that it eventually will want to acquire them. There is much that the West and especially the United States can do to shape Iranian incentives in the direction of not wanting to acquire them. While not giving up the goal of a non-nuclear-weapons-armed Iran (which is not the same as an Iran with no nuclear program), we need to take a much more sober approach to the prospect of what Iran and the Middle East would look like if that goal is not achieved—more sober than has been true of most discourse on the subject.

Specifically, the attitude that "there would be nothing worse than a nuclear armed Iran" needs to be firmly and decisively discarded. I can think of many things, including many things in the Middle East, that would be worse. One thing that would be worse is a military strike in the name of setting back the Iranian nuclear program. Such an action would not kill the program, it would increase Iranian incentives for accelerating the program (rather like Iraq's response to the Israeli strike on its nuclear reactor in 1981), it would lead Iran to show us what it really means to be the "no. 1 state sponsor of terrorism," it would kill for probably another decade or more any chance of the kind of U.S.-Iranian relationship that could be the core of a more stable Persian Gulf, it would erase what repair to the standing of the U.S. in the Muslim world the United States has begun by committing to a withdrawal from Iraq, and it would throw the oil market into at least short-term turmoil. A military strike against Iran would be folly.

Among all the vague talk about the ill effects on Middle Eastern security of an Iranian nuclear weapon, one hears almost no specific and convincing strategic logic about exactly how Tehran would use its possession of such a weapon in a damaging way. No plausible scenarios come to mind where terrorism comes into play, or where Tehran ever would have any reason to share nuclear capability with a terrorist client. The same is true with questions of how Iran would try to exert influence in the Persian Gulf region. It would have no advantage in any conflict escalating to a level where nuclear weapons became relevant. To use Cold War terminology, the United States (and Israel) would retain escalation dominance. Iranian leaders (unlike Kim Jong-Il) have been risk-averse in their foreign policy for the last couple of decades. And they are not suicidal. The principles of deterrence are not repealed just because one of the parties in a deterrent relationship happens to wear a turban and a beard.[76]

One has to be an ostrich with an especially long neck stuck in the ground to ignore the obvious evidence that Iran wants nuclear weapons. How Iran would use such weapons is shown by the way it uses its conventional arms: as a psychological club to bludgeon and blackmail neighbors. That is why Egypt and Saudi Arabia will almost immediately begin a crash nuclear program if Iran keeps moving inexorably toward its bombs. It is amazing that people familiar with arms control issues—Pillar and his ex-boss George Tenet—were not more worried about Iranian–North Korean nuclear weapons and their proliferation to other state terror regimes or terror organizations. When they were not visibly concerned—as is shown by the 2007 National Intelligence Estimate—it was a strong sign they had abandoned serious analysis for wishful thinking or for political one-upsmanship. It indicated that their intelligence lacks local and regional roots as well as any ability to learn from history. This is not intelligence but pseudohistorical imbecility.

Syria's construction of a nuclear reactor with Iranian and Korean help—thankfully destroyed by another Israeli preemptive strike in 2007—should also silence the snickers from Pillar about "rogue regimes" or an "Axis of Evil." It should also silence the gab reflex of Pillar, Scheuer, and some of their colleagues, who reflexively claim that Western military moves are unwise and self-defeating and that talking always works with authoritarian regimes and terror organizations. Isn't it amazing that the Arab world did not rise up as one to condemn Israel for destroying the

Syrian-Iranian–North Korean weapon of mass destruction? Isn't it amazing that there was a similar lack of solidarity with Hamas in 2008, with
Hizballah in 2006, or with the PLO when Israel attacked them after
being attacked by them? Doesn't the Arab-Islamic world's reaction—
unwillingness to justify Hamas, fear of Hizballah, and loathing for the
PLO—show that even in the Arab-Islamic world there is some respect
for the principle of a Western country defending itself against a demon-
strable threat?

But divorcing oneself from reality is evident in another Pillar article,
where the CIA's former top regional analyst pats himself and the CIA on
the back for supplying great intelligence on the Middle East in general
and particularly in Iraq. True, the CIA warned that the postwar reconstruction would be difficult.[77] This is partially true, particularly the dangers
in postwar Iraq, but Pillar's version of events and CIA successes seems
deliberately prevaricative. CIA field intelligence in Iraq, for example, was
dismally bad, but its field record in Washington, D.C., was impressive. In
2004, the *Wall Street Journal* showed how Pillar selectively leaked intelligence material but hid CIA errors as part of an "insurgency" against then-
President George W. Bush. Pillar and the CIA, the *Journal* said, wanted
not just to thwart Bush policies but also to help John Kerry beat Bush in
the 2004 U.S. elections, observing "his [Pillar's] corner of the CIA has
long claimed that the 'secular' Baathists in Iraq would never do business
with the fundamentalist al-Qaeda. Tell that to Abu Musab al Zarqawi
and the Baathists now cooperating in Fallujah. "[78] Pillar claims the Bush
administration was hell-bent on war in Iraq, ignored CIA advice, and
pretended that Iraq had a connection to Al-Qaeda and weapons of mass
destruction. True, Bush erred in many aspects of the Iraq war. Yet, there
was more than one Saddam-Al-Qaeda link, there was an Iraqi WMD
program, and there was an anthrax attack on America at the same time
as 9/11. Moreover, Al-Qaeda allied itself with Saddam, and the defeat
of the Al-Qaeda forces in Iraq was a major defeat for Osama bin-Laden,
severely weakening Al-Qaeda. Pillar has a long pattern of touting supposed CIA successes in the Middle East over the years, but he is weaving
together many half-truths and complete falsehoods, again hiding many
CIA mistakes. He repeats the line by former CIA director Richard Helms
(who advised President Lyndon Johnson) that, before the 1967 war, the

CIA predicted Israeli military success within a matter of days. This, too, is a very partial truth, and sometimes even a partial truth can be a full-fledged lie.[79] As the British poet Blake once said: "A truth that's told with bad intent / Beats all the lies one can invent."

Thomas Powers, who studied the CIA, has written tellingly about how it has a way of burying disturbing details or those who might reveal them, noting that "no one should underestimate the tenacity with which an intelligence organization like the CIA will hold on to the secrets that can cause real trouble."[80]

Pillar is right to suggest that the Bush administration's democratization ideas and postwar planning were unrealistic and fuzzy. Some of this was probably the CIA's fault. Yet it may take years for historians to unravel—if they can at all—what the CIA told the Bush administration and vice versa. The CIA was clearly not happy with some Bush policies, and many of its officials were leaking broadly and selectively to hurt the Bush position. Such a bureaucratic battle over foreign policy is not new in Washington, as Morton Halperin illustrated more than thirty years ago.

"The decision to leak information to the press is taken by those who are dissatisfied with the decision being taken within the executive branch."[81] Yet it is rare to see any country's government so attacked in the media by intelligence officials currently employed by that country. In general, one can say that the Bush administration was never particularly skilled in press relations. However, Bush policies were crippled most by intelligence officials who got their version of events reproduced and adopted by the *New York Times, Washington Post, Newsweek, New Yorker,* CNN, NBC, and other prime media outlets.

President Bush never really presented a cogent case for his anti-terror policies. Bush held only four press conferences in eight years,[82] and he was repeatedly treated as a kind of caricature, lampooned as someone who could barely speak English. Vice President Dick Cheney was tight-lipped, giving relatively few press appearances,[83] and Secretary of Defense Donald Rumsfeld largely avoided the press, too.

One of the worst accusations against the Bush administration was that it distorted intelligence data and fabricated a case that Iraq had weapons of mass destruction.[84] However, congressional committees and independent inquiries dismissed the fabrication charges as baseless.

Several foreign intelligence services corroborated information on Iraqi WMD in 2002, and there is still evidence that at the time of the 2002 war, there was at least an ongoing Iraqi WMD program and links with the Al-Qaeda organization. Former federal agent Dave Gaubatz has described three large concrete weapons bunkers that he believes held WMD but that were not excavated by U.S. forces in time, and were looted by Iraqis.[85] In addition, a view strongly different from Pillar's is presented in at least five separate, well-researched books by, respectively, former CIA field agent Bob Baer and former undersecretary of defense Douglas Feith, as well as investigative journalists Stephen F. Hayes, Kenneth Timmerman, and Rowan Scarborough.[86] Rather than relying on Pillar and his reflexive defenses of the CIA, we'd do better to look at these well-based critiques of U.S. intelligence in the 1990s as well as solid academic analysis.

Amy Zegart, for example, is not arguing (as Pillar charges) that good organization solves all intelligence problems. Zegart cites remarks by Senator Henry Jackson to the National War College in 1959 that are just as valid today. "Organization by itself cannot assure a strategy for victory in the cold war. But good organization can help, and poor organization can hurt."[87] Worse than just bad organization is the "organization man" syndrome, or, as Zegart says, "entrenched bureaucrats in existing agencies pose the most serious obstacles to reform."[88]

Zegart also interviewed CIA officers from the Directorate of Operations, also known as the Clandestine Service. She found that many admitted that there was tremendous bureaucratic resistance inside the CIA to using even the most basic techniques to penetrate terror organizations, such as the use of NOCs (pronounced "knocks"). These are nonofficial covers (for example, concealing one's identity as "businessmen" or as "anti-American activists") that enable officers to move more freely and quietly in and out of countries and perhaps gain contact with hard-to-contact groups. But as one such officer told Zegart, "We were resistant to change. We had a comfort zone and we were going to stay right there." But it is hard to penetrate terror organizations while working solely out of embassies and attending diplomatic cocktail parties, especially if your target groups don't go to cocktail parties.

INTELLIGENCE AND HUMILITY

"Who is the wise man? He who learns from every man." This Talmudic aphorism sums up the link between intelligence and humility. Members of the U.S. intelligence community—and this also includes legislative oversight committees—could do themselves a favor by exercising a little humble self-examination.

Intelligence agencies that get bogged down in groupthink and static approaches should heed the special message of Marc Bloch, a historian who was executed by the Gestapo after working for the French Resistance. Bloch wrote tellingly about the importance of the failure of intelligence in strategic defeat: "What drove our armies to disaster was the cumulative effect of a great number of different mistakes. One glaring characteristic is, however, common to all of them. Our leaders, or those who acted for them, were incapable of thinking in terms of a *new* war. In other words, the German triumph was, essentially, a triumph of intellect—and it is that which makes it so peculiarly serious."[89]

The 9/11 attacks, bad as they were, could have been worse, if one of the hijacked planes had reached the White House or the Capitol, or if the planes had hit the World Trade Center an hour later, when more people were at work. A little healthy "fear of the consequences," a lot more "imagination" (as suggested by the 9/11 Commission), and a more humble attitude should prompt Western government intelligence services to imagine even bolder terror plots.[90]

One key to stopping those plots is human intelligence—a solution with two sides:

- Preparing Western intelligence with more and better-trained personnel
- Seizing personnel from the terrorists and getting them to supply information

This second part of the solution could have been more quickly and easily implemented after the West went to war against Al-Qaeda and the Taliban, as described by one key Pentagon official: "To prevent the next 9/11, U.S. officials needed intelligence on the organizations and plans of jihadist terrorists, and the most promising source of intelligence was the pool of terrorists already captured."[91] After all, HUMINT—human intelligence—is still the best defense against terrorism. Human intelligence is not oxymoronic, nor moronic, if we find the best humans and train them for one of the most important jobs in any free society.

Reporter and CIA historian Tim Weiner ends his book with an interesting idea:

> Two years ago, a National Intelligence University was created—on paper. It remains a blueprint for an insular bureaucracy. It should become a real university, the equivalent of West Point and the National War College. Government programs created in 1991 to train new national-security officers have received an annual budget of $2 million for undergraduates and $2 million for graduate students—a ridiculously low investment when the nation is spending $2 billion *a day* on the military. Two billion dollars a year would enable thousands of undergraduates to become fluent in the language, history, and culture of the nations of Islam and the future great powers. The students might grow up to be diplomats, or military officers, or seek their fortunes elsewhere. But some might choose to serve their nation in dirty, dangerous places where real intelligence work is done.[92]

A similar educational effort should be made in several Western countries because Arab-Islamic terror is not likely to disappear even though Osama bin-Laden has been killed. He has already inspired many other copycat terrorists, some of whom are already residing inside Western countries. The war on Arab-Islamic terror is likely to last many years, and the best way to shorten the war and lower the casualties is to have good education and intelligence.

Strategic surprise comes from bad intelligence and wishful thinking. Terrorists and dictators send mixed messages. They promise peace while preparing for war. After attacking, they offer truces they never mean to uphold. They entice elected leaders with sweet words while exhorting their own supporters to war. This is not a new strategy. Terrorists and dictators share a tendency that Hannah Arendt once described as threatening truthfully: "would-be totalitarian rulers usually start their careers by boasting of their past crimes and carefully outlining their future ones."[93] Later, they learn how to mask their message. We must remove that mask.

One can always find a leader or "intelligence expert" who says, "They don't really mean what they say" or "They will moderate, once they've been in power for a while." In 1992, CIA's Mideast analyst, Graham Fuller, said of the Islamist surge in Algeria: "It is time to demystify the phenomenon of Islamic fundamentalism and to see it for what it is: a movement that is both historically inevitable and politically 'tamable.'"[94] About two hundred thousand people died in Algeria in the period after Fuller said that, many murdered by Islamists who beheaded whole towns and villages—all of them Muslims.

There will always be a wishful-thinking analyst or politically correct pundit who is patient with rabid forms of Islamism, tribalism, and nationalism, those who buy the lines of Arafat, bin-Laden, Saddam, and Iranian ayatollahs. Hitler, a master of radio and the grand public speech, understood this. Osama bin-Laden, a student of oratory who mastered the videocassette, also understood this. Both achieved surprise. Their enemies should have known better.

"One obvious conclusion to draw is that Hitler understood the French and the British governments better than those governments understood him," observed Ernest May. Hitler found the weak spot of democracies. "The reason for his better understanding included the fact that he focused on political leaders and public opinion rather than on apparent national interests or capabilities; and the companion fact that his assessments of those governments were not negotiated assessments."[95]

The real genius of the talented tyrant—terrorist or dictator—is in playing on the "genius" of the democratic societies who could oppose his aims: courting their wishful thinking, seducing their delusions, promising them what they want to hear.

As British historian Sir John Wheeler-Bennett put it: "Except in cases where he had pledged his word, Hitler always meant what he said."[96]

Much the same can be said for Arab-Islamic terror organizations and their state sponsors. We must understand *their* motives and goals, not invent a set of our own.

7

THE IDEOLOGIES, METHODS, AND
MOTIVES OF ARAB-ISLAMIC TERROR

"How can you tell when someone is just devout or when he has become extreme and might be turning to terror?"

It was a direct, almost naïve question—not the kind usually heard in a government forum or the halls of academia. The first time I was asked this question in the early 1990s, the query was in Hebrew. I was giving tips to an Israeli undercover unit training to get close to and then capture Arab terrorists. The unit, code-named Shimshon, was one of several units known as *mista'arabim*—the Hebrew term for people who masquerade as Arabs. Such units help Israel control terror with relatively low casualties and low firepower.

The next time I was asked the question, it was at a meeting with police, FBI, and prosecutors who were part of the Joint Illinois-Missouri Terrorism Task Force in 2008. Both times the question was better than any answer I could give, because there is no single framework for religious practice and no exclusive profile of Arab-Islamic terrorists.[1] Still, I tried to give an answer that works much of the time.[2]

Terror is really a chain, not a flash. It is a series of events and personalities—ideology, fund-raiser, planner, supplier, bomber—that ends in an attack. We want to stop the attack, but that means more than just one question or one answer. To break the chain requires breaking only one link, but to keep the chain broken and from being repaired requires an analysis that is a kind of chain itself: a series of queries and responses, starting with the following questions:

- What makes someone an Arab-Islamic terrorist?
- Is it something psychological or is it political?
- Is there a sociological element? Is there an economic factor?
- Is it religious ideology or does it show religious deviancy?
- Is there a medical factor, perhaps a hormonal imbalance? Is it perhaps the result of some repressed sexual impulses?
- And, why is answering these questions important for the war against terror?

Let's try to answer the last question first: Almost all wars reach a stage where the will to win determines the ability to win, and this is especially true of a terror war. When one side loses heart, it gives up, well before it is physically defeated—well before its cities fall or all its members are arrested. If we can understand the factors that cause a man or a woman to enlist with the terrorists or to lose faith in their cause, we may be able to thin out the terrorists' ranks by deterring or dissuading new enlistees. If we know the factors that tempt people to join terror groups, we can find ways to make terrorism less enticing. If we see how religious arguments, political ideology, or external forces (socioeconomic or political stimuli) sway potential terrorists, we may be able to blunt or redirect the power of these forces.

PROFILING THE TERRORIST MIND

There is no single factor that determines if someone will be a terrorist. We know this from interviews with terrorists (including suicide terrorists whose bombs misfired or who changed their minds at the last minute) and with their friends and family.[3] Just being angry, being poor or rich, being single or married or unlucky in love, or being frustrated about the job picture is not enough. Everyone has a gripe, but not everyone becomes a terrorist. Still, there have been attempts to provide a terrorist model.[4]

Actually there are *several* formulae—*several* recipes—that produce a

terrorist, even a highly unusual terrorist we usually call a "suicide bomber."
Why?

First, a terrorist is a bit like a walking explosive, and it usually takes a *combination* of compounds to make an explosive.[5] Second, there are several kinds of explosives, just as there are several kinds of terrorists. That is why it is not possible to "profile a terrorist" based on one isolated factor. Yet there is a *set* of identifiable factors, which, when taken together, point to certain people becoming terrorists. These factors can lead someone to join a terror group or to become a lone terrorist, but there appear to be differences between the way these factors play out in different areas and also among men and women. For example, researchers have found that many of the Palestinian women suicide bombers (or would-be bombers who got caught) were driven to their actions by a kind of social blackmail after being ostracized for some sexual or social sin that caused shame to their families.

Some women were suspected of having an affair before marriage, or cheating on their husbands or fiancés after marriage or betrothal. In at least one case, a woman was divorced and abandoned by her husband following a miscarriage that left her barren. The woman, Wafa Idris, a nurse by profession, was the first Palestinian female suicide bomber.[6] Idris the nurse was smuggled into Jerusalem with her bomb aboard a Palestinian ambulance. Idris and other women had a "choice" between a "heroic death" and a life of shame and isolation or even being murdered by members of their own family in what are called "honor killings." This "choice" drove them to choose *istish-haad*[7]: to martyr themselves, regaining face for themselves and family. This behavior, incredible to a typical Westerner, has been solidly documented.[8] (The phenomenon of "honor killings" is part of tribalism—a behavior or ideology that is still prevalent in the Middle East and which will be discussed later in this chapter.)

There were several other dynamics that appeared in the exploitation and development of Palestinian women suicide bombers for the Fatah organization of Yasser Arafat, such as the need to find ways to compete and outdo the Islamic group Hamas[9] and the shortage of male suicide bombers.[10] Another researcher has shown that the use of women suicide bombers spurred millions of dollars in donations for Fatah by a Saudi Arabia television "terror telethon."[11]

One French filmmaker has shown that many of the young Arab men who became suicide bombers did so out of sexual repression combined with the promise of eternal life in paradise being treated by seventy-two virgins.[12] The propaganda films of the Palestinian Authority under Arafat regularly featured beautiful women beckoning young men to join them in paradise after becoming "martyrs." In one such film, which I have recorded, a gorgeous young woman, dressed in gossamer robes, seduces a man away from his attractive (but older) wife. One would-be Palestinian suicide bomber captured before he could blow himself up was found to have swathed his genitalia in protective gauze because he was looking forward to those seventy-two virgins, and he wanted his equipment intact. As Daniel Webster once said, "There is nothing as powerful as the truth, and nothing so strange."

In these cases, the sexual or sociological factor did not act alone. Rather there was a reinforcing ideology—religious, political, and even tribal—that served as important "background music." This background music is often overlooked or misunderstood by Westerners, especially by many in the press, academia, and government/intelligence services. Many of these elites still insist, for example, that poverty and "frustration" are prime motivators of terror. Western officials or pundits regularly ascribe poverty and social "frustration" as the motivators of terror. Repeated research has shown that this is not so. Indeed, Princeton University researcher Claude Berrebi, now at the RAND Corporation, demolished the idea in a detailed study.

"Many people in today's global society, including many of its most prominent leaders and academics, maintain that terrorist activity is the result of ignorance and/or poverty," wrote Berrebi. "As such, unless a more subtle mechanism is at play, we should expect individual terrorists to predominantly be impoverished or ill educated."[13] However, his research showed the opposite. Terror organizations seemed to thrive on wealthy and well-educated terrorists. "If income level and education are linked, at the micro level, to participation in terrorist activities, it is probably to the opposite effect of what the popular conventional wisdom assumes."[14]

Another frequently claimed motivator, the need to throw out foreign occupiers, was proven *not* to be a major contributory factor. As Mia Bloom asked, why was suicide terror not used against the Soviets in Afghanistan during an eleven-year occupation, and why was it such a frequently used tactic inside Iraq (by Sunnis against Shiite civilians, for example) or in Pakistan (again against Pakistani civilians)?[15] In fact there are a variety of factors that are directly related to terror, especially in the Arab-Islamic community. Perhaps the most important overarching factor, described by Bloom, was an air of societal approval: "Certain trends in suicide terrorism have become evident to most of us [researchers] . . . that as long as certain religious authorities justified and provided credibility for this form of violence, it will likely persist throughout the Islamic world."[16]

In fact, it is necessary to broaden Bloom's observation, because suicide bombers in Lebanon, Israel, the West Bank, Gaza, and Egypt have also gotten not just religious approval but broader additional ideological or societal authorizers for their actions. (Similar societal approval was given by imperial Japan to its kamikaze suicide pilots.)

In order to isolate these factors, we must examine what has moved Arab-Islamic terror in the last century—the *ideas* and the *way* they were transmitted.

One way to jump into our subject is by a seemingly indirect route, by asking a somewhat incongruous question: What do Osama bin-Laden, Yasser Arafat, and Napoleon Bonaparte have in common?

WATANIYYA: LOCAL OR HOMELAND PATRIOTISM

The answer is that each of them influenced political thinking and tactics in the Arab-Islamic world. Moreover, each of them had an important role in political communication—the media lever that multiplies the effects of actions and thoughts. Napoleon conquered Egypt in 1798, introducing the printing press and Western notions of nationalism for the first time to the Arab world. Both were significant.

When Napoleon came to Egypt, he came with a team of experts, calling on Egyptians—in Arabic—to join him as Egyptian patriots. "O ye Egyptians,"[17] he said, addressing sons and daughters of the Nile, urging them to break from the Ottoman Empire. In three years, Napoleon set up a local patriotism focused on the homeland or *la patrie* (fatherland in French) and *watan* in Arabic—hence the name *wataniyya*.

It was a simple concept—France for the French, Egypt for the Egyptians. Such feelings were common in Europe: the French had *la patrie*, the Russians *Rodina* (motherland), and the Germans *Vaterland* (Fatherland).

But this was a new idea for the Middle East, where the idea of a nation-state and fixed national borders was really quite novel. Local Arab feelings became what Arabs call *wataniyya*—local or *homeland* nationalism. Years later, Egyptian leader Anwar Sadat broke with other Arabs to make a separate peace with Israel, resurrecting the local nationalist theme under the slogan *Misr Awalan, Misr Daiyman*: "Egypt First, Egypt Always."

Today, any time an Arab leader—whether a Sadat, a Saddam, or an Arafat—pledges never to give up "one grain of sacred sand" or "our precious soil," he should also salute that diminutive French general whose short rule in Egypt left a lasting impression. "The Napoleonic invasion of Egypt in 1798 was an aftermath of the French Revolution. While, militarily, the invasion failed, yet the ideas for which the French Revolution stood remained."[18]

Today, some Arabs prefer to ignore Western influence on Arab political thought, but it was not Napoleon's only contribution in three years of rule. Napoleon also left a printing press and newspapers. Egypt became the political center and communications hub of the Arab world.[19] Western impact on Arab politics and communications spread in the 1800s under an Egyptian viceroy, Mehmet Ali. He and his children studied French culture and governance, sending several missions to France. They also nearly conquered Istanbul and the Ottoman Empire itself, until dissuaded by the British fleet.

When Britain evicted Napoleon from Egypt, it placed a tight hold, especially on the Suez Canal (completed in 1876)—the strategic link to the British Empire in India. Egyptian desires for self-rule exploded in rebellion in 1880, and returned in the 1900s with Saad Zaghlul, the leader of the Wafd Party. Zaghlul, a local patriot, asked Western powers to grant real Egyptian independence in line with their promises after World War I.[20] The British, however, fought self-rule, continuing to rule behind the scenes, clinging to the Suez Canal as a special British-run preserve. In 1952, anti-British sentiment grew after young army officers ousted the corrupt, corpulent King Farouk, last vestige of the now-flabby monarchy that Mehmet Ali had founded. Colonel Gamal Abdul-Nasser, the unofficial leader of the young officers, established a new assertive Arab political nationalism known as *qawmiyya*.[21]

This ideology had a strong anti-Western undercurrent because the colonial powers in the Middle East were from Western Europe: Britain, France, and Italy.[22] In 1954, Abdul-Nasser signed a treaty with Britain limiting Britain to special rights only in the Suez Canal Zone. However, a member of the Muslim Brotherhood felt even this concession was too much, and he tried to murder Abdul-Nasser for betraying religious and national rights. Indeed, despite their bloody rivalry, Abdul-Nasser and the Muslim Brothers shared many inclinations, such as anticolonialism and vague notions of social justice. When Abdul-Nasser seized the Canal in July 1956, this led to the Anglo-French attack on Suez in the October 1956 war, in which Israel directed a land conquest of the Sinai Peninsula. The 1956 war, like the reassertion of Arab rights over the Suez Canal Zone, actually enshrined Abdul-Nasser as the leader of Arab anticolonial nationalism. "In retrospect," as a close friend of Abdul-Nasser later wrote, "a clash of arms between the British . . . and the forces of Arab nationalism, which Nasser came to personify, can be seen to have been inevitable."[23]

QAWMIYYA: PAN-ARAB NATIONALISM

Gamal Abdul-Nasser and his fellow officers did not have a clear economic or sociopolitical philosophy, but rather "a series of improvised programmes."[24] They eventually drifted toward centralized planning they called "Arab Socialism." As Mohamed Heikal, a close confidant of Abdul-Nasser, wrote, "apart from getting rid of the King and his corrupt associates, the Free Officers had few plans."[25] The officers wanted Egypt to master its own fate, to remove traces of foreign rule in Egypt. They also wanted to remove the corruption that they felt was at the root of the Egyptian-led Arab defeat at the hands of Israel in 1948. In many respects, the largely secular pan-Arab movement recalled (and drew inspiration from) the highly secular anti-Ottoman movement of Mustafa Kemal (Attaturk[26]), which unseated the vestiges of the corrupt and ailing Ottoman Empire.[27] "Attaturk viewed Islam as a vestige of the Ottoman past he was seeking to eradicate," observes Peter Mandaville. "Islam for him was backwards, anti-modernist, and an obstacle to the Westernizing future he dreamed of for Turkey."[28] Like Attaturk, Colonel Abdul-Nasser and his officers reacted out of a sense of shame over the failure of their old, traditional, religious leaders and monarchs on the field of battle and in the arena of ideas. They responded with modern, secular, nationalistic, and military-oriented regimes. Generals and technocrats would replace kings, imams, and sheikhs. (Years later, the Islamic resurgence would also be driven by anticorruption impulses.)

NATIONALIST GENERALS VS. TRADITIONAL KINGS AND IMAMS

Traditional Islam, with its caliphates and sheikhdoms, was fine for most Arabs and Muslims when Islam was ascendant, when the Ottomans twice almost conquered Vienna. But the dramatic decline of the Otto-man Empire changed all that. Western military might transformed the Arab-Islamic world into a figure of derision even in the eyes of Arabs and Muslims themselves. Western diplomats had formerly paid their respects at the area known as the Sublime Porte, the grand open court in Istanbul's Topkapi Palace, home of the sultan who ruled the Ottoman Empire. But now the Sublime Porte had become a doormat, and the sultan and his empire were known as "the Sick Man of Europe." Arab nationalism—*wataniyya* and *qawmiyya*—essentially replaced the traditional role of Islam: a system of rule as well as a religion.

"Ottoman and Arab concern with the West," as historian C. Er-nest Dawn observed, was "dominated by an obsession with power and glory." The various strains of Arab nationalism shared a "common crucial theme"—frustration with a situation in which "the power and glory has passed from the Moslem East to the Christian West."[29]

"What tended to make the educated, conscious, modern Muslim something of a fanatic was the shocking discrepancy between the stu-pendous claims of Islam and the golden moments in its history on the one hand and its present deplorable state on the other," observed Nissim Rejwan, who chronicled modern Arab intellectual history.[30]

Throughout the nineteenth and the twentieth centuries, there were visible trends and many salient events—wars, occupations, regime collapses —that underscored the decline of the Arab-Islamic community. These included the failure of Turkey in World War I (1914–18) and the demise of the last caliphate when the Ottoman Empire fell in 1924. "It was the defeat that befell the Turks in World War I that awakened the Arabs and stimulated Arab nationalism," observed Abd al-Rahman Azzam, the first secretary-general of the Arab League, adding that "the collapse of the last Islamic Empire was another important factor which stimulated Arab nationalism."[31] This yearning for former Arab-Islamic power and glory is an underlying theme of almost all ideologies in the Arab-Islamic sphere today.

Abdul-Nasser melded Egyptian pride, Arab honor, and anticolonialism into a nationalistic package. The unifying glue for this nationalism was Arabness or the Arabic language. Still, it would be inaccurate to say *qawmiyya* was a doctrine that was totally different from the previous local nationalism or totally averse to Islamic sensibilities. All three doctrines spoke of Arabs recapturing pride, independence, and glory. Though avowedly Pan-Arab, Egyptian-led *qawmiyya* envisioned *Egypt* leading the Arabs. Though secular, it was not anti-Islamic, but its linguistic/secular stance allowed Christians and other non-Muslims to be devotees of the doctrine.[32]

"It must be remembered that Nasser, who had inaugurated a socialist revolution, made a point of publicly displaying his great devotion to Islam."[33] Despite strong ties to the Soviet Union, Abdul-Nasser never called himself a communist, because this would have been tantamount to being an atheist: something unacceptable in the Arab world. His example was not unique. Libya's Muammar Qadhafi, Iraq's Saddam Hussein, the PLO's Yasser Arafat, and, before them all, Haj Amin al-Husseini, all borrowed elements from local patriotic nationalism, pan-Arab and Islamic motifs.

This is crucially important for Westerners—particularly Americans—to remember, because there is a tendency to try to classify Middle Eastern phenomena into neat categories, or convenient boxes with neat right angles. But a Pan-Arabist like Saddam, Arafat, or Abdul-Nasser could exploit Islamic themes when convenient, just as Sunni and Shiite terrorists may make joint cause against a common enemy.

Using his powerful radio station, the "Voice of the Arabs," Abdul-Nasser reached a huge audience from Morocco on the Atlantic to Iraq on the shores of the oil-rich Gulf. His dramatic radio presence swayed Arabs the way Franklin Roosevelt or Winston Churchill stirred Western audiences a few years earlier.[34] Abdul-Nasser's tall, youthful, athletic appearance enhanced his status as a media idol with star power and political clout. He used the Egyptian propaganda machine—even Egypt's film industry—to magnify his power and to destabilize other countries.[35] He attacked Arab rulers—the kings of Jordan and Saudi Arabia or the Christian president of Lebanon—as being mere vassals of the British and the Americans. Several regimes toppled before his media blitz: Lebanon and Jordan in 1958 were rescued by British and American support. Clearly, Egypt's leader could propel events and destabilize even remote regimes though his broadcast charisma. Abdul-Nasser's appeal transcended Egypt in three concentric circles he called the Egyptian Circle, the Arab Circle, and the Nonaligned Circle.[36] He was the uncontested leader of the Arab world. Years later, his media methods were consciously copied by other Arab leaders, such as Yasser Arafat and Saddam Hussein, as they sought to broaden their base.[37]

In the end, Abdul-Nasser's *qawmiyya* and other Arab doctrines (Iraqi/Syrian Baathism and Jordanian/Saudi/Moroccan monarchism) failed to mesh collectively or get results individually. They all flunked the subject of economics. Though Europeans killed each other for centuries, they succeeded in forming NATO and a common market. The Arabs, great merchants for centuries, could not even form an economic union. "One of the most obvious, yet nevertheless striking features of inter-Arab politics during the system's formative years," wrote one perceptive observer, "was the insignificance of the economic dimension," and, indeed, "the only examples of genuine Arab economic integration were those imposed by foreigners."[38]

George Bernard Shaw once joked that the British and the Americans were two peoples separated by a common language. In the case of the Arabs, it was nineteen or twenty states separated by a common language, and it was in the language that the failures reverberated. Pan-Arabism—the majestic linguistic bond of Arabic—highlighted and accentuated failure. It was a bombastic language full of pretensions and delusions, where virtuoso demonstrations of style overrode content, and where failures were always blamed on non-Arab outsiders. "The invented nationalist historiography of the Arab kind has always pointed outward: It accused others—Ottomans, Europeans, and others—of causing the ills of the Arab world."[39] Later, Arab failures in development and war were all explained by nefarious plots by Israel or the CIA.

The "Palestine Question" overtook all Arab imaginations and imposed itself on all discussions.[40] In their hearts, most Arab leaders could not care less about the Arabs of Palestine, and yet, "Increasingly, a leader's position on the Palestine question came to be the litmus test for fidelity to pan-Arab ideals, in both the domestic and the regional spheres."[41] "Fighting for Palestine" was a slogan that framed a barren policy of impotent men flexing their rhetorical muscles, but the rhetoric sometimes escalated to real violence.[42] Years later, Osama bin-Laden and Ayman Zawahiri periodically raised the Palestine issue. For them, too, it was not a sincere core issue, merely a convenient slogan or fund-raising device forged in the crucible of pan-Arab rhetoric—a time-tested rallying cry designed to elicit a Pavlovian response. As Michael Barnett has observed, "because their legitimacy, popularity, and sometimes even survival depended on whether they were viewed as adhering to the norms of Arabism, Arab leaders expended considerable energy conveying the image that they were genuine disciples of Arab nationalism."[43]

The Arab League, set up by Britain in 1945, was really quite a joke. It was a huge, hollow, and half-baked lemon meringue pie: fluff on top, empty inside. It lent an image of surface Arab unity beneath which there was complete disunity and total inability to unite on any real political or economic policy except hating Israel. Visions of Arab nationalism and unity crashed into the reality of Arab particularism.[44] Overall, Arab nationalism's failings did not appear suddenly overnight but over years. Partly, the various nationalisms failed because the national idea was so new to the Arab theater, unlike Europe, where the national idea had developed over hundreds of years. Even the borders of the Arab states were foreign inventions, imposed by European powers. Arab nationalism and nation-states floundered also because Arab leaders had only vague policy ideas and fuzzy notions of their own group identity. They even tried formal mergers—such as Egypt and Syria joining in the so-called United Arab Republic, which was anything but united or a republic.[45]

Israel defeated the joint Arab armies under the command of Abdul-Nasser in June 1967: the ultimate, symbolic defeat of Pan-Arabism. The world called it "the Six-Day War." The Arabs called it *al-Naksa*[46]—the Relapse or the Reversal. For Abdul-Nasser it was what Waterloo was for Napoleon—a dead end. For the Arabs, it was a turning point, slowly moving away from nationalism and returning to the call of Islam and

Pan-Islam. However, just as nationalism did not collapse overnight, so the shift away from nationalism and toward Islam did not occur overnight, but over years.

THE SAUDIS, ISLAMISM, AND PAN-ISLAM

Saudi Arabia is the world's only country named for a family—the House of Saud. Imagine the United States as Clintonia or Bushland, its citizens "Clintonites" or "Bush-men." Saudi Arabia radiates the ideology of pan-Islam and the failure to implement it well. Pan-Islam is the desire to unite the world under the belief in and rule of Allah. The Saudi regime is the fruit of an alliance, made in 1744, between Muhammad Ibn Saud, an Arabian chieftain, and Muhammad Ibn Abd al-Wahhab, a grim theologian for whom Wahhabism is named.[47] As theology, Wahhabism is highly dogmatic, antireform, anti-Christian, and anti-Jewish. It emerged in the stark Arabian hinterland of the Najd Plateau: an extremely austere and severe interpretation of Islam claiming to bring the Arabs and their faith back to the ancient truths of Muhammad.

For decades, Saudi-Wahhabi forces fought to conquer all of Arabia, until their wiry horsemen and desert fighters defeated the British-backed Hashemite family that controlled the Islamic shrines of Mecca and Medina in 1924.[48] The alliance spawned an even more fanatical internal faction known as the Ikhwan, "Brotherhood."[49] They were the Saudi shock troops whose bestial combat tactics became legend.[50]

The Ikhwan said foreign ideas had corrupted Islam, even in Arabia, sapping its energy. Wearing plain white head cloths, they literally averted their eyes from foreigners. They spent *their* energy attacking Arabs and Muslims for not being real Arabs and true Muslims. They destroyed the dome at the tomb of Muhammad, Islam's messenger, stripping all decoration at the site, declaring worship at a grave site was but paganlike worship of saints and polytheism—known in Arabic as *shirk*.[51]

After seizing Mecca in 1924, the Saudis became all they had once despised. They called themselves kings and formed a dynasty of three to five thousand princes, with wives, ex-wives, fleets of luxury cars and yachts, sumptuous homes in Arabia and abroad—all staffed by non-Arab servants. Young Arabs' anger and disgust for Saudi rulers is understandable when one compares the Arab ideal with what the Saudis had become.

In the words of Yaroslav Trofimov, "The rot seemed to come from above.
. . . Crown Prince Fahd was gaining a reputation as a pro-American playboy. Following Fahd's example, slews of lesser princes—and these now
numbered in the thousands—had taken to escaping Wahhabi restrictions
in the French Riviera or Spain's Costa del Sol, where stories proliferated
about their gambling, drinking, and whoring exploits."[52]

Philip K. Hitti writes:

> The Arabian in general and the Bedouin in particular is a born demo-
> crat. He meets his sheikh on an equal footing. . . . But the Arabian is
> also aristocratic as well as democratic. He looks upon himself as the em-
> bodiment of the consummate pattern of creation. To him the Arabian
> nation is the noblest of all nations. The civilized man, from the Bedouin's
> exalted point of view, is less happy and far inferior. In the purity of his
> blood, his eloquence and poetry, his sword and horse, and above all his
> noble ancestry, the Arabian takes infinite pride.[53]

The Saudi regime owns a mixed image of false piety and real licentious-
ness that is indelibly etched. For many of the 23 million Saudi citizens,
it is a source of great shame. Nonprinces like Osama bin-Laden grew
disgusted by their leaders' dissolute and profligate lifestyles—a factor that
spurred rebels to seize Mecca's Grand Mosque in 1979, where hundreds
died.[54] Saudi youth seethe as hypocritical Saudi princes gamble in Monte
Carlo but pose as the "keepers of the holy shrines" in Mecca, where gambling is a grave sin. Rather than pass the dice, Saudi princes cover all bets,
erecting mosques from Pakistan to London and from Jakarta to New
York. The playboy dynasty funds expensive and extensive religious outreach programs collectively known as *al-Dawa* (the "call"). Preachers and
proselytizers go forth to convert the world to Wahhabi Islam. Discs and
books are sent to re-Islamize secular Turkey,[55] chaplains to recruit soldiers
in Western armies and to draft prisoners in British and U.S. penitentia-
ries.[56]

This religious machine was not built for God. It was built for a man:
to repulse the vicious attacks of Abdul-Nasser's sophisticated propaganda
apparatus. It was erected also to co-opt internal foes of the Saudi regime,
exporting the fanatics abroad like crude oil, to convert non-Muslims and

to reclaim Muslims who had strayed too close to foreign ideas. The global outreach was also meant to cover up the wanton and besotted behavior at the very top of the Saudi pyramid, as one observer noted:

> Appearances matter for Saudi kings. . . . In the early 1960's, King Saud's tarnished religious reputation roused the *ulama* and eventually led to his ouster. In addition, there were widespread rumors of the royal family's corruption, that Fahd and his brothers earned under-the-table commissions from many of the kingdom's arms purchases. . . . So in order to retain a free hand in foreign affairs, King Fahd's government had to satisfy the needs of the Wahhabi clerics. Saudi Arabia, therefore embarked on a massive campaign to bring Wahhabi Islam to the world.[57]

Oil prices rose sharply in 1974 (a fourfold increase in a few months), and as oil flowed out, money flowed into Saudi Arabia, widening the surreal gulf separating Saudi ideals and Saudi reality, between Saudi citizens and Saudi leaders. Social tensions grew in Arabia as the country became a "kleptocracy," where officials stole money on all government operations, such as oil transactions and lucrative arms deals, according to Robert Baer, a decorated, Arabic-speaking former CIA field agent. He said that on the eve of 9/11, "the royal family's grotesque corruption and thousand-and-one-nights lifestyle had started to take a real toll on the Saudi street. Popular preachers all over Saudi Arabia were openly calling for a jihad against the West—a metaphor, I assure you, that includes the royal family."[58]

The leading world exporter of petroleum, Saudi Arabia also became the world's top exporter of religious extremists, extremist ideologies, and their "by-products." With U.S. approval, the Saudis sent money and manpower for jihad against the Soviets in Afghanistan in the 1980s. The well-oiled Saudi religious machine turned into a pipeline unleashing waves of people, ideas, and money to mosques and madrassas (religious schools) around the world. Millions of dollars every year propelled the Saudi-Wahhabi vision of an as-yet-incomplete-and-therefore-unending jihad that had to continue outside Arabia and outside the Middle East. Visions of endless jihad swept aside more moderate interpretations of Islam at schools and mosques in London and Virginia, Paris and Michigan. Though only a minority perspective, Wahhabism became the establishment view in Pakistan (whose émigrés went to Britain), surged to greater popularity in Turkey (whose émigrés went to Germany), and even crested the shores of Indonesia, Malaysia, and the Philippines.[59] America helped this process along. One diversion point for Saudi religious funds was, of course, Afghanistan, where American officials encouraged contributions to those fighting the Soviet Union in the 1980s.[60] This is a facet of the narrative that some CIA and State Department officials like to forget.

Many who fought the Soviets in Afghanistan in the 1980s became popular mosque speakers in the 1990s, urging jihad in Finsbury Park in London and Atlantic Avenue in Brooklyn. After major terror attacks in New York, Madrid, and London and the abortive Southeast Asian plots (for example, the Bojinka affair, and a plan to kill Clinton), Saudi funds were traced to mosques and schools that became centers for terrorism—in London, Hamburg, and New York and New Jersey. This began well before 9/11.

A moderate Muslim preacher, Sheikh Muhammad Hisham Kabbani, told U.S. officials in 1999 that 80 percent of the mosques and Islamic charities in America had been "taken over" by extremists who were getting Saudi support and guidance.[61] Saudi funds supposedly for religious education (even though extreme education) were also siphoned into warfare, sabotage, and terror, beginning in the 1950s. The Saudis sent aid to the Muslim Brotherhood in Egypt, a group whose personnel and ideology were linked to Saudi Arabia's own Wahhabi doctrines, through the teachings of Hassan al-Banna, founder of the Muslim Brotherhood. Al-Banna was a disciple of Muhammad Rashid Rida, who studied Wahhabism in Saudi Arabia. The Egyptian Muslim Brotherhood—Ikhwan al-Muslimoun —became something like an overseas unit of Saudi's own Ikhwan shock troops of yore. This time, however, instead of flashing swords on horses in the desert wastes, Egypt's Ikhwan preached and occasionally fired revolvers, set off bombs, and carried out assassinations. Al-Banna and the Brotherhood did not see a separation between mosque and state. For them, Islam itself was a political path whose constitution was the Quran: "When asked for what it is you call, reply that it is Islam, the message of Muhammad, the religion that contains within it government. . . ."[62]

The lasting influence of al-Banna and his successor Sayyid Qutb on the doctrines and thinking of various Arab-Islamic terror groups—from Al-Qaeda to Hamas—is evident in almost all the documents issued by these groups. For example, the Hamas Charter of 1988 (slogan, and article 8) almost echoes the cadences of al-Banna in 1928: "Allah is our goal, the Prophet our model, the Quran our Constitution, Jihad our path, and death for the sake of Allah our most sublime belief."

The Brotherhood led militant Muslim groups attacking and sometimes assassinating Egyptian officials: Prime Minister Mahmoud al-Nukrashi Pasha in 1949, several failed attempts to kill Abdul-Nasser in the 1950s, and, of course, the murder of Anwar Sadat in 1981.[63] When Egypt cracked down on Brotherhood members, the Saudis welcomed them back, giving them refuge in Arabia.

"As part of his pan-Islamic outreach, King Faisal also invited into the kingdom thousands of members of the Muslim Brotherhood, the secretive fundamentalist organization that preached the destruction of secular Arab regimes."[64] This was like Dr. Frankenstein inviting home for dinner the monster he created. When Egypt executed al-Banna in 1949 and Qutb in 1966, the Saudis welcomed home Muhammad Qutb, Sayyid's brother, who became a teacher. Qutb was the beloved instructor of men who commandeered Islam's holiest shrine, the Grand Mosque, in Mecca in 1979. Qutb also taught Osama bin-Laden.

ISLAMIC CAMOUFLAGE AND CREATIVE AMBIGUITY: *TAQIYYA*

Taqiyya is a tenet of Muslim ideology and method often neglected by Westerners. A great Islamic writer said a Muslim without *taqiyya* was naked and unprotected before his enemies. "*Takiyya* is a cloak for the believer: he has no religion who has no *Takiyya*."[65] For modern Arab-Islamic terrorists, this cloak of concealment is a central part of the terrorists' arsenal. So what is it?

Originally, it is clear, *taqiyya* was a defensive idea: lying or concealing one's true identity or intentions in order not to be killed or hurt. The Quran offers a number of cases, the most famous of which is that of Ammar, son of Yasser, who pretended not to believe in Muhammad so that the pagan Arab tribesmen who captured him would not murder him, as they had murdered his parents. Muhammad forgave Ammar because he had not betrayed Islam in his heart, but only to survive. Another case of justified dissimulation in Islamic scripture is that of the Israelite high priest Aaron, who cooperated with rebellious Israelites who forged a golden calf because otherwise the rebels would have killed him.[66]

This *defensive* use of *taqiyya* is common in the lands of Islam, as when even Shiites passing through Sunni areas or Druze passing through Shiite areas (and so on) may need to "blend in," lest they be attacked or subject to persecution. Sometimes concealing one's real name and religion is a matter of life and death. In addition, a Muslim may drink wine, normally prohibited, if this is required to save one's life.[67]

Taqiyya also is used for what one might call "white lies"—stretching the truth and even lying in order to reconcile a husband and wife or two people who have had a dispute. Many guides to Islam say a Muslim may lie in order to make peace or for reconciliation, to "persuade a woman," and to save life.[68] In fact, *taqiyya* goes well beyond this approach, and it includes lying for strategic offensive purposes.

Using deception to hurt an enemy, even when one is not threatened, also appears in the Quran and in the Hadith (the oral traditions about Muhammad's life and sayings). Indeed, in the offensive mode, *taqiyya* is basically lying for the sake of Allah.

According to the Islamic tradition, the Prophet Muhammad called for volunteers to assassinate a poet, Kab bin Ashraf, who was making fun of him. Kab's stepbrother, Muhammad bin Maslama, said he would kill the poet, but asked if he could lie in order to get Kab out of his fortress. Islam's prophet replied affirmatively,[69] and he later praised the stepbrother when he brought him the head of the offensive poet.

Muhammad himself used deception several times to secure the surrender and then subsequent beheading, enslavement, or banishment of his enemies. The entire Jewish tribe Banu Qurayza (also sometimes written Kuraiza), between six hundred and nine hundred men and boys, their hands tied behind their backs, were beheaded in a daylong ceremony in the market of Medina. All women and prepubescent children of the Jewish tribe were enslaved. Muhammad chose one of the women to be one of his wives.[70]

TAQIYYA AS LYING IN WAR AND PEACE

In short, Islam's highest authority—Muhammad—justified a lie in order to kill an enemy. Muhammad used deception as a strategic device several times, and it has been cited by many Arab and Islamic political leaders. Indeed, Muslim legal scholars accept this view. For example, religious authority Imam Abu Hamid Ghazali said: "Speaking is a means to achieve objectives. If a praiseworthy aim is attainable through both telling the truth and lying, it is unlawful to accomplish through lying because there is no need for it. When it is possible to achieve such an aim by lying but not by telling the truth, it is permissible to lie if attaining the goal is permissible."[71]

A good example of a terrorist leader using Muhammad to justify his lying is Yasser Arafat. When opponents accused him of selling out the Palestinian cause, Arafat rightly cited the tactics and strategy of Muhammad, who made self-effacing concessions to his foes from the tribe of Quraysh. Later, he turned the tables on them. When Muhammad signed a truce agreement with the Quraysh, his antagonists insisted he erase the title "messenger of God." Muhammad agreed. Two years later, when he had grown stronger, Muhammad used a pretext to abrogate the treaty and to kill or enslave many of his opponents. This event is known as the Treaty of Hudaibiya. It was a strong recurring theme in many of Arafat's speeches.[72]

Arafat's use of *taqiyya* is not surprising, for many reasons. Objectively speaking, terrorists are usually weaker than the regimes they attack. Most terrorists will also contend that they were attacked or were defending themselves or their party from attack. This dovetails with the view of *taqiyya* in the defensive mode, a doctrine of self-preservation for a weak party. What is interesting is that Arafat also consciously spoke of the offensive *taqiyya* doctrine, reminding his listeners how Muhammad turned the tables on his foes when he had the upper hand, often without any mercy.

Taqiyya is often mistakenly spoken of as a tool only of Shiites, who were a minority and weaker than Sunni Muslims. As shown, *taqiyya* is widely accepted and used throughout the Sunni Muslim community—and in the aggressive and offensive mode, too. The great expert on Islamic theology Ignaz Goldziher said that it was the strategic inferiority of the Shiites that led them to stress this doctrine, which put an emphasis on "a subversive rather than a fighting propaganda."[73]

Goldziher's remark seems particularly appropriate for the changes in Arafat's media approach over the years. When Arafat had a secure physical base and believed he would win the "armed struggle" outright, he used "fighting propaganda." As it became clear he would need to wage his battle in a series of stages where he would periodically fight and periodically talk, he adopted a different strategy of propaganda. Indeed, when Arafat was getting territory from Israel, he muted his "fighting propaganda" while whispering the subversive propaganda in closed rooms or by speaking in codes or in internal memos.

Raymond Ibrahim, then the Islam specialist at the Library of Congress, said the concept of *taqiyya* is "often euphemized as 'religious dissembling,' though in reality [it] simply connotes 'Muslim deception vis-à-vis infidels.'"[74] Ibrahim, who has edited a book on the texts of statements by Osama bin-Laden and other Al-Qaeda leaders, gave long and detailed testimony on the use of *taqiyya*, to which insights Western leaders and students of Arab-Islamic terror should pay heed. He cites the view of *taqiyya* in the eyes of two of the most authoritative legal commentaries, Al-Tabari and Ibn Kathir:

> Al-Tabari's (d. 923) famous *tafsir* (exegesis of the Koran) is a standard and authoritative reference work in the entire Muslim world. Regarding [Quran verse] 3:28, he writes: "If you [Muslims] are under their [infidels'] authority, fearing for yourselves, behave loyally to them, *with your tongue*, while harboring inner animosity for them. . . . Allah has forbidden believers from being friendly or on intimate terms with the infidels in place of believers—except when infidels are above them [in authority]. In such a scenario, let them *act* friendly towards them."
>
> Regarding 3:28, Ibn Kathir (d. 1373, second in authority only to Tabari) writes, "Whoever at any time or place fears their [infidels'] evil may protect himself through outward show." As proof of this, he quotes Muhammad's close companion, Abu Darda, who said, "Let us smile to the face of some people [non-Muslims] while our hearts curse them."

Today, an especially effective method of *taqiyya* used by terrorists is medical fraud. They use ambulances to ferry arms and men, put bombs under bandages or prosthetic devices, sneaking them into hospitals in Afghanistan, Israel, or Iraq, where they blow up. Al-Qaeda, Hamas, Fatah, and Hizballah have all used this tactic.

For example, twenty-one-year-old burn victim Wafa Samir Ibrahim al-Biss tried to smuggle more than twenty pounds of explosives under her bandages in order to blow up Soroka Hospital in Beersheva, Israel, on June 20, 2005.

This tactic has another terroristic benefit. When police, soldiers, or security guards check the bandages of people going into the hospital or going through roadblocks, the terrorists have "proof" of how hard-hearted, cruel, and anti-Muslim the West is. Phony atrocity stories are another element of *taqiyya* that has become part of the standard operating procedure of Arab-Islamic terrorists.

THE MIND, THE HEART, AND THE GUTS
BEHIND THE MASK OF TERROR

"La-illaha illa allah, wa Muhammad rasuul-allah." This Arabic chant is sung from the towers of mosques throughout the world: "There is no God but God, and Muhammad is the messenger of God."

This is the heart of the Islamic faith. All Muslims and nearly all Arabs agree that there is only one God. Jews, Christians, Ahmadis, Bahai, and Druze adherents also believe in one God, but they hold a special place for a leader or prophet, for example, for Moses, Jesus, Bahu-allah, al-Nabi Shu'ayb, etc.

The problem is not primarily about belief in God but in determining who is *the messenger* of God and what is *the path* for believers to take. This disagreement reigns even inside the Muslim community, where bloody disputes have led to thousands and even millions of deaths. After Muhammad died in 632, there was an immediate and fierce struggle for power among his followers. It was an epic fight that lasted more than a hundred years, dividing the community of Islam into many factions vying to set Islam's spiritual path and its more mundane political path.

MUHAMMAD'S HERITAGE:
THE WARS INSIDE THE ARAB-ISLAMIC WORLD

No one dared to try to fill Muhammad's shoes as a prophet, because Muhammad was *hatim al-anbia'a*: the seal of the prophets, the final prophet. Rather, would-be heirs sought to interpret Muhammad's sometimes conflicting messages, and they sought to inherit his powers as a temporal ruler—*Amir al-Mu'minin*: the Prince of the Faithful.

Muhammad was not just a prophet, but a politician and a warrior who had begun to carve an empire, first conquering all of Arabia[75] and thence, through his followers, a huge empire from today's Persian Gulf all the way to the Atlantic Ocean. Unlike Jesus, Muhammad foresaw his own role as way beyond being the leader of a persecuted minority. Unlike Moses, Muhammad's goals far surpassed leading newly freed slaves to a small, promised land. In essence, Muhammad's promised land was the entire planet, and his tool was jihad.

"The basis of the obligation of *jihad* is the universality of the Muslim revelation," according to Islam historian Bernard Lewis. "God's word and God's message are for all mankind; it is the duty of those who have accepted them to strive (*jahada*) unceasingly to convert or at least to subjugate those who have not. This obligation is without limit of time or space. It must continue until the whole world has either accepted the Islamic faith or submitted to the power of the Islamic state."[76]

The late Islamic scholar Carl Brockelmann was even more direct: "The Muslim may show only hostility to infidels when encountered: war against them is a religious duty. Idol worshipers must always be attacked without more ado, Jews and Christians, however, only after they have ignored a summons, made three times, to accept Islam." Brockelmann said "the obligation of the Holy War is merely postponed" by truces with Jews and Christians.[77]

In other words, the jihad goals of bin-Laden and other Islamist terrorists—to conquer the world for Islam—are not completely foreign to the mainstream of Islam. Surveys of attitudes of Muslims in Islamic and Western countries in the last decade show large Muslim support for bin-Laden's interpretation. For example, Pew Research found 20 percent of Egyptians, 23 percent of Indonesians, and 34 percent of Jordanians held "favorable views of al Qaeda" in 2010. Right after 9/11, the support was even higher, reaching 60 percent in Jordan. In Nigeria, 49 percent supported Al-Qaeda in 2010. As for specific support for suicide bombing and attacking civilians, 20 percent of Egyptians, 20 percent of Jordanians, and 15 percent of Indonesians said they supported those acts "often" or "sometimes," as opposed to "rarely" or "never." More than 70 percent of Lebanese

Muslims backed suicide attacks in 2002.[78] Fifteen percent of Muslim Americans under age thirty said suicide bombings were justified.[79] The Pew poll figures are not unique.

Gallup surveys in the last decade show very strong unfavorable reactions to the United States and other Western countries. In Saudi Arabia, 64 percent held an unfavorable view of the United States in 2001, and this grew to 79 percent in 2005. In Jordan, 62 percent disfavor rose to 65 percent from 2001 to 2005. In Morocco, the unfavorable view of the United States went from 41 percent to 49 percent in 2001 and 2005, respectively. In Turkey, where the Islamic government grew stronger, the anti-U.S. view climbed from 33 percent to 62 percent.[80]

Given these findings, it is wrong and pathetic when Western officials or academics offer blanket apologies for all Muslims or for Islam in all forms. One prominent apologist is Karen Armstrong, whose shallow, popular books on Islam are not based on any primary research or even basic knowledge of Arabic.[81] She is not alone. In a book claiming to be based only on empirical research and the scientific method, Marc Sageman, a former CIA and State Department official, makes a rather bold statement. He contends "not only is global Islamist terrorism utterly distinct from Islam, but the Quran contains far more verses supporting peace than the very few that support violence."[82] Sageman's assertion of Islamic terror being "utterly distinct" from Islam is utterly unproven by sources in Sageman's text. His claim about Islam's overriding peaceful intentions are also not supported by evidence.[83] If Sageman were more familiar with Arab culture and the Arabic language, he probably would not have made the assertion. Even the greeting *Al-salaam 'aleikum* (peace be upon you) is *not* meant to be given to non-Muslims.[84] If a non-Muslim offers "salaam" to a Muslim, the Muslim is supposed to *not* offer it in return. Rather, he is supposed to say "peace be upon the believers" or "peace be on whosoever follows the guidance of God."[85] *Salaam*—peace—"was only for Muslims and those who embraced Islam."[86]

Years before the major Arab-Islamic terror attacks, several researchers refuted politically correct but factually inaccurate Islam-is-peace-and-never-terror assertions. Samuel Huntington, in his article, then book on "the clash of civilizations," devoted an entire section to what he called "Islam's Bloody Borders."

"Some Westerners, including President Bill Clinton, have argued that the West does not have problems with Islam but only with violent Islamist extremists," averred Huntington. "Fourteen hundred years of history demonstrate otherwise."[87]

Professor Huntington added that "wherever one looks along the perimeter of Islam, Muslims have problems living peaceably with their neighbors." Professor Philip Carl Salzman cites and endorses these germane observations by Huntington, noting how they have been confirmed (one could argue even amplified) in the wake of the September 11, 2001, attacks on the United States.[88]

> . . . The overwhelming majority of fault line conflicts, . . . have taken place along the boundary looping across Eurasia and Africa that separates Muslims from non-Muslims. . . . Intense antagonisms and violent conflicts are pervasive between local Muslim and non-Muslim peoples. . . . Muslims make up about one-fifth of the world's population, but in the 1990s they have been far more involved in inter-group violence than the people of any other civilization. The evidence is overwhelming. There were, in short, three times as many inter-civilizational conflicts involving Muslims as there were between non-Muslim civilizations. . . . Muslim states also have had a high propensity to resort to violence in international crises, employing it to resolve 76 crises out of a total of 142 in which they were involved between 1928 and 1979. . . . When they did use violence, Muslim states used high-intensity violence, resorting to full-scale war in 41 percent of the cases where violence was used and engaging in major clashes in another 39 percent of the cases. While Muslim states resorted to violence in 53.5 percent, violence was used by the United Kingdom in only 1.5 percent, by the United States in 17.9 percent, and by the Soviet Union in 28.5 percent of the crises in which they were involved. . . . Muslim bellicosity and violence are late-twentieth-century facts which neither Muslims nor non-Muslims can deny.[89]

This was written several years before major attacks on New York, London, Madrid, Mumbai, and Washington—more than a decade before Sageman's bold statement. A careful researcher on Islamic terror should pay attention to comments on the role of Islam in world conflicts from the world's best-known political scientists. Huntington's view was not unique. In 1991, British scholar Barry Buzan raised serious concerns about the inherent Islamic-Western rivalry and the potential for violence:

> By its conspicuous economic and technological success, the West makes all others look bad (i.e. underdeveloped, or backward or poor, or disorganized or repressive, or uncivilized or primitive) and so erodes their status and legitimacy. The tremendous energy, wealth, inventiveness and organizational dynamism of the West, not to mention its crass materialism and hollow consumer culture, cannot help but penetrate deeply into weaker societies worldwide. As it does so, it both inserts alien styles, concepts, ideas and aspirations—"Coca-Colaization"—and corrupts or brings into question the validity and legitimacy of local customs and identities. In the case of Islam, this threat is compounded by new patterns of global security, geographical adjacency, and historical antagonism, and also the overtly political role that Islam plays in the lives of its followers. Rivalry with the West is made more potent by the fact that Islam is still itself a vigorous and expanding collective identity. In combination, migration threats and the clash of cultures make it rather easy to draw a scenario for a kind of societal cold war between the centre and at least part of the periphery, and specifically between the West and Islam, in which Europe would be in the front line.[90]

Similarly, Steven Fish found a statistical correlation between Arab-Islamic regimes, authoritarianism, and the abuse of women.[91] None of these researchers is saying all Muslims are bad, but their findings suggest more than a casual and coincidental link between Arab-Islamic terror and a version of Islam that has many adherents within the community of Islam.

DOWNSIZING JIHAD TO FIT POLITICAL CORRECTNESS

Judaism and Christianity have the Ten Commandments. Jihad is actually the equivalent of the "eleventh commandment" of Islam. That is because Islam has "five pillars"—central religious duties. Jihad is the *sixth* pillar, but without the canonical status of the first five.[92] These five pillars— *khamsat arkaan al-Islam*—are basic commandments: (1) affirmation of faith, (2) daily prayer, (3) charity, (4) pilgrimage to Mecca, and (5) the monthlong fast of Ramadan. Jihad is the strong number six.

It is impossible to imagine the Arab tribes moving away from their traditional habits of small raids (*ghazwa*) and going on to empire building, as Islamic scholar Montgomery Watt observed, without the command of jihad. Islam's tremendous territorial expansion "from the Atlantic and the Pyrenees in the West to the Oxus and the Punjab in the East" would have been impossible politically and practically. "It seems certain that without the conception of the *jihad* that expansion would not have happened."[93] In other words, jihad was not just some esoteric notion but a clear religious and political-military duty—an offensive concept, not a defensive concept—that was repeatedly put into practice over generations. Muhammad himself is said to have participated in about six hundred battles, almost all of which were offensive, aimed at expanding the boundaries of Islam.[94] Most classical Islamic scholars say that this injunction—to expand the "house" of Islam (*dar-al-Islam*) at the expense of the realm of the nonbelievers (*dar al-harb*)—continues unabated to this day.

"Before political correctness took over, Western scholars routinely explained *jihad* as warfare to extend Muslim domains," observes Islamic scholar Daniel Pipes.[95]

This kind of plain-spoken assessment of ongoing jihad was condemned by Edward Said and avoided and obfuscated by John Esposito. They preferred not to give too clear a picture of Arab-Islamic terror, its agents, and its jihadist roots.

Today many speak and think wishfully of Islam as a religion of peace, but Islam was born in fire. It has a terrifically violent heritage from its formative period, when Muhammad consciously chose to spread Islam by the sword. The watchword for Islam in this period was *sabil allah fi-al-saif*: the path of God is by the sword.

This was the age of jihad. It is this age and this message that today's Islamists and terrorists have stressed and copied. Whether they identify as followers of Osama bin-Laden's Al-Qaeda, Arafat's Fatah, Hamas, or the pro-Iranian Hizballah, they call their dead agents *shouhada*—martyrs. They do not think of themselves as fundamentalist Muslims but as being "fundamentally Muslim" or "true Muslims."[96] We can call them "jihadis" or "salafists" or "neo-jihadis" or whatever, but they think they are returning Islam to its true, original, and triumphant path.

Another factor promoting the violent heritage in the lands of Islam was that Islam's messenger did not leave a clear law of succession. The four men who succeeded Muhammad in leading the Muslim community as caliphs[97] were known as "the righteous caliphs"—*al-rashidoun*—but at least three of the four were assassinated, all of them at prayer or as they entered a mosque.[98] This was only a small part of the violent heritage bequeathed by Muhammad, and early Islamic violence has left a huge rift inside the community of the Islamic faithful. About 20 percent of the Islamic community today are patrons of Ali, the fourth caliph, who was the nephew and son-in-law of Muhammad. They even call themselves Shiite or Shia—which is short for *shi'at Ali*: the faction of Ali.[99] Ali was brutally murdered, as was his son Hussein, and today's Shiites mark the martyrdom of both men.

Today, glib politicians and superficial journalists[100] make one-to-one comparisons between the lives and teachings of Muhammad-Jesus-Moses on one hand and the faith of Islam-Judaism-Christianity on the other. However, the milieu and evolution of the faiths are quite different. Muhammad serves as a role model for Muslims far beyond what Moses or Jesus can be for Jews and Christians. Some Christians may say, "What would Jesus do?" and Jews habitually study biblical accounts of prophets and patriarchs, analyzing their mistakes or faults as told in scripture or in legend. But there is no detailed record of their lives. For many Muslims there is a record of Muhammad, and it is unthinkable to criticize Muhammad or his actions. Those who are critical are often condemned to punishment and even death.

Muslims are expected to emulate Muhammad's *sunnah*—his customs and habits—in ways that Jesus and Moses cannot be emulated. We have, however, pretty detailed biographical accounts of Muhammad written and passed down by contemporary chroniclers. These accounts form the body of *hadith*—"traditions" of Muhammad and contemporaries, what one scholar calls "a veritable record of Muhammad's activities."[101] We know how many women he married (and at what ages), what he took as booty in war, and even the punishments he meted out to those who insulted him. Muhammad had several poets murdered because they satirized him. An old woman, Umm Qirfa, was brutally executed for cursing him: she was ripped in half, her limbs tied to two camels driven in opposite directions. Since Muhammad killed those who satirized him, it is clear why many Muslims believe any satirizing of Muhammad and any skeptical commentary in newspapers, books, or movies is a capital crime. Almost any treatment of Muhammad beyond the classical Islamic view of Muhammad can be very dangerous. That is why Yale University Press published a book about the controversy over Danish newspaper cartoons of Muhammad *without the cartoons.* European politicians and filmmakers who criticize Muhammad or radical Islam have been attacked, have had to hire bodyguards, or have been forced to leave Europe.[102]

Islam means submission—man to God, but in the Islamist view, it also means submission of non-Muslims to Muslims. Islam's prophet was not someone to turn the other cheek, as Jesus taught his followers. Nor did Muhammad ask God to pick someone else to be the prophet or to do the job, as Moses, Elijah, and later, Jonah, did.[103] Muhammad did not shy away from power. He wielded power. Muhammad also envisioned limitless vistas for his faithful, not a clearly demarcated home for his faithful, as Moses preached for Israel. In classical terms, Islam is a religion that tries to convert the world, and if necessary, by the sword.

Yes, after about 150 years of conquest and battles, the jihad relaxed. Treatment of non-Muslims within the realm of Islam also improved. Despite persecution, non-Muslims under Islam (though treated as second-class *dhimmis*) fared better than non-Christians in Christendom.[104] But in those periods, Islam was confident and triumphant, while Christendom was backward and in retreat. Today the Arab-Islamic world is not the pride of the planet in any field. The UN's Arab Human Development Report, compiled by Arab intellectuals, shows that "Arab societies are being crippled by a lack of political freedom, the repression of women and an isolation from the world of ideas that stifles creativity."[105] Literacy levels and freedom levels are lower even than in Africa. The UN report, issued in 2002, noted a lack of curiosity and readiness to learn from others. For example, the entire Arab World (300 million people) translated into Arabic less than one-fifth the number of books that Greece (with a population of 11 or 12 million) translated into Greek. To say these things is not to be anti-Arab or anti-Muslim. Charles Issawi, a prominent Arab historian, compared Western

readiness to learn from Arabs and Muslims with the dearth of Arab intellectual curiosity and mental insularity.[106] Nevertheless, many Muslims
want intellectual exploration, and they are willing, even eager, to learn from
Western ideas and experience. We see this manifested in the tempestuous
antigovernment protests of 2009 and 2011 in Iran and Egypt as well as
in earlier demonstrations in 1991. This yearning was also visible in early-
twentieth-century political and literary modernization movements[107] and
in recent articles and books produced in the Arab-Islamic world.[108] Clearly,
many Arabs and Muslims do not wish to return blindly to the first years of
Islam, slavishly imitating the *salaf*—the cohort around Muhammad. But
many Muslims—perhaps many more Muslims—disagree.

"Modern and contemporary Arab discourse," as one student of Arab
thought perceived, "is in truth a discourse of memory, not a discourse of
reason."[109]

How many are there in each camp? We do not know. One prominent
scholar of Islam has suggested that 15 percent of the world's Muslim
population holds Islamist—radical Islamic—views, such as wanting to
impose Shariah, Islamic religious law, on society.[110] The 15 percent figure
is a sensible estimate, but Pew organization polls cited earlier suggest that
the Islamist tendencies may be higher. If 20 percent or more in Jordan or
Egypt hold such views, hard-core Wahhabi areas such as Saudi Arabia
and Pakistan (where bin-Laden had many backers even inside the government) may be two or three times that high. These figures may actually *understate* the problem, because people being surveyed in the Arab-Islamic
sphere often hide their true views, especially when talking to foreigners.
This does not translate into immediate support for terror, because there is
no one-to-one correlation between Islamist views and support for terror,
but there appears to be a strong link. If even *only* 15 percent support Al-
Qaeda and suicide terror, this means one in seven Muslims support terror.
If the true figure for Islamist belief is 15 percent pro-Islamist, then, in a
world of 300 million Arabs and 1.3 to 1.6 billion Muslims, there are huge
numbers of people who can form the base for terror acts.

Yet these numbers are not astounding, because they reflect unsurpris-
ing attitudes held by established Islamic jurists applauding terror. Scholars
at Cairo's Al-Azhar University, the foremost Islamic center in the Sunni
world, have stated:

He who sacrifices himself [a *fidaai*] is he who gives his soul in order to come closer to Allah and to protect the rights, respect and land of the Muslims. . . . On the other hand, he who commits suicide loses his soul and kills himself, because of his desperation . . . and in order to escape from life, and not for a higher goal, whether religious or national, or for the sake of the liberation of his robbed land. . . . When the Muslims are attacked in their homes and their land is robbed, the Jihad for Allah turns into an individual duty. In this case, operations of martyrdom become a primary obligation and Islam's highest form of Jihad.

"These operations are the supreme form of Jihad for the sake of Allah," declared Sheikh Yousef Qaradhawi, perhaps the most influential Muslim jurist in the world. Qaradhawi cited a verse in the Quran stating that one must be prepared to "spread fear among one's enemies and the enemies of Allah." Sheikh Qaradhawi is a member of the Muslim Brotherhood and head of Islamic studies at the University of Qatar. His speeches are seen and heard by millions on Al Jazeera satellite TV. The sheikh says "the term 'suicide operations' is an incorrect and misleading term, because these are heroic operations of martyrdom,[111] and have nothing to do with suicide. The mentality of those who carry them out has nothing to do with the mentality of someone who commits suicide."[112] Sheikh Qaradhawi is enunciating what is in the hearts and minds of many Muslims: what Westerners call "suicide attacks" are, in many Muslim eyes, "glorious and heroic acts" when non-Muslims are attacked for the sake of Allah.

Addressing these thoughts may not be politically correct, but it is strategically prudent. Confronting these ideas is important. Wishful thinking is the worst guide for strategic planning, and we must keep hard facts and realistic fears in mind when trying to find solutions to the Arab-Islamic terror situation.

TRIBALISM AND THE CULTURE OF VIOLENCE

Before Arab nationalism and before Islam, the areas we now call the Arab-Islamic world were governed by a set of codes that are still influential today. When you hear Arab statesmen speak of "honor" or "revenge," or when we see a multimillion-dollar Arab television network dispensing the flowery Arabic of bin-Laden on videocassettes, they are all paying homage to a pre-Islamic and prenational culture whose codes might best be called "tribal." When a Muslim in Missouri or New Jersey, or in a British suburb or an Israeli Arab town, slaughters a daughter or sister who wanted to date boys or wear nontraditional dress, the murder is not committed out of Arab nationalist ideology or Islamic ideology or law,[113] but rather out of something deeper, much more primitive, and probably more lasting: tribalism.

Among pre-Islamic Arab tribes, one of the highest forms of entertainment was reciting poetry recounting great feats or warning an enemy. Bin-Laden's taped messages recall this motif. For the Bedouins, who were the original Arabs, when someone in the family has been killed, wounded, or insulted by a neighbor, there is a "group debt" or a "blood debt" that is not going to be settled by any Arab government or any Islamic *kadi,* or "religious judge." The aggrieved clan or the *hamoulah* avenges the injury or death by exacting retribution, unless the offending family agrees to a stylized admission of guilt and a monetary payment as part of a *sulhah*— literally a peace settlement. This is a primitive but effective doctrine of group responsibility and group deterrence under which "all group members may be called to fight in order to defend a member in a conflict, or to seek vengeance in the case of loss of property, injury, or death, or to pay compensation in the case of a group member causing injury to another, or would be a legitimate target for a member of the opposing group."[114]

This tribal code is not usually discussed in government position papers or university courses, but it is still very real. The 2011 upheavals in Libya, Syria, and Yemen are all about tribal divisions, not just political differences. This is the tectonically unstable ground on which much of the modern Middle East is built. Tribalism is a major reason certain aspects of modern statehood—tax collection, building codes, sewage disposal, law enforcement—have never worked or have collapsed in many areas of the Mideast. Tribalism is a force often greater than state agencies in many Mideast countries, and its power often exceeds that of even the most venerated religious authority.

The lasting frameworks and customs of tribal society explain why even countries whose educational and legal systems were established by European powers regressed so quickly after achieving independence, according to anthropologist Philip C. Salzman:

Tribes operate quite differently from states, which are centralized, have political hierarchies, and have specialized institutions—such as courts, police, and an army, with tax collectors providing the means of support. . . . Members of tribal societies understandably resisted being incorporated into states, preferring their independent and egalitarian communal lives to exploitation by an arrogant and brutal elite.[115]

What Salzman calls "the tribal spirit" produces an "us-versus-them" mentality that he says instills "rule by group loyalty, rather than rule by rules." This undermines modern concepts such as civil society, encourages factionalism, and spurs a predilection to despotism and "might makes right."[116] Salzman sees Islam as preserving many tribal elements.[117] Journalist Lee Smith sees Arab nationalism "as a tribal pact raised to a supranational level: in projecting unity, it seeks to obscure local enmities and keep Arabs from making war against each other."

In brief, the Arab-Islamic community is still driven by a kind of tribal behavior, an unspoken but well-understood tribal ideology. The fourteen centuries of Islam and the decades of Arab nationalistic rhetoric have sublimated, but not eliminated, this factor. Arab-Islamic terrorists who feel they do not need to answer any man-made law may actually be heeding a kind of tribal code of their own.

CONNECTING IDEOLOGIES AND TERRORISTS

What is the common ground between the Arab-Islamic ideologies and the personal mind-sets of the Arab-Islamic terrorists?

These worldviews try to recapture, as one historian observed, "the power and glory [that] has passed from the Moslem East to the Christian West."[118] The cure for what ails the Arab-Islamic world, these ideologies assert, is, in historian Albert Hourani's phrase, a "return to the institutions of the real or imagined golden age."[119]

This quest for something that is missing or lost on the national or communal level may dovetail with a personal quest by a terrorist trying to capture a sense of glory, a sense of belonging, or simply to remove a stain on reputation (as seen in the cases of women suicide bombers). Most serious academic and professional studies make clear that bombers are not throwing their lives away out of increasing suicidal impulses. We are not witnessing sharp increases in the incidence of suicides in Afghanistan, Iraq, Pakistan, or Gaza. We do not see people hanging themselves, taking poison, or slashing veins in bathtubs, etc. There are no signs supporting the frequently cited conventional wisdom that terrorists are motivated by frustration and deprivation.

Generally, terrorists are *not* driven by poverty or sadness over social deprivation. Many terrorists are well-to-do—not just leaders like Osama bin-Laden and Ayman Zawahiri—but also terrorists in the field. What motivates them, what they *need*, is an ideology. It needs to be a socially approved ideology, as Mia Bloom suggests—an ideology with significant community backing. This is a primary need, not a secondary factor, as claimed by Sageman. A reinforcing social network helps, as Sageman observes, but it is not necessary, especially not in the case of "lone wolves."

Ignoring or downplaying ideology, however, actually increases the danger of terror.

POLITICAL CORRECTNESS AS
AN IDEOLOGY TEACHING US TO IGNORE IDEOLOGY

Ignoring or belittling the extremist ideologies sparking terrorism is itself an ideology—the Western ideology of political correctness. This ideology has already cost many lives, according to a bipartisan Senate investigative report released in February 2011. The Senate Homeland Security Committee report was largely ignored by top Western media. It said the Fort Hood terror attack of November 2009 could have been prevented easily, if officials in the FBI, the army, and the Defense Department had not been guided by political correctness.[120]

The ninety-one-page report painstakingly showed how Major Nidal Hasan had bragged about his ideological leanings. Far worse, he had been in continuing contact with terrorists who were already part of several U.S. government probes.[121] The report said U.S. officials were willfully oblivious to a massacre in the making. In effect, the Senate report said politically correct U.S. officials had blood on their hands.

"This is not a case where a lone wolf was unknown to the FBI and the Department of Defense," asserted Senator Susan Collins, the top minority Republican on the committee. Major Hasan's extremely bizarre behavior over several years reached the attention of a joint agency terror task force that produced "a woefully inadequate investigation" lasting three or four hours, said Collins, adding that the heart of the matter was an unwillingness to face and to name an ideological danger.

"Our investigation found that employees of the Department of Defense and the FBI had compelling evidence of Nidal Hasan's growing embrace of violent Islamist extremism in the years before the attack that should have caused him to be dismissed from the military," declared Senator Joseph Lieberman, chairman of the Homeland Security Committee. Hasan, he said, because of his contact with known terrorists, should have been regarded as "a clear and present danger" or "a ticking bomb." Instead, he was promoted.

"America's enemy today is not terrorism or a particular terrorist organization or a particular religion. The enemy is the ideology, the political ideology of violent Islamist extremism," declared Lieberman. "The ideology that inspired 9/11 and other attacks and plots around the world continues to motivate individuals to commit terrorism, and that now increasingly includes Americans both inside and outside America—people we now call homegrown terrorists."

Lieberman said the United States needed to confront the rising threat of ideologically driven homegrown terror, despite criticism from some Muslim groups who felt American Muslims were being scapegoated. "Unless you know your enemy and describe it," he said, "you are not going to be able to meet it and defeat it."[122]

Lieberman and Collins said many U.S. government agencies were careful not to mention the term *Islam* in their discussions. As columnist Dorothy Rabinowitz observed, "In November 2010, each branch of the military issued a final report on the Fort Hood shooting. Not one mentioned the perpetrator's ties to radical Islam."[123]

Several European leaders have recently shown that they are moving away from the politically correct path that avoids criticizing Islamic extremism and has instead enshrined it as part of multiculturalism. German chancellor Angela Merkel, French president Nicolas Sarkozy, and British prime minister David Cameron, each of whom has a large Muslim minority in their country, have now said that path is a dead end.

After the London bombings, then–prime minister Tony Blair said the war with Arab-Islamic terror was a battle whose roots were ideological:

"This is the battle that must be won, a battle not just about the terrorist methods but their views. Not just their barbaric acts, but their barbaric ideas. Not only what they do but what they think and the thinking they would impose on others."[124] Fortunately, a growing number of Western leaders is starting to recognize ideology as a key to Arab-Islamic terror. To fight terror we need also to combat these ideological motivators directly in what has sometimes been called the battle of ideas. We will discuss some of them briefly in our summary of prospective solutions in this book's final chapter.

8

COUNTRY CASE STUDIES:
OPERATIVE LESSONS

Before we explore operative solutions, we must pause and ask what can be learned from the experiences of individual countries battling terror around the world. This chapter is not meant as an exhaustive study. It surveys the history and anti-terror policy of several states, drawing salient practical lessons from them.

Europe is both the cradle and crossroads of Western civilization, but it is also the incubator, cradle, and way station for Arab-Islamic terror aimed at the West. However, terror attacks in India, Bali, Kenya, the Philippines, and Argentina show that Arab-Islamic terror has also reached diverse parts of Asia, Africa, and South America.

TERROR IN WESTERN EUROPE: AN OVERVIEW

Well before Al-Qaeda sparked the terror millennium in September 2001, terrorists of many stripes frequented Europe's corridors and alleyways. From the nineteenth century through the end of the twentieth, terror was advanced by anarchists, separatists, Nazis, and communists, from Russia and Italy to Germany and Spain. Among these terrorists were Italy's Red Brigades, Germany's Baader-Meinhof gang, the Irish Republican Army, and the Basque ETA. Some of them formed working partnerships with

Arab terror groups in the late 1960s and into the 1970s. As Europe grew more dependent on Arab oil and more supportive of Arab-Islamic political tendencies, it sometimes saluted Arab goals by winking at Arab terror and releasing terrorists captured by Britain, France, Germany, Italy, and other countries. In the 1980s, Europe appeased Arab terror often. Libyan despot Muammar Qadhafi bragged about using Libya's embassies in Europe—known as "people's bureaus"—to murder Libyan dissidents abroad. "In 1980 alone 11 persons were killed in 14 separate incidents carried out by Libya in 11 different countries."[1] In 1984, Qadhafi's "diplomats" in the London embassy shot at street demonstrators, killing a British policewoman, Yvonne Fletcher. In 1986, Syrian diplomats helped Nizar Hindawi, who tried putting a bomb on an El Al plane in London, but the device was intercepted. Britain broke diplomatic ties with Libya and Syria "but there was never any prospect that EC [European Community] partners would follow suit."[2]

As Europe grew slavishly reliant on Arab oil, it also grew more reliant on Arab-Islamic sources of labor: workers from Algeria and Morocco in France and Spain, from Pakistan and India in Britain, and from Turkey in Germany. "Europe is not the central focus of the jihad," said a Spanish official, but "it is an increasingly attractive arena for recruitment in Muslim communities and theatre for operations against the allies of the United States." Moreover, "it is this intersection between jihadism and immigration that makes jihadism a formidable threat."[3]

Today's Europe prides itself on free movement, and today's terrorist thrives on it. Open borders are meant to show that the great conventional wars of the past are indeed a thing of the past. However, the wars of the twenty-first century are likely to be dominated by terror—not large nation-state armies trampling borders by invading, but small terror groups without uniforms going under and over the fence. This creates a mental hurdle for European opinion makers—government, academia, and media—because they have framed terror as a police/law enforcement issue, and, after all, "terrorists can go across borders, but police do not go across borders."[4]

Borders signal nationalism, and Europe, scarred by two great twentieth-century wars, avoids strident nationalism. The European Union (EU) has a common flag and a common currency. Open borders aspire to a brighter, peaceful future. Open borders also frame an EU anti-terror approach that is less militant and less military than the U.S. or Israeli mind-set. This prompts some to ask, "Is Europe soft on terror?"[5]

The answer is not simple. European leaders like to explore diplomatic options when facing terror.[6] The U.S. approach, first enunciated by President Richard Nixon, is "we don't talk to terrorists"—a claim that has been broken many times. Both Europe and America talk to terrorists all the time. Recently, U.S. forces in Afghanistan badly bungled an effort to talk to a supposed Taliban leader who was actually an impostor. Today, European leaders are less willing "to make deals with terrorists" than they were in the 1970s–90s, but the United States talks more to terrorists than it wants to admit,[7] and it has made deals of which it is ashamed.[8]

Still, there are contrasts in European and American views of counterterrorism. The United States wants "to deliver," while Europe wants "to deliberate." Europe prefers the multilateral approach. The United States wants to lead, or, if needed, "to go it alone." Europeans used to call this "Americans playing cowboy." U.S. officials used to say Europeans treat terrorists like hot potatoes, releasing them or moving them anywhere else so as not to be burned themselves. Europeans sometimes say the United States bites off more than it can chew. This is not just rhetoric. It is reflected in policy.

In 1986, after Libya targeted Americans in Europe, President Ronald Reagan ordered attacks on Qadhafi's Libya. No NATO country except Britain allowed U.S. aircraft to refuel for the attack. In another example, Secretary of State Madeleine Albright chided Germany and Italy for not capturing Abdullah Ocalan, the Kurdish terror leader, when they had the chance. "Implicit in Albright's message was a warning against a return to patterns of behavior that prevailed throughout the 1970s and 1980s, when Europe, fearful of potential reprisals, seemed more inclined to provide a safe haven for international terrorists than to seek their apprehension."[9]

In 1996, America clashed publicly with both France and Germany over this issue at the Group of Seven summit meeting of foreign and security ministers held in Paris. Although the conference produced a 25-point multilateral program to counter terrorism, America's initial insistence on measures to isolate state sponsors of terrorism such as Iran, Iraq, Libya, and Sudan cast a cloud over the proceedings. Members of the French delegation in particular chided their American counterparts for being preoccupied with "old forms" of terrorism—arguing that state-sponsored terrorism was no longer the menace that the Americans portrayed it to be. From France's point of view, loose associations of self-funded, transnational groups, such as radical Islamic cells, encapsulated the "new forms" of terrorism against which the West must prepare. Although largely dismissed at the time, this argument proved to be remarkably prescient given the meteoric rise of bin-Laden and his transnational Al Qaeda network.[10]

After 9/11, joint U.S.-EU anti-terror policy improved, but some habits persist. In 2010, the EU suspended the Terrorist Finance Tracking Program monitoring bank data of suspected terror-linked money transfers. EU officials haggled for seven months about resuming the program that already had captured terrorists, such as the leader of the 2002 Bali terror attack that murdered 202 people and wounded 240.[11]

After credible warnings of imminent attacks on targets in Europe in autumn 2010, the United States quickly issued alerts, but some EU states hesitated. These are clear contrasts in approach and enforcement, especially in the area of borders and cross-border travel.

"Al Qaeda [also] exploited relatively lax internal security environments in Western countries, especially Germany," stated the 9/11 Commission Report.[12] The 9/11 plotters set their operations base, later known as the "Hamburg Cell," in Germany, before moving to the United States. Other Al-Qaeda plots were based on loose security and pre-check-in procedures between Europe and North America, especially from Britain to the United States. Easy travel within Europe (and then to Asia and North America) has been exploited in major terror attacks such as the 2004 Madrid train bombings and the 2005 London transport bombings, as well as in the aborted millennium bombing of Los Angeles International Airport. Terrorists can go from Greece on the Mediterranean to Britain, France, and Norway on the Atlantic with scarce inspections.

European security officials face a huge challenge, because it is relatively easy to mount a huge threat in Europe today. Arab-Islamic terrorists do not have to mass armies the way the Ottomans besieged the gates of

Vienna in 1529 or 1683. After all, there are large Arab-Islamic populations already inside Europe's gates.

The mostly nonviolent European Muslims have not assimilated
into European life. They do not flow in the European mainstream, but
stand apart as rocky islands of sullen separatism, easy targets for extremist manipulators. Foreign Islamist leaders, such as Turkish leader Recep
Erdogan, actually abet separatism of Muslims.[13] Other Islamists go further. Iran's leaders exhort Muslim immigrants to remake Europe into an
Islamic republic, and the Islamist fascination with Europe goes beyond
speeches. More than five thousand veterans of the anti-Soviet Afghan
jihad came to Europe to fight in and re-Islamize Bosnia, hoping it would
be a takeoff point for the rest of Europe.[14]

The root of Europe's Islamic crisis is that Europe's Muslims do not
share the European dream. Most have rejected the European idea of a
modern and multicultural life, as German chancellor Merkel recently asserted. They live in separate, crime-ridden communities often off-limits
to outsiders, alienated from their host country. Well-financed forces want
to recruit these Muslims for battle against the "decadent West." On Internet sites, they warmly encourage terror, even offering ways to assault
or kill politicians. In May 2010, a young British Muslim woman, Rosho-
nara Choudhry, answered the call, stabbing parliament member Stephen
Timms twice in the stomach as he met constituents one-on-one in his
office.[15]

"We ask Allah for her action to inspire Muslims to raise the knife of
Jihad," declared one website that, like others, had published "hit lists" of
European politicians or businesspeople deemed legitimate targets for Eu-
ropean Muslims.[16] In some European countries, radical mosque preachers
publicly recruit volunteers and solicit money for holy war. Meanwhile,
Islamic voting blocs have reached 5 and 10 percent of the total population.
This inhibits European politicians, wary of losing major voter blocs, from
acting strongly against those supporting jihad.

"Europe has become an incubator for Islamist thought and political
development," says Lorenzo Vidino, an Italian scholar who specializes in
radical Islam. "Since the early 1960s, Muslim Brotherhood members and
sympathizers have moved to Europe and slowly but steadily established
a wide and well-organized network of mosques, charities, and Islamic

organizations." Muslim militants have seized leadership slots. "Unlike the larger Islamic community," their aim was not simply "to help Muslims 'be the best citizens they can be,' but rather to extend Islamic law through-out Europe and the United States."[17] From London to Berlin and from Lille to Bosnia, these radical Muslim leaders also specialize in the art of *taqiyya*[18]—the Islamic tenet of camouflage, dissembling, and even outright deceit when dealing with non-Muslims.

"With moderate rhetoric and well-spoken German, Dutch, and French, they have gained acceptance among European governments and media alike," says Vidino. "Politicians across the political spectrum rush to engage them whenever an issue involving Muslims arises or, more pa-rochially, when they seek the vote of the burgeoning Muslim community. But, speaking Arabic or Turkish before their fellow Muslims, they drop their facade and embrace radicalism."[19]

To a great extent, Europe brought this danger upon itself. From the 1960s to today, Europe's political and academic elites appeased even the most radical elements in the Arab-Islamic world. These run the gamut of the Sunni-Shiite spectrum from oil-rich Saudis who finance and train the most rabid mosque speakers to the ayatollahs in Iran who export ter-rorists. Indeed, revolutionary leader Ruhollah Khomeini found refuge and freedom to plan the Iranian Revolution while living in France. What caused Europe to open its doors to Arab-Islamic extremism and terror?

Europe sought "a cheap solution to protect itself from Arab terrorism; for assuring its energy supplies; dominating Arab markets; and turning Arab jihadists against Israel and the USA by adopting" a pro-Arab-Islamic stance, especially on Arab-Israeli affairs.[20] With growing depen-dence on Middle Eastern oil and labor, and with growing Arab-Islamic militancy, Europe's leaders surrendered to oil's crude clout. Beginning in 1967, Charles de Gaulle led Europe as it embraced the Arab-Islamic world, kissing it on both cheeks. De Gaulle also denounced what was most unpopular among Muslims and Arabs—Israel and America:

> His verbal attacks against Israel sometimes included anti-Semitic state-ments. In his press conference on 27 November that year, de Gaulle called the Jews "an elitist and domineering people" in a much-publicized remark. This is often considered the post-Holocaust reintroduction of

anti-Semitism at the highest levels of mainstream European democratic society. With this breaking of the postwar taboo, de Gaulle paved the way for other European statesmen who would go much further in later years. Greek Socialist Prime Minister Andreas Papandreou, and Swedish Socialist Olaf Palme on his way to the prime ministership [*sic*], would compare Israelis to Nazis by 1982.[21]

Arab terrorists were freed from jails in France, Britain, and Germany. Even in 2010, Britain released a Libyan terrorist convicted of murdering 270 people—"for health reasons." Simultaneously, some European states (for example, Britain and Belgium) allowed prosecutors or citizens to file arrest warrants or charges against officials from Israel and America for fighting, respectively, Hamas terror in Gaza or Al-Qaeda in Iraq.

Europe's face changed. Huge populations of Muslim workers drawn from Morocco to Turkey supplanted Europe's own aging and dwindling population, replacing natives who were decreasingly productive and re-productive. Entire sections of cities, from London and Malmo (Sweden) to Paris and Berlin, became enclaves of Muslim foment, crime, and anti-Western hatred. The most common name for boys born in Europe is no longer Bill or Jack or Guillaume or Jacques. It is Muhammad.

Egyptian-born writer Bat Yeor foretold this scenario years ago. She saw Europe morphing into Eurabia, a continent that grew more Arab-Islamic politically and demographically. European elites dismissed Bat Yeor's idea as a preposterous myth or conspiracy theory. The *Economist* of London called it scare-mongering,[22] but after the terror attacks in London and Madrid in 2004 and 2005, Bat Yeor's idea, says historian Niall Ferguson, "seems somewhat less risible."

> A hundred years ago—when Europe's surplus population was still cross-ing the oceans to populate America and Australasia—the countries that make up today's European Union accounted for around 14 percent of the world's population. Today that figure is down to around 6 percent, and by 2050, according to a United Nations forecast, it will be just over 4 percent. The decline is absolute as well as relative. Even allowing for immigration, the United Nations projects that the population of the current European Union members will fall by around 7.5 million over

the next 45 years. There has not been such a sustained reduction in the European population since the Black Death of the 14th century.[23]

Many European Muslim communities display a confidence reaching bravado. Aggressively recruiting religious converts from local European populations, they unabashedly try to Islamize local laws and education systems, boasting in public demonstrations that Islam will conquer Europe. Some threaten a sad fate for Jews.

"There are already areas in France, Belgium, the Netherlands, Germany, and Britain where Muslim children constitute the majority of the school population. In addition, there are growing numbers of converts to Islam in major European countries such as France and Britain—50,000 in each in the past decade."[24]

BRITAIN

Shakespeare described Britain as a "teeming womb of royal kings,"[25] but today the British Isles are teeming with Arab-Islamic terrorists and sympathizers. In 2004, "a British government report estimated that between 10,000 and 15,000 British Muslims are supporters of Al Qaeda or related groups," declared Peter Bergen, an investigative journalist, after the London attacks in 2005.[26] British writer Melanie Phillips restated that estimate in 2006, when she observed, "According to British officials, up to sixteen thousand British Muslims either are actively engaged in or support terrorist activity, while up to three thousand are estimated to have passed through al-Qaeda training camps, with several hundred thought to be primed to attack the United Kingdom."[27] This later estimate may still be too low. Bergen says the earlier estimate was "based on intelligence, opinion polls and a report that 10,000 Muslims attended a 2003 conference held by Hizb ut-Tahrir, described by the Home Office as a 'structured extremist organization.'" Bergen, who was raised in Britain, cited "Britain's relatively permissive asylum laws" allowing the entry of Arab-Islamic fighters from Afghanistan. As a result, "Arab militants living in London sometimes jokingly refer to their hometown as Londonistan."[28]

When British author Salman Rushdie published *The Satanic Verses* in 1988, Iran's leader Ayatollah Khomeini pronounced him an apostate to Islam. Iran put a price on his head. British Muslims in the town of

Bradford protested against Rushdie, and they staged a ritual burning of Rushdie's book, demanding the author's death or trial for "blasphemy." It was a moment that defined the radical Islamization of Britain.

For Britain's Muslims, it was a time to step out of the closet, to be proud. Conversely, for many British non-Muslims, it was a time to shrink back into the shadows, backing away from confronting the emerging power of Muslims in the United Kingdom, some of whom were protesting publicly and loudly, demanding the death, no less, of a noted British author. British Muslims themselves said it was their "defining moment," crystallizing a sense of community and political power. The Muslim Council of Britain (MCB), which grew out of the UK Action Committee on Islamic Affairs (UKACIA), described its own development:

> The UK Action Committee on Islamic Affairs (UKACIA) was formed in September 1988 in the wake of the publication by Viking Penguin of Rushdie's profane and abusive book "The Satanic Verses." At about the same time, a federation of the Khoja Shia Ithna-Asheri Communities (KSIMC) was formally instituted. The Muslim Parliament, which grew out of the Muslim Institute for Research and Planning, was launched in 1992. Thus by the mid-1990s, a variety of representative bodies had evolved within the British Muslim community to respond to both general and specific concerns and crises. The need to coordinate efforts on wider issues of common concern became apparent in the course of the Rushdie affair.[29]

Even more striking than the bald incitement to kill Rushdie, a British subject, was the fact that British elites largely excused, minimized, or overlooked the organized call for the murder of an innocent man. This again happened in September 2011, when a British Muslim group issued a not-too-veiled threat to British singer Cheryl Cole for the "crime" of entertaining British troops in Afghanistan: "We say to Cheryl Cole that if you cherish your life, you should dissociate yourself from the British army and its occupation in Afghanistan, condemn the British government for its murderous war in Afghanistan and demand that all British troops withdraw from Muslim Lands." Can one imagine what Americans would have done if a U.S. protest group had threatened Bob Hope and his troupes entertaining American soldiers in Vietnam? But British elites did not jump to defend Cheryl Cole in 2011, just as Prince Charles did not defend one of his subjects from the threats of a foreign tyrant in 1988. Rather than defend Rushdie's freedom of speech, Charles reacted to the death decree by reflecting on the positive features that Islam had to offer the spiritually empty lives of his countrymen. In one speech, Prince Charles held up Muslim states as good examples of fair treatment of women: "Islamic countries like Turkey, Egypt and Syria gave women the vote as early as Europe did its women—and much earlier than in Switzerland! In those countries women have long enjoyed equal pay, and the opportunity to play a full working role in their societies."[30]

Sadly, Prince Charles is not alone in this tendency to excuse tyrants and terrorists. Leading members of the British ruling class—the media and government—consistently blame Britain and its policies (social welfare, foreign support for the United States and Israel[31]) for the unrepentant and repeated calls for violence by a sizable portion of British Muslims. A parliamentary report in September 2009 said "a failed social policy" caused Muslim militancy. It argued that monitoring Muslim extremists "threatens to alienate already marginalized Muslim communities from mainstream society."[32] Some pushy politicians eagerly embraced the extremists who were tied to the Muslim Brotherhood and pushed them to leadership positions in the Muslim Council of Britain.

"The idea was taken up with particular alacrity by Jack Straw, always with an eye to his Muslim constituents in Blackburn," wrote British journalist Martin Bright. When the MCB was officially founded in November 1997, "Straw championed its cause, first as Home Secretary and then, after the 2001 election, as Foreign Secretary."[33] The MCB itself, Bright proved, was driven by leaders wedded to an extremist version of Islam that had arisen in Pakistan: "Iqbal Sacranie, the recently retired head of the MCB, and its press spokesman Inayat Bunglawala have both expressed their admiration for Maulana Maududi, the founder of Pakistan's Jamaat-e-Islami party which is committed to the establishment of an Islamic state ruled by Sharia law." Documents leaked to Bright from inside the British Foreign Office showed that many civil servants were troubled that the British government, both in foreign and domestic affairs, was "pursuing a policy of appeasement towards radical Islam that could have grave consequences for Britain."[34] Other signs of an Islamized England include:

- The British press has reported that some British schools have cut back on study of the Holocaust, lest this offend Muslims, though UK education authorities say the reports were exaggerated.[35]
- Muslim bus and cab drivers warn the blind not to bring "unclean" dogs on board.[36]
- One London neighborhood is mandating the use of only halal meat in its schools, and British Airways is considering a similar decision, as well as allowing Muslim crew members to wear veils, but not permitting crucifixes on Christian staff.[37]

Rather than restraining violent radical Muslim activities, security officials and politicians have bent over backward to allow them, according to the *Sunday Times*: "Scotland Yard has bowed to Islamic sensitivities and accepted that Muslims are entitled to throw shoes in ritual protest—which could have the unintended consequence of politicians or the police being hit."[38] British comedians say they fear making certain jokes, lest they be attacked by Muslims, hardly an idle threat. A Dutch filmmaker was murdered, and Danish cartoonists have been attacked by European Muslims. Meanwhile, inside British prisons, already a growing source of radical Islamic manpower (for example, the 2001 "shoe bomber," Richard Reid), Muslim gangs regularly force inmates into Islamic practices and even conversion.

England's Muslims are confident and get policy initiatives passed on their behalf, because they are the fastest growing community in Britain by far, already almost 5 percent. Within a decade, one of ten Britons will likely be Muslim. They are one of the few groups in Britain whose numbers are growing—30 percent in four years. The Islamic population growth compares with a non-Muslim British birth rate of about 1.5 children per family: less than the replacement rate. The confidence and militancy of the British Muslim community has driven demands for codifying Shariah law as part of British law. About one hundred such Islamic courts already operate in Britain.

Several prominent mosques—the East London Mosque and the

Finsbury Park Mosque—became centers for the militant Wahhabi philosophy, getting money from radical Saudi donors. The Finsbury Park Mosque is now known as the North London Mosque. Some of its more moderate mosque trustees asked British officials for help. They felt that extremists (veterans of combat in Afghanistan or the bloody Algerian civil war) had hijacked the mosques that were built with the aid of top British leaders, such as Prince Charles and the mayor of London.[39] British officials did not get involved. Meanwhile, these mosques featured "preachers" promoting anti-Western terror, overturning Western governments, and beating women for such offenses as wearing perfume. One was Omar Mahmoud Othman, better known as Abu Qatada. His itinerary-cum-résumé is typical of many of the "preachers":

- Wanted for terror crimes in Jordan for which he was convicted.
- Recruited from Islamist forces in Afghanistan, deemed close to Al-Qaeda.
- Traveled on a forged United Emirates passport.
- Aided terrorist plots in Britain, Germany, and the United States, including 9/11.
- Gained political asylum in Britain under false pretenses.[40]

Abu Qatada reportedly counseled the 9/11 Hamburg cell of Muhammad Atta, as well as advising Zacarias Moussaoui and Richard Reid. Various courts in Europe found significant evidence against him, and a Spanish judge concluded he was "Osama Bin-Laden's right-hand man in Europe."[41] Yet the EU's Human Rights Court awarded him compensation and barred Britain from deporting him, citing possible infringement of rights.[42] A British court let him out on bail in 2007.

Another colorful preacher on the British scene was a burly man known as Abu Hamza, who had an especially checkered (and nonreligious) past. The real name of this born-again Egyptian preacher was Mustafa Kamel Mustafa. Like many Arab terrorists, he entered the West on a student visa, seeking education as an "engineer."[43] Clearly he was not a great student, losing both hands and an eye while setting or dismantling bombs. He bears scars and burn marks from combat in Bosnia and Afghanistan. Despite his lost eye, he was once a bouncer at a British peep show.

Abu Hamza[44] gestures during his speeches with a hook that replaced a right hand. The British press like to poke fun of him as a Captain Hook figure, but he is no joke. In one speech he called for attacking a G-8 summit in order to kill U.S. president George W. Bush. For a decade he spewed screeds of hatred until British officials finally arrested him. In 2006, Abu Hamza was convicted of "soliciting murder," terror and conspiracy, getting a seven-year sentence, only part of which he served.[45] In fact, there is proof the British and European judicial systems have been protecting him (like Abu Qatada), while the British welfare system has coddled him. Europe's Court of Human Rights banned his transfer to the United States to face terrorism charges until it is sure he will not be "treated inhumanely." The EU bars extraditing terrorists who face a death penalty, something not allowed in the EU. So, if Osama bin-Laden had somehow managed to gain safe harbor in Europe, his life would have been safe.

Europe's flaccid judicial approach to terror (and its effect on national courts in Britain) was foreseen by former British prime minister Margaret Thatcher a decade ago. Thatcher showed how the European Convention on Human Rights was used to protect the allegedly infringed rights of Irish terrorists who were shot before they could complete an attack on British-controlled Gibraltar. Thatcher said awarding compensation to dead terrorists' families was an example of "judgments that seem to many people in Britain incomprehensible or just plain wrong." One can imagine what Thatcher thinks of compensating the new wave of Arab-Islamic terrorists such as Abu Qatada and Abu Hamza, both high-maintenance felons. Abu Qatada reportedly gets £1,000 monthly health payments. Abu Hamza gets thousands of pounds in free health care and disability payments. His eight children (several convicted for terror-related crimes) also live off the public purse. "The Tax Payers' Alliance estimates father-of-eight Hamza has cost Britain £2.75million in welfare payments, council [public] housing, NHS [National Health Service] and prison bills, trials and legal appeals. It is feared his fight against deportation could take five years and cost another £250,000."[46] Is it any wonder that when Abu Hamza arrived at Britain's Heathrow Airport, his gateway to Europe, he chuckled that he had gotten to "a paradise, where you could do anything you wanted"?[47]

Another agent of terror who preached in British mosques was Anwar al-Awlaki, a leader of "Al-Qaeda in the Arabia Peninsula." Al-Awlaki was linked to two of the 9/11 bombers, and he was implicated in the abortive Christmas Day bombing over Detroit and the Fort Hood attacks in 2009. In a London mosque sermon filmed by Andrew Gilligan of Channel Four in Britain, al-Awlaki coaches listeners to a martyr's death and its mythical rewards: "Think about the final moments of entering into paradise, or entering into hellfire."[48]

A British-born preacher, Anjem Choudary, led a group called "Islam 4 the UK." Choudary has appeared on BBC, CNN, and other television programs gloating that Buckingham Palace and the White House would be turned into mosques, while Nelson's Column in Trafalgar Square would be removed, because it was an example of idol worship. Speaking in a fine British accent, Choudary said he was using the Internet to recruit people to attack the United States and other Western countries. Choudary asseverated the uncompromising view that anyone who was not a Muslim could not be considered "innocent" in the eyes of God. Therefore, he said, any non-Muslim Westerners killed in attacks by Muslims were not innocent victims.

"There are two camps in the world—one who believes that sovereignty belongs to Man and who believes that sovereignty belongs to God. . . . One is represented by Barack Obama and one is represented by Osama Bin-Laden. I am in the camp of Sheikh Osama Bin-Laden." Asked if he was trying to recruit for attacks against the United States, he answered: "Of course." Asked if he supported the 9/11 and 7/7 attacks and further assaults, he said, "They are going to give you a taste of your own medicine. You send them bombs! What do you expect them to send back, chocolates?"[49]

When CNN television interviewer Eliot Spitzer heard Choudary's remarks, he called on U.S. prosecutors to have him arrested and put on trial. It is testimony to the impotence of the British-European-U.S. anti-terror system that Choudary has avoided incarceration in the same Britain he is working so hard to transform and/or destroy.

HARDENING OF SECOND-GENERATION BRITISH MUSLIM VIEWS
Choudary was a living reproof to hopes that homegrown second-generation British and European Muslims would become more moderate and less politically militant.

If anything, Muslim groups and movements have become more visible on the European political stage and are becoming more adept at using national media and political channels to pursue a wide range of agendas. For example, the Muslim Association of Britain, an affiliate of the Muslim Brotherhood, became a major player in Britain's anti–Iraq War movement by partnering with disaffected members of the British Labor Party and the Stop the War Alliance.[50]

This active role by second-generation British Muslims is not just political. Three of the four suicide bombers of the London underground and bus system on July 7, 2005, were Muslims born in Britain who swore allegiance to Osama bin-Laden and Al-Qaeda. Fifty-two people died in those simultaneous attacks and seven hundred were injured. Two weeks later, another set of British-born Muslims tried again to blow up four sites on London trains and buses, but the detonators malfunctioned. One year after the London bombings, a survey of British Muslims found 15 percent felt suicide bombings were sometimes justified. Most British Muslims (56 percent) denied that Arabs had carried out the attacks on the United States in September 2001.[51]

Surveys by Pew, the *Times* of London, and the *Daily Mail* actually showed a *hardening* of views by British Muslims when asked if they justified terror acts or if they would report terror preparations to authorities. The numbers of those supporting the July 7 train-bus attacks rose from the single-digit range to 23 percent in a poll by the *Daily Mail*: "Almost a quarter of British Muslims say the July 7 attacks can be justified because of the Government's support for the 'war on terror.'The shocking 23 percent figure is the equivalent of 370,000 of the 1.6m Muslims living in the UK."[52]

British analysts say these developments impact far beyond British shores. According to Nile Gardiner, "Britain, for years a safe haven for Islamic militants across the world, has become a hornet's nest of Islamic terrorists. The United States must apply concerted pressure on the UK and other major European countries with large Muslim populations to crack down on Islamic extremists, who through the visa waiver program have easy access to the United States. It will take extensive U.S.-European cooperation to ultimately defeat the scourge of terrorism in an increasingly globalized world."[53]

Peter Bergen writes:

> Here's the problem for the United States: Under our Visa Waiver
> Program, residents of Londonistan who hold a valid British passport
> can board a plane for the United States without an interview by an
> American consular official. This program also applies to more than a
> score of other European countries, like France, Germany, the Nether-
> lands and Spain, that meet the criteria for visa-free travel to the United
> States. Unfortunately, while these countries may enjoy a low visa refusal
> rate, grant reciprocal visa-free travel to Americans and issue machine-
> readable passports—all criteria for inclusion in the waiver program—
> many of them have also had a hard time integrating their growing Mus-
> lim populations. . . . [There is] plenty of evidence from episodes like the
> Madrid bombings in 2004 that these countries contained sleeper cells
> with the ability and motivation to carry out major terrorist operations
> and even, perhaps, to attack the United States itself.[54]

These analyses are well founded. For example, U.S. and British authorities
foiled a British-based terror plot hatched before 9/11 but almost as ambitious in its goal to sow death and destruction in New York and Washington. A sophisticated British terror team, led by a British convert to Islam,
planned to attack the New York Stock Exchange, the World Bank, and
the International Monetary Fund, specifically "to collapse buildings by
detonating limousines packed with explosives and to set off a radiation
bomb."[55] The group used advanced video surveillance to map out targets
in England, Washington, D.C., and New York, reconnoitering the New
York financial district several times. After 9/11, the British group put
its American bombing plans on hold, concentrating instead on British
targets.

"I think that we woke up as a society in 2005 to the idea that people
were prepared to commit suicide and carry out atrocities in Britain because of the perversion of an ideology," declared Sir Norman Bettison,
chief constable for West Yorkshire, home for three of the 7/7 train bombers. Asked in a BBC interview how long Britain would have to fight Islamic terror, he averred: "I think this is generational. I think for the next
generation. . . . Just as dealing with any infection, it will take a generation

of treatment to prevent the infection from spreading. . . . I think it may take 20 years."[56]

FRANCE

Since Charles de Gaulle came to power in 1958, France has pursued an independent course in its diplomacy and security policies, not just vis-à-vis the United States but also regarding its European partners. De Gaulle pulled France out of its military links with NATO, building an independent French nuclear component known as Force de Frappe. Even French communications use an independent SECAM system rather than the standardized European PAL system for television signals. It is not surprising that French leaders—De Gaulle, Pompidou, d'Estaing, Mitterrand, and Chirac—all steered a path clearly apart from America, Britain, and much of Europe. This is also true of French attitudes to the Arab-Islamic sphere, for which France's large Arabic-speaking population was a factor. France's Arab population is, officially, about 3.6 million people or about 5.7 percent—the second highest percentage in Europe. Unofficially, some observers feel there are at least six million Muslims in France—10 percent of the population—far and away the largest Islamic enclave in Europe.

Most of the Arabic-speaking citizenry is from the former French colony of Algeria, where France fought a bloody war against rebels in the 1950s. French opposition to Arab nationalists first informed a pro-Israeli stance in the mid-1950s, but when De Gaulle withdrew from Algeria, France's view of the Arab-Islamic world changed. The pro-Arab policy tilt deepened after De Gaulle's pique with Israel in 1967.

This new policy meant not just avoiding a fight with the growing Arab sector, but also giving in to demands from Palestinian organizations in the 1970s and 1980s, freeing captured terrorists or allowing them to escape. France hoped to keep its channels open to markets in the Arab world and also to preclude terror in its territory. But these prayerful thoughts did not prove correct. France was witness to several Arab-Islamic terror attacks even before 9/11, including the 1980 assault on the Jewish community in Rue Copernic. A bicycle laden with more than twenty pounds of explosives blew up outside a synagogue, killing four people and wounding dozens.

Inside France, hopes that second-generation immigrant families would assimilate into French life did not materialize. In 1995, Algerian violence again spilled over when the second Algerian civil war—between Algerian Islamists and secularists—reached the French mainland. Four Algerian terrorists hijacked an Air France plane, killing three passengers, before a force of French gendarmes overcame them, killing four hijackers. During 1995, there were scores of terror attacks across France, even bombs on high-speed rail lines. An attack on the St.-Michel station in Paris killed eight people and wounded 150. A car bomb attack at a Jewish school wounded seven children. Radicalized Algerian forces (the Armed Islamic Group, or GIA) also assassinated Imam Abdelbaki Sahraoui of the Islamic Salvation Front in his Paris mosque. Sahraoui was deemed too "moderate" because he opposed bringing the Algerian war to France.

FRENCH MEDIA COVER UP ARAB VIOLENCE

Arab riots erupted in 2005 after two Arab boys electrocuted themselves when they hid out in an electric junction station, trying to evade police. In the riots, between nine and ten thousand vehicles and about three hundred buildings and stores were burned down in various cities and towns. The French media—newspapers and TV—hid the full scope of the mayhem for political reasons. Jean-Claude Dassier, head of LCI news service, said, "Politics in France is heading to the right and I don't want right-wing politicians back in second, or even first place because we showed burning cars on television."[57]

Many of the riots also took on an anti-Semitic character, as Jews and their property were singled out for attack. Anti-Jewish aspects of the attacks were downplayed both by French authorities and the French and British press. In a 2006 attack, Ilan Halimi, a Jew, was tortured for days by an Algerian gang demanding a ransom from his family: "If you don't have money, then go to the synagogue and get some," the kidnapper-torturers said as they chanted verses from the Quran in the background. After days of torture—being burned and stabbed by fifteen gang members—Halimi's body was found handcuffed around a tree. The French newspaper *Le Figaro* and the British newspaper the *Observer* declined to tell readers about the anti-Jewish side of the attack, but the *Observer* did report the French prosecutor's statement that the murder was a response to U.S. mistreatment of prisoners at the Abu Ghraib prison in Iraq. French politicians did not want to discuss the anti-Semitic aspects of the case, saying the motive was money. Essentially they repeated what they had done after another brutal Muslim murder of a Jew two years earlier.[58] France's relative impotence in the face of Arab violence sparked fears among France's Jews, especially in cities such as Lille and Lyon with large Arab populations. Many French Jews have emigrated to Israel and Canada for fear of attack. "The Jewish Agency, the quasi-governmental body responsible for settling immigrants, reported a doubling in the number of French Jews" who came to Israel in 2002, for example, as compared to 2001.[59]

Even French police admit they fear entering many Arab neighborhoods, including in Paris. There are officially 751 such urban "no-go zones" or *zones urbaines sensibles*. That means about 8 percent of France's total population—about five million people—basically live in the *realm of Islam*, while living in France. In some French towns like Lyon, the police have even demonstrated to protest the criminal violence aimed at them, prompting one observer to say, "Things have reached a pretty sad state when the police have to demonstrate in the streets against the criminals."[60]

CHANGING EUROPEAN PERSPECTIVES

Since 9/11, 3/11, and 7/7, Europe felt a rise in terror and has begun altering its view, slowly. The French approach has shifted, too—especially with the rise to power of Nicolas Sarkozy, a former interior minister familiar with the rising militancy in the Arab-dominated suburbs. France's ban on women wearing the full-body burqa in public is part of the French majority's anger at being pushed around.[61] Having terror and Islamic extremism pursue its citizens, European leaders have gained a new perspective, thanks partly to the rise of Angela Merkel in Germany. She and Sarkozy do not share de Gaulle's distaste about working with the United States and Britain. They and British prime minister David Cameron grew skeptical of the multicultural gestalt that was once Europeanism. Still, French and German leaders retain a different counterterror mind-set than the

United States. They pursue national goals and prefer joint action against terrorism, but they have tended to be less insistent on fighting state sponsors of terror, preferring to confront freelance or semiconnected terror groups. However, the 2011 fighting in Libya and the Obama administration's aloof posture may be changing even this long-standing perspective. Sarkozy and Cameron have been more assertive than the United States in exploring military options against Libya's Qadhafi. The dramatic Arab political foment starting in Tunisia and moving to Egypt and Libya has goaded European leaders to worry about violence on their doorstep. Refugee flows greatly concern Italy, France, and Britain, particularly more than ten thousand in the Italian island of Lampedusa, which is so close to Tunisia.[62]

GERMANY

As a free Germany entered the third millennium, there were more than four million Muslims on her territory, most of them Turkish workers and their families seeking a better life.[63] This hardly sounds like a profile for Arab-Islamic terror, and yet Germany was probably the center of Arab-Islamic terror activity in Europe.

German and American investigators say Egyptian-born Muhammad Atta's Hamburg Cell was the nucleus of the 9/11 attacks. The cell consisted of eight members: three suicide pilots, three logistical planners, and two others—Egyptians and Saudis steeped in the ideology of the Muslim Brotherhood.[64] The Hamburg Cell was hardly the only Arab-Islamic terror group inside Germany. In 1992, Iran's German embassy was the operational base to track down and murder four leading Kurdish opponents of the clerical regime in a bloody Mafia-style attack on the Mykonos Café in Berlin. In 1991, an Iranian hit team (with diplomatic cover) assassinated former Iranian prime minister and regime critic Shahpour Bakhtiar in Paris.[65] These were not isolated acts, because "the Iranians established a special operations centre in 1986 to coordinate terrorism in Europe from the sixth floor of the Bonn embassy, run by a permanent staff of 20 elite 'Revolutionary Guards.'"[66]

The question is how did Germany, particularly democratic West Germany, become a haven for Arab-Islamic terrorists?

Part of the answer is the systematic importation over forty years of cheap labor from Muslim countries—Morocco, Tunisia, and especially Turkey. Another part of the answer is connected to communist-run East Germany having been a Soviet training and operations base. Terrorists of a particular pedigree were nurtured and protected by the East German regime. They included "Carlos the Jackal" (Illich Ramirez Sanchez) and Palestinian terrorists working for Yasser Arafat's Fatah organization, including Abu Daoud, who planned the 1972 Munich Olympics attack. East Germany also aided Palestinian terrorist Abu Nidal and George Habash's Popular Front for the Liberation of Palestine: left-oriented Arab terrorists, supported by "revolutionary" states like Libya, Syria, and Gamal Abdul-Nasser's Egypt.

Capitalist West Germany, unaware that they were not just poor political refugees, often gave refuge to the rightward-oriented militants of Islam who fled these countries—most of them graduates of the Muslim Brotherhood. "When Egypt and Syria established diplomatic relations with the communist government, Bonn decided to welcome Syrian and Egyptian political refugees. Often, these dissidents were Islamists. Many members of the Muslim Brotherhood were already familiar with Germany. Several had cooperated with the Nazis before and during World War II. Some had even, reportedly, fought in the infamous Bosnian Handschar division of the Schutzstaffel (SS)."[67]

Even when there was evidence of extremist activity or even a clear case of terror, Germany, like most European states, did not choose an aggressive, American-like approach. During the 1972 Munich attack, West German authorities wanted to avoid use of force. They badly mismanaged a rescue mission, leading to the deaths of eleven Israeli athletes and one policeman.

At Munich, it would be easy to say German officials were cowardly or inept. But five years later, a special German police anti-terror unit recaptured a Lufthansa plane that Arab terrorists hijacked to Somalia—without any hostages or police being hurt. So, Germany has successfully used force against terror. Its GSG-9 anti-terror unit is one of the world's best. Still, Germany has unique historical and constitutional reasons *not* to use force: its laws prevent using the army against the population inside Germany. Its laws prohibit acting against groups based on their religious faith. Like postwar Japan, Germany shuns militarism and using the army, especially inside its own borders. For Germans, "the concept of 'terror' since 1945 has historical connotations that are linked not only to extremist groups but also to the state, which had abused its power for unspeakable evil in the 1930s and 1940s."[68] Therefore, says Peter Katzenstein, "terrorism is typically viewed not as a military but as a policing problem." Terrorism is "placed in a broader political and social perspective that seeks to comprehend and cope with both its manifestations and its roots." Military force "is politically taboo for reasons of history and identity." Therefore, Germany traditionally favors joint police work and economic incentives.

Yet there is a new spirit in Germany, reflected in the views of Angela Merkel, the German chancellor, who grew up in communist-ruled East Germany. Merkel is soberly starting to face the problem. She threw away political correctness and discussed the social morass represented by the large Muslim workforce, noting that at "the beginning of the 60's our country called the foreign workers to come to Germany and now they live in our country." The chancellor asserted: "We kidded ourselves a while. We said: 'They won't stay, sometime they will be gone,' but this isn't reality. And of course, the approach [to build] a multicultural [society] and to live side-by-side and to enjoy each other . . . has failed, utterly failed."[69]

RUSSIA

Tyrants enjoy some advantages when using or facing terror.

Russia's bloody modern history proves this. Vladimir Lenin and Joseph Stalin used their secret police known as the Cheka. It was essentially a "terroristic counter-revolutionary militia"[70] to terrify and destroy rivals at home.[71] Later, Soviet leaders employed terror as an instrument of foreign policy, training and financing terrorists.

Beginning with the Bolshevik Revolution, Soviet officials ordered mass murder, sometimes just to fill quotas. Often they did not even pretend to know the nature of the "crimes" or the names of those executed: "You are charged with the task of exterminating 10,000 enemies of the people. Report results by signal."[72] "Heads rolled by the thousands, the tens of thousands, probably even the hundreds of thousands. A process of terror and panic, mutual denunciation and mutual extermination, was set in motion which is probably without parallel in modern history. In a vast conflagration of mock justice, torture, and brutality, at least two thirds of the governing class of Russia literally devoured and destroyed itself."[73]

The Bolshevik Revolution's use of *krasniy terror*—the red terror—was a tool to keep the revolution moving. This was a lesson drawn from the French Revolution and the terror unleashed by Robespierre and his comrades. Both revolutions and their revolutionaries were often swallowed by the voracious appetite of the terror. However, Russian foes of the Soviets also used terror, seriously wounding Lenin in a 1918 assassination attempt. Russia set the modern pattern of regime terror and antiregime terror, bequeathing it to others.

The Nazis copied Soviet terror methods, cowing domestic rivals and then decimating resistance movements in Nazi-occupied Europe.[74] Iran's ayatollahs have used the Basij militia and the Revolutionary Guards to suppress foes, at home and abroad, in the Soviet manner. Many South American regimes have been similarly inspired, causing their domestic opponents to disappear by the thousands.

RUSSIA'S MIND-NUMBING TERROR POLICIES

For decades, Russians did not question their Soviet leaders' policies. Citizens were unaware of many events. The safest course for them was to say, "*Ya nee znayoo, ee-nee-khachoo znatye*"—"I don't know, and I don't want to know."[75]

Stalin's despotic rule is long gone, but some habits linger even in "the New Russia." Under the tough rule of Vladimir Putin, an ex-colonel in the Soviet secret police (KGB), Russian citizens and journalists are dissuaded from asking about policy against terrorism. Such terror is more widespread than Russian leaders would like to admit, and so is the pattern of mysterious murders of a score of Russian journalists.[76] Even Russian officials are careful not to know or say too much. This affects Russian counterterror policy. Authorities use almost limitless force to fight terror, but they strangle information so much that the application of force is incredibly inefficient. Sometimes even *they* do not know what is happening, leading to tactical confusion.

One glaring case was the seizure of one thousand hostages in a Moscow theater in 2002. At least 130 hostages died from gas used by Spetsnaz forces, not by the terrorists.[77]

Authorities also bungled the siege of a school in Beslan in September 2004. More than a thousand students and teachers were imprisoned. After a three-day standoff, 330 people died and 728 were wounded in a botched rescue. At least 186 children were killed, as were ten members of special forces. Only one terrorist was captured alive.

During the standoff in Beslan, in the southern region of North Ossetia, Russian officials seemed spectacularly disorganized, failing to seal off the hostage area. Hysterical parents looked on helplessly from outside the besieged school. Some parents attempted—and a few succeeded—in sneaking into the school to save their children.

There were many warning signs before the Beslan attack. Ten weeks earlier, about forty terrorists broke into a government armory in the Ingushetia region and stole 1,177 firearms. At least eighty people were killed and 106 wounded in that attack, most of them law enforcement officials. Worse, many weapons and much ammunition used in the subsequent Beslan attack had been prestored inside the school itself. The regime's networks had been alerted to the infiltration of terrorists in the Beslan region.

"Despite credible warnings concerning an impending terrorist attack, School Number 1, with its large number of students and teachers, was left completely undefended on opening day, 1 September 2004—a ceremonial occasion in which a number of parents traditionally accompany their children to school," recounts researcher John Dunlop.[78]

Beslan was not atypical. A week earlier, on August 24, 2004, two Russian airliners crashed mysteriously. "It took two and a half days for Russia's security service to announce what virtually everyone else believed from the moment two domestic passenger airlines plunged to earth simultaneously," reported the *New York Times*, five days later: "Russia had suffered yet another gruesome blow from terrorists."[79]

Russian fears of knowing too much or letting others know too much are one reason even sparse details of several major terror attacks in Russia in the last decade have not fully emerged. These fears of knowing may have also hurt Russian abilities to thwart terror even when officials already had intelligence regarding impending attacks.

This is a Russian tradition. It appears that there was also antiregime terror activity under the Soviets, but the full scale of terrorist activity against the previous communist regimes of Lenin, Stalin, Khrushchev, Brezhnev, et al. was never known, because the communist regimes hid the facts.[80] A similar but slightly less severe pattern has emerged today: the neocommunist regime of Vladimir Putin also hides the scale of terror and the regime's occasionally catastrophic counterterror policies.

"Terrorist attacks tend to quickly disappear from the public discourse, if not its collective consciousness," observed reporter Steven Lee Myers. "That is in large part because of the Kremlin's near absolute control of politics and of the state media, including all the national television networks."[81] Even the cast of characters—the names and origin of the terrorists—is shrouded in mystery. In a major terror attack in 1999, at least 243 people were killed in the explosion of three apartment buildings in Moscow and Volgodonsk. Russian leaders blamed Chechens, always convenient targets, but none of the nine people arrested in the attacks was a Chechen.

Clearly, Russia's terror problem goes far beyond the Chechens, a Muslim minority already persecuted for centuries by the czars. The communists, too, blamed the Chechens for separatist aspirations and for being Nazi sympathizers in World War II. However, Russia's ethnic and nationalist foment is extensive and multi-faceted. There are calls for self-determination and separatist movements in the regions of Ossetia, Ingushetia, as well as Dagestan, Adygea, Kabardino-Balkaria, Karachay-Cherkessia, and Bashkortostan. The possibility of foment looms among the large and heretofore quiescent population of Tatars. Other groups and neighbors of Russia who feel hurt by her policies include Armenians, Azeris, Ukrainians, and Georgians.

INCONCLUSIVE COUNTERTERROR POLICIES

"Nothing more exemplifies the agony of Russia's post-Soviet transition than its bloody, inconclusive involvement in two wars in Chechnya," observes Donald Jensen. "Tens of thousands of civilians were killed during years of fighting and over 500,000 displaced."[82] Russia's anti-terror policy has been most effective when it concentrates on "decapitating" terror leaders. Too often it has been scattershot.[83] After destroying the Chechen capital of Grozny, Russia withdrew most of its forces in 2009, but anti-Russian terror grew in the Caucasus region and even in Moscow.[84] Two women blew themselves up on the Moscow metro in March 2010. Recently, the European Court of Human Rights said Russian officials in the region still use torture and assassination as a policy tool, feeding "the nefarious cycle of violence."[85] Sixteen people were killed in a suicide bomb attack in the city of Vladikavkaz in September 2010, and 138 were wounded.[86] Russian leaders Putin and Dimitri Medvedev vowed to keep fighting the "monsters." A month later, heavily armed terrorists invaded the Russian-ruled Chechen parliament, killing three people, before killing themselves or being killed.

Some analysts contend Putin's anti-terror policies have widened terror, uniting and radicalizing diverse separatist movements into a larger jihadist movement. Putin prefers to depict himself as a chivalrous knight on a white horse,[87] slaying jihadist dragons, rather than as subverting sincere self-determination by minorities. Still, Putin is aware of the danger of seeming Islamophobic. He has cultivated Russia's Islamic neighbors, such as Iran. He was the first non-Muslim leader to address the fifty-seven-state Islamic Conference in October 2003, declaring that Islam preceded Christianity in Russia.[88] Despite such overtures, Muslim groups are transforming Russia's terror threat. Terror acts in the Caucasus increased 100 percent in 2010.[89]

"Russia is experiencing the beginning of an Islamist jihad," writes Gordon M. Hahn, who studies terror by ethnic groups in Russia.[90] This Islamic awakening has awesome implications, due to the location of Islamic foment: "Except for Pakistani Islamic fundamentalists and Islamists, none of the world's other radical Muslims live in such close proximity to so many stockpiles of materials and weapons."[91]

Abroad, Russia's record on terror is less colorful but no less important. Post-Soviet regimes have a KGB hue and cast,[92] aiding tyrants and terrorists in attacking targets around the world. Russia has sold advanced weapons and nuclear technology to Iran and to North Korea, the world's two worst terror-assisting regimes, who spread weapons of mass destruction.

Russia has blocked strong diplomatic sanctions or military action against North Korea and Iran. Therefore, Russia enables terror significantly, though its indirect aid may appear less harmful than past Soviet policy of actively training and exporting terror, especially Arab terror from 1968 through the 1980s.[93]

SPAIN

Unlike other Western European countries, Spain's supply of cheap Muslim labor—and potential Arab-Islamic terror—lies just across the border in Morocco. There is a built-in closeness and animosity to the Spanish-Moroccan relationship that is reinforced by the fact that many Muslims regard Spain as Al-Andalous, the part of Europe that was once Muslim. To this day, it is doted on by some Muslims as part of Dar al-Islam: the House of Islam. This cannot be overstressed.

The Strait of Gibraltar symbolically separates Arab-Islamic Morocco from what had been the Arab-Islamic foothold in Europe—an area wrested from the Christians in the years 711–28. For this reason, Spain is seen by many Muslims, especially radicalized Muslims, as part of the Islamic *wakf*—Islamic endowment, Islamic property. In many mosque sermons around the world, extremist Muslims say they want to return as sovereigns to Al-Andalous. For Spaniards, La Reconquista (the reconquering of Spain for Christendom) was completed, after seven hundred years of struggle, by King Ferdinand and Queen Isabella in 1492—the same monarchs who, in the same year, dispatched Christopher Columbus to America and who banished Spain's Jews.

However, until the Madrid commuter train bombings of 2004, most Spaniards, if asked about terror, would not have spoken of Arab-Islamic terror. Rather, they would have pointed to the Basque separatist organization known as ETA—the Basque Fatherland and Freedom Party (Euskadi Ta Askatasuna). The Basques are a distinct linguistic and cultural minority living in southern France and northern Spain.

ETA was founded in 1959, when it broke away from the much larger Basque Nationalist Party (Partido Nacionalista Vasco, or PNV). It only began its terror campaign a decade later. Over the span of forty years, about eight hundred people were killed in various bombings and assassinations, with ETA first concentrating on police and civil guard officials as well as Spanish military and political targets. It assassinated Spanish prime minister Admiral Luis Carrero Blanco in 1973. At its height, ETA is said to have had no more than five hundred active members. ETA lost much of its communal Basque support because of its bloody policy, including the murder of nonmilitary targets, especially children. Partly as a result, ETA has several times declared unilateral cease-fires in its terror program.

Only three days before national elections, bombs exploded on ten Spanish commuter rail lines on March 11, 2004, killing 191 and wounding 1,800. It was probably natural for the Spanish government of José María Aznar, who once miraculously survived an ETA bombing of his car, to assume that ETA was again attacking. Even the opposition socialist party made the same initial assumption. But as evidence emerged of Arab-Islamic terror, Aznar repeated his mistaken view on the subject. This alienated voters who felt he was hiding the truth only days before the 2004 Spanish elections. Aznar had strongly supported America's counter-terror policy and the U.S. assault on Saddam's Iraq—positions that were not popular in Spain. The misplaced blaming of ETA and the Basques only helped Aznar's party lose.

José Luis Rodríguez Zapatero, the socialist party leader and new prime minister, reversed Spain's policy on terror, to the consternation of the United States and some of its allies. The election results seemed to give the impression that the Madrid train bombing—executed by Arab-Islamic bombers allied with Al-Qaeda—had convinced Spanish voters to reverse Spain's role in the U.S.-led war on Arab-Islamic terror:

> Were the Socialists certain Al Qaeda was involved? No, but saying so made it easier to convince voters that the bombs had been placed by Muslims angry that Spain had sided with the United States in the war—and that the only way to make things right would be to get out of Iraq. Whatever their motivation, the Socialists' argument was fundamentally flawed. Osama bin-Laden and other Islamists had identified Spain as a priority target years before the Iraq war. Under Muslim law, no land conquered by Islam may legitimately come under non-Muslim rule. For the fanatics, Spain is still Al Andalus of the Middle Ages, which must be re-claimed for Islam by immigration and intimidation.

> Even if the bombs were placed by Islamists, the idea that Spain was at-
> tacked solely because of Mr. Aznar's support for the Iraq war is simply
> wrong.[94]

The Madrid bombings of March 11 were not a one-shot deal by Arab-
Islamic terrorists. Even after the attacks, and even after the election of the
new government, the same terror organization was planning to blow up
the high-speed rail line at Seville on April 2, "making use of similar explosive substances and detonators," said one investigator, adding that the
same cell set up safe houses and accumulated a financial reserve of more
than 1.5 million euros—fifteen times what it cost to mount the Madrid
attacks.[95] Seven members of the cell were killed or blew themselves up
and an eighth escaped during a police raid on April 3, 2004. "The subsequent police investigation found that they had accumulated information
on new targets in and around Madrid, such as a Jewish recreational facility
for children and young people, a Jewish school, British educational centres
and a national public institution."[96]

What should Spain do about the possibility of more Arab-Islamic
terror? Perhaps the best answer is to look at the success of Spain's anti-
ETA terror policy, which has been coordinated with other states. In May
2008, Francisco Javier López Peña, the political-military head of ETA,
was arrested in Bordeaux, France. In November 2008, French police arrested ETA military chief Miguel de Garikoitz Aspiazu Rubina, alias
"Txeroki." A month later, his successor was arrested—a blow to ETA's
leadership.

IRAN'S TERROR FOOTHOLD IN LATIN AMERICA:
ARGENTINA AND VENEZUELA

Argentina has a tradition of tolerating and even supporting tyrants, terrorists, and totalitarian doctrines. This includes Nazis of various ranks
such as Adolph Eichmann, who planned the mass murder of Europe's
Jews. Like Eichmann, they found easy refuge in Argentina and several
other countries in Latin America. Later, these Nazis and their sympathizers helped form the support base for various military juntas.

The Argentine area also has a tradition of welcoming immigrants from the Middle East, including many Shiite Muslims. The former president of Argentina, Carlos Menem, descended from a Syrian family. Argentina's "tri-border region"—where Argentina, Brazil, and Paraguay come together—is favored by drug smugglers and money launderers. It also welcomes certain kinds of Middle Easterners, particularly from Iran and its terror subcontractor, the Hizballah militia, which staged two major terror attacks in Buenos Aires in 1992 and 1994.

On March 17, 1992, a bomb-laden truck driven by a suicide bomber deliberately crashed into the Israeli embassy building in the Argentine capital of Buenos Aires, destroying the building and damaging a nearby school and Catholic church. Twenty-nine people were killed, many of them children, most not Israeli. Two hundred forty-two people were wounded. The truck-bomb, suicide-driver method was typical of Hizballah and its attacks in Lebanon against foreign embassies and peacekeeping forces. The investigation of the attack was slow and unproductive, but it was renewed after another bombing—this time of the AMIA Jewish Community Center in Buenos Aires on July 19, 1994. In that attack, eighty-seven people died and about two hundred were injured.

A big break in both cases occurred in 1998 when a telephone call intercepted from the Iranian embassy in Argentina showed conclusively how Iran was involved in the embassy attack. Menem's government expelled six of the seven Iranian diplomats in Argentina. None of the diplomats was questioned, and further details were blocked. An Argentine court that had been investigating the case for seven years issued quick, superficial, and shoddy findings blaming Imad Mughniyeh, mistakenly identified as a leader of Islamic Jihad in Lebanon (he was actually in Hizballah).

"The temptation to look for culprits abroad proved irresistible to the government, and for good reason," observed Argentine journalist Sergio Kiernan. "As the experts quoted by the court said, both the embassy and the AMIA bombings were carried out by foreign operatives working in Argentina with the support of Argentines. President Menem and his officials were always reluctant to explore 'local connections.'"[97]

Much later, local police, prosecutors, and judges charged that President Menem (1989–99) deliberately blocked both inquiries.[98] In return for stalling investigations, Menem allegedly got sizable bribes (at least $500,000 and reputedly as much as $10 million) that were placed in his Swiss bank account.[99]

After trying to get an illegal third term, Menem left office in 1999, and the inquiries proceeded. They revealed details proving that the embassy and AMIA attacks were Iranian operations. The Argentine State Intelligence Agency identified the suicide driver in the embassy attack as Ibrahim Hussein Berro, a young Lebanese Hizballah fighter from the Shiite-dominated Baalbek region of eastern Lebanon, bordering Syria.[100] In 2005, Argentine president Néstor Kirchner formally accused Iran of the attacks. Kirchner said Menem had obstructed the truth. In March 2007, Interpol issued red alerts for suspects named in the Argentine report, including Hizballah terror planner Imad Mughniyeh,[101] Iran's former president Hashemi Rafsanjani, Iran's ex-intelligence chief Ali Fallahijan, and Ali Akbar Velayati, a former minister.

Even as Iranian terrorist-directing diplomats left Argentina, Iran's terror and weapons proliferation machine penetrated several other countries in South America. In 2007, Iranian president Mahmoud Ahmadinejad led a five-day official visit to Venezuela, Nicaragua, and Ecuador. His visit coincided with the inaugurations of Nicaragua's newly elected president Daniel Ortega and Ecuador's Rafael Correa. Iran also began working closely with Cuba, which shares Iran's opposition to U.S. policies. But the Iranian move into Latin America was not just based on ideology. In 2010, Iran signed a pact giving nuclear technology to Bolivia in return for uranium for Iran. Venezuela, led by Hugo Chávez, also sends uranium to Iran. Both Bolivia and Venezuela are breaking international sanctions decreed by the United Nations. Iran began direct flights from Tehran to Venezuela, and there are growing reports of Hizballah cells operating in Venezuela, mostly on Margarita Island. The direct flights to Venezuela can be used—like Iran's direct flights to Damascus and Beirut—to transfer men and equipment, including Iranian Revolutionary Guard trainers.

Iran is reportedly setting up missile bases in Venezuela, and it is apparently selling at least three different models of intermediate-range missiles and rockets to that country.[102] A German newspaper says Iran will staff the base with its own missile officers and soldiers, and this happens at the same time as Russia is selling Venezuela sophisticated air-defense SS-300 missiles of the kind it first agreed to sell Iran. Russia has since delayed sending the anti-aircraft missiles to Iran (missiles that could be used to defend Iranian nuclear sites from Western attack). It is not a far stretch to believe that Venezuela—perhaps with a wink from Russia—might be planning to resend the SS-300s to Iran on one of those direct air flights from Caracas.[103]

INDIA

India has been facing terror for many years—but not just Islamic terror. Strife between India's Hindu majority and its Muslim minority is the root cause of the 1947 partition of the Indian subcontinent into India and Pakistan (which later subdivided into Pakistan and Bangladesh). Partition, however, did not stop the strife or the terror. Hindus and Muslims still fight, as does the Sikh minority.[104]

Indeed, four of the world's most lethal terror attacks in the last forty years have involved Indian targets—attacks by Islamic extremists and assaults by murderous Sikh separatists. This terror has included strikes at Indian planes in midair, Indian commuter trains, and commando assaults on Indian tourist complexes. The single most lethal terror assault on Indian targets was the attempt to blow up three Air India planes in midair simultaneously in 1985—one near Ireland, one over Canada, and one leaving Japan.[105] Three hundred thirty-one people died and four people were wounded in the attack that would have been even deadlier had not two of the bombs exploded prematurely on the ground rather than in midair.[106] Police blamed Sikh separatists. In July 2006, terrorist bombs blew up seven commuter trains in Mumbai, killing 209 and wounding more than seven hundred people. Indian officials said the murderous attack was carried out by Islamic terror groups known as Lashkar-e-Taiba and Student Islamic Movement of India, with support from Islamic terrorists based in Pakistan. Indian officials asserted the terrorists were also helped by Pakistan army personnel who want to destabilize India, some of whom are sympathetic to Al-Qaeda. This is not just an Indian claim, according to experts on Southwest Asia:

> On the one hand, the weakness of the state [Pakistan] has permitted sectarian terrorism to flourish in recent years. On the other hand, the staff of agencies of the state, most notably the Inter Services Intelligence (ISI) directorate of the Pakistan Armed Forces, have played a role in nurturing terrorist groups committed to advancing Pakistan's geopolitical interests with respect to its eastern neighbour India and its western neighbour Afghanistan.[107]

Despite India's long history of facing terror and despite its emergence as an economic power, the world's second most populous country has a rather poor counterterror record. For example, despite its early intelligence advisory on the planned 2008 Mumbai attack, the fitful and feeble Indian counterterror response to the commando assault was appallingly bad. At least 173 people died and more than three hundred were wounded in assaults on more than nine different targets in the Indian city. A RAND Corporation study of the events found "exposed numerous weaknesses in India's counter-terrorism and threat mitigation structure." Worse, the report said, it was clear that "planning for the attacks began as far back as mid-2007. The terrorists were heavily armed, and had detailed maps and information about each of the targets they hit. The multiple targets were carefully chosen for their religious, political, and cultural values in order to make a statement."[108] This last item is a reference to the terrorists' choice of a Jewish community center as one target.

In the last three years, India has often warned Pakistan against allowing terror attacks on India from its territory. India has also asked other states for counterterror assistance, including the United States, Israel, and Germany. The threat to India, however, is not just coming from across the border in Pakistan. "Although it long insisted that Islamic extremism had not developed among its Muslim communities, India is now having to accept that a small section of its 160-million-strong Muslim community—the second largest after Indonesia's and accounting for 14 percent of the largely Hindu population—has become radicalised."[109]

ISRAEL

As the nation with the most experience fighting Arab-Islamic terror, Israel is living proof that counterterror success is linked primarily to mental attitude, creativity, imagination, and intelligence. Necessity is the mother of invention, and Israel needed to be inventive in fighting terror in order to survive. This began when the Jews of the British-run Palestine trust territory confronted unrelenting terror even before Israel's official birth in 1948. The pre-Israel Jewish community in Palestine, known as the Yishuv, faced Arab-Islamic assaults from 1920 onward. This terror morphed and mutated from attacks on roads to well-organized hijackings of airliners to suicide bombings in malls and public transportation. Today's terror threats to Israel include biological, chemical, and nuclear variants. With such a wide array of dangers, Israel has developed excellent technological and human responses. It reaped great counterterror successes by destroying Saddam Hussein's nuclear option in 1981 and Syria's secret atomic reactor in 2007, and by using airborne drones to kill Hamas operatives and leaders.[110] Sadly, Israel has also reaped some ignominious counterterror failures.

Looking at some successes, Israel stopped cross-border terror infiltration in the 1950s, and it defeated the airport and airline terror that threatened to isolate it in the late 1960s and early 1970s. Similarly, it shut down suicide bombers who targeted buses, restaurants, and malls from 1993 to 2003. Israeli planes, bus depots, and public buildings are considered among the safest in the world. It is breathtaking to see how Israel reversed a tidal wave of suicide terror in 2001–2002 (with 100 to 450 fatalities a year), reducing such attacks almost to zero.

Unfortunately, Israel has also given terror organizations a new lease on life by the politically motivated release of hundreds and even thousands of convicted Arab terrorists from jail in return for a handful of Israelis.

NOTABLE ISRAELI-PALESTINIAN DEALS FOR RELEASING TERRORISTS

March 14, 1979—Israel releases 70 convicted Palestinian terrorists in return for an Israeli soldier captured when he crossed into PLO-ruled territory in southern Lebanon.

November 23, 1983—Israel releases 4,765 (4,700 security detainees in Lebanon and 65 convicted terrorists in Israel) in return for six soldiers taken prison in fighting in Lebanon.

> May 21, 1985—Israel releases 1,150 convicted terrorists in exchange for three Israeli soldiers taken as prisoners of war by Palestinian groups during fighting in Lebanon.
>
> January 29, 2004—Ariel Sharon orders the release of 427 convicted terrorists in return for the release of the bodies of three Israeli soldiers and Elhanan Tannenbaum, an Israeli drug dealer who had been a personal friend of Sharon.

Surveys of six major terrorist-hostage swaps show that between 12 percent and 60 percent of the convicted terrorists released return to terror. Israel's security services estimate that about 180 people have been killed by convicted terrorists released since the year 2000, and hundreds more from earlier deals with terror groups.

"Since 1985 the State of Israel has freed over 10,000 Palestinians who were serving prison sentences for hostile activity or terror actions, and this resulted in the murder and death of hundreds of Israeli citizens," observes historian Nadav Shragai. "Some of the Palestinian terrorists were freed in the framework of deals with terror organizations that involved the exchange of a few isolated Israelis who were taken captive by the terrorists, for hundreds and thousands of terrorists. Another portion were freed in the framework of what were termed diplomatic 'goodwill gestures.'"[111]

Israel's biggest counterterror failure probably was saving Yasser Arafat and his moribund Fatah/PLO organization from ignominious exile in Tunisia. Yitzhak Rabin and Shimon Peres signed treaties with the PLO in 1993, hoping for peace, but Arafat was never interested in peace, preferring *al-kifaah al-musallah*: "the armed struggle." The PLO chief broke the various treaties immediately, smuggling weapons into the West Bank and Gaza in his personal vehicles (plane, helicopter, cars). Arafat also sent huge bulk arms shipments by boat from Iran. Captured PLO documents show Arafat never deviated from planning and executing terror against Israeli targets.[112] Over the next twelve years, twelve hundred Israelis and tourists were murdered by terrorists—more than the combined total of the four previous decades.

FATALITIES IN PALESTINIAN TERROR ATTACKS (1920–2009)[113]

Year	Number of Deaths	Year	Number of Deaths
1920	9	1965	10
1921	24	1966	10
1922	5	1967	16
1923	0	1968	55
1924	4	1969	33
1925	1	1970	74
1926	1	1971	18
1927	1	1972	46
1928	0	1973	27
1929	119	1974	67
1930	0	1975	39
1931	2	1976	14
1932	4	1977	9
1933	0	1978	57
1934	0	1979	10
1935	1	1980	16
1936	44	1981	14
1937	10	1982	6
1938	94	1983	21
1939	26	1984	9
1940	137	1985	27
1941	14	1986	14
1942	4	1987	11
1943	1	1988	16
1944	3	1989	40
1945	1	1990	33
1946	28	1991	21
1947	152	1992	34
1948	379	1993	45
1949	37	1994	65
1950	52	1995	29
1951	41	1996	56
1952	40	1997	41
1953	46	1998	16

1954	41	1999	8
1955	30	2000	43
1956	53	2001	207
1957	19	2002	457
1958	15	2003	213
1959	10	2004	124
1960	11	2005	56
1961	8	2006	29
1962	10	2007	13
1963	7	2008	36
1964	9	2009	8

Of Israel's many leaders over the years, several have had direct counterterror field experience, but few have had the overall impact of Ariel Sharon. As a young colonel, Sharon helped develop Israel's assertive responses to terror incursions in the 1950s. As a defense minister in 1981–83 and as a prime minister in 2001–2005, he was the author of some of the most important strategic decisions in Israeli history—overreaching in Lebanon in 1982 and the unilateral Israeli exit from Gaza in 2005.

Sharon claimed his Gaza pullback promoted peace, but it was a unilateral move that came out of thin air, without any serious strategic planning by Israel. It was executed without coordinating with Egypt, which therefore was not inclined to help Israel with any unforeseen problems, such as increased weapons smuggling. It was also done without the agreement of the Palestinian Authority led by Mahmoud Abbas, Arafat's seemingly more moderate successor. It thus weakened Abbas, and it helped Hamas rout the ruling Fatah regime. Indeed, the hastily conceived pullout led to the establishment of an Iranian-aided Islamic terror base in Gaza just ten to fifteen miles from the ports of Ashdod and Ashkelon, twenty miles from metropolitan Tel Aviv and Israel's vulnerable coastal plain. The pullback also spurred more Hamas attacks on Israel, as Hamas tried to prove it had "forced" Israel out of Gaza. It took Israel almost six years to develop some technological answers to the low-flying rockets.[114]

In effect, Israel ceded the entire Gaza-Sinai frontier to terrorists, returning Gaza to what it had been in the early 1950s: an area of uncontrolled terror infiltration. But the *fedayeen* of the 1950s were not as well organized or trained as the new generation of terrorists from Hamas and Islamic Jihad, who came equipped with rockets, mortars, and Iranian-supplied explosives and night-vision equipment. More than five thousand Gaza-based rockets and mortars struck Israeli towns from 2005 to 2011. Major fighting in 2006 and the Gaza war of 2008 were testimony to Sharon's strategic debacle.

TERRORIST ROCKET AND MORTAR ATTACKS FROM GAZA

- In 2001, 249 rockets and mortar shells are fired by Palestinian terrorist groups (245 mortars and 4 rockets).
- In 2002, 292 rockets and mortar shells are fired by Palestinian terrorist groups (257 mortars and 35 rockets).
- In 2003, 420 rockets and mortar shells are fired by Palestinian terrorist groups (265 mortars and 155 rockets).
- In 2004, 1,157 rockets and mortar shells are fired by Palestinian terrorist groups (876 mortars and 281 rockets).
- In 2005, 417 rockets and mortar shells are fired by Palestinian terrorist groups (238 mortars and 179 rockets).
- In 2006, 968 rockets and mortar shells are fired by Palestinian terrorist groups (22 mortars and 946 rockets).
- In 2007, 2,312 rockets and mortar shells are fired by Palestinian terrorist groups (1,263 mortars and 1,049 rockets).

Those familiar with Israel's counterterror policy sometimes liken it to a two-edged sword with which Israel hacks its enemies but sometimes ends up cutting itself: one edge exhibits tremendous creative thinking, but the other edge is ad hoc thinking often without even minimal planning. Ariel Merari, a psychologist who is one of Israel's most respected and most experienced anti-terror experts, summed this up when he said that "Israel has always preferred to leave the conceptual initiative to its adversaries."

As surprising as it may seem, Israel has never formally devised a comprehensive doctrine or strategy for dealing with Palestinian political violence. In agglomeration, however, the measures that Israel has taken to fight terrorism amount to a *de facto* strategy. For better or for worse, Israel has developed countermeasures to respond to problems as they have arisen, rather than conducting an assessment of the overall threat and then planning a comprehensive set of responses.[115]

For almost a century, Israel has faced unremitting danger from a wide and changing array of tyrants, terror regimes, and terror organizations. These have included the Pan-Islamic/Pan-Arab Mufti Haj Amin al-Husseini, the secular Pan-Arab regimes of Baathist Syria and Iraq, Marxist terror groups like the Popular Front for the Liberation of Palestine, the Islamist/nationalist Fatah organization of Yasser Arafat, the Islamist Hamas, the Iranian-backed Shiite organization Hizballah, and most recently, contingents of Al-Qaeda that staged terror assaults simultaneously against Israel and Jordan. Due to Israel's narrow borders and lack of strategic depth, and due to the ample sanctuary for terrorists, intelligence—in every sense of the word—has assumed an even greater role in Israel's defense than in other countries.

Intelligence, creative thinking, and imagination are the key to Israel's success in counterterror policy, but there are also some huge failures, which must be examined.

In 1967, Israel succeeded dazzlingly in what came to be known as the Six-Day War, smashing three Arab air forces in a matter of minutes, while Israeli armor and infantry achieved dramatic victories on three fronts. In 1973, the country suffered nearly three thousand dead and a near-systemic collapse because of lack of mental preparation and bad intelligence. The average Israeli referred to this in Hebrew as *ha-mehdal*—the Debacle—or *ha-konseptzia*—the Concept. These are references to the Israeli security community's wishful thinking and overweening complacency.[116] Israelis often lament the 1973 war's lapse in mental acuity and imagination. Its recurrence is the nightmare that Israeli security planners and counterterror experts cite as the thing they fear the most. And yet, it has recurred, not in a conventional war, but in more limited conflicts with terror groups that have become Israel's regular fare.

Israel destroyed the PLO's terror infrastructure in the 1982 Lebanon war, denying Yasser Arafat his sanctuary and base next to Israel, and also pushing Syrian forces back. However, Israeli defense minister Ariel

Sharon misplayed his hand. Rather than evicting Yasser Arafat quickly, Sharon got bogged down in a siege of Beirut. Israel then overstayed its welcome in Lebanon, trying to install a pro-Israeli regime led by Maronite Christian leader Bashir Gemayel, who was murdered by pro-Syrian forces. Israel got stained by its Maronite allies' revenge massacre of Palestinians at Sabra and Chatilla, which we examined in an earlier chapter. It got sucked into internal Lebanese politics, helping spark Shiite hostility and the rise of the Iranian-backed Hizballah organization. Later, Israel's hasty and sloppy pullbacks from Lebanon emboldened a resurgence of Palestinian terror.

"The manner of Israel's withdrawal from southern Lebanon signaled a vulnerability to violence," observes Ira Sharkansky, echoing thoughts of many Israeli army officers. "By some analyses, the Palestinians began their intifada in keeping what they thought was a Lebanese model; that chronic threats against soldiers, settlers, and civilians would produce Israeli pressure on the government to withdraw completely from the land the Palestinians claimed as theirs and perhaps offer other concessions."[117]

In the 1990s, Israel's elites—in academia, media, and intelligence—swallowed the wishful thinking that Arafat wanted peace, that he would rein in Islamic terror. Israeli leaders Yitzhak Rabin and Shimon Peres said Arafat would "take care" of Islamic radicals without what Rabin called the kid-glove treatment mandated by Israel's legal system. When Arafat was caught speaking of "jihad," Peres said that Arafat only meant it metaphorically, not a real war. Besides, Rabin said, terror was not "an existential problem" for Israel. Both men were proven wrong on all counts.

Arafat, who got control of Gaza and much of the West Bank, did not become Israel's anti-terror warrior. Instead, terror became the number-one issue inside Israel. Indeed, despite the rivalry between Arafat's Fatah group and the Islamist Hamas organization, Arafat praised Hamas suicide bombers, and he cooperated with Hamas's leader Sheikh Ahmad Yassin. Hamas and Fatah had a kind of friendly competition to see who could murder more Israelis.[118] Hamas initiated the suicide bombings, but in 2002, at the height of the bombings, Arafat's Fatah actually staged more suicide attacks and caused more deaths than Hamas. Arafat's Fatah also pioneered the use of women as suicide bombers. Moreover, Arafat's Fatah (sometimes through its Al-Aqsa Martyrs Brigade or Tanzim units) linked up with Hamas and Islamic Jihad as well as the PFLP in many "joint operations." Despite the conventional wisdom in the Western press and academia that Fatah was more "moderate" than Hamas, this was not so. Arafat had only mastered the art of pleasing divergent audiences simultaneously.

ISRAEL'S TWILIGHT ZONE OF TERROR:1993–2001

One thing countries do not need in intelligence officers is a surplus of conventional wisdoms and political correctness. Yet Israeli leaders chose those traits during Israel's entente with the PLO during the years 1993 to 2001. Prime ministers Rabin and Peres picked men of questionable background and often scant operational experience for the most challenging intelligence jobs in any democratic society.

Shin Bet director Yaakov Peri supported Rabin's decision to sign a revolutionary accord with Arafat's PLO. Peri swept aside doubts raised by top army commanders[119] and intelligence experts in Israel about the wisdom of signing a deal with Arafat.[120] Publicly and privately, Peri said Israel could rely on Arafat to maintain peaceful ties with Israel and to control anti-Israel terror by Islamic groups such as Hamas and Islamic Jihad. Peri even certified that Israel could depend on the PLO for intelligence data on groups seeking to attack Israel.

Israel's intelligence acquisition continued to deteriorate, and the terror casualties in Israel mounted successively during the era of phony peace. About 1,200 Israelis and tourists were murdered in this period. More died from terror in the decade of "peace" from 1993 to 2002 than in all of Israel's previous history, 1948–92.

In this period of Israeli-Palestinian "peace," the Mossad external intelligence service was turned over to Major General Danny Yatom, formerly Rabin's military aide, a man who lacked salient intelligence skills or experience. Rabin and Peres then bequeathed their intelligence chiefs to Benjamin Netanyahu, who defeated Peres in the 1996 elections, and one of their biggest fiascos was the botched assassination of Hamas leader Khaled Mishal in Jordan in 1996. Two Mossad agents "bumped into" Mishal and injected him with a slow-acting poison.[121] The operation was handled clumsily, and the agents were captured by Jordanian police. To assuage Jordanian anger, Israel had to supply an antidote—to save the

Hamas official. Israel was also forced to release Hamas leader Ahmad Yassin from an Israeli jail. It was as if terror went to the racetrack and won the daily double.

When Ariel Sharon was elected prime minister in 2001, he reinvigorated Israel's intelligence services and operations, picking leaders with proven analytical skills and operational experience. Sharon chose former major general Meir Dagan, a veteran special operations commander and Arabic speaker, as the Mossad head. The Shin Bet was turned over to seasoned Arab affairs experts like Avi Dichter and Yuval Diskin.

These men took a no-nonsense approach to terror, not looking through rose-colored lenses nor intoning politically correct tunes. This stance was critically needed. Israel had been slowly strangled by fear of suicide bombers in the late 1990s and especially in 2000–2002. There were sixty suicide attacks in 2002—more than an attack a week.

Parents were afraid to let their children ride on public buses that might explode at any moment. Adults were skittish about going out for dinner or to shop at malls.

Waves of bombings in Israel's cities compelled Sharon to launch a ground invasion of the West Bank. Israel recaptured vital territory, and it reestablished its own security presence and intelligence networks. Israel intercepted several Iranian arms ships laden with thousands of weapons bound for PLO gunmen and bombers—as part of deals arranged by Yasser Arafat himself with the Iranian regime.[122] About the same time, Israel closed down Orient House, a PLO center in Jerusalem, confiscating thousands of documents that also showed Arafat's direct involvement in financing and planning terror. Sharon then announced that he would isolate Arafat himself in the PLO leader's compound in the West Bank town of Ramallah.

Israel's intelligence services regained the upper hand in the war against terror. From sixty suicide bomb attacks in 2002, Israel saw fewer than thirty in 2003, thirteen in 2004, and nine in 2005. There were *no* such attacks in 2008 and 2009.

Israel stopped the terror wave by uniting high-tech with a personal touch: terrorists got special-delivery booby-trapped gifts from trusted friends or surprise parties when Israeli infantrymen and special forces took them from their beds at night. Naval commandos intercepted their arms shipments at sea. Sometimes the Israeli air force used remote-controlled drones—a technique pioneered by Israel—or missiles from helicopters or two-thousand-pound bombs dropped by jet fighters.

The targeted killings spurred a steep drop in terror, crippling the leadership and trained manpower of the terror groups. Hamas's Sheikh Ahmad Yassin and Abdel-Aziz Rantissi were killed. Fatah's West Bank leader, Marwan Barghouti, surrendered and was convicted of mass murder.

This was exactly the opposite of what Israeli pacifists and left-wing activists had predicted. The pacifists were backed by anti-Israel politicians from Norway, Sweden, Britain, and Spain who predicted that the Israeli policy would spawn a new generation of suicide bombers and vastly increased Israeli casualties.[123] They were wrong.

"The number of Israelis killed after Yassin's death, in particular, was far lower than most observers expected."[124] Editorialists at the *New York Times* and spokesmen at the U.S. State Department had warned that Israel's tough policies would "fuel the cycle of violence." They were completely wrong. In the West Bank town of Jenin, for example, a shopping mall replaced the headquarters of Fatah suicide bombers. Not only did suicide bomb attacks drop from sixty a year in 2002 to zero in 2008, 2009, and 2010, but even when a terror attack occurred, it was far less effective, producing fewer casualties, less trauma.[125]

"Israel's experience suggests that targeted killings can help manage terrorism," observes counterterror analyst Daniel Byman, who stops short of wholesale endorsement of Israel's methods. Byman advises other countries to recognize that such a policy "cannot by itself resolve the [terror] problem. Thus any killings must be embedded in a broader counterterrorism program with better defenses and improved intelligence."[126] One almost wants to say "Fair enough," but the overall Israeli record is such that one cannot logically deny that putting terrorists on the defensive is the best way to keep them from taking the offensive.

Even abroad, Israel's counterterror posture has seemed to improve with the more activist approach. Many in the Israeli security community say, for example, that some of the "accidents" in Iran's nuclear program—from computer viruses to assassinated scientists—are probably connected to a more aggressive Mossad operational policy.

So, in sum, what can we learn from Israel's experience with Arab-Islamic terror? The theoretical and operational lessons from Israel's history are clear:

- Arab-Islamic terror can be defeated, if one is determined and imaginative.
- Arab-Islamic terror cannot be won over by concessions.
- Terror cannot be fought by subcontractors or solely by remote-control devices.
- There is no substitute for training and selecting counterterror staffs based on proven ability and knowledge of Arab-Islamic subject matter, not politically correct blather.
- Hands-on, aggressive intelligence is a must.

9

SCENARIOS AND SOLUTIONS

"The supreme irony of this age of power is its impotence to deal with determined or fanatical minorities." So wrote *New York Times* columnist James Reston on September 11, 1970—thirty-one years to the day before 9/11.

Impotent rage is a typical reaction to a terror attack. But we can do better than that, as shown by the much-delayed and much-deserved dispatch of Osama bin-Laden, and by Israel's superb triumph over Palestinian Islamic bombers in 2002–2003.

The heart of terror is the mind: our mind versus their mind. This means at least three different kinds of intelligence: intelligence or data on the terror enemy; the intelligence or wisdom to use the right methods and strategies against the enemy; and the kind of emotional intelligence that bespeaks confidence without cockiness, not easily dismayed by periodic setbacks but doggedly assertive for the long-haul battle.

Western elites have hindered the battle against terror. Our "best and brightest"—journalists, academics, and officials—have minimized the threat or even made light of the *sense* of danger rather than curbing the danger itself. For example, John Mueller of Ohio State University wrote a book whose title said it all: *Overblown: How Politicians and the Terrorism Industry Inflate National Security Threats, and Why We Believe Them.*

Mueller was hosted by the *New York Times* and the prestigious journal *Foreign Affairs,* inviting favorable review from Harvard's Jessica Stern, Sara Lawrence's Fawaz Gerges, and the *Atlantic*'s James Fallows.[1] None of these "experts" apologized after subsequent Arab-Islamic terror attacks and abortive plots proved Mueller was as wrong about terror—after 9/11—as Columbia's Edward Said, Georgetown's John Esposito, London's Fred Halliday, and Gerges himself (then of Johns Hopkins) had been before 9/11. They returned to the journals and TV studios where, before 9/11, they said terror was a myth or an exaggerated threat, to opine sagely that Al-Qaeda and its copiers were merely, to use Gerges's term, "a dangerous nuisance."[2] But as Princeton's Alan Krueger once observed: "Experts can be dead wrong, but they are rarely called to account."[3]

Stern derided the "inflammatory" comments of Representative Peter King (R-N.Y.), who chaired the April 2011 congressional hearings into the U.S. homegrown Islamic threat. "King's rhetoric is [so] dangerous," Stern asserted. Sounding like a disciple of Edward Said, she added that "non-Muslim domestic terrorists are greater in number than Muslim ones." Her contentions were misleading and inaccurate. There are many non-Muslim extremists in the United States, but since 9/11, there have been few (if any) deaths caused by them. Stern lauded Representative Keith Ellison (D-Minn.), a Muslim congressman who condemned the hearings into the Islamic threat and who staged a phony and tearful performance at the hearings themselves, trying to brand them a "witch hunt."[4]

Witches are not real and do not fly. Terrorists are real, and we know how they fly.

When the sky indeed fell on us—in New York and Washington—and when death came from the trains, the buses, or the sea—in London, Madrid, Mumbai, and Jerusalem—the danger was clear and manifest. Yet our elites often undermined the moral justice of fighting hard against terror. They educated us and our youth that fighting was futile because there was no way we could really win, or that our strenuous efforts were as bad as the means used by the terrorists themselves.

This summation chapter will try to concentrate on the lessons of the mind and on practical, down-to-earth ways to limit the rising dangers from Arab-Islamic terror.

Terrorism is a disease whose modern mutation is especially virulent. There is probably no one-time, stop-all cure, but there are ways to control the malady and its damage. Here is a short review of some suggested ways to curb the terror disease.

COMPROMISE AS AN OPTION

Eons ago, a great Chinese strategist said the highest form of warfare was to win without fighting, especially to turn one's enemy into one's friend.[5] This advice, both noble and wise, is embraced by many who want nonviolent solutions to terror. Unfortunately, terrorists have other plans, especially the Arab-Islamic terrorists of today: the Muslim Brotherhood, Al-Gema'at al-Islamiyya, Takfir Wa-Hijra, Hamas, Hizballah, the Taliban, and Al-Qaeda with its imitators. Their minimum aim, on a local level, is regime change. On a global level, their jihad is aimed at nothing less than civilizational change—spreading Islam worldwide—*their* brand of Islam.

By definition, these are groups and individuals whose strategic goals do not allow for compromise or moderation. Nevertheless, some academics, diplomats, strategic planners, intelligence officials, and journalists have suggested that a revamped and more "moderate" Taliban-run Afghanistan, for example, or a "more mature" Hizballah-run Lebanon or a "pragmatic" Hamas-run Gaza will become more "reasonable" over time. The U.S. director of national intelligence, Lieutenant General James Clapper, told Congress in February 2011 that the Muslim Brotherhood was a mostly nonviolent and moderate group of secular social reformers: "The term 'Muslim Brotherhood' . . . is an umbrella term for a variety of movements, in the case of Egypt, a very heterogeneous group, largely secular, which has eschewed violence and has decried Al Qaeda as a perversion of Islam. . . . They have pursued social ends, a betterment of the political order in Egypt, et cetera. . . . In other countries, there are also chapters or franchises of the Muslim Brotherhood, but there is no overarching agenda, particularly in pursuit of violence, at least internationally."[6]

Clapper said the Brotherhood could be approached by the United States, but admitted its members were not enthusiastic supporters of the Egyptian peace treaty with Israel. When asked by Senator Dianne Feinstein of California whether the Brotherhood is committed to the

"Egyptian-Israeli peace agreement," Clapper answered, "I would assess that they're probably not in favor of the treaty."[7]

This analysis cannot be classified as intelligence, but only as an insult to intelligence. As shown earlier, the Muslim Brotherhood is the modern pioneer of Islamist terror and the godfather of many Islamist terror groups. One offspring is Al-Qaeda. Osama bin-Laden studied with Muhammad Qutb, a senior member of the Muslim Brotherhood and brother of the Brotherhood's main ideologue, Sayyid Qutb.

For any intelligence official to call the Muslim Brotherhood "secular" or possibly "moderate" is like a zoologist confusing a Nile crocodile with a camel. So describing the worst terror groups goes way beyond *politically correct but factually inaccurate*. To hear policy and intelligence officials, think tank analysts, and media pundits repeatedly call bloodthirsty Arab-Islamic terrorists moderates is to witness an unusually correct prediction of Karl Marx: history repeats itself first as tragedy and then as farce.[8]

Sadly, this farcical view of terrorists as moderates is quite widespread among European officials and even within the U.S. intelligence community and military, and it has gotten worse in the first years of the Obama administration. "'We shouldn't be afraid of Islam in the politics of these countries,' said a senior administration official, speaking on the condition of anonymity to describe internal policy deliberations," according to the *Washington Post*. "'It's the behavior of political parties and governments that we will judge them on, not their relationship with Islam.'"[9]

This was not the flip remark of a minor official. It accurately reflects the Obama administration view—from Obama himself to his director of national intelligence, James Clapper, and to his senior aide on counterterrorism, John Brennan. They think Islamist governments and organizations are not anathema. The Obama administration feels the United States can make a deal, a compromise, with these regimes and organizations. President Obama feels these regimes and groups should be engaged and embraced, as shown by a recent *Washington Post* report containing details of an administration study:

> As the Arab revolutions unfold, the White House is studying various Islamist movements, identifying ideological differences for clues to how they might govern in the short and long term. The White House's

internal assessment, dated Feb. 16, looked at the Muslim Brotherhood's and al-Qaeda's views on global jihad, the Israeli-Palestinian conflict, the United States, Islam in politics, democracy and nationalism, among others. The report draws sharp distinctions between the ambitions of the two groups, suggesting that the Brotherhood's mix of Islam and nationalism make it a far different organization than al-Qaeda, which sees national boundaries as obstacles to restoring the Islamic caliphate.

In short, the Obama administration and U.S. intelligence agencies are trying to parse the contrasts and explore the variant nuances between the Muslim Brotherhood and Al-Qaeda, without seeing the vast areas of agreement: primarily their unending hostility to the West, particularly the United States. Is there a better example of "experts" overlooking the existence of the forest while examining the leaf of a tree?

The sheer folly of this recent search for compromise where there can be none was well described by Barry Rubin: "It is bad enough for U.S. and European policies to do nothing in the face of the greatest challenge of our time, but to assist actively in the coming to power and flourishing of enemies is incredibly foolish. The bottom line is that this goes beyond appeasement. It is a strategy of actively helping the enemy grow stronger in the belief that this is a brilliant idea."[10]

Some U.S. Army analysts have suggested dialogue with the Taliban or Hizballah, and accepting their demands. For example, Sami Hajjar, then-head of Middle East studies at the U.S. Army War College, urged acceptance of many of Hizballah's demands and recognizing its "pragmatic" leaders: "Under Nasrallah's leadership, Hizballah continues to pursue a strategy of pragmatism, accommodation, and engagement in the Lebanese political system and causes."[11]

That was written in 2002, before Hizballah murdered former Lebanese prime minister Rafik Hariri, before it violated all agreements against holding a separate armed militia, and before it started a major war with Israel in 2006 by invading Israeli territory to kill and kidnap several Israeli soldiers. Yet many U.S. and European officials *still* entertain the notion of embracing or "engaging" Hamas and Hizballah—and their state sponsors, Iran and Syria. Even as the Syrian regime of Bashar Assad was slaughtering opponents, Paul Pillar, the ex-CIA and State Department counterterror expert, urged the United States to keep "doing business" with Assad and Company: "There is underestimation of how much worthwhile business could be conducted with the incumbent regime, however distasteful it may be."[12] There is a long, ugly tradition of Western officials, academics, and journalists who feel Arab-Islamic terror groups and states are "tamable," are democratically oriented "reformers" and modernists.[13]

"Islamically oriented political actors and groups should be evaluated by the same criteria that are applied to any other potential leaders or opposition party," observed John Esposito of Georgetown University, where many State Department and CIA officials get their training. Esposito said that even though Islamist regimes and groups will generally be anti-American and anti-Western, "they will generally operate on the basis of national interests and demonstrate a flexibility that reflects the acceptance of the realities of a globally interdependent world."[14]

This is the worst kind of wishful thinking. Its "logic" has been shattered by the conduct of Islamist states such as Iran (the world's foremost state sponsor of terror) and Sudan (the world's current champion of mass murder, slavery, and genocide) and by terror groups such as Hamas, Hizballah, and the Taliban. Such terror states and terror groups sometimes offer a *hudna*, or temporary truce, when cornered. They feign interest in UN talks or multiparty accords, using any respite to rebuild forces and reignite war at their convenience. Israel's record with Palestinian terrorists set free by political deals and U.S. experience with terrorists freed from Guantánamo show that few hardened terrorists are ever rehabilitated. This is especially true of terrorists who say becoming a "martyr" is their greatest wish. Compromise with them is not an option.[15]

CONTAINMENT AS AN OPTION

When Soviet communism collapsed after seventy years, the victory was ascribed to the Western doctrine of "containment." It was a long-term strategy used by successive U.S. governments and U.S. allies in Europe over forty years. Like communism, Islamism also seeks world dominion, and some analysts have suggested containment may be used against Islamism and the Arab-Islamic terror that it fuels.

Containment was proposed in 1947 by George Kennan, a prescient

U.S. diplomat. President Harry Truman and subsequent presidents of both political parties modified it. The heart of the doctrine was putting slow, steady pressure on the communist empire of Soviet Russia and its satellite states in Eastern Europe. Containment was meant to block communist expansion with a variety of political, economic, and even military means, but stopping short of full-scale combat with the Soviets.

"Containment was intended to prevent Soviet expansion without saddling the United States with unsustainable global military obligations," observes Ian Shapiro of Yale, who has offered containment as a model for twenty-first-century counterterrorism.[16] Kennan's Containment Doctrine, Shapiro avers, was based on the view that "appeasement of their [Soviet] ambitions would be disastrous for America's vital interests, and that a direct assault on the USSR or its client states was unnecessary and would be counterproductive." Containment seems, at first glance, a completely apt doctrine also for the Arab-Islamic terror drive for world domination:

1. It costs less—in lives and resources—than full-scale war, and this is especially appropriate at a time when Western economies are strapped and the U.S. military is already overextended.
2. A full-scale war produces unwanted consequences. In the Soviet era, it could have led to nuclear Armageddon. Today, a full-scale war against Islamists might antagonize large sectors of Arab-Islamic opinion, hurting U.S. and Western interests, perhaps even sparking more terror.

On the other hand, there are some key differences between the Soviets and the Arab-Islamic terror groups and regimes. These differences make containment a questionable strategy. As Shapiro acknowledges, "The Soviet Union was a single 'it,' whereas today we face dangerous threats from a variety of hostile regimes."[17] Indeed, Shapiro's admission does not go far enough. He does not discuss the wide variety of terror organizations and substate actors outside of the multiple state sponsors. Shapiro's mention of "hostile regimes" sloughs over the fact that the Arab-Islamic terror danger goes far beyond several direct state sponsors of terror—Iran, Syria, and Sudan, for example—and includes a broader field of states, some of them failed states, that cooperate with Arab-Islamic terror (North Korea and Lebanon), offer diplomatic cover for terrorists and terror regimes (China and Russia), or offer funds and sanctuary (for example, Pakistan, Saudi Arabia, and Taliban-run Afghanistan).

Containment is a conservative and gradual approach suited for well-defined and cumbersome states like the Soviet Union led by plodding seventy-year-old leaders. It is not built for fleet-footed terrorists who can kill fifty thousand people without encircling Berlin with tanks. Though communism was a revolutionary doctrine, Soviet leaders were quite cautious and rational in their policy choices, because they believed that communism would eventually defeat capitalism. Why risk world war when Soviet ideology saw an inevitable dialectic leading to Western decline and communist triumph? The Soviets therefore rarely made or supported sudden or rash attacks.[18] This is not the case with Arab-Islamic terrorists. Many of them crave death. Indeed, many of them say the key to their kind of world must come through a devastating period of war. Yasser Arafat and Osama bin-Laden yelled repeatedly that they would love a martyr's death. So too has Iran's president, Mahmoud Ahmadinejad, who hopes to spur a world cataclysm that will usher in the age of the *mahdi,* the Islamic messiah. Soviet leaders Joseph Stalin or Leonid Brezhnev never made such remarks.

Sheikh Yousef Qaradhawi, the Muslim Brotherhood preacher whose sermons draw millions on Al Jazeera television, said he would love to die a martyr's death, even if he had to do it from his wheelchair. He yearned for "martyrdom" in front of a huge crowd of protesters in Cairo. This shows how the ideology of Islamism reinforces the power and strategic reach of Arab-Islamic terrorists. Islamists want Islamic law to rule the world. Many Islamists idealize suicide terror and death as the way to get close to God—*istish-haad*: actively seeking martyrdom. True, not *all* Islamists support terror, and not all Arab-Islamic terrorists are Islamists, but there is a growing congruence between the two groups. Al-Qaeda attack planner Ramzi Yousef did not live an Islamic lifestyle, but he was glad to help Al-Qaeda spread Islam by the sword and impose Shariah, Islamic law, wherever possible.

This cataclysmic view of effecting change is common to Al-Qaeda, Hamas, Hizballah, the Muslim Brotherhood, and other groups in both Sunni and Shiite Islam. Perhaps more importantly, this cataclysmic view includes Iranian president Ahmadinejad and Iran's supreme leader,

Ayatollah Ali Khamenei, both followers of Twelver Shiism. This is a belief that the messiah or *mahdi* is the twelfth, hidden imam who will return from hiding into a world consumed by terrible conflagration.

To prevent a conflagration or a major terror attack, Western countries cannot rely solely on slow-acting containment and similar tactics such as the use of sanctions. In the 1980s and 1990s, the United States declared a "dual containment" policy against the ayatollahs' Iran and Saddam's Iraq, using sanctions against both, as well as against Muammar Qadhafi's Libya. These methods failed miserably and repeatedly.

"American enthusiasm for using economic sanctions to advance U.S. foreign policy interests reached its peak with the passage of the Iran-Libya Sanctions Act in 1996," remarked Michael Armacost, president of the Brookings Institution and a former senior State Department official. However, he added, many U.S. officials "have come to view that propensity as misplaced."[19] Sanctions may have some use against small, isolated, or primitive countries like Sudan or Syria, but against bigger or stronger countries, they often "prove feckless," according to another study.[20]

Containment and the use of sanctions, therefore, are not a real option.

DETERRENCE AS AN OPTION

Can the West use a strategy of deterrence, a good tool in the East-West rivalry, against Arab-Islamic terror groups and terror states?

Thomas Schelling gave the classical definition of deterrence doctrine: "In addition to seizing and holding, disarming and confining, penetrating and obstructing, and all that, military force can be used to *hurt*. . . . Hurting, unlike forcible seizure or self-defense, is not unconcerned with the interest of others. It is measured in the suffering it can cause and the victims' motivation to avoid it."[21]

Deterrence is really a kind of refined form of terror or instilling the kind of fear that dissuades someone from a particular course of action, and the question is, can we terrorize terrorists?

The problem is that terrorists are not typical enemies. Their psychology and values are far different from ours or those of the old Soviet Union or even Nazi Germany.

Arab-Islamic terrorists do not seek incremental gains in territory or prestige. To put it in the parlance of Western sports: they do not want to win the championship. They want to own the stadium or, if needed, burn it down.

This is hard for most Westerners to understand. Most of us have been educated and acculturated to achieve incrementally and to avoid violence. Early on, our parents taught us things like "force never solves anything." Even in war, Western countries usually play by certain rules (for example, the Geneva Conventions and the various treaties about weapons) that are meant to inhibit civilian casualties or bestial behavior. The modern Western way to solve disputes in our daily lives is compromise through negotiation, arbitration, and the like. When all else fails, we go to court. This does not mean that there is no crime or no violence in Western societies, but that violence is not the ideal, not the norm. For terrorists, the abnormal is normal. Violence and threats are the norm. Endangering civilians is de rigueur: blowing up buses and buildings, poisoning water or air, or shooting a gun or a rocket and then hiding behind a baby carriage. So, what might deter us might not deter a terrorist.

Will severe manpower losses in a terror group or in a terror state army or its own civilian population base serve as a strategic deterrent? Experience with several Arab-Islamic terrorists and tyrants shows that deterrence is difficult:

- Yasser Arafat (Amman, 1970; siege of Beirut, 1982; Jenin and Ramallah, 2000–2002) showed he was willing to sacrifice entire cities for his goals.
- Saddam Hussein (Iran-Iraq War in 1980–88, Kuwait war in 1990, U.S.-Iraq war of 2003) was not deterred by the direct threats of the United States and its allies.
- Muammar Qadhafi and his son Saif-al-Islam declared they were willing to destroy most of Libya in order to stay in power in 2011, but Qadhafi temporarily pulled back from terror after seeing what the United States did to Saddam.
- Abdullah Azzam, the Palestinian Islamist leader who inspired Osama bin-Laden and the Arab fighters in Afghanistan, said he was willing to have entire Muslim populations in Afghanistan or Bosnia die of starvation for the sake of jihad.

- Osama bin-Laden and Ayman Zawahiri were clearly not deterred from their long-term objectives by massive assaults on their bases.

On a tactical or short-term basis, however, deterrence may work, if the pain causes operational incapacitation or shutdown of terror groups. Israel used targeted killings at various times to incapacitate Hamas. Many Hamas leaders did not fear death or even the deaths of their families. But they were worried they would lose the ability to act at all. Likewise, Israel achieved temporary deterrence against Hizballah in 2006 when the Iranian-aided organization verged on losing its political base in central Lebanon and its military base in southern Lebanon entirely.[22] Hizballah, Al-Qaeda, and other terror groups recruit followers, claiming the West causes Muslim death and suffering, but they themselves are sensitive to charges that *they* are hurting Muslims.[23]

Threats of violence or pain, in the abstract, are not usually effective in getting terrorists to change direction. It is a little bit like trying to threaten a drunk or a drug addict. Only "functional pain" works—the kind that keeps them from standing up. For most Arab-Islamic terrorists or tyrants, pain and violence are their daily currency. Therefore, strategic deterrence of terrorists has only limited and temporary effect.

CONQUEST AS AN OPTION

On a gut level, conquering terrorists and destroying their bases has great appeal. There are, however, many drawbacks. One is intrinsic Western distaste for fighting, especially a long fight. In Western societies violence is only extolled—and sublimated—in violent entertainment and sports, but we understand that this is not meant to be the real world. Violent Western sporting events where there can be only one ultimate winner—from football to ice hockey—are decided in what is called "sudden death." But we do not really mean *sudden death*. We do not expect the losing team in the Super Bowl, the World Series, or the Stanley Cup Finals to give up their lives.[24] The contests are measured in points and goals. Yes, only one side gets the trophy and the big money, but, as the saying goes, "there is always next year."

In resolving political conflicts, labor disputes, and even sports confrontations, we are trained to expect compromises and imperfect resolutions that may be changed by future discussion, next year's season, or next year's parliament or congress. That is not true with the terrorists and the regimes they would install. Some of them pretend to have democratic hopes, but they do not believe in "one-man, one-vote." To borrow the phrase of Bernard Lewis, they want "one-man-one-vote-ONE-TIME-ONLY." *Once in power, they will not relinquish it.* Iran and Sudan are good examples of Islamist regimes—one Shiite, one Sunni—that will use any measures needed to stay in power. Likewise, terror-based groups and regimes will do almost anything to get power and to stay in power. Of course, Western regimes and states have, over time, used brutal tactics, too, sometimes against their own citizens. Still, the overall pattern is that Western democracies do not slaughter their own citizens, nor wipe out or enslave the entire population of the enemy. The United States imprisoned and relocated Japanese-Americans during World War II, but did not try to kill or enslave all Japanese when it conquered Japan. The atomic bombings of Hiroshima and Nagasaki were meant to shorten the war in the face of huge casualties and Japanese suicide tactics.

Since World War II and the establishment of the United Nations in 1945, the trend to search for peaceful solutions has deepened. Westerners have been trained to try to work out disputes "rationally." However, our "rational" and their "rational"—or if you will: our rationale and their rationale—are quite different. Western children, particularly in Europe, are taught to avoid fights and to seek compromise. That is not what Arab-Islamic terrorists and tyrants teach *their* children. They are taught to fight to the death, and never to settle for a compromise, though, as a ploy, terrorists hint they are willing to make truces. That is one reason historian and counterterror analyst Walter Laqueur once said the best way to deal with a terrorist was to kill him.

Killing all or most terrorists has great appeal on a moral plane. Frankly, the terrorists deserve to die because they want to shake the very foundations of society, and use despicable means for unspeakable ends. Killing them also appeals to us on a utilitarian level. Removing terrorists permanently is much safer than putting them in jails where they can escape or be released in hostage deals. *That is the real reason Osama bin-Laden was killed.* But there are problems with the killing-terrorists option, as shown by wars in Iraq and Afghanistan:

- Unlike dictatorships, Western democracies do not have the stomach for killing, fortunately, and do not like to fight long wars.
- Western societies do not have unlimited manpower and funds. A terrorist bomb or mortar is usually much cheaper than the West's high-tech countermeasures.[25]
- Terrorists can hide behind civilian populations or seek sanctuary, even hopping from country to country, looking for failed states or failing states that can serve as hosts for their parasitic lifestyle.
- To pursue the conquest option or the kill-the-terrorist option, democratic states have to be well prepared, well financed, and equipped with enough manpower to carry the task to completion as quickly as possible, and not get sidetracked by laudable but difficult goals like bringing democracy to Iraq or women's rights to Afghanistan.[26]

The United States once had a two-and-one-half-war profile. This meant the ability to fight several wars simultaneously. That was before budget cutbacks of the 1990s shrank U.S. strategic reach. The United States has fought in Iraq and Afghanistan with troops often drawn from reserve units. This stretched military capacity to the breaking point. With recent financial crises, such problems are even deeper. While the conquest option or the killing-all-terrorists option appeals to us on many levels, it is not a real policy option to "be the world's policeman" in most cases and at most times.

DECAPITATION AND TARGETED KILLING AS AN OPTION

America's liquidation of Osama bin-Laden in Abbottabad, Pakistan, is the most salient example of the use of targeted killing as part of the war on terror. Few but the United States could carry out such an operation so far from home, and few but America would be able to overcome criticism of such a clear violation of national sovereignty even for the just cause of bringing an archterrorist to justice. But as the great Israeli humorist Ephraim Kishon once said after yet another condemnation of Israel: better to have your condemnation than your condolences.

Killing Osama bin-Laden had huge symbolic and moral impact, though he was probably not a serious operational factor in Al-Qaeda terror in the last five years, especially not in the terror by Al-Qaeda imitators.

The important operational roles moved to younger, more active people whose names are not well-known to the general public. Yet eliminating these younger, more active, and less prominent terrorists will probably have an even greater impact on lowering the level of terror.

There is much political and operational hypocrisy on the subject of targeted killings of terrorists and tyrants—sometimes called "assassinations" by the media and some governments. The United States has an official policy against "assassination," for example, until it gives itself approval to do so. The best example of an active policy of targeted killings against terror groups is what Israel has periodically used very successfully against Fatah, Hamas, and even against Hizballah. These anti-terror strikes were very effective in curbing the terror-making capacity of the targeted group, but the Israeli acts have often been decried even by the United States, Britain, France, and other Western countries that applauded bin-Laden's demise. Even when such anti-terror strikes are clean, surgical affairs that take place in Gaza, they are often condemned. Such attacks are especially censured when they occur in a sovereign state such as Jordan or Syria or when they also kill or injure neighbors or family members of the terrorists.

DEFENSE AS AN OPTION

Marc Sageman, a former CIA and State Department expert, has said that the West has largely defeated Al-Qaeda and now faces a "leaderless jihad," a group of ragtag forces that can be mopped up.[27] This observation has been advanced by several analysts,[28] and it has an element of truth, but it is also very dangerous. For example, Jessica Stern, a highly regarded counterterror analyst, recently referred to the phenomenon of Islamized Western youth being recruited by Internet as a mere "fad," adding, "And like all fads, this one too shall pass."[29]

Yes, Al-Qaeda has been wounded, and some of its operational plans have been thwarted or thrown into disarray by the U.S.-led strikes against it. Unfortunately, Sageman's analysis and Stern's somewhat flippant remark are both too optimistic and premature. Spanish anti-terror expert Fernando Reinares, for example, has shown conclusively that the 2005 attacks in Madrid were executed by well-entrenched and well-financed Al-Qaeda cells that were planning additional attacks. Reinares painstakingly reviewed the evidence of the Madrid bombings, and he was critical of media reports and the optimistic counterterror analysts: "The conventional wisdom that soon emerged about the 3/11 attacks was that it [*sic*] was a prototypical example of a local terrorist cell at work: self-recruited, leaderless jihad—a 'bunch of guys,' as one analyst put it." Reinares added that "the media has astonishingly contributed to this [perception of] Al Qaeda as an amorphous phenomenon."[30] Actually, it is a deadly pathogen that can change form, a set of surprisingly advanced organisms (some Sunni, some Shiite, some Arab, some non-Arab, and some mixed) that can metastasize, that is, transmit pathogenic microorganisms or terrorist cells from an original site—Cairo, Jerusalem, Riyadh, Mecca, Kabul—to one or more sites around the world: New York, Madrid, London, Buenos Aires, Nairobi, Mumbai. Some of these organisms can also be sleeper cells that were put in place well before 9/11, 7/7, or 3/5.

Despite our best efforts, we must assume some attacks or plots—perhaps major attacks—will escape detection and be carried out. This is not a worst-case scenario, but in fact a prudent scenario. We must prepare active and passive defenses to block, minimize, and absorb attacks that get by our preventive measures.

Israel has done this for sixty years. Though better known for its aggressive preventive counterterror measures, Israel has heavily and successfully invested in defensive and risk-reduction methods. This is the reason that, "unlike Lebanon, no sizeable car bomb has ever been detonated in Israel."[31] Israel has also known that Palestinian terrorists and state sponsors wanted to crash a jetliner into a building in Tel Aviv. This, too, has been prevented in Israel, because of basic commonsense precautions. For more than forty years, Israeli plane cockpits have remained locked during flight. That is one reason the Palestinians moved to the two-legged missiles known as human bombs or suicide bombers.

Sensitive public buildings and even small private businesses have been "hardened," with several rings of defensive measures. The common idea is to "push the defense perimeter outward." If all else fails, a suicide terrorist, for example, is to be intercepted outside a building, rather than inside it. Why?

The reason is that an explosion in a crowded interior space can be ten to twenty times more deadly because of the concussive blast effect of shock waves, not to mention fire and shrapnel. People coming to

Ben-Gurion Airport are screened by several rings of security, for example, and even Israelis entering restaurants and shopping malls are screened or "eyeballed" by guards and/or cameras. That is also why there are concrete barriers outside certain public buildings in Washington, D.C.: they are meant to stop car and truck bombers. Such sights and such practices are ugly necessities. So are identity cards and better barriers against illegal immigration.

MORAL AND LEGAL QUESTIONS IN TERROR DEFENSE

We justifiably love our civil liberty, but the most important human right is life. Typical rules of civil procedure and criminal law do not apply, because we are dealing with a particularly uncivil phenomenon and with the kinds of crimes that must be prevented, not punished. When we fight terror, we are protecting not just the life of the individual baker, bricklayer, nurse, and doctor, but the collective life of society threatened by terror. We are used to moving about freely, but we have to accept some minimal delays and limitations on our total freedom of movement and our absolute freedom of privacy. Again, we can learn from several countries how and what to do and what not to do—especially in times of tension. Some of these techniques are already being employed in the United States, Britain, France, Germany, India, and Israel.

More than twenty years ago, Israel wrestled with the question of whether suspected or captured terrorists could be treated roughly. Israeli Supreme Court chief justice Moshe Landau set up a commonsense protocol of limited rough stuff such as shaking the terrorist but not harsher methods from authoritarian societies, such as electric shock treatment or other forms of torture. Israeli courts also recognized increased latitude when terrorists were part of a "ticking bomb" situation or a "clear and present danger" justifying quick coercive pressure to prevent imminent loss of life. At such times, I believe that waterboarding is not only permissible but necessary. Several top U.S. officials have confirmed that such methods have prevented major terror strikes in the United States.

"Rules governing coercive interrogation must be crafted in a way that gives clear guidance so that these methods do not approach torture," cautions law professor Philip Bobbitt, adding, we must "pay more attention to our vulnerabilities."[32] At a time when terrorists send signals and instructions via email and Internet, this means having sensible monitoring of electronic communication. The USA Patriot Act and other legislation have codified proper safeguards on such methods, and the matter should not be turned into a partisan political episode by politicians or news media trying to grab a quick headline.

SUGGESTED APPROACHES TO FIGHTING TERROR

A full and detailed discussion of operative counterterror options is beyond the scope of this book. Indeed, it would require an entire new book, but there are some options that can be discussed and enumerated in general terms.

Eclectic Tactics and Combined Arms Theory

We are fighting terrorists who defy easy classification. They change form, change tactics, and come from diverse backgrounds. That means individual countries facing terror will not be able to use only one set of arms or one set of tactics to fight terrorists—nor fight them all by themselves. Just as countries cooperate to stop the spread of biological and chemical dangers—for example, plagues of *E. coli* from Germany to Holland, or rabies from Jordan to Israel—states must unite to stop cross-border terror.

Western nations need to combine elements of several options at different times and in different places—sometimes using drone aircraft or commandos for targeted killing of terrorists or using multilateral actions to interdict terrorists or their arms.

In some cases, conquering terror sanctuaries *will* be a viable option either for a single country, such as the United States, Britain, France, or Israel, operating in a relatively easy theater of operations such as Libya or Gaza, for example. However, long-term conquests and nation building in failed states must be avoided, especially in large and hard-to-rule areas such as Afghanistan. In any event, Western democracies will have to help each other, sharing resources, sharing manpower, sharing intelligence. The old games of diplomatic one-upping will have to be cast aside.

Sometimes, the conquering option may be pursued by a coalition of forces, as in the wars for Kuwait or Iraq or parts of former Yugoslavia. Experience shows that forming such coalitions and using ad hoc military cooperation will be very hard. One possible solution is for NATO or the

European Union or countries of the Organisation for Economic Co-operation and Development to form combined anti-terror forces that can begin training together.

Rebuilding Military Options

The end of the Soviet Union led to hopes for "a new world order" (George H. W. Bush) and for a "peace dividend" (Bill Clinton), with the contraction of Western military forces. Those hopes were embraced and exaggerated by intellectuals and pundits as diverse as Francis Fukuyama (*The End of History*) and Michael Mandelbaum (*The Ideas That Conquered the World*) but none as much as Thomas Friedman of the *New York Times*. "The next big idea was that globalization would bring harmony" and a surge of human rights.[33] Rarely has such a loudly delivered prediction proved so hollow so quickly.

Several Western countries, especially the United States, will need to rebuild part of their strategic reach: navies, standing armies, and especially field intelligence and rapid deployment forces. This does not mean launching outlandish construction of fleets of stealth ships or numerous nuclear-fueled aircraft carriers, but it means an investment in equipment and manpower that will be more than repaid if it helps stop one or more attacks of the magnitude of 9/11 or worse.

Defensive Options

Aside from heightening awareness and hardening security at sensitive installations and public sites, Western countries need to develop more anti-terror and anti-WMD technologies such as devices to detect radiation, dangerous chemical precursors, biological agents, and airborne and waterborne poisons. Some of these will need to be deployed at airports, at seaports, and at mass transit nodes.

While the general public is aware of scanners at airports, one of the greatest areas of weakness is our seaports, through which many dangerous materials may reach our shores. In the United States, most ship cargoes today are simply not examined in any way.

The United States and its allies, particularly Israel, are already investing in active defense techniques such as devices to intercept or damage incoming rockets, missiles, and other nonballistic projectiles carrying conventional explosives and nonconventional payloads. The United States should push ahead with this research and implementation, as is Israel, even over the objections of countries such as Russia and China, both of which are indirectly and directly helping Arab-Islamic terror groups and state terror sponsors.

We must also step up protection of our cyber networks from attack from hacking as well as from electromagnetic pulse disturbance. Several countries have already suffered serious cyberattacks in 2010 and 2011.

Weakening Our Terror Foes Economically

A common element of most Arab-Islamic terror groups is that they were helped by oil money, particularly from Saudi Arabia and Iran. We must try to intercept and disrupt funds for these groups, but the best long-term way to cripple terror finances is to stop throwing money at the ayatollahs or Saudi billionaires who finance terror. We can do this by reducing our dependency on foreign energy sources, particularly oil. This has to be done in a variety ways, first by developing the flexible fuel option in Western vehicles—cars, buses, and trains that can run on fuels other than just oil-based gasoline: ethanol, methanol, coal-derived methanol mixtures, hybrid electric, shale-derived mixtures, hydrogen, and natural gas.[34]

Demographic Policy and Immigration Reform

John Kennedy once called the United States "a nation of immigrants." This is a badge of honor that can be worn today by many Western states, but it is also dangerous. Just as Lenin once laughed that Western capitalists would sell rope to the revolutionaries who would hang them, so Arab-Islamic terrorists brag about using the liberal immigration and welfare policies of the West to destroy the West and its liberalism from within.

We must reject softheaded immigration policies and "sanctuary" movements in places such as New York, San Francisco, London, and Tel Aviv. Immigration from Arab-Islamic countries should be *strongly vetted and reduced.* Immigration from places with a history of producing terror should be especially cut. Policies should be changed so that anyone convicted of complicity in major crimes or immigration fraud can be summarily deported along with his or her family. An Egyptian cleric who wants to bomb the World Trade Center should not be allowed to stay in New York because he claims that someone in Egypt wants to hurt him.

Meanwhile, Western countries—especially in Europe—should encourage their own population to start having more children, rather than importing foreign labor forces that become sullen bases for crime and terror. Most European countries are not even replacing themselves demographically, but this can and should change.

Rebuilding Intelligence and Education

As Samuel Huntington and Margaret Thatcher each observed more than a decade ago, the Arab-Islamic sphere generates most of the global threats and violence today. We need to reverse the "black hole" of ignorance at Western universities and think tanks regarding this arena. Middle East studies—languages, culture, history, politics, anthropology—need to recapture the respectful place from which they were routed by the anti-Orientalist ideology and anti-area-study approach launched by Edward Said. Also, we cannot allow the curricula and staff of Western universities to be determined by authoritarian Arab regimes and their donations. We see what happens to young Western minds tutored by Edward Said and John Esposito.

As *New York Times* intelligence reporter Tim Weiner suggested, Western intelligence agencies and armies should build and enlarge their own academic capacities, even their own universities, specializing in intelligence skills and area studies. Yonah Alexander, one of the foremost scholars of world terror, also supports establishing specially trained and educated national and international counterterror units, because 9/11 and other attacks prove "the built-in vulnerability of modern societies and their infrastructure."[35] As a short-term measure, American forces should ask for help from friendly and reliable Middle Eastern allies such as Israel and Jordan, to help in the area-study education process. Just as British and even U.S. diplomats once got Arabic immersion in Lebanon, special programs may be established at Hebrew University, the Shalem Center, or Jordan University.

In Eastern martial arts systems, defensive measures include "hard" techniques as well as "soft" techniques. Fighting terror also requires using "soft power"—using words and ideas to defeat terrorists.

Soft Power, Smart Power, and the Battle of Ideas

America and the West should extend a hand of friendship to all regimes, groups, and religions who are willing to live in peace and settle disputes by talking. Particularly, the West must focus on Muslims and stress that Muslims who are willing to accept non-Muslims are welcome. To do this, the West must initiate and expand information programs via radio, TV, libraries, and social media such as the Internet.

Sadly, the United States has often done the opposite. For years it cut back on its U.S. Information Service. This needs to be reversed. Young Arabs and Muslims need to know what the West can offer, and that the West is *not* inimical to many of the East's traditional values. Robert Satloff, who studied this subject, stresses three elements:

a. "explaining U.S. policy, candidly and without apology";
b. "providing alternative sources of credible, factual, relevant information, especially abut the wider world but also about the local countries in which listeners and viewers live";
c. "projecting those core U.S. values that characterize U.S. society, especially tolerance, openness, meritocracy, and civic activism."[36]

This will be a slow process. As Satloff admits, it will be hard "to drain the swamp" because "even if one were to accept a low-end estimate of the number of Islamists worldwide (say, 5 percent of all Muslims) and a low-end estimate of the number of terrorists and their activist sympathizers—financiers, logistical supporters, ideological advocates—among them (say, 1 percent of all Islamists), then there are at least 600,000 hard-core radicals fishing for followers in a sea of at least 60,000,000 potential recruits."[37] Indeed, the scale of the problem may be even more daunting because the number of Islamist/terror sympathizers may be four or five times higher than Satloff estimates. Moreover, information campaigns sometimes backfire. Sayyid Qutb, the seminal guide of the Muslim Brotherhood, became more anti-American and anti-Christian after months in a cultural exchange program in the United States in the 1950s.

Above all, U.S. and Western information programs must radiate strength as well as friendship. The Arab-Islamic world respects strength, and Osama bin-Laden himself and other terrorist leaders like Hizballah chief Hassan Nasserallah scorn weakness. They have been emboldened when they perceive weakness. "When people see a strong horse and a weak horse, by nature, they will like the strong horse."[38] The West must be wary never to let itself sound like a coterie of whining apologists.

Public diplomacy is not a totally new approach. The United States used it during the Cold War against the Soviet Union. "Policymakers understood the link between engagement with foreign audiences and victory over ideological enemies and considered cultural diplomacy vital to U.S. national security," observes Helena Finn, a veteran U.S. foreign service officer.[39] While fighting terror, the United States must wage a hot war as well as using soft-power Cold War techniques. These methods are known today by the various terms *soft power, smart power,* and *public diplomacy.* This means basic education about the West. It also may require elements of propaganda and psychological warfare. We should not be ashamed to use these means. Officials should not be deterred from using Arab newspapers, Internet, and TV by hostile or sarcastic editorials in the *Washington Post* or *New York Times.*

Arabs and Muslims respect those who respect themselves. They respect those who are loyal to friends. They respect strength. The United States should not, as President Obama has done, apologize to the Arab-Islamic world for anything. The United States should not apologize to the Arab-Islamic community, because it is counterproductive and because the apology is not warranted by facts. The United States has not colonized the Arabs or the Muslims. The United States has *not* fought wars for the sake of Israel, but, on the contrary, it has sacrificed its own blood and treasure to save Arab and Muslim populations in Kuwait, Iraq, Lebanon, Bosnia, and Afghanistan in the last few years. Obama's apologetic version of "engagement" has not won ideological converts or policy concessions from tough Arab regimes, and public opinion surveys show it has actually repelled the Arab man in the street.

Similarly, the United States should not abandon traditional allies, hoping that superficial gestures will yield a quick public opinion payoff. Obama and his aides hastily undercut Egypt's Hosni Mubarak, and, as problematic as he was, the replacement will be disappointing. The Obama administration also helped isolate Israel, America's only steady ally in the Middle East. Polls in the Arab sector show such gestures do not win friends and influence people. Even Hizballah leader Nasserallah publicly laughed at Obama for his actions.

When the United States killed Osama bin-Laden, it should not have given him any kind of proper funeral. He was a mass murderer, not a regular criminal, certainly not a soldier. For U.S. authorities to get involved with "Muslim burial" or "ritual bathing" was a ridiculous show of ignorance or weakness—probably both. When Israel executed Adolph Eichmann, it disposed of his ashes at sea. He did not deserve burial, and neither did bin-Laden. Disposal of ashes at sea is a good option.

Terrorists who are executed for mass murder have lost most of their privileges as human beings. We should not deliberately desecrate their bodies or make light of their deaths, not because of them, but rather because it would diminish us. In this respect, President Obama is correct that showing close-up pictures of dead terrorists or tyrants or video footage of their execution is not part of our tradition.

Suspected terrorists should be tried in military courts or special tribunals. They should not be allowed to turn civilian courts into expensive and time-consuming public relations circus events. They should not be treated like civilian criminals or like prisoners of war. They are in a different category not covered by Geneva Conventions. At the same time, they should not be subject to debasement or torture.

Looking to the Future

We are facing an ever-changing terror virus or cancer that has adopted different forms in different locales. The terrorists have an underlying unified purpose to change the landscape of the world by promoting an extreme Islamist agenda—destroying or changing non-Islamic governments in the Middle East and the Western states that they believe have helped promote the Western corruptive influence on "true" Islam.

As Margaret Thatcher observed, "it is the connection between Islam and violence that is so disturbing. Apart from North Korea, all of the states classed as 'rogues'—Iraq, Syria, Libya, Iran, and Sudan—are mainly, and in some cases militantly, Muslim."[40] Of course, not all or even most Muslims are supporters of Arab-Islamic terrorism, but Muslims—particularly Arab Muslims—have been at the heart of most terror acts and most conflict since the early 1990s. This prompted Samuel Huntington to use the term

"Islam's Bloody Borders."[41] Indeed, the Arab-Islamic world has hardly distinguished itself in condemning or isolating its terrorists, particularly those who attacked New York and Washington. "The Islamic world is not responsible for what bin-Laden did," declared Thatcher. "But in the past too many influential Muslims have failed to speak out openly against what he and his kind represent."[42] Many Muslims, unfortunately, are supporters of terror, including even a few members of Western military and law enforcement agencies. Some of these supporters aid terror actively (by passing funds or information) and many more support terror in more indirect ways (refusing to report terrorists' movements, etc.) or by cheering the terrorists' actions at rallies.

Part of the challenge in fighting Arab-Islamic terror is that many politicians, professors, and pundits hide the real problem under a layer of euphemisms and obfuscation. They call it "global terrorism" rather than Arab-Islamic terrorism. Especially in academia, serious examination and criticism of the Arab-Islamic world, serious ability to warn about disturbing trends, has been stymied by certain fashions in thought that regard the West as guilty of the all the evils in the Third World.

Monitoring Mosques and Islamic Organizations

Most Arab-Islamic terror attacks on the West in the last decade involved a stage of recruitment or radicalization involving mosques and/or Islamic organizations as well as their websites. Therefore, Western law enforcement and intelligence must monitor these institutions and their media. This is not McCarthyism, and this is not a witch hunt. It is only common sense. The people investigated—and often unfairly hounded—by Senator Joseph McCarthy had never supported terror attacks. We can have no confidence that the same is true of the Jersey City Mosque or the Atlantic Avenue Mosque and the Kifayah Organization in Brooklyn or the Finsbury Park Mosque in London. And, there is evidence that these mosques and organizations were not alone in championing radical Islamist policies. As cited earlier, Sheikh Muhammad Hisham Kabbani, a moderate Muslim preacher, told U.S. officials in 1999 that most mosques and Islamic charities in the United States had been "taken over" by Saudi-funded extremists.[43]

Most Muslims in America, Britain, and France are not involved in terror. They should be the first to want to remove the scourge of religiously sanctioned hatred from their *minbars,* minarets, and mailing lists. Militant Muslim groups accusing Western governments of wholesale racism may act as front organizations for radical Islamists. *They*—their top officials and finances—should be investigated thoroughly.

"We must gather intelligence about likely threats," Philip Heymann, who was deputy attorney general in the Clinton Justice Department, wrote in 1998, in a statement that reflects the gap between the idea and its execution. "We must monitor organizations that urge political violence as a tactic and have the capacity to use it." Heymann added his view that "this effort will inevitably inhibit free speech and political organization at the outer borders of political discussion" and that such a policy must be conducted "with a concern to minimize that inhibition."[44] Heymann's observations came three years before 9/11, more than a decade before Fort Hood and other domestic U.S. terror attacks by Arab-Islamic terrorists.

Events showed that the Clinton administration's misgivings about monitoring terror threats, its self-imposed limits about sharing intelligence between various law enforcement agencies (for fear of violating privacy rights), and its reticence about even appearing to be using any form of profiling actually helped terrorists escape detection.[45] In a passage that would virtually be repeated by the 9/11 Commission, Heymann writes, "We cannot afford to have the FBI deny the CIA information it has obtained, or the CIA to deny the FBI the information it has."[46] Of course American Muslims and their brothers and sisters in faith in Britain, France, Israel, Germany, Spain, and elsewhere are entitled to complete freedom of religion and freedom of speech, but that does not mean that terrorists should be given sanctuary in mosques.

A PERSONAL NOTE

My own personal hunch is that terrorists who are about to strike have a need to feel that their action is not futile. Those "martyrs" who are set to give their life need to know that their act is likely to have some effect, at least cumulatively. This view emerged from my own thirty-plus years as a student, reporter, and official in the Middle East. It also derived from some conversations with former Israeli prime minister Yitzhak Shamir, who well understood the motives and pressures of terror groups, because he led one. Shamir suggested strongly in one of his final interviews as prime minister that the best way to fight a terrorist was to make sure that the terror was futile, that the terrorist understood that the democratic society would not surrender.[47]

As someone who was once a terrorist and who put his own life on the line, Shamir was quite blunt, telling friends: "A man who goes forth to take the life of another whom he does not know must believe only one thing—that by his act he will change the course of history."

So, if we convince terrorists that their acts are going to be futile, there is a good chance we can prevent many acts of terror—by winning the battle of the mind.

NOTES

INTRODUCTION

1 This is a partial list based on a map prepared for hearings at the House Homeland Security Committee, April 2011, and earlier testimony by law enforcement officials.

2 Testimony of FBI director Robert S. Mueller III, Senate Committee on Homeland Security and Governmental Affairs, September 30, 2009.

3 Jessica Stern, a respected researcher at Harvard and the Council on Foreign Relations, made the comment in "Muslims in America," *National Interest*, April 19, 2011.

4 U.S. national crime statistics compiled by the FBI since 2001, cited in more detail later, show a relatively low level of anti-Islamic crimes, which are still in terms of number only a fraction of anti-Jewish activities annually, but there are regular media reports and allusions to anti-Islamic hysteria.

5 Obama interview in July 2010 by Bob Woodward for Woodward's book *Obama's War*. See Steve Luxenberg, "Bob Woodward Book Details Obama Battles With Advisers Over Exit Plan For Afghan War," *Washington Post*, September 22, 2010, p. 1, also at http://www.washingtonpost.com/wp-dyn/content/article/2010/09/21/AR2010092106706_pf.html, and Woodward–Diane Sawyer interview, September 27, 2010, ABC TV, http://abcnews.go.com/WN/bob-woodward-tells-diane-sawyer-book-obamas-wars/story?id=11738879 and http://www.realclearpolitics.com

/video/2010/09/27/woodward_jumped_in_chair_after_obamas_absorb_
terrorism_remark.html.

6 See Peter Grier, "Times Square Bomber Joins the Growing List of Inept
Terrorists," *Christian Science Monitor,* May 4, 2010.

7 I have never been a devotee of elites as a key element in political or sociological theory, such as in C. Wright Mills's *The Power Elite.*

8 Paul Pillar, *Terrorism and U.S. Foreign Policy* (Washington, DC: Brookings
Institution Press, 2001), p. 5.

9 *The 9/11 Commission Report* (official title, *Final Report of the National Commission on Terrorist Attacks upon the United States*), Executive Summary,
2004, p. 14.

10 Marius H. Livingston, preface, in Livingston et al., eds., *International Terrorism in the Contemporary World* (Westport, CT: Greenwood Press, 1978),
collecting papers from a symposium of world leaders and academics on
fighting terror held at Glassboro State College, 1976.

11 This is the title of the book the *Times* produced after 9/11. Richard Bernstein and the staff of the *New York Times, Out of the Blue: The Story of September 11, 2001, From Jihad to Ground Zero* (New York: Times Books, 2002).

12 The fourth plane hijacked on 9/11 crashed in Pennsylvania, due to resistance
by passengers, but it is believed to have been aimed at the White House.

13 Hannah Arendt, *The Origins of Totalitarianism* (New York: Meridian, 1958),
p. 307.

14 I will hereafter use the common shorthand "9/11" for the date.

15 Larry C. Johnson, "The Declining Terrorist Threat," *New York Times,* July 10,
2001, p. A19, http://www.nytimes.com/2001/07/10/opinion/the-declining
-terrorist-threat.html?scp=1&sq=%22the%20declining%20terrorist%20
threat%22&st=cse.

16 Peter Chalk, "Grave New World," *Forum for Applied Research and Public
Policy* 15, no. 15 (Spring 2000), p. 13.

17 See, inter alia, John L. Esposito, *The Islamic Threat: Myth or Reality?* (New
York: Oxford University Press, 1992); Elaine Sciolino, "The Red Menace Is
Gone, But Here Is Islam," *New York Times,* January 21, 1996; Fred Halliday,
Islam and the Myth of Confrontation: Religion and Politics in the Middle East
(New York: St. Martin's Press, 1995); Fawaz A. Gerges, *America and Po-
litical Islam: Clash of Cultures or Clash of Interests?* (Cambridge: Cambridge
University Press, 1999); and, of course, many of the books and articles of
Edward Said, the late prominent professor at Columbia University.

18 See comments by Bernard Squarcini, "Terrorisme: 'La menace n'a jamais
été aussi grande'" (Terrorism: "The Menace Has Never Been Greater"), *Le
Journal du Dimanche,* September 10, 2010.

19 Marko Langer, "Geheimdienst-Aktion: Terroranschläge auf Europas
Metropolen Vereitelt" (Terror Attacks on European Cities Thwarted),

Deutsche Welle, September 29, 2010, http://www.dw-world.de/dw/article
/0,,6055742,00.html; Tamara Cohen, "'Mumbai-Style' Al Qaeda Terror Attacks Planned on UK, France And Germany Are Uncovered," *Daily Mail*,
September 29, 2010, http://www.dailymail.co.uk/news/article-1315992
/Mumbai-style-terror-attacks-planned-UK-France-Germany-uncovered
.html. The death toll of 174 at Mumbai includes nine terrorists.

20 "India, Germany to push anti-terror, economic pacts on Tuesday,"
    Times of India, February 1, 2010, http://timesofindia.indiatimes.com/india
    /India-Germany-to-push-anti-terror-economic-pacts-on-Tuesday/article
    show/5524236.cms.

21 Francis Fukuyama, "The End of History and the Last Man," *National Inter-
    est*, Summer 1989.

22 Michael Mandelbaum, *The Ideas That Conquered the World: Peace, Democracy,
    and Free Markets in the Twenty-First Century* (New York: PublicAffairs,
    2002), p. 377.

23 At the millennium, a partial list of despots who employed their own terror
    or who used terror groups as subcontractors would include: Syria's Assad,
    Korea's Kim, Iraq's Saddam, and Iran's ayatollahs.

24 For a transcript, see http://www.whitehouse.gov/the_press_office/Remarks
    -by-the-President-at-Cairo-University-6-04-09/ and "President Obama
    Addresses Muslim World in Cairo," *Washington Post*, http://www.wash
    ingtonpost.com/wp-dyn/content/article/2009/06/04/AR2009060401117
    .html.

25 See September 11, 2010, interview with *Christian Science Monitor*, where
    Napolitano saw an increased "home grown terror threat."

26 Speech by John O. Brennan, Center for Strategic and International Stud-
    ies, August 6, 2009, http://www.whitehouse.gov/the_press_office/Remarks
    -by-John-Brennan-at-the-Center-for-Strategic-and-International
    -Studies/.

27 See, for example, Michael Howard, "What's In a Name? How to Fight
    Terrorism," *Foreign Affairs* (January/February 2002), pp. 8–13, where How-
    ard, an esteemed British military historian, argues that Osama bin-Laden
    should be called a criminal.

28 See Philip Bobbitt, *Terror and Consent: The War for the Twenty-First Century*
    (New York: Knopf, 2008).

29 Interview with Barack Obama, on *GPS*, hosted by Fareed Zakaria, CNN,
    July 13, 2008.

30 John O. Brennan, remarks at New York University, February 13, 2010.
    No official transcript was produced by NYU or the White House, but
    numerous accounts and video clips of the ninety-one-minute-long re-
    marks, reviewed by the author, were available on the Internet at the
    following sites, inter alia, http://www.whitehouse.gov/photos-and-video

/video/john-brennan-takes-questions-national-security, http://www.tren
tonian.com/articles/2010/02/15/opinion/doc4b79b1439bb89311492260
.prt, http://www.politico.com/blogs/joshgerstein/0210/Brennan_unruffled
_talks_terror_at_NYU.html.

31 Obama has clearly been influenced by the writings of Columbia professors Edward Said and Rashid Khalidi, the latter a close friend of Obama.
Among Said's works is Edward W. Said, *Covering Islam: How the Media
and the Experts Determine How We See the Rest of the World* (New York: Pan-
theon, 1981; rev. ed., New York: Vintage, 1997).

32 White House Transcript, President Barack Obama, "Remarks by the President at the Closing of the Tribal Nations Conference," November 5, 2009,
http://www.docstoc.com/docs/15378602/Transcript-of-President-Obama
-Speech-on-Fort-Hood-Tragedy.

33 Literally, the words in Arabic mean "God is great"; the phrase is used both
as a call to prayer and as a battle cry in the Arab-Islamic community.

34 Obama's academic records have not been made public, but he has acknowledged the influence of Said's ideas as well as those of another Palestinian
academic, Rashid Khalidi, a personal friend of Obama, and who became
the Edward Said Professor of Middle Eastern Affairs at Columbia.

35 Two hundred fifty-nine people were killed aboard Pan-Am flight 103 over
Lockerbie, Scotland, in 1988, and another eleven people were killed on
the ground by plane fragments. Britain released Libyan intelligence officer
Abdel Basset al-Megrahi, convicted of the terror, into Libyan custody. He
got a hero's welcome in Libya.

36 President Barack Obama, remarks at memorial of 9/11 attacks, White
House, September 11, 2010.

37 The Egyptian government of Gamal Abdul-Nasser, for example, organized
fedayeen—men of sacrifice—for terror attacks against Israel in the 1950s,
but Abdul-Nasser eventually had to crack down against the Muslim Brotherhood when one of its members tried to assassinate him. Saudi Arabia
has spent billions exporting Islamic radicalism, partly against other Arab
governments, only to find itself attacked by Islamists who took over Islam's
holiest shrine, the Grand Mosque in Mecca, in 1979.

38 The reference is to Michael Scheuer, whose ideas are discussed in the chapter on intelligence.

39 The term was first used by radical socialist terrorists in nineteenth-century
Europe, but it is especially true of Arab-Islamic terrorists like Osama bin-
Laden and Ayman Zawahiri, for whom the symbolic nature of statements
and actions is particularly important. See J. Bowyer Bell, *Dragonwars:
Armed Struggle and the Conventions of Modern War* (New Brunswick, NJ:
Transaction Books, 1999), p. 151. See also Walter Laqueur, *The Age of Ter-
rorism* (Boston: Little, Brown, 1987), pp. 48–51.

CHAPTER ONE: TERROR AND ACADEMIA: SABOTAGING THE WESTERN MIND

1 Bush critics like Richard Clarke, for example, cite what they see as his failure to heed intelligence warnings about Osama bin-Laden, while critics of
   Clinton cite failure to arrest bin-Laden in Sudan or Saudi Arabia before
   9/11. We will discuss these and other claims later in detail.

2 Donna Robinson Divine, introduction to Philip Carl Salzman and Donna
   Robinson Divine, eds., *Postcolonial Theory and the Arab-Israel Conflict* (London and New York: Routledge, 2008), p. 1.

3 For example, Chomsky had three books listed in slots 5, 17, and 35—
   following Kuhn, Joyce, Frye, and Wittgenstein—in "The Fifty Twentieth-
   Century Works Most Cited in the Arts & Humanities Citation Index,
   1976–1983," cited by Eugene Garfield, *Essays of an Information Scientist*,
   vol. 10, 1987, retrieved at http://home.comcast.net/~antaylor1/fiftymost
   cited.html. MIT's press office bragged that his "3,874 citations in the Arts
   and Humanities Citation Index between 1980 and 1992 make him the
   most cited living person in that period and the eighth most cited source
   overall—just behind famed psychiatrist Sigmund Freud and just ahead of
   philosopher Georg Hegel." MIT said that "from 1972 to 1992, Professor
   Chomsky was cited 7,449 times in the Social Science Citation Index—
   likely the greatest number of times for a living person there as well. . . ." See
   MIT Tech Talk 36, no. 27 (April 15, 1992). The 2007 rankings for books in
   the humanities show Chomsky and Said ranked 15 and 21, respectively. See
   Thomson Reuters ISI Web of Science, http://www.timeshighereducation
   .co.uk/story.asp?storyCode=405956&sectioncode=26.

4 See Edward W. Said, "Defamation, Zionist-style," *Al-Ahram Weekly* (English edition), no. 444 (August 26–September 1, 1999), as well as Edward
   W. Said, "Between Worlds," *London Review of Books* 20, no. 9 (May 7,
   1998). The term "Professor of Terror" was applied to Professor Said by
   Professor Edward Alexander in "Critical Inquiry into Terror," *Commentary*,
   August 1989, pp. 49–50, and in "'Professor of Terror': An Exchange: Edward Alexander, Critics," *Commentary*, December 1989, pp. 2–15.

5 A protester threw a tear gas canister into Hurok's office that set off a fire in
   which Kones died.

6 Kahane was an Orthodox rabbi but, in his youth, he had occasionally masqueraded as a non-Jew, as "Michael King," joining some far-right-wing
   groups and even serving as a kind of government informant. Although
   his ideological doctrines called, among other things, for the prevention of
   intermarriage with non-Jews, Kahane himself had not always practiced
   what he preached. See Michael T. Kaufman, "Remembering Kahane, and
   the Woman on the Bridge," *New York Times*, March 6, 1994. In the article,
   Kaufman described an earlier (January 24, 1971) profile article by him on
   Kahane in the *New York Times* that unearthed much negative background

material on the militant Jewish leader. Kahane acknowledged to Kaufman that the material was true but asked the reporter not to disclose some of it. The United States and the State of Israel, as well as others, list several of the organizations founded by Rabbi Meir Kahane and his followers as illegal terrorist organizations, for example, KACH, Kahane-Hai, and the JDL. The Brooklyn-based Kahane moved to Israel and was elected to the Knesset, Israel's parliament, in 1984. The U.S. State Department revoked Kahane's passport in 1985, claiming his actions violated his American citizenship, but the action was overturned by a federal court in 1987 that said that the State Department had no authority to foreclose the recognized right to hold dual citizenship. Kahane's KACH Party was banned from the 1988 Israeli elections because its ideology called for banishing all Arabs from Israel.

7   Kahane's party got only two seats (out of 120) in its best showing, and the Knesset finally banned his participation in elections because of racist planks in his platform.

8   Andrew J. McCarthy, "Prosecuting the New York Sheikh," *Middle East Quarterly* 4, no. 1 (March 1997).

9   See John Miller and Michael Stone with Chris Mitchell, *The Cell: Inside the 9/11 Plot, and Why the FBI and CIA Failed to Stop It* (New York: Hyperion, 2002), esp. pp. 38–56.

10 Ibid., p. 46.

11 Nosair's acquittal in the Kahane murder came in 1991, and the subsequent conviction for conspiracy came in 1996.

12 Lawrence Wright, *The Looming Tower: Al-Qaeda and the Road to 9/11* (New York: Vintage Books, 2006), p. 201.

13 See ibid., p. 206, and Peter Lance, *Cover Up: What the Government Is Still Hiding About the War on Terror* (New York: ReganBooks, 2004), p. 25.

14 Major Hasan also displayed Islamist behavior that was overlooked or forgiven by his superiors.

15 For an example of this disdainful tone, see, for example, Michael A. Sheehan, *Crush the Cell: How to Defeat Terrorism Without Terrorizing Ourselves* (New York: Crown, 2008), pp. 26–27, where Sheehan describes the first World Trade Center attack as an "amateur operation" and the other Al-Qaeda attacks of the 1990s as replete with "incompetence and downright idiocy." Dumb, perhaps, but smart enough to kill hundreds of people. A similar attitude by other officials will be discussed in detail later. The subtitle of Sheehan's book—"how to defeat terrorism without terrorizing ourselves"—is testimony to the influence of Said on him and other officials at CIA, State, and NSA who did not want to be seen as "hysterical" in their view of an "Islamic" terror threat.

NOTES303

16   Stephen F. Hayes, *The Connection: How Al-Qaeda's Collaboration with Saddam Hussein Has Endangered America* (New York: HarperCollins, 2004), p. 51. See also Lance, *Cover-Up*, p. 184.

17   For an additional source on possible Saddam involvement with the first World Trade Center attack see Christopher Dickey, "Seeing the Evil In Front of Us," *Newsweek*, September 9, 2002, http://www.newsweek.com/id/65578/page/1.

18   Richard Bernstein, "U.S. Portrays Sheik as Head of a Wide Terrorist Network," *New York Times*, May 6, 1994.

19   Bill Gertz, *Breakdown: The Failure of American Intelligence to Defeat Global Terror*, rev. ed. (New York: Plume, 2003), p. 28.

20   Robert S. Mueller III, "The New FBI: Protecting Americans Against Terrorism," remarks prepared for delivery at the American Civil Liberties Union 2003 Inaugural Membership Conference, June 13, 2003.

21   Heather MacDonald, "Keeping New York Safe from Terrorists," *City Journal* 11, no. 4 (Autumn 2001), Manhattan Institute for Policy Research. See also http://www.homelanddefense.org/journal/articles/HeatherMacDonald.htm.

22   The tensions between the Jewish and black communities exploded two years later in the Crown Heights riots after a Jewish driver was beaten by a black crowd following a traffic accident in which a young black boy was killed.

23   Edward W. Said, *Orientalism* (New York: Random House, 1978). The reference is p. 14 in the Vintage paperback edition. All subsequent references are from the same edition.

24   Richard Bernstein, "Edward Said, Leading Advocate of Palestinians, Dies at 67," *New York Times*, September 25, 2003, p. 1, http://www.nytimes.com/2003/09/25/obituaries/25CND-SAID.html?ex=1082088000&en=5a aff97cef45a8ba&ei=5070.

25   Michael Smerconish, "Listen to Lehman," *National Review Online*, April 15, 2004, http://www.nationalreview.com/comment/smerconish200404150849.asp.

26   *National Review* interview with John Lehman, August 6, 2004, http://corner.nationalreview.com/post/?q=ZTE3ZDNhYWFiOGY5M2ZjOW Y4MGEyZTI5NzJjOGEwYzI=, partly available at http://www.national review.com/corner/83581/irrepressible-john-lehman/rod-dreher.

27   See, inter alia, Said, *Orientalism*, p. 107, and Said, *Covering Islam: How the Media and the Experts Determine How We See the Rest of the World* (London: Routledge & Kegan Paul, 1981), pp. 86–88, as well as Bernard Lewis, "The Return of Islam," *Commentary*, January 1976, pp. 39–49.

28   Said, *Orientalism*, p. 317.

29 One basic element of this ideology is spreading Islam from *dar al-Islam* (the House of Islam) or *dar al-salaam* (the house of peace) to the non-Muslim areas of the world, known as *dar al-harb* (the house of war), by means of jihad.

30 Said, *Covering Islam*, pp. 84–86.

31 Bari Weiss, "The Tyrannies Are Doomed," *Wall Street Journal*, April 2, 2011, p. A13, http://online.wsj.com/article/SB10001424052748703712504576234601480205330.html?mod=WSJEUROPE_newsreel_opinion.

32 In this kind of concentric ideological opposition to the West, Edward Said probably owes a debt to Gamal Abdul-Nasser's "Three Circles" philosophy, in which the Egyptian dictator saw himself as standing as an anti-imperialist leader within concentric Arab, Islamic, and nonaligned power groups.

33 PLO chief Arafat became an icon at Third World protests and even at anti-globalization rallies.

34 In the Lebanon war of 1982, Israel directly targeted the PLO, and the entire Arab world did not intervene in any appreciable way—not by force of arms and not with any economic boycott.

35 See, for example, Fouad Ajami, "The End of Pan Arabism," *Foreign Affairs* 57 (Winter 1978–79), pp. 355–73, and *The Arab Predicament: Arab Political Thought and Practice Since 1967* (Cambridge: Cambridge University Press, 1981); and see also Michael Barnett, *Dialogues in Arab Politics: Negotiations in Regional Order* (New York: Columbia University Press, 1998), p. 13, where Barnett discusses how Arab politics moved away from the Palestinian and Pan-Arab themes.

36 Edward W. Said, *The Question of Palestine* (New York: Times Books, 1979), p. 229.

37 The Arabist phenomenon includes romantics such as Gertrude Bell, Freya Stark, and of course, Colonel T. E. Lawrence ("Lawrence of Arabia"), as well as American diplomats who developed close ties with the Arab world. For a brilliant documentation, see Robert D. Kaplan, *The Arabists: The Romance of an American Elite* (New York: Free Press, 1993). Another fine and more recent work is Mitchell Bard, *The Arab Lobby: The Invisible Alliance That Undermines America's Interests in the Middle East* (New York: Harper, 2010).

38 Until 1973, various Arab states—such as Egypt and Jordan—claimed to represent the Palestinians.

39 Widlanski interview with Dr. Denis MacEoin, March 26, 2011.

40 The Qadhafi doctorate was questioned even by many of LSE's own professors. Saif Qadhafi went on Libyan TV to broadcast threats to dissidents in a coarse Arabic that exceeded even his father's rhetoric. Katherine Sellgren, "LSE Investigates Gaddafi's Son Plagiarism Claims," BBC, March 1, 2011, http://www.bbc.co.uk/news/education-12608869.

41 Centre for Social Cohesion, London, *Radical Islam on UK Campuses: A Comprehensive List of Extremist Speakers at UK Universities,* 2010, p. v, http://www.socialcohesion.co.uk/files/1301651215_1.pdf.

42 Dana Harman, "Hunting For Witches In An Ivory Tower," *Haaretz,* March 18, 2011.

43 Fidel Sendagorta, "Jihad in Europe: The wider context," *Survival* 47, no. 3 (2005), pp. 63–72, http://dx.doi.org/10.1080/00396330500248029.

44 "LSE 'has links with Chechen terrorists,'" *Guardian,* February 21, 2001, http://www.guardian.co.uk/uk/2001/feb/21/chechnya.world.

45 "Suicide bombing in Sweden: Latest terrorist attack exported from UK," Centre for Social Cohesion Briefing, December 13, 2010, http://www.social cohesion.co.uk/files/1292344510_1.pdf.

46 On LSE, see the article by LSE student union representative Emmanuel Akpan-Inwang, "The LSE's Libya Connection Is Only the Tip of the Iceberg," *Guardian,* March 4, 2011, http://www.guardian.co.uk/commentisfree/2011/mar/04/lse-howard-davies-libya-uae. For Harvard material, see Ralph Ranalli, "Harvard to Return $2.5m Given by Arab President," *Boston Globe,* July 28, 2004, http://www.boston.com/news/local/articles/2004/07/28/harvard_to_return_25m_given_by_arab_president/. For Columbia material, see "President Bollinger's Statement about President Ahmadinejad's Scheduled Appearance," http://www.columbia.edu/cu/news/07/09/ahmadinejad2.html and Nahal Toomsi, "Ahmadinejad Questions 9/11, Holocaust," *Huffington Post,* September 24, 2007, http://www.huffingtonpost.com/huff-wires/20070924/iran-us/.

47 A rabbi in St. Louis asked me to appear at St. Louis University, a Catholic school, "to try to add some balance" during a "Palestine Week" held in 2008.

48 Video of the event, which took place at UCSD on May 10, 2010, is available at http://www.newsrealblog.com/2010/05/11/for-it-msa-student-confesses-she-wants-a-second-holocaust/ and http://www.foxnews.com/story/0,2933,592993,00.html.

49 Fawaz A. Gerges, *America and Political Islam: Clash of Cultures or Clash of Interests?* (Cambridge: Cambridge University Press, 1999), p. 53.

50 Elaine Sciolino, "The Red Menace Is Gone, But Here Is Islam," *New York Times,* January 21, 1996.

51 This was a way of dismissing Professor Samuel Huntington's "clash of civilizations" approach, too.

52 Umar Farouk Abdulmutallab, a Nigerian student radicalized at UCL, tried to blow himself up on a Northwest Airlines flight on Christmas Day 2009, and Ahmed Omar Saeed Sheikh, who attended LSE, was convicted and sentenced to death for his role in the murder of *Wall Street Journal* reporter Daniel Pearl. BBC, "Profile: Omar Saeed Sheikh," July 16, 2002, http://news.bbc.co.uk/2/hi/uk_news/1804710.stm. See also Karla Adam, "British

Universities Sometimes Seen as Breeding Grounds for Radical Islam," *Washington Post,* January 1, 2010, http://www.washingtonpost.com/wp -dyn/content/article/2009/12/31/AR2009123102332.html.

53   John L. Esposito, "Political Islam and the West," *Military Technology* 25, no. 2 (February 2001), p. 92. In a later book, *Unholy War: Terror in the Name of Islam* (New York: Oxford University Press, 2002), pp. ix–x, Esposito apologized for bin-Laden as "a product of his upbringing," and said Arab-Islamic terror followed a pattern seen "in the history of every world religion."

54   Gerges, *America and Political Islam,* p. 14. See also Fred Halliday, *Islam and the Myth of Confrontation: Religion and Politics in the Middle East* (New York: I. B. Tauris, 1996).

55   John L. Esposito, *The Islamic Threat: Myth or Reality?* (New York: Oxford University Press, 1992). For some of Professor Esposito's other noteworthy remarks, see the website of Campus Watch, http://www.frontpagemag .com/articles/Printable.asp?ID=2651.

56   Esposito, *Unholy War,* p. x.

57   There is also the Al-Qaeda attack on the USS *Cole* in Yemen and evidence of Al-Qaeda involvement in the attacks on Khobar Towers in Saudi Arabia.

58   Esposito, *Unholy War,* p. x.

59   Edward Said, "The Phony Islamic Threat," *New York Times Magazine,* November 21, 1993, pp. 62–68.

60   Martin Kramer, *Ivory Towers on Sand: The Failure of Middle Eastern Studies in America* (Washington, DC: Washington Institute for Near East Policy, 2001), p. 56.

61   Bulliet cited in Gerges, *America and Political Islam,* p. 46, and Kramer, *Ivory Towers on Sand,* p. 51. His claim that Muslims were victims of anti-Semitism was essentially an echo of Said's own rhetoric.

62   Jessica Stern, *The Ultimate Terrorists* (Cambridge, MA: Harvard University Press, 1999), p. 66. See also Dave Williams, "The Bombing of the World Trade Center in New York City," *International Criminal Police Review,* pp. 469–471, INTERPOL, 1998, originally available at http://www.interpol .int/Public/Publications/ICPR/ICPR469_3.asp and now at http://turner network.com/online/documents/wtc1993.shtml.

63   Richard Bulliet, ed., *Under Siege: Islam and Democracy,* Occasional Papers 1 (New York: Middle East Institute of Columbia University, 1994), p. iii.

64   The Bay Ridge sermon followed a massacre of Arabs by a Jewish settler, five days earlier, in the biblical town of Hebron. See Yehudit Barsky, The Brooklyn Bridge Shooting: An Independent Report and Assessment, New York, The American Jewish Committee, November 2000. Earlier, Baz had heard a guest sermon at Brooklyn College from Sheikh Wagdi Ghuneim, who taught listeners a song comparing Jews to apes, as well as calling for jihad.

65 Andrea Elliot's series, published March 5–7, 2006, did not mention the Baz trial or bridge attack. It called Shata "flexible," not a "firebrand," citing his views on oral sex between married couples. See http://www.nytimes.com/2006/03/05/nyregion/05imam.html?r=1&ref=muslimsinamerica. For a biography of Sheikh Reda Shata and his sermons in English, see his website at http://www.redashata.com/English/index.php and "Why They Hate Us" at http://www.redashata.com/English/index.php?page=sermons.

66 U.S. Department of Justice, Federal Bureau of Investigation, Counterterrorism Threat Assessment and Warning Unit—National Security Division, *Terrorism in the United States—1998,* Washington, DC, 1999, p. 24, states, "There were no incidents of terrorism in 1994." See also FBI 1999 terror report released in 2000: *Terrorism In The United States—1999,* and http://www.fbi.gov/about-us/partnerships_and_outreach/community_outreach/dcla/2009/newyork.

67 Uriel Heilmann, "Murder on the Brooklyn Bridge," *Middle East Quarterly* 8, no. 3 (Summer 2001), pp. 29–37, http://www.meforum.org/77/murder-on-the-brooklyn-bridge.

68 When an immigrant Pakistani terrorist tried to blow up a car bomb in the middle of teeming theater crowds in Times Square on Saturday night, April 30, 2010, the *New York Times* forced itself not to use the words "Muslim" or "terrorist" in its coverage. When the terrorist was indicted two weeks later, the *Times* continued to be antiseptically indirect in its descriptions, saying Faisal Shahzad was indicted "on five felony counts." One had to go five paragraphs into the *Times* article to discover that Shahzad, a 30-year-old Pakistani immigrant, was accused of terrorism, attempted mass murder, and using a weapon of mass destruction. The *Times* minimized the danger from the "crude car bomb" and the terror network behind the bomber, who had been trained overseas and who was caught fleeing the country. Almost exactly a year later, in May 2011, the New York Police arrested two men from Morocco who planned to attack churches, synagogues, and the Empire State Building. Once again, the *New York Times* refrained from using the words "Muslim" or "terror" to describe Ahmed Ferhani and Mohamed Mamdouh, both immigrants from Morocco. The *Times* buried the item on page 21. See, inter alia, Al Baker and Karin Henry, "Car Bomb Leads To Evacuation In Times Square," *New York Times,* May 2, 2011, p. 1, http://www.nytimes.com/2010/05/02/nyregion/02timessquare.html; "Times Square Bomb Attempt (May 1, 2010)," http://topics.nytimes.com/top/reference/timestopics/subjects/t/times_square_bomb_attempt_may_1_2010/index.html?scp=1&sq=Times%20Square%20bomber&st=cse; Mark Mazzetti, Sabrina Tavernise and Jack Healy, "Suspect, Charged, Said to Admit to Role in Plot," *New York Times,* May 4, 2010; Andy Newman and Colin Moynihan, "Faisal Shahzad Arraigned on Terror Charges," May 18, 2010,

at http://cityroom.blogs.nytimes.com/2010/05/18/faisal-shahzad-to-be
-arraigned/; and Al Baker, "Two Men Arrested in New York Terror Case,"
New York Times, May 12, 2011, p. A22. William K. Rashbaum and Al Baker,
"Suspects in Terror Case Wanted to Kill Jews, Officials Say," *New York Times,*
May 13, 2011, p. A21.

69 Anne D. Neal and Jerry L. Martin, "Defending Civilization: How Our
Universities Are Failing America and What Can Be Done About It,"
Defense of Civilization Fund, American Council of Trustees and Alumni,
Washington, DC, February 2002. See http://www.goacta.org.

70 IAP was established in Chicago by three men: Al-Arian; Musa Abu Mar-
zook, who became head of the political wing of Hamas and later foreign
minister of the Hamas regime in Gaza; and Khalid Meshal, later director of
Hamas's operations based in Damascus. See Andrew McCarthy, *The Grand
Jihad: How Islam and the Left Sabotage America* (New York: Encounter
Books, 2010), p. 129. ICP and WISE were set up at USF in Tampa with
Ramadan Shallah, Khalil Shikaki, and Basheer Nafi, from Islamic Jihad.
Al-Arian befriended both Sunni and Shiite terrorists, inviting Egyptian
sheikh Omar Abdul-Rahman for a talk, but also visiting Iran to raise funds
from its regime, court evidence shows.

71 One frequently published periodical in Arabic was *Al-Mujaahid* (The Warrior).

72 Steven Emerson, *American Jihad: The Terrorists Living Among Us,* pbk. ed.
(New York: Free Press, 2003), p. 111.

73 Harvey Kushner, *Holy War on the Home Front: The Secret Islamic Terror Network in the United States* (New York: Sentinel, 2004), p. 14, and
BBC, "Accused academic speaks out," February 26, 2003, http://news.bbc
.co.uk/2/hi/uk_news/2802427.stm.

74 Al-Arian was tried before a civilian jury whose identities were kept secret.
The jury was hung on many charges brought under the USA Patriot Act.
To avoid a costly retrial that might have jeopardized classified intelligence
sources in Israel and the United States, the U.S. government and al-Arian
signed a plea agreement. Al-Arian pleaded guilty in 2006 to conspiracy
to raise funds for Palestinian Islamic Jihad. Federal district judge James
Moody sentenced him to a longer sentence than even prosecutors had re-
quested. He refuted al-Arian's claim of concern for destitute families, saying
al-Arian's "only connection to widows and orphans is that you create them."
See Jennifer Steinhauer, "19 Months More in Prison for Professor in Terror
Case," *New York Times,* May 2, 2006, p. 14.

75 Harvey Kushner, *Terrorism in America: A Structured Approach to Understanding the Terrorist Threat* (Springfield, IL: Charles C. Thomas, 1998), p. 38.

76 Marzook, when pressed, claimed he was not tied to Hamas's "military
wing," and he later became foreign minister in the Hamas regime in Gaza.

77   Kushner, *Holy War on the Home Front*, p. 14.

78   Said, *Orientalism*, p. 32.

79   Said's discussion in *Orientalism* is built around Lord Balfour, who said that he did not take a "superior" attitude to the denizens of the Middle East, particularly Egypt. Perhaps it is just chance that Said and the Palestinians view(ed) Balfour as a great villain for other reasons, such as the Balfour Declaration recognizing the right for a Jewish homeland in Palestine. See pp. 31–35 in the chapter titled "Knowing the Oriental."

80   The reference is to the 1978 Vintage edition of *Orientalism* and others.

81   Said, *Orientalism*, p. 311.

82   The quote is from the 1964 movie *Dr. Strangelove or: How I Learned to Stop Worrying and Love the Bomb*: General Jack D. Ripper, a rabidly right-wing character, contends that fluoridation programs are government conspiracies. The general launches a nuclear strike against the Soviet Union to stop the communist infiltration that he fears will "sap and impurify all of our precious bodily fluids." This theme has been adopted by others. See Ronald Bailey, "'Impurifying our precious bodily fluids': Fear of fluoridation takes a left turn," *Reason Online*, December 5, 2001, http://reason.com/rb /rb120501.shtml.

83   Said, *Orientalism*, p. 105, berates the "cultural synthesis" espoused by P. K. Holt and others.

84   Edward Said, "The Morning After," *London Review of Books* 15, no. 20 (October 21, 1993).

85   R. Hrair Dekmejian, "Islamic Revival: Catalysts, Categories, and Consequences," in Shireen T. Hunter, ed., *The Politics of Islamic Revivalism: Diversity and Unity* (Bloomington: Indiana University Press, 1988), p. 3.

86   Ali Hilal Dessouki, "The Islamic Resurgence: Sources, Dynamics, and Implications," in Dessouki, ed., *Islamic Resurgence in the Arab World* (New York: Praeger, 1982), p. 8.

87   Peter Beinart, "Teach-In," *New Republic*, November 12, 2001, and Kramer, *Ivory Towers on Sand*.

88   Said, "A Stupid War," *Al-Hayat* (English-language website), April 14, 2003. The same material also appeared, word for word, in "The Academy of Lagado," *London Review of Books* 25, no. 8 (April 17, 2003).

89   Ibid.

90   Ibid.

91   Edward W. Said, "The Arab-American War: The Politics of Information," in Edward Said, *The Politics of Dispossession: The Struggle for Palestinian Self-Determination, 1969–1994* (New York: Vintage Books, 1994), p. 300. The chapter originally appeared as an article in the *London Review of Books*, March 7, 1991.

92   Saul Bellow, *Mr. Sammler's Planet* (New York: Viking, 1970), p. 34.

CHAPTER TWO: TERROR AND THE PRESS: THE DEVIL'S BARGAIN

1 Walter Laqueur, *The Age of Terrorism* (Boston: Little, Brown, 2007), p. 121.

2 Marvin Kalb and Carol Saivetz, "The Israeli-Hezbollah War of 2006: The Media as a Weapon in Asymmetrical Conflict," Joan Shorenstein Center on the Press, Politics and Public Policy, Harvard University, Research Paper Series #R-29, February 2007. Quotation is from abstract available at http://www.hks.harvard.edu/presspol/publications/papers/research_papers /r29_kalb.pdf.

3 Later examination showed tremendous inconsistencies and fabrications in Hizballah claims, including movement of bodies and placement of "props" such as baby pacifiers, along with deliberate inflation of casualty figures. Claims of more than fifty dead, for example, were cut in half, and it was not at all clear that an Israeli plane had dropped a bomb on the village or whether it might have been Hizballah's own bombs. The same phenomenon has occurred with Hamas and Fatah, where early detonation of bombs is often blamed on Israeli air strikes.

4 The level of real human rights at the UN Human Rights Council is demonstrated by its members, including Saudi Arabia, Cuba, Russia, and Bangladesh in recent years, as well as Libya. Its predecessor, the UN Human Rights Commission, disbanded in 2006, included Sudan, a country where hundreds of thousands were slaughtered in religious terror warfare and thousands were regularly sold into slavery—all without any UN condemnations or reports.

5 Israeli officers, soldiers, and policy makers feared being hauled into courts in Belgium, Britain, Holland, and Spain under the "universal jurisdiction" of "war crimes" charges. See Richard Goldstone, "Reconsidering the Goldstone Report on Israel and War Crimes," appearing first in the online edition of the *Washington Post,* April 1, 2011, http://www.washington post.com/opinions/reconsidering-the-goldstone-report-on-israel-and-war -crimes/2011/04/01/AFg111JC_story.html?hpid=z3. It appeared in the print edition of the *Post* on April 3, 2011, p. A21.

6 Internet sites serving Al-Qaeda and documents and testimony from other groups such as Hamas and Fatah also corroborate this terrorist tactic.

7 CNN, "Newsweek Backs Off Quran Desecration Story," May 16, 2005, http://articles.cnn.com/2005-05-15/world/newsweek.quran_1_newsweek -editor-mark-whitaker-qurans-afghanistan?_s=PM:WORLD.

8 Eleven soldiers and officers were convicted on charges of abuses, mostly involving dereliction of duty or sexual debasement of prisoners rather than actual physical torture. Sergeant Ivan Frederick received an eight-year sentence for punching a prisoner and forcing three others to masturbate. Specialist Charles Graner and Specialist Lynndie England were sentenced to ten years and three years in prison, respectively.

9 "The flow of information between the United States and the Arab world is overwhelmingly one way, West to East. Arab audiences know much more about America than Americans know about Arabs," observes William Rugh, in *Arab Mass Media: Newspapers, Radio and Television in Arab Politics* (Westport, CT: Praeger, 2004), p. ix. What Rugh says about the United States is true of the West in general, and what he says about the Arab audiences is even truer of Arab-Islamic terrorists.

10 Both Al-Qaeda and their Taliban hosts were defeated in early 2002, but Al-Qaeda has since gotten sanctuary in parts of Pakistan and Yemen, and the Taliban had a resurgence when America turned its attention to Iraq.

11 Arafat was evicted from southern Lebanon and Beirut by Israel in 1982, and he was banished from northern Lebanon and nearly killed by Syria in 1983. He regained the world stage by harnessing the media energy of the Palestinian-Israeli war of attrition that came to be known as "Intifada" in 1987–88. Hamas similarly survived the near-total liquidation of its leadership by claiming Israel had committed "atrocities" against innocent people in Gaza.

12 During the 1990s Osama bin-Laden's personal worth was "guesstimated" at $300–500 million—the legacy of his father's construction business, which was patronized by the Saudi royal family. But after the 1998 U.S. embassy attacks and after 9/11, the Saudis and other governments have sequestered or seized most of bin-Laden's known wealth. This means that even bin Laden had cash flow problems.

13 See Brigitte L. Nacos, *Mass-Mediated Terrorism: The Central Role of the Media in Terrorism and Counterterrorism*, rev. ed. (Latham, MD: Rowman & Littlefield, 2007). Nacos describes how reporters and anchormen and anchorwomen have sought out terrorists such as Timothy McVeigh and Osama bin-Laden, often turning them into celebrities and cult figures.

14 Ibid., p. 102.

15 An honorific Arab nickname of this kind—for example, Abu Muhammad means "father of Muhammad"—is like calling someone "Uncle Louie" and is a sign of respect and affection.

16 Nacos, *Mass-Mediated Terrorism*, p. 100.

17 It is known to Muslims as the Ibrahimiyya Mosque because Abraham (Ibrahim) is buried there along with other important personages from scripture: Sarah, Isaac, Rebecca, Jacob, Leah (and Adam and Eve, according to Jewish tradition, as well as Isma'il or Yishmael, according to Muslim lore).

18 This is based primarily on the author's reporting for the *New York Times*, including an interview conducted in 1981 by *Times* bureau chief David Shipler and the author with Adnan Abu Jaber, the leader of the four-man

Fatah terror squad. Additional reporting was done by Ehud Yaari of Israel Television Channel 1.

19 See Steven Lacroix's analysis of Zawahiri's writings in "Introduction: Ayman al-Zawahiri: Veteran of Jihad," esp. pp. 157–58 and 166, in Gilles Kepel and Jean-Pierre Milelli, eds., *Al-Qaeda in Its Own Words* (Cambridge, MA: Harvard University Press, 2008).

20 Walter Cronkite, *A Reporter's Life* (New York: Knopf, 1996), p. 317.

21 Gay Talese, *The Kingdom and the Power: The Story of the Men Who Influence the Institution That Influences the World*—The New York Times (New York: World, 1969), p. 2.

22 William L. Shirer, *The Rise and Fall of the Third Reich* (New York: Simon & Schuster, 1960), p. 234.

23 Deborah Lipstadt, *Beyond Belief: The American Press and the Coming of the Holocaust, 1933–1945* (New York: Free Press, 1986), p. 51.

24 Shirer, *The Rise and Fall of the Third Reich,* p. 245.

25 Ibid., pp. 247–48.

26 Lipstadt, *Beyond Belief,* p. 23.

27 Ibid., p. 30.

28 See J. N. Westwood, *Russia, 1917–1964: A History of Modern Russia from the 1917 Revolution to the Fall of Khrushchev* (New York: Harper & Row, 1966), p. 87: "About 10 to 15 million people died in the 1932–34 famine and its attendant epidemics."

29 See Whitman Bassow, *The Moscow Correspondents: Reporters on Russia from the Revolution to Glasnost* (New York: William Morrow, 1988), p. 69.

30 Robert Conquest, *The Great Terror: A Reassessment* (New York: Oxford University Press, 1990), p. 468.

31 Bassow, *The Moscow Correspondents,* pp. 69–70.

32 Shirer, *The Rise and Fall of the Third Reich,* p. 279.

33 The *New York Times* also produces daily inserts for many newspapers around the world.

34 Talese, *The Kingdom and the Power,* p. 278. Richard Shepard also covers the events in his book.

35 See *John F. Kennedy: The Great Crises,* vol. 1, ed. Timothy Naftali, The Presidential Recordings (New York: Norton, 2001), pp. 186–90.

36 Richard F. Shepard, *The Paper's Papers: A Reporter's Journey Through the Archives of* The New York Times (New York: Times Books, 1996), p. 196.

37 Michael T. Kaufman, "The Complex Past of Meir Kahane," *New York Times,* January 24, 1971, p. 1.

38 Michael T. Kaufman, "Remembering Kahane, and the Woman on the Bridge," *New York Times,* March 6, 1994, sec. 4 (Week in Review), p. 1, http://www.nytimes.com/1994/03/06/weekinreview/remembering-kahane -and-the-woman-on-the-bridge.html.

39 From 1948 to 1984, the *Times* also had a policy of not sending a Jew as a correspondent to Israel.

40 Talese, *The Kingdom and the Power,* pp. 58–59.

41 Shepard, *The Paper's Papers,* p. 303.

42 Yasin escaped to Iraq, and the United States placed a $25 million bounty on his head.

43 The source here is a *Times* article based on an interview on the CBS show *60 Minutes* by Leslie Stahl. See Tina Kelly, "Suspect in 1993 Bombing Says Trade Center Wasn't First Target," *New York Times,* June 1, 2002, p. A10, http://www.nytimes.com/2002/06/01/us/suspect-in-1993-bombing-says-trade-center-wasn-t-first-target.html?scp=1&sq=%22world%20trade%20center%20bombing%20in%201993%22&st=cse.

44 Christopher Wren, "Bomb Trial Jurors Say Panel Had No Doubts," *New York Times,* September. 9, 1996, p. B2, http://www.nytimes.com/1996/09/09/nyregion/bomb-trial-jurors-say-panel-had-no-doubts.html. Yousef was also the planner of the 1993 World Trade Center attack. His Bojinka Plot was uncovered when the chemicals he was mixing set off smoke, alerting neighbors.

45 The *Times* almost never uses the words *murder* or *terror* to describe attacks by Fatah, Hamas, or Hizballah on unarmed Israeli civilians. The agent of the attack is *not* identified as Fatah, Hamas, PLO, or Hizballah but "Car Bomb Kills 2," or "Shots Kill 3," whereas when Israel kills armed terrorists who have bragged about murdering unarmed Israelis, the *Times'* headline and content are unmistakably hostile and direct, and the results are described as "deadly" and "bloody." Such an article is usually accompanied by a dramatic picture. See, for example, Ethan Bronner, "Israeli Military Kills 6 Palestinians," December 26, 2009, which adds, in the first paragraph, "It was the deadliest day in the conflict in nearly a year." The article does not mention that the "deadliest day" occurred after a tremendous escalation in Palestinian assaults on Israeli civilians: ten different Palestinian attacks in three days—including a large rocket attack on the southern city of Netivot. There was no coverage of the rocket attack, nor of most of the other attacks that were apparently timed to celebrate the founding of Fatah, commemorated on the week leading to and following the official January 1 holiday.

46 Laurel Leff, *Buried by* The Times*: The Holocaust and America's Most Important Newspaper* (Cambridge: Cambridge University Press, 2005), p. 108.

47 Ibid.

48 Susan E. Tifft and Alex S. Jones, *The Trust: The Private and Powerful Family Behind the* New York Times (Boston: Little, Brown, 1999), p. 215.

49 Ibid., p. 237.

50 Ibid.

51 The plan was to detonate car bombs by phone, while at the same time launching Stinger missiles at Air National Guard planes flying in the Newburgh, New York, base.

52 The *Times* went out of its way to run a politically correct but factually misleading "correction" saying of the men that "none are Arabic [*sic*] descent," even though that was not mentioned in the original story: Al Baker and Javier C. Hernandez, "4 Accused of Bombing Plot at Bronx Synagogues," *New York Times*, May 20, 2009. The only Arabic in the story was the alias each man took for himself, according to the federal criminal complaint: Abdul-Rahman, Hamza, Daoud, and Amin. The fact that all four men were Muslims was mentioned at the bottom of the ninth paragraph in one story. It was not mentioned in most follow-up articles on the terror plot. See http://topics.nytimes.com/top/reference/timestopics/people/c/james_cromitie/index.html?scp=1-spot&sq=%22JAMES%20CROMITIE%22&st=cse.

53 See James Dao, "At Fort Hood, Reaching Out to Soldiers at Risk," *New York Times*, December 23, 2009.

54 Robert Wright, "Who Created Major Hasan?" *New York Times*, November 22, 2009, p. 11.

55 Charles Krauthammer, "Medicalizing Mass Murder," *Washington Post*, November 13, 2009, p. A21, http://www.washingtonpost.com/wp-dyn/content/article/2009/11/12/AR2009111209824_pf.html.

56 Russ Braley, *Bad News: The Foreign Policy of the* New York Times (Chicago: Regnery-Gateway, 1984), p. 365; "Marxist Leader of Commandos—George Habash," *New York Times*, June 13, 1970, p. 12.

57 The symbol for the Popular Front was a map of Palestine (including Jordan) with the word *jabha* (meaning "front" in Arabic) showing an arrow moving from the Jordanian desert westward to the Mediterranean.

58 For a good account of the fighting in Jordan, see Braley, *Bad News*, pp. 359–77. Braley, a reporter for the *New York Daily News*, also describes the policy of PLO and PFLP press intimidation inside Jordan.

59 Widlanski conversation with Markham in *New York Times* office in Jerusalem, August 1981, during a period when Markham was filling in for vacationing Jerusalem bureau chief David K. Shipler.

60 The KGB named the school for Lumumba, a communist leader in the Congo who was assassinated.

61 The term "Abu Mazen," in addition to being a friendly nickname or *kunya*, is also Abbas's *laqab* or nom de guerre inside the Fatah organization. Western media often appear clueless about this, unaware that this is a very tendentious and affectionate reference, like calling Joseph Stalin "Uncle Joe" in a news bulletin or referring to Nikita Khrushchev as "Nikita Sergeivitch"—the friendly Russian patronymic. The misuse and overuse

of Arabic nicknames is apparent when news reports say "PLO leader Abu Mazen arrived in our capital today. Mazen is in town for meetings with officials"—treating Mazen as a family name and Abu as a surname. When Peter Jennings, who had spent some time in Beirut, called Arafat Abu Ammar, it was an obvious moment of journalistic sycophancy.

62 The term is often mistranslated as "uprising," but it is from the Arabic root *n-f-D* (emphatic *d*), meaning "shaking off."

63 Robert Fisk, *Pity the Nation: Lebanon at War,* paperback ed. (Oxford: Oxford University Press, 2001), p. 411. Other reporters have made similar comments.

64 Christiane Amanpour, "Israeli Troops Surround Arafat Compound," March 29, 2002, http://transcripts.cnn.com/TRANSCRIPTS/0203/29/bn.26.html.

65 Arafat made it to page 8 of *Al-Ahram,* though the Egyptian newspaper actually misspelled his name as "Farhat." See Andrew Gowers and Tony Walker, *Behind the Myth: Yasser Arafat and the Palestinian Revolution* (London: W. H. Allen, 1990), p. 9.

66 The Israeli police seized more than five hundred thousand documents in 2002 at Orient House, a Jerusalem complex that was the PLO's forward base inside Israel. The author edited these documents.

67 Jillian Becker, *The PLO: The Rise and Fall of the Palestinian Liberation Organization* (London: Weidenfeld & Nicolson, 2004), p. 157.

68 Ibid.

69 The PLO and Hizballah exert a great deal of control on "stringers"—locally hired reporters. In recent years, the *New York Times* and *Washington Post* have had a few reporters who studied Arabic.

70 Robert I. Friedman, "Journalists under the gun in Beirut," *Nation,* no. 239 (December 15, 1984), p. 641(3).

71 See John Kifner, "Reporter's Notebook: Fear is Part of the Job in Beirut," *New York Times,* February 22, 1982, p. A4. See also Fisk, *Pity the Nation,* pp. 407–8. Fisk purports to know the identity of Toolan's paramours and how much the hit men were paid. Neither Kifner nor Fisk cites a source. Ze'ev Chafets, *Double Vision,* pp. 92–93 and 114–15, demonstrates conclusively that other Beirut journalists (*Los Angeles Times, Maclean's* magazine, the Associated Press) reported Toolan was murdered for political reasons, probably because of the ABC documentary that angered the PLO. The PLO told ABC that anyone who worked on the documentary was in danger. Several of its workers—Jerry King, Barbara Newman, and Geraldo Rivera—all left Lebanon before the film's airing. Chafets, who interviewed many who served in Beirut in the 1970s and 1980s concluded (p. 109) that it was "a depressing chapter in Western journalism—the willingness of important news organizations to bow to Arab terror and to play an active part in hiding it from the public."

72   Becker, *The PLO*, p. 159. See also Jerry Gordon, interview with Timmerman, *New English Review*, March 2011, http://www.newenglishreview.org/custpage.cfm/frm/83653/sec_id/83653.

73   Other Lebanese journalists mention the deaths of Mark Tryon, Free Belgium Radio; Jean Lougeau, correspondent for French TF-1; Tony Italo, Italian journalist; and Graciella Difaco, Italian journalist. Fisk mentions the death of al-Lawzi on p. 165 but has apparently forgotten this by pp. 408–9, perhaps excluding it because he feels the Syrians, not the PLO, murdered him, or that al-Lawzi ought not be deemed a "Western journalist" because of his Arabic name, though his newspaper was in London.

74   Fisk, *Pity the Nation*, p. xi.

75   Ibid.

76   Ibid., p. 127.

77   See Alain Gresh, *The PLO: The Struggle Within: Towards an Independent Palestinian State*, trans. A. M. Berrett (London: Zed Books, 1988), p. 227. Gresh, a Cairo-born French journalist close to the PLO, stresses political aspects of the PLO but notes that Arafat had more than twenty thousand men at arms, most in Lebanon. The figures on PLO and Syrian casualties are from Chaim Herzog, *The Arab-Israeli Wars* (Tel Aviv: Steimatzky, 1984), p. 361, and other Israeli sources. The figures were casualties incurred between June 6, 1982, and May 1983, though most of the fighting was actually from June to September 1982.

78   Herzog, *The Arab-Israeli Wars*, p. 361.

79   Ze'ev Schiff and Ehud Yaari, *Israel's Lebanon War* (New York: Simon & Schuster, 1984), p. 228. See also Herzog, *The Arab-Israeli Wars*, p. 383, according to which the PLO had more than fifteen thousand fighters in southern Lebanon alone. We know the exact evacuation figures because the Palestinian and Syrian evacuees were counted by Israel and the United States.

80   Fisk, *Pity the Nation*, p. xi. Fisk not only seems to follow the direction of Said and Chomsky but actually to employ their style and "facts."

81   See http://www.nationmaster.com/encyclopedia/1982-Lebanon-war#Casualties. It is quite amazing that for a source on military history the CIA would use Chomsky, who, along with his coauthor Edward Hermann, has repeatedly minimized the role of Pol Pot and his communist regime in the mass murder of two to three million of his own people in Cambodia. Chomsky has great difficulty calling Pol Pot or Yasser Arafat a murderer or a dictator or a terrorist, but these are titles he readily applies to U.S. president Ronald Reagan or to former Israeli prime minister Shimon Peres, the man who made more concessions to Palestinians than perhaps any other Israeli leader.

82   Fisk, *Pity the Nation*, p. 390.

83 Ibid., p. 391.

84 Ibid., pp. 2–5.

85 Sharon was effectively banned from top cabinet posts for years. General Eytan would have been dismissed if not for the fact that his term ended anyway.

86 "News Gathering Under the Gun," *Time,* March 1, 1982, http://205.188 .238.109/time/magazine/article/0,9171,922824-2,00.html.

87 Friedman, *From Beirut to Jerusalem,* p. 70. Friedman did not mention that Kifner's comment about fear was literally forced out of him and the *Times* by revelations from an Israeli official charging a *Times* cover-up of terrorism. The article, "Reporter's Notebook: Fear Is Part of the Job in Beirut," was prompted by the charges. Fuller comments on the article appear below. Some of the other stories and jokes regarding the fear of reporters in Beirut are also taken from the same Kifner article that appeared February 22, 1984, on page A4 of the *Times.*

88 The real atrocity of Sabra and Chatilla, where about three hundred were murdered by the Phalange militia, was preceded by many phony atrocity stories about how Israel had destroyed Damour (it had been destroyed the Palestinians several years before), the alleged napalming of civilians, or the supposed destruction of all of southern Lebanon's housing, purportedly leaving 600,000 homeless in an area where fewer than 600,000 actually lived.

89 Cited by Professor Richard Landes of Boston University in his media-monitoring website, http://www.theaugeanstables.com/2007/11/12/media -intimidation-dossier/.

90 Ze'ev Chafets, *Double Vision* (New York: William Morrow, 1985), pp. 85–87, 96–103. A fuller version of the story appears here because I was a reporter in the *Times* Jerusalem bureau at the time of the events, hearing about them firsthand. See "News Gathering Under the Gun," *Time,* March 1, 1982, op. cit, http://205.188.238.109/time/magazine /article/0,9171,922824-2,00.html, in which reporters were quoted as saying "We made an informal agreement that we would not write about the incident."

91 When I left the Israeli army in September 1982, the *Times* asked me to help out in the Jerusalem bureau before I took up my new job as a correspondent for Cox Newspapers' *Atlanta Constitution.*

92 Friedman, *From Beirut to Jerusalem,* p. 70.

93 When Begin led the Irgun Tzvai Leumi—or ETZEL—in pre-1948 Palestine, he ordered an attack on British military headquarters at the King David Hotel, but he never attacked reporters or diplomats. After his election in 1977, Prime Minister Begin never used his powers against domestic rivals.

94 Other Phalange leaders of later generations, Amin Gemayel and Michel Aoun, also made their deals with Syria in order to be selected as president and

in order to survive. The Maronites, however, had actually invited Syrian intervention in Lebanon in 1976 after the Phalange suffered losses in fighting.

95 "U.S. Presses Israel to Let U.N. Troops Move Into Beirut," *New York Times*,
September 20, 1982, p. 1.

96 One wonders how a Norwegian doctor in Beirut could so easily identify
Haddad, who was hardly a prominent figure on the Beirut scene. My own experience is that many Scandinavians who work for international organizations
such as UNRWA or pro-PLO nongovernmental organizations have adopted
the pan-Arab or PLO viewpoint. From the Fisk and Friedman articles, it
seems Palestinians in Beirut were eager to have Haddad and Israel blamed
directly for the massacres. Similarly, in 1996 and 2006, Hizballah used bogus
findings by Lebanese health officials, charging Israeli massacres at Qana.

97 During a 1987 trip to Shifa Hospital in Gaza with my colleague Bob
Slater of *Time*, I asked the doctors if they had remnants of the "dum-dum"
bullets—projectiles that are designed to explode or come apart inside the
body of the person who was shot. They had none. I asked how they were
sure they had treated dum-dum bullets. They described "big holes" in the
victims, consistent with exit wounds for a rifle bullet such as the 5.56 from
an M-16 or the 7.62 Kalashnikov bullet. Three other brief similar examples:
1) The first woman Palestinian suicide bomber was smuggled into Jerusalem in an ambulance; 2) prosthetic devices were sometimes used to hide
bombs and weapons; 3) PLO health officials also claimed radiation devices
were used against Palestinians.

98 The article can be retrieved at http://www.nytimes.com/1982/09/26/world
/the-beirut-massacre-the-four-days.html?&pagewanted=5. I accompanied
Friedman on a short tour of southern Lebanon, including an interview with
Major Saad Haddad.

99 The interview was conducted in southern Lebanon as Friedman returned
from Jerusalem to Beirut. I and *Times* correspondent James Clarity accompanied Friedman to the interview, and we were both taken aback by the
manner in which it was conducted.

100 In 1982, far less than half the SLA was composed of Shiites. Haddad died
of cancer in 1984 and was succeeded by Lebanese general Antoine Lahad,
who increased the Shiite component of the SLA.

101 Friedman did not even say "good morning" or "good-bye" in Arabic before
or after the interview.

102 Formally, Friedman has studied some Arabic and Hebrew, but I have been
witness to a number of events—such as the resignation of Israeli finance
minister Yitzhak Modai at a Jerusalem press conference—where it was
clear that Friedman, then the *Times'* Jerusalem bureau chief, could not follow the train of events.

103 James Clarity, another *Times* correspondent who speaks several languages and who was also at the interview, agreed with my view that he had never seen an interview technique like this before.

104 The PLO also had Shiites, including 'Imad Mughniyeh, later the top terror planner of Hizballah. He began his career working for Yasser Arafat's elite "Force 17" unit.

105 Boxing champion Muhammad Ali and nineteenth-century Egyptian leader Mehmet Ali, for example.

106 Both FBI and CIA officials have described how the Saudi royal house, which had links to bin-Laden, refused to allow serious investigation of several terror attacks on Americans in Saudi Arabia, including the Khobar Towers attack of 1998.

107 Thomas Friedman, "An Intriguing Signal From the Saudi Crown Prince," *New York Times*, February 17, 2002, http://www.nytimes.com/2002/02/17/opinion/17FRIE.html?ex=1173330000&en=e90435530dc4d8fc&ei=5070.

108 See Thomas L. Friedman, "Abdullah II: The 5-State Solution," *New York Times*, January 27, 2009, http://www.nytimes.com/2009/01/28/opinion/28friedman.html.

109 Turkey aided the Islamist IHH (İnsan Hak ve Hürriyetleri ve İnsani Yardım Vakfı), a terror front organization whose leader, Bülent Yildirim, has sworn to help end "the virus of Zionism."

110 Thomas L. Friedman, "When Friends Fall Out," *New York Times*, June 2, 2010, p. A25, http://www.nytimes.com/2010/06/02/opinion/02friedman.html.

111 Obama insisted on a total freeze on Israeli building in the West Bank and Jerusalem before talks proceeded—something that even Yasser Arafat never demanded. Arafat's successor, Mahmoud Abbas, could not afford to seem less Palestinian than Obama. So Abbas refused even to meet Israeli leaders.

112 Friedman, "Abdullah II: The 5-State Solution."

113 Thomas L. Friedman, "America Vs. The Narrative," *New York Times*, November 28, 2009.

114 In the case of Al-Qaeda, it is the attacks on New York and Washington, the financial and political heart of America, and in the case of Hizballah, it is to attack the industrial center of Haifa and to threaten rockets on Tel Aviv, Israel's cultural and financial center.

CHAPTER THREE: CNN: CERTAINLY NOT NEWS

1 Gil Merom, *How Democracies Lose Small Wars: State, Society, and the Failures of France in Algeria, Israel in Lebanon, and the United States in Vietnam* (Cambridge: Cambridge University Press, 2003), pp. 14–15.

2   The term was originally coined in a 1938 editorial by *Time* magazine publisher Henry Luce, trying to get America to emerge from isolationism.

3   Merom, *How Democracies Lose Small Wars,* p. 15.

4   Israel had informed King Hussein of Jordan of its plan to attack, and Jordan notified Arafat, lest Hussein later be accused of conniving with the Israelis. Later, one assumes, after Arafat tried to take over Jordan, Hussein may have regretted his actions.

5   Syria and the Palestinians stood behind several attacks on the U.S. embassy in Beirut as well as the October 1983 attack on the U.S. and French peacekeeping forces in which 241 U.S. marines, sailors, and soldiers and 59 French soldiers were killed.

6   Anthony H. Cordesman, with George Sullivan and William D. Sullivan, *Lessons of the 2006 Israeli-Hezbollah War* (Washington, DC: CSIS Press, 2007), p. 43.

7   I use the term "mostly spontaneous" because it became clear that activists from Palestinian Islamic Jihad—not Arafat's Fatah, and not Hamas—had sparked some of the early riots by planting stories that a fatal road accident at a Gaza road junction was a deliberate act of revenge by an Israeli truck driver for the Palestinian terror hang-glider attack from Lebanon about ten days earlier.

8   As noted earlier, the term means "shaking off" in Arabic, not uprising.

9   Widlanski interview with Rabin and coverage of meeting with delegation from Florida, 1988.

10   Both Jordanian and Egyptian television showed less footage of Intifada protests in 1987 and 1988 than Israel State Television did because of their fear that *their* publics would be inflamed.

11   This was written many months before the food and gasoline riots of Tunisia and Egypt in 2011.

12   Cell phones and social media have further increased the process in the last decade.

13   Jim Lederman, *Battle Lines: The American Media and the Intifada* (New York: Henry Holt, 1992), p. 135. The book is probably the single best analysis of media tactics during the "Intifada," written by a reporter who worked for Canadian broadcasting and U.S. National Public Radio.

14   Mark D. Alleyne, *News Revolution: Political and Economic Decisions about Global Information* (London: Macmillan, 1997), p. 9.

15   Ibid.

16   Turner analyzed his change of views from conservative to "progressive, not liberal" on *The O'Reilly Factor,* Fox News, December 10, 2008, http://www.foxnews.com/story/0,2933,465124,00.html. There and in interviews with PBS's Charlie Rose, he discussed his donations to the United Nations, his opposition to the Vietnam War, the views he shared with his wife, the

actress and activist Jane Fonda, his respect for Cuban dictator Fidel Castro, his support of Barack Obama, and his distaste for George W. Bush. See http://www.charlierose.com/view/interview/9019.

17 Howard Kurtz, *Media Circus: The Trouble with America's Newspapers* (New York: Times Books, 1993).

18 This account is based on the author's interviews with then-CNN reporter Jay Bushinsky and then-CNN field producer Shabtai ("Shabi") Simantov.

19 Mitzna was largely regarded as a failure as West Bank commander, trying fitfully to contain the violence by hiding the news and by enforcing inane rules of engagement. For example, Mitzna ordered his soldiers not to fire on those who were throwing gasoline bombs at them, unless they threw more than one, unless the bombs actually ignited, and unless the bomb throwers were not running away. Mitzna later went into politics, becoming mayor of Haifa, and he subsequently ran for prime minister as Labor Party candidate against Ariel Sharon in 2003, suffering the worst election defeat in Israel's history: a two-to-one trouncing. His policy of trying to micromanage the media was surprisingly similar to Sharon's policy of blocking Israel-based reporters from entering Lebanon in the first days of the 1982 war. Both policies backfired, giving media prominence to the Palestinians.

20 There are a variety of sources on this matter. The Palestinian Human Rights Group gives the figure, saying it is roughly equivalent to the number of Palestinians killed by Israelis in the same period, but some Israeli sources claim Palestinian fatalities caused by Palestinians were actually close to double the number of those caused by Israelis. This pattern was similar to the 1936–39 Arab Revolt.

21 While reporting in the West Bank, the author made the same mistake on at least two occasions.

22 Mark Seager, "I'll have nightmares for the rest of my life," *Sunday Telegraph,* October 15, 2000.

23 Roberto Cristiano, advertisement in Arabic, "Tawdih Hass Min al-Televizyon al-Italki al-Rasmi" (A Special Clarification from Official Italian Television), *Al-Hayat al-Jadeeda,* October 16, 2000.

24 Abu Rahma and France 2 correspondent Charles Enderlin (who was in the West Bank at the time) changed the details of their account several times, and consistently refused to show film covering an incident that supposedly lasted more than twenty minutes. They only had about a minute of shot film and could not really explain why. When they were accused by a French media expert, Philippe Karsenty, and an Israeli physicist, Nahum Shahaf, of misleading the public and probably forging the scene, they sued their accusers. A French appeals court decided in 2008 that the accusers had not committed libel.

25   James Fallows, "Who Shot Mohammed al-Dura?" *Atlantic,* June 2003, http://www.theatlantic.com/doc/200306/fallows.

26   An examination of both films shows that the boy being buried at the funeral is not the same one in the France 2 film of the supposed crossfire.

27   "The Muhammad Al-Dura Blood Libel: A Case Analysis: Interview with Richard Landes," Jerusalem Center for Public Affairs, October 2008, http://www.jcpa.org/JCPA/Templates/ShowPage.asp?DBID=1&LNGID =1&TMID=111&FID=381&PID=470&IID=2658.

28   Jews murdering and even eating the flesh of Muslim children is a common theme in Palestinian newspapers and cartoons, especially in the Fatah-owned *Al-Hayat al-Jadeeda.*

29   The first agreement, known as the Declaration of Principles, was signed in September 1993. Other agreements on economic ties, security matters, media resources, etc., were signed thereafter and are collectively called the Oslo Accords.

30   The message was: be like Muhammad and go throw rocks and maybe you can become like him, a revered martyr.

31   Direct quotation from Stephanie Gutmann, *The Other War: Israelis, Palestinians, and the Struggle for Media Supremacy* (San Francisco: Encounter Books, 2005), p. 252. General observations from Gutmann, *The Other War,* pp. 248–57, from Lederman, *Battle Lines,* and the author's own experience in the West Bank as well as interviews with Daniel Seaman, director of the Israel Government Press Office.

32   Israel was attacked on two fronts, by Hizballah from Lebanon and Hamas from Gaza, almost simultaneously. Hamas struck into Israel on June 25, 2006, killing two soldiers and kidnapping a third, Gilad Shalit. Hizballah struck on July 12, 2006, killing several Israeli soldiers and kidnapping two others, who later died of their wounds.

33   UN Secretary-General Kofi Annan accepted Hizballah's figure of fifty-four or fifty-six dead: "Preliminary reports say that at least 54 people have been killed, among them at least 37 children." A later count showed only twenty-eight bodies, several of which had clearly been unearthed from graves or brought from refrigerated storage. "Secretary-General Urges Security Council to Condemn Israeli Attack on Qana," July 30, 2006, http://www.un.org/News/Press/docs/2006/sgsm10580.doc.htm. See also Marvin Kalb and Carol Saivetz, "The Israeli-Hezbollah War of 2006: The Media as a Weapon in Asymmetrical Conflict," Shorenstein Center Policy Paper, Harvard University, February 2007, p. 4, and note 11, citing Kim Murphy, "Warfare in the Middle East; Officials Say 28 Die in Qana, Not 54," *Los Angeles Times,* August 4, 2006. Israel said it had not bombed in the Qana area on the day in question. This left the distinct possibility that an explosion in Qana may have been caused by Hizballah's own mortars or

Katyusha rockets falling short and landing on Hizballah-controlled southern Lebanon, or Hizballah munitions exploding inside Qana, or even an
anti-aircraft missile falling back on the village. All of these mishaps have
previously occurred with both Hizballah and Hamas. Both groups have
blamed Israel when actually they had been the cause of an explosion that
injured or killed their own people.

34   Lederman, *Battle Lines*, p. 301.

35   For example, in his *Live From Baghdad* (New York: St. Martin's, 2002),
     Wiener (p. 296) gratuitously insults three U.S. presidents, especially George
     W. Bush, who, he says, "has about as much foreign policy know-how as my
     pet cat." The book was turned into an HBO movie featuring Michael Ke-
     aton as Robert Wiener.

36   Ibid., p. 296.

37   See for example the litany of incidents and discoveries by UNSCOM and
     the International Atomic Energy Agency described by Australian professor
     Timothy L. H. McCormack in his book *Self-Defense in International Law:
     The Israeli Raid on the Iraqi Nuclear Reactor* (New York: St. Martin's Press,
     1996).

38   Eason Jordan, "The News We Kept to Ourselves," *New York Times*, April
     11, 2003, p. A25, http://www.nytimes.com/2003/04/11/opinion/11JORD
     .html.

39   Interview of Eason Jordan by Bob Garfield, *On the Media*, WNYC, October
     25, 2002, http://www.onthemedia.org/yore/transcripts/transcripts_102502
     _jordan.html.

40   Peter Collins, "Corruption at CNN," *Washington Times*, April 15, 2003,
     http://www.washtimes.com/op-ed/20030415-91009640.htm.

41   Jordan, "The News We Kept to Ourselves."

42   Franklin Foer, "CNN's Access of Evil," *Wall Street Journal*, April 14, 2003,
     http://www.opinionjournal.com/extra/?id=110003336.

43   The English signs at the factory, showing the words "Baby Milk," looked
     hastily prepared.

44   Franklin Foer, "Air War," *New Republic*, October 28, 2002.

45   Ken Ringle, "Peter Arnett, the Ultimate War Horse," *Washington Post*,
     January 20, 1991, p. F1.

46   My former *Times* boss, David Shipler, was a Vietnam reporter and re-
     counted some experiences.

47   See Henry Kissinger, *Ending the Vietnam War: A History of America's In-
     volvement in and Extrication from the Vietnam War* (New York: Simon &
     Schuster, 2003), p. 46.

48   Don Oberdorfer, *Tet!* (Garden City, NY: Doubleday, 1971), p. 329 ff.

49   This is certainly what Arafat meant when he said he learned from Vietnam.
     Hizballah and Al-Qaeda leaders have made similar comments.

50 Mona Charen, "Peter Arnett: Whose Man in Baghdad?" April 1, 2003, http://townhall.com/columnists/MonaCharen/2003/04/01/peter_arnett _whose_man_in_baghdad.

CHAPTER FOUR: JOURNALISTS AS LAPDOGS

1 Larry C. Johnson, "The Declining Terrorist Threat," *New York Times*, July 10, 2001, p. A19, http://www.nytimes.com/2001/07/10/opinion /the-declining-terrorist-threat.html?scp=1&sq=%22the%20declining%20 terrorist%20threat%22&st=cse. Johnson was identified as "a former State Department counterterrorism specialist" but apparently did not read the U.S. government's own tepid annual reports on global terror, which showed increasing attacks in the 1990s.

2 A search of *Times* archives showed no mentions in the regular news or opinion pages. Pipes is a prolific writer of journal articles and op-ed pieces, founder of *Middle East Quarterly*, and the author of more than a dozen books, including *Militant Islam Reaches America* (New York: Norton, 2002). Kushner is deemed one of the top experts on domestic terrorism and criminology and is the author of several books.

3 Harvey Kushner, *Terrorism in America: A Structured Approach to Understanding the Terrorist Threat* (Springfield, IL: Charles C. Thomas, 1998), pp. 11–12.

4 Marcelle S. Fischler, "Helping to Lift the Cover Off Terrorism," *New York Times*, Long Island Edition, December 27, 1998, pp. LI 13–14, http://www.nytimes.com/1998/12/27/nyregion/long-island-journal -helping-to-lift-the-cover-off-terrorism.html?scp=8&sq=hARVEY%20 kUSHNER&st=cse.

5 Nacos, *Mass-Mediated Terrorism*, p. 104.

6 Ibid., p. 95.

7 This approach, which is both superficial and factually inaccurate, has also been employed by a number of academic authors such as Daniel Benjamin and Steven Simon (*The Age of Sacred Terror*) and Mark Juergensmeyer (*Terror in the Mind of God*), among others.

8 The first episode of the three-part series, dealing with Jews, was first aired on August 22, 2007.

9 The 2008 Peabody Award, the 2009 Alfred I. Dupont Award from Columbia University, and a special Television Academy Honor for "television with a conscience," first awarded in May 2009.

10 Dan Abrams, "Live With Dan Abrams," MSNBC, August 27, 2007. See Felix Gillette, "MSNBC's Dan Abrams' War of Faith Against CNN," September 4, 2007. See also http://newsbusters.org/blogs/brad-wilmouth /2007/08/28/msnbcs-abrams-hits-cnns-amanpour-defending-islamic -fundamentalism.

11 *Fox and Friends,* Fox News, September 30, 2007.

12 Daniel Byman, "Homeland Insecurity," *Wall Street Journal,* December 15, 2009, p. A16.

13 Material here is from U.S. private intelligence consulting firm STRAT-FOR and the *Wall Street Journal.* See "For Terror Suspect, a Life of Contradictions: Heroin Conviction in '90s Was Turning Point From Decadence to Devotion, but Headley Partied in Mumbai in '08, Authorities Say," *Wall Street Journal,* December 12, 2009, p. A6, http://online.wsj.com/article /SB126057977267688241.html; Scott Stewart, "Tactical Implications of the Headley Case," http://www.stratfor.com/weekly/20091216_tactical _implications_headley_case?utm_source=SWeekly&utm_medium =email&utm_campaign=091216&utm_content=readmore.

14 Three people were killed in the attack. An alert security guard prevented bomber Asif Muhammad Hanif, twenty-two, from entering the club where the explosion would have been far more lethal. A second British citizen, Omar Khan Sharif, twenty-seven, tried to set off his own bomb, but the detonator failed. He fled the scene, injured. Later, his body was found floating in the nearby Mediterranean Sea. Both men had been escorted into Israel by a journalist from Gaza. That is likely why they were not better scrutinized at the checkpoint, a later investigation showed.

15 See "For Terror Suspect," *Wall Street Journal,* December 12, 2009, and Stewart, "Tactical Implications of the Headley Case."

16 Much of the case is secret, but there is evidence that Zazi, who had lived in Flushing, Queens, New York, was planning to blow up a sports stadium or attack the New York City subway.

17 FBI annual hate crime statistics, http://www.fbi.gov/ucr/ucr.htm#hate. The last yearly figures, for 2009, were issued in November 2010, at http:// www2.fbi.gov/ucr/hc2009/index.html.

18 "The Truth About American Muslims," editorial, *New York Times,* April 1, 2011, http://www.nytimes.com/2011/04/02/opinion/02sat2.html? ref=opinion, print edition, April 2, 2011, p. A18.

19 William McGowan, *Coloring the News: How Political Correctness Has Corrupted American Journalism* (San Francisco: Encounter Books, 2002), p. 251.

20 Ibid., p. 252.

21 The establishment media gave great coverage to the trial and execution of Timothy McVeigh, the American-born terrorist who blew up a government office building in Oklahoma City. However, only a local Oklahoma television reporter pursued interesting clues that showed that McVeigh was in contact with Arab-Islamic sources. McVeigh also used a truck bomb similar to the one used in the New York attack of 1993 and in many of the terrorist attacks in the Middle East.

22 McGowan, *Coloring the News,* pp. 254–57.

23 Lorenzo Vidino and Josh Lefkowitz, "The enemy within: Islamic terrorists infiltrate opposing forces," *US Armed Forces Journal,* January 1 and January 13, 2005, http://www.investigativeproject.org/338/the-enemy-within.

24 The term "Black Muslim" is used to refer to "The Nation of Islam"—a group originally founded by Elijah Muhammad and now controlled by Louis Farrakhan.

25 Richard Miniter, *Losing Bin-Laden* (Washington, DC: Regnery, 2003), pp. 36, 171. Passages from Miniter's book also appeared verbatim under the headline "An Unheeded Warning" in the *Wall Street Journal* on September 30, 2003. See also Lawrence Wright, *The Looming Tower: Al-Qaeda and the Road to 9/11* (New York: Vintage Books, 2006), p. 206, and Peter Lance, *Cover Up: What the Government Is Still Hiding About the War on Terror* (New York: ReganBooks, 2004), p. 25.

26 Interview with General George Casey by John King, *State of the Union,* CNN, November 7, 2009.

27 We have spoken earlier, in the chapter on intelligence, of the role played by Ali Muhammad, a former Egyptian officer who worked for Al-Qaeda and trained bin-Laden's bodyguards but also served as an intelligence advisor to the U.S. Army and American intelligence.

28 A similar narrative, downplaying terror, was featured on NBC's *Meet the Press* and on the *New York Times'* front page that same day, as in the lead-in on NBC: "The *New York Times* reports this morning that investigators have tentatively concluded that the shooting rampage was not part of a terrorist plot."

29 Casey appeared on ABC's *This Week* with George Stephanopoulos, on NBC's *Meet the Press,* and on CNN.

30 Casey, remarks on CNN's *State of the Union* program.

31 Casey, remarks on NBC's *Meet the Press,* November 8, 2009, http://www.msnbc.msn.com/id/33752275/ns/meet_the_press/.

32 Carolyn Plocher, "PC News: Networks Downplay Terrorism, Muslim Connection in Ft. Hood Attack," November 11, 2009, http://newsbusters.org/blogs/carolyn-plocher/2009/11/11/pc-news-networks-downplay-terrorism-muslim-connection-ft-hood-attac.

33 Andrea Elliott, "Complications Grow for Muslims Serving in U.S. Military," *New York Times,* November 9, 2009, p. 1, http://www.nytimes.com/2009/11/09/us/09muslim.html?_r=1&ref=global-home. The *Times* suggested Hasan suffered some traumatic response to being assigned to overseas duty: http://www.nytimes.com/2009/11/09/us/09muslim.html?_r=1&scp=1&sq=Muslims%20Serving%20in%20U.S.%20Military&st=cse.

34 The *Washington Post* also fell into this kind of agitprop legalese in some of its articles, headlines, and photo captions. For example, one caption on November 17, 2009, showed recruits from Fort Hood getting ready to go overseas, asserting that their "preparations come just weeks after Maj. Nidal

Malik Hasan allegedly went on a shooting rampage that left 13 people
dead and 37 others wounded." Hasan did not allegedly shoot and kill
people. He really murdered them. See caption at http://www.washington
post.com/wp-dyn/content/gallery/2009/11/21/GA2009112100066.html.

35 Carrie Johnson, Spencer S. Hsu, and Ellen Nakashima, "Hasan Had In-
tensified Contact With Cleric, FBI Monitored E-Mail Exchanges," *Washington Post*, November 21, 2009, http://www.washingtonpost.com/wp-dyn
/content/article/2009/11/20/AR2009112004381_pf.html.

36 *Times* correction, November 11, 2009: "An article on Monday about difficulties for Muslims serving in the American armed forces described incorrectly the background of Michael A. Monsoor, a member of the Navy Seals.
Mr. Monsoor was a Christian of Lebanese and Irish descent, not a Muslim.
The article also described incorrectly the act that earned him a Medal
of Honor. It was for falling on a grenade and saving at least three team
members—not for pulling a team member to safety. (Saving a team member in an earlier incident earned him a Silver Star.)"

37 Brent Kendall, "FBI to Assess Actions Before Hood Shooting,"
Wall Street Journal, December 9, 2009, http://online.wsj.com/article
/SB126029116310482127.html.

38 Joel Mowbray, "How military missed signs," *Washington Times*, November 16, 2009, http://www.washingtontimes.com/news/2009/nov/16/how
-military-missed-signs//print/.

39 Bernard Goldberg, *Bias: A CBS Insider Exposes How the Media Distort the
News* (Washington, DC: Regnery, 2002), p. 199.

40 See Edward J. Epstein, "The Andropov Hoax," *New Republic*, February
7, 1983, pp. 18–21, http://www.edwardjayepstein.com/archived/andropov
.htm. Epstein does a delightful job detailing the various tall tales and preposterous accounts swallowed by leading Western media.

41 This same "liberal" Syrian leader has prevented his own people from using
the Internet freely, and he conspired with Iran and North Korea to try to
build a weapons-oriented nuclear reactor in 2007. In 2011 the "moderate
mask" was stripped from Assad as his troops killed scores of unarmed protesters.

42 Joan Juliet Buck, "Asma al-Assad: A Rose in the Desert," photographed by
James Nachtwey, *Vogue*, February 25, 2011, http://www.vogue.com/vogue
-daily/article/asma-al-assad-a-rose-in-the-desert/.

43 Letter by Salim Za'anoun (former head of Palestinian National Council)
summing up agreement between Arafat and Yassin, edited and translated
into English by Michael Widlanski, at the time strategic advisor to the
ministry. A copy of the letter in Arabic along with the translation appears
in the appendix of documents attached to the author's doctoral disserta-
tion: "The Palestinian Broadcast Media: Models of Influence and Control,"

Bar Ilan University, 2004. The letter was published by the Israeli Ministry of Public Security in April 2002 after first being offered, with other exclusive documents, to the *New York Times,* which did not show any interest in the far-reaching documentation. The three-page handwritten cooperation framework agreement for confronting Israel was hammered out in several meetings in late July and early August 2000 between Salim Za'anoun, speaker of the Palestine National Council, and Sheikh Ahmad Yassin, the spiritual leader of the Hamas movement. Za'anoun writes that he has been personally delegated by Arafat to speak to Yassin. The agreement, in the form of a letter from Za'anoun to Yassin, was forwarded in its handwritten form (apparently for reasons of secrecy) to Faisal Husseini, Arafat's personal emissary in Jerusalem as well as a member of the PLO's highest body, its thirteen-man Executive Committee. The Za'anoun-Yassin letter of strategic cooperation was dated August 10, 2000, the same day Husseini sent out a letter calling for all his Orient House employees and families to take part in a drill practicing confrontation with Israel at the Temple Mount/Al-Haram Al-Sharif. Both documents underscore the amount of Palestinian planning that preceded the supposedly spontaneous outbreak of Arab violence that followed Ariel Sharon's visit to the Temple Mount plaza area. The documents essentially destroy many of the facile contentions made by journalists about Fatah and Hamas.

44 The *Times* took the right position in 1971, though its publisher at the time, Arthur Ochs Sulzberger, was a former U.S. marine, and even though its executive editor, Abe Rosenthal, was fairly conservative in his political views, staunchly anticommunist, and had even supported U.S. involvement in Vietnam.

45 The decision was reached in consultation with Minister of Public Security Uzi Landau, who directed the police.

46 Sharon never even got close to the actual mosque area, and he certainly did not enter it with shoes on. Still, the Palestinian Authority propaganda machine called his action *Tadnees*—defilement.

47 The *Times* also refused to cover incitement to hatred—even to suicide attacks—in the official Palestinian media, though this, too, was a major violation of treaties. The *Times* published, however, an article on how the PA was "moderating" hateful propaganda (whose presence the *Times* never covered). See Greg Myre, "On the Air, Palestinians Soften Tone on Israelis," *New York Times,* December 15, 2004, p. A1.

48 James Bennet interview, *McNeil-Lehrer News Hour,* PBS, March 21, 2002, at http://www.pbs.org/newshour/bb/middle_east/jan-june02/talks_3-21.html.

49 The Associated Press and *Haaretz* ran articles on the documents, but neither could devote the space and the prominence to the story that the *New York Times,* the "paper of record," should have done.

50   Nacos, *Mass-Mediated Terrorism*, p. 222.

51   Ibid.

52   Walter Laqueur, *The New Terrorism: Fanaticism and the Arms of Mass Destruction* (London: Oxford University Press, 1999), p. 44.

53   Alex P. Schmid and Janny deGraaf, *Violence as Communication: Insurgent Terrorism and the Western News Media* (London: Sage, 1982), p. 9.

54   "John Burns: 'There Is Corruption in Our Business,'" interview with John Burns, September 15, 2003, *Editor & Publisher*, http://www.editorand publisher.com/eandp/news/article_display.jsp?vnu_content_id=1979014.

55   The Burns remarks are from a 2,300-word selection, of which the first and final paragraphs are offered here. The full interview is in Bill Katovsky and Timothy Carlson, eds., *Embedded: The Media at War in Iraq—An Oral History* (Guilford, CT: Lyons Press, 2003).

56   Turner's view that poverty breeds terror is still a common one among journalists and policy makers even though it has been vitiated by strong and unambiguous academic research.

57   Gerald M. Carbone, "Turner urges students to save world," *Providence Journal*, February 12, 2002. The story was also distributed by the Associated Press, but it originally appeared at the now-defunct URL http://www.projo .com/report/html/07029261.htm. A nearly identical account of Turner's remarks appeared in Brown University's *Brown Daily Herald*: http://www .browndailyherald.com/stories.cfm?ID=6169. Turner later tried to explain that his remarks were taken out of context. See also Media Research Center, "Ted Turner Called Terrorists 'Brave,' Blamed 9/11 on Poverty, Denounced Bush as 'Julius Caesar,' Forecast Environmental Collapse," http:// www.mrc.org/cyberalerts/2002/cyb20020212_extra.asp. See also http:// www.foxnews.com/story/0,2933,45376,00.html.

58   Tifft and Jones, *The Trust*, p. 499.

59   I once experienced this side of the elder Sulzberger, a trustee at Columbia University, who sent a donation for *The Columbia-Barnard Course Guide*, of which I was the editor. The donation was accompanied by a short personal note that was obviously personally typed and signed by Sulzberger himself—including a small typographical error.

60   The nickname was due to Arthur's sister, Judy, and the two were known as "Punch and Judy," in reference to a popular English puppet show. Reporters liked Punch Sulzberger, although his views were more conservative than those of many of his staffers.

61   President Lyndon Johnson, who ordered escalation in Vietnam, was a Texan, like George W. Bush.

62   Bob Kohn, *Journalistic Fraud: How The New York Times Distorts the News and Why It Can No Longer Be Trusted* (Nashville, TN: WND Books, 2003), p. 31.

63 In his career, Raines had spent only one year abroad, in London. This was in marked contrast to previous *Times* editors such as Abe Rosenthal, Joe Lelyveld, and even Max Frankel.

64 David Margolick, "The *Times*'s Restoration Drama," *Vanity Fair*, August 2003, p. 140.

65 Tifft and Jones, *The Trust*, p. 649.

66 Dowd's oeuvre offers many examples, but these comments are from "Oil Man Plays Ozone Man," February 4, 2006, http://select.nytimes .com/2006/02/04/opinion/04dowd.html?pagewanted=print; "Drunk on Rummy," September 28, 2003, http://www.nytimes.com/2003/09/28 /opinion/28DOWD.html.

67 Maureen Dowd, "Who's Your Daddy?" *New York Times*, September 4, 2002, p. 21, http://www.nytimes.com/2002/09/04/opinion/04DOWD.html.

68 Tifft and Jones, *The Trust*, p. 620.

69 David Margolick observes that Sulzberger's editor, "[Howell] Raines began killing stories by some of the *Times*'s best journalists. He also went to war with the small team of reporters doing long-term investigative stories, showing little interest in projects which, he felt, took too long." See Margolick, "The *Times*'s Restoration Drama."

70 See "Eliminating Hidden Weapons: Illusory Inspections in Iraq," editorial, *New York Times*, August 28, 1998, p. A24, http://www.nytimes .com/1998/08/28/opinion/eliminating-hidden-weapons-illusory-inspections-in-iraq.html?pagewanted=1. Two months later Congress passed the Iraq Liberation Act, calling for removing Saddam from power.

71 At the time of the Dowd article, Saddam had already violated eleven UN Security Council resolutions and had totally corrupted the UN's Food for Peace Program so that its monies propped up his regime while enlarging the accounts of several corrupt UN officials in New York.

72 Dowd, "Drunk on Rummy."

73 More than one metric ton of weapons-grade uranium was found in Iraq after 2002, as were artillery shells with sarin gas.

74 Arnold M. Howitt and Robyn L. Pangi, *Countering Terrorism* (Cambridge, MA: MIT Press, 2003), p. 1. One of the most overlooked elements of Arab-Islamic terror is the fact that America was also hit by a series of anthrax attacks in the weeks around 9/11, and Iraq was known to have such capabilities. Similarly, Iraq provided safe haven and documents to members of the jihad/Al-Qaeda groups, including participants in the 1993 World Trade Center attack.

75 See Stephen F. Hayes, *The Connection: How Al-Qaeda's Collaboration with Saddam Hussein Has Endangered America* (New York: HarperCollins, 2004), pp. 9–12, 15, 47–50.

76 James Risen and Eric Lichtblau, "Bush Lets U.S. Spy on Callers Without Courts," December 16, 2005, http://www.nytimes.com/2005/12/16/politics/16program.html?scp=1&sq=national%20security%20wiretaps&st=cse. The original news article indicated that the *Times'* decision to delay and then publish was also based on a desire to defend civil liberties as well as to gain more newsworthy information. *Times* editorials said the Bush administration acted unlawfully: "What Mr. Bush wants is to be able to listen to your international telephone calls and read your international e-mail whenever he wants, without a court being able to prevent it or judge the legality of his actions." ["The Intelligence Cover-Up," March 16, 2008, http://www.nytimes.com/2008/03/16/opinion/16sun2.html?ref=wiretappingandothereavesdroppingdevicesandmethods.] For a contrary view of *Times* motives, see, inter alia, Rowan Scarborough, *Sabotage: America's Enemies Within the CIA* (Washington, DC: Regnery, 2007), pp. 65–69, and Kenneth Timmerman, *Shadow Warriors: The Untold Story of Traitors, Saboteurs, and the Party of Surrender* (New York: Three Rivers Press, 2007), pp. 249–57. Both Scarborough and Timmerman make the case that the *Times* did not act just out of concern for civil liberties but rather out of antiwar feelings and also to hurt the Bush administration. The policy consideration of Bush and Vice President Dick Cheney, who supported the Terrorist Surveillance Program (TSP) and liberal interpretation of the existing Foreign Intelligence Surveillance Act (FISA), as well as their feelings about the *Times* decision are clear from their memoirs. See George W. Bush, *Decision Points* (New York: Crown, 2010), especially pp. 162–64, 172–74, and 176–81; for Cheney's views on a variety of surveillance and interrogation programs, see Dick Cheney, *In My Time* (New York: Threshold Editions, 2011), pp. 348–57, where Cheney says of the TSP (p. 353) "this program is one of the things of which I am proudest. I know it saved lives and prevented attacks."

77 Charges of widespread torture of captured suspected terrorists were disproved, as well as charges of deliberate falsification of intelligence data. Similarly, the charge that Bush or Cheney had tried to sabotage the career of Ambassador Joseph Wilson and his wife, CIA employee Valerie Plame—both critics of Bush policies—was also disproved. Similarly, charges by *Newsweek* that U.S. jailers defaced a Quran or flushed it down a toilet were disproven and recanted by the magazine, but not before scores were wounded and several killed in worldwide anti-American riots. For the *Times* account on bank records see, Eric Lichtblau and James Risen, "Bank Data Is Sifted by U.S. in Secret to Block Terror," *New York Times,* June 23, 2006, http://www.nytimes.com/2006/06/23/washington/23intel.html. Congress eventually approved several laws allowing many of the techniques

sought by the Bush administration, but the public debate alerted the terrorists to be wary of those very techniques.

78 Another precedent breaker was the *Times'* firing of several reporters and editors caught in acts of fraud and plagiarism, the most infamous of which was the scandal involving Jayson Blair.

79 Maureen Dowd, "Captain Obvious Learns the Limits of Cool," *New York Times*, January 10, 2010, p. 11, http://www.nytimes.com/2010/01/10/opinion/10dowd.html.

CHAPTER FIVE: PROTECTING THE CIA AND BOOSTING BIN-LADEN

1 The notion that intelligence is a critical factor in the outcome of a war has been challenged recently by British historian Sir John Keegan. See his *Intelligence in War: Knowledge of the Enemy from Napoleon to Al-Qaeda* (New York: Knopf, 2003). Despite Keegan's point that force is more important than knowledge, and despite Henry Kissinger's analysis that national will is often the most critical factor, this author believes that intelligence is a critical factor in fighting terrorists—perhaps the most critical factor.

2 Gary Berntsen, *Jawbreaker: The Attack on bin Laden and Al-Qaeda: By the CIA's Key Field Commander* (New York: Crown, 2005), p. 33.

3 Robin W. Winks, *Cloak and Gown: Scholars in the Secret War* (New York: William Morrow, 1987), p. 323.

4 "Anti-Terror War's Missteps Detailed By NSC Staffers," *Washington Post,* October 2, 2002, http://www.washingtonpost.com/wp-dyn/articles/A30061-2002Oct1.html.

5 Ronald Kessler, *The CIA at War: Inside the Secret Campaign Against Terror* (New York: St. Martin's Press, 2003), pp. 9–10.

6 Clinton and Vice President Al Gore were probed for allegedly getting illegal foreign donations, and Clinton was also being investigated on charges ranging from financial and executive improprieties to alleged perjury about sexual misconduct. President Clinton was eventually impeached for his misconduct by the House of Representatives, but he was acquitted by the Senate.

7 Gorelick has denied the charges, saying she only enforced existing rules. The charges against her were lodged by John Ashcroft, attorney general under President George W. Bush. It seems Ashcroft's account is closer to the truth—that Clinton-Reno-Gorelick stiffened the "wall" preventing sharing intelligence information. The *9/11 Commission Report* largely sidesteps the issue.

8 Elsa Walsh, "Louis Freeh's Last Case," *New Yorker,* May 21, 2001, http://www.newyorker.com/archive/2001/05/14/010514fa_fact_walsh. See Mike Wallace interview with Freeh, *60 Minutes,* CBS, October 9, 2005, in which Freeh says Clinton was reluctant and ineffectual in getting Saudi government cooperation with the U.S. investigation. Freeh says he was forced to

get former president George H. W. Bush to ask the Saudis for help, and they then agreed. Both Freeh and Wallace refer in detail to Freeh's book, *My FBI: Bringing Down the Mafia, Investigating Bill Clinton, and Fighting the War on Terror* (New York: St. Martin's Press, 2005).

9   The 9/11 Commission discusses some of this material, but it is related in detail—with additional examples—in independent accounts. See Kenneth Timmerman, *Shadow Warriors: The Untold Story of Traitors, Saboteurs, and the Party of Surrender* (New York: Three Rivers Press, 2007), p. 67; Emmy Award winner Peter Lance's *Cover Up: What the Government Is Still Hiding About the War on Terror* (New York: ReganBooks, 2004); Steve Coll, *Ghost Wars: The Secret History of the CIA, Afghanistan, and Bin Laden, from the Soviet Invasion to September 10, 2001* (New York: Penguin Books, 2004); Wright, *The Looming Tower.*

10   Tim Weiner, *Legacy of Ashes: A History of the CIA,* rev. ed. (New York: Anchor Books, 2008), p. 401.

11   John Ranelagh, *The Agency: The Rise and Decline of the CIA from Wild Bill Donovan to William Casey* (New York: Simon & Schuster, 1986), p. 597.

12   See Bill Gertz, *Breakdown: The Failure of American Intelligence to Defeat Global Terror,* rev. ed. (New York: Plume, 2003), pp. 24–28, 36.

13   John Miller and Michael Stone with Chris Mitchell, *The Cell: Inside the 9/11 Plot, and Why the FBI and CIA Failed to Stop It* (New York: Hyperion, 2002).

14   Final Report of the National Commission on Terrorist Attacks Upon the United States, Official Government Edition, April 2007, http://www .gpoaccess.gov/911/Index.html.

15   Ernest R. May, "When Government Writes History: A Memoir of the 9/11 Commission," *New Republic,* May 23, 2005, p. 33.

16   Ibid.

17   Ibid., p. 30.

18   *9/11 Commission Report,* chap. 8, p. 2.

19   Ibid., Executive Summary, p. 13. May explains that the historical detail was meant to give a strong factual underpinning to the narrative, delaying for as long as possible the political maneuvering about the report's findings and language.

20   Israel's commission was known as the Agranat Commission, because it was chaired by Israeli Supreme Court chief justice Shimon Agranat. It found fault with the Israeli army's lack of readiness and lack of intelligence, but it excused the political leaders, especially Prime Minister Golda Meir and Defense Minister Moshe Dayan. The Israeli public, however, protested against these leaders, forcing their resignations. Subsequent Israeli commissions of inquiry for the 1982 and 2006 Lebanon wars were much more penetrating in their discussion.

21 Tenet began service as "acting director" in 1996 after Clinton appointee John Deutch resigned under a cloud of charges.

22 Gertz, *Breakdown*, p. 67.

23 Robert Baer, *See No Evil: The True Story of a Ground Soldier in the CIA's War on Terrorism* (New York: Three Rivers Press, 2002), p. xviii.

24 Thomas Powers, *Intelligence Wars: American Secret History from Hitler to Al-Qaeda* (New York: New York Review of Books, 2004), pp. 386–87 and 416. See Robert Baer, *See No Evil*, pp. 3–7, op cit, for Baer's view on what prompted the charges that were eventually dropped. See also Timmerman, *Shadow Warriors*, op cit, pp. 20–27, for additional discussion of turf wars and personal differences that may have served as motives for bringing the charges. See also, Gertz, *Breakdown*, op cit, pp. 56–57, where Gertz describes Anthony Lake using Baer as "his whipping boy."

25 See Kenneth Timmerman, "The Murky Depths of Anthony Lake," *American Spectator*, April 1997, pp. 36–41. He compares Lake's ideas to those of Oliver North in the Iran-Contra affair.

26 *9/11 Commission Report*, chap. 3, p. 20.

27 Rowan Scarborough, *Sabotage: America's Enemies Within the CIA* (Washington, DC: Regnery, 2007), p. 114.

28 *9/11 Commission Report*, chap. 3, p. 20. "DCI" means director of central intelligence, or head of the CIA. This commission statement puts a good face on a terrible situation. Congress moved very slowly to re-upgrade CIA manpower, and the CIA was clumsy and unfocused in enlisting language specialists.

29 Deutch was incredibly sloppy with classified material, for example, putting it on his home computer that was linked to unscrambled Internet connections. Tenet worked together to block a serious investigation of the matter together with Senator Carl Levin (D-Mich.), who blocked the Senate Intelligence Committee deliberations on the subject.

30 The *9/11 Commission Report* covers this with some interesting euphemistic passages, including: "The Clandestine Service felt the impact of the post–Cold War peace dividend, with cuts beginning in 1992" (chap. 3, p. 20). To be fair, one must note that Clinton's first CIA director, James Woolsey, tried to resist congressional pressure for budget cuts. It is also apparent that the administration of George H. W. Bush and his secretary of state James Baker also seemed to be adherents of the view that the collapse of communism would lead to a "peace dividend."

31 Kessler is the author of three separate books on the CIA, one on the FBI, and one on the U.S. Secret Service. These remarks are from Kessler's blog at Newsmax, "Obama Has Paralyzed the CIA," April 27, 2009, http://www .newsmax.com/kessler/obama_cia/2009/04/27/207740.html.

32   Torricelli was running for Senate in 1996, but after 9/11, he was challenged during his reelection campaign in 2002 for having hurt American intelligence efforts. See David Kocieniewski, "Challenger to Torricelli Attacks Curbs on the C.I.A.," *New York Times,* September 17, 2002, http://www.nytimes.com/2002/09/17/nyregion/challenger-to-torricelli-attacks-curbs-on-the-cia.html.

33   Congressional testimony of James Woolsey, hearings on bioterrorism, September 13, 2002.

34   See, inter alia, Baer, *See No Evil,* pp. 40–41, 271, and Berntsen, *Jawbreaker,* pp. 32–33, for changes in CIA agent recruitment policy. See also Timmerman, *Shadow Warriors,* p. 179.

35   Bob Woodward, *Veil: The Secret Wars of the CIA, 1981–1987* (New York: Simon & Schuster, 2007), p. 112.

36   Berntsen, *Jawbreaker,* p. 9.

37   Ibid., p. 32.

38   Baer, *See No Evil,* p. 267. The entire book, which was redacted and severely censored by a CIA review board, is still full of examples where evidence of cooperation between Iran and Fatah or between Osama bin-Laden and Hizballah was not really pursued by the United States.

39   The heart of these charges is that Bush and Vice President Richard Cheney pushed intelligence agencies to claim that Saddam Hussein's Iraq was bent on developing weapons of mass destruction—a case that Bush and Cheney used as grounds to invade Iraq after attacking Al-Qaeda in Afghanistan.

40   Powers, *Intelligence Wars,* p. 386.

41   Bush made the same mistake when he first announced the nomination of his friend and counsel Harriet Miers to the Supreme Court. He withdrew her name when she was seen as not qualified. Bush also hired Michael D. Brown, a friend, to be head of the Federal Emergency Management Agency. Brown resigned in September 2005 after what was seen to be his mishandling of Hurricane Katrina.

42   Dana Priest, "Former Chief of CIA's Bin Laden Unit Leaves," *Washington Post,* November 12, 2004, p. A04, http://www.washingtonpost.com/wp-dyn/articles/A43899-2004Nov11.html.

43   Donilon worked at Fannie Mae, the semipublic housing conglomerate that was one of Obama's big campaign donors, and whose corrupt practices helped trigger the U.S. market meltdown in 2008. Carol E. Lee and Gordon Lubold, "Tom Donilon to Replace James Jones As National Security Council Chief," *Politico,* October 8, 2010, http://www.politico.com/news/stories/1010/43323.html#ixzz1Khsam1wv. See Terence O'Hara, "Donilon Oversaw Relations With Regulators, Congress," *Washington Post,* April 16, 2005, p. E01, http://www.washingtonpost.com/wp-dyn/articles/A57900-2005Apr15.html.

44 National Public Radio, "Political Insider's Ascent to Top NSC Job," October 8, 2010, http://www.npr.org/templates/story/story.php?storyId=130442444; Tom Fitton, "Fannie Mae Lobbyist to Head Obama's National Security Council," *Washington Examiner,* October 18, 2010, http://washington examiner.com/node/516012#ixzz1Khoxvk5r.

45 Muhammad's Battle of Badr victory essentially confirmed his status as prophet, signaling his success and easing his recruitment of followers, while Arafat's spinning of "victory" at the Battle of Karameh in 1968 essentially made him the undisputed leader of the PLO. See Michael Barnett, *Dialogues in Arab Politics* (New York: Columbia University Press, 1998).

46 J. Bowyer Bell, *Dragonwars: Armed Struggle and the Conventions of Modern War* (New Brunswick, NJ: Transaction Books, 1999), p. 151. See also Walter Laqueur, *The Age of Terrorism* (Boston: Little, Brown, 1987), pp. 48–51, where Laqueur discusses the role of "the propaganda of the deed" among socialist revolutionaries and anarchists in nineteenth-century Europe.

47 Michael Scheuer ("Anonymous"), *Imperial Hubris: Why the West Is Losing the War on Terror,* rev. ed. (Washington, DC: Brassey's, 2007), pp. xiii, 266.

48 See Scheuer's statement that "bin-Laden is in the Islamic mainstream," in ibid., p. 2.

49 Ibid.

50 Ibid., p. 270.

51 The author believes that the Bush administration objectives of "democratization" or "nation-building" are noble but were not sufficiently thought through.

52 The full name of Medina is *madinat al-nabi*: the city of the Prophet.

53 Yasser Arafat, who wanted to emphasize the importance of Jerusalem, frequently referred to Jerusalem in Arabic as *oola al-qiblatein*: the first of the two directions of prayer. Later interpretations of Quranic verses have attempted to imply that Jerusalem's Al-Aqsa mosque was part of the miraculous "night journey" mentioned in the Quran.

54 The ideology of the Brotherhood is discussed in detail in a later chapter, including its links to the Wahhabi ideology of Saudi Arabia.

55 Lieutenant General James Clapper, testimony to House Intelligence Committee, February 10, 2011.

56 There are many examples of writers, even good ones, who make this mistake. See for example, Wright, *The Looming Tower,* p. 91, where Wright describes the moderate or "tolerant and accepting view of Islam" from another Brotherhood figure, Hassan Hudaybi, who opposed the immediate murder of believing Muslims who did not agree with the Brotherhood. Hudaybi still advocated converting the world to Islam by force, if needed, but he was a bit more patient than his colleague Qutb. Still worse is the cavalier way Daniel Byman, a respected student of terror and member of the 9/11

Commission, refers to the Brotherhood as a group "that has flirted with violence repeatedly." See Daniel Byman, *The Five-Front War: The Better Way to Fight Global Jihad* (Hoboken, NJ: Wiley, 2008), pp. 56–57.

57 Haniyeh's comments were seen and recorded from various Arab and Israeli TV outlets, May 2, 2011. The comments appeared also in Arabic and English on various Hamas websites.

58 Members of Fatah, such as the Al-Aqsa Martyrs Brigade, also saluted bin-Laden and condemned the United States, though their comments were not widely reported in the Western media.

59 R. Stephen Humphreys, "The Contemporary Resurgence," in A. H. Dessouki, ed., *Islamic Resurgence in the Arab World* (New York: Praeger, 1982), p. 72.

60 Ali Hilal Dessouki, "The Islamic Resurgence: Sources, Dynamics, and Implications," Dessouki, ed., *Islamic Resurgence in the Arab World*, p. 3.

61 Gilles Kepel, *Jihad: The Trail of Political Islam* (Cambridge, MA: Harvard University Press, 2002), p. 28.

62 Sayyid Qutb, *Social Justice in Islam*, first English translation by John Hardie, 1953, American Council of Learned Societies, and revised translation by Hamid Algar (Oneonta, NY: Islamic Publications International, 2000), 263.

63 Ibid., trans. Algar, p. 157.

64 Algar, introduction to ibid., p. 5.

65 Ibid.

66 Bernard Lewis, *The Crisis of Islam: Holy War and Unholy Terror* (New York: Modern Library, 2003), p. 24.

67 See, for example, Professor Albert Bergesen's introduction, in Albert J. Bergesen, ed., *The Sayyid Qutb Reader* (New York: Routledge, 2008), p. 5. The Palestinian Hamas movement has been critically influenced by the Brotherhood and Qutb's writings.

68 It is not clear how or why Scheuer made this mistake. Perhaps it is because Muhammad is the most common Arab name. Sayyid Qutb actually had a younger brother named Muhammad who went into exile in Saudi Arabia after his older brother's fate. This younger brother taught in Saudi universities and may have taught the young Osama bin-Laden. See Yaroslav Trofimov, *The Siege of Mecca* (New York: Anchor/Random House, 2007), p. 22, and Dore Gold, *Hatred's Kingdom: How Saudi Arabia Supports the New Global Terrorism* (Washington, DC: Regnery, 2003), pp. 91–95. But the younger Qutb was *not* the philosopher and ideologue of the Muslim Brotherhood who was hanged by the government of Gamal Abdul-Nasser. In his book, Scheuer hangs the wrong brother. Nine years later, Scheuer, in his fourth book, suddenly discovers Sayyid Qutb, after mentioning him parenthetically in his second book and not at all in his third book. He "discovers" Qutb apparently only because someone has called his attention to the embarrasing mistakes of the 2002 book, and also because serious

scholars of Islamic politics (e.g., Raymond Ibrahim, Gilles Kepel, and many others) as well as serious journalists who interviewed bin-Laden or studied him closely (Yaroslav Trofimov, Peter Bergen, Lawrence Wright, and others) highlight the impact of Qutb on Al-Qaeda: "In an earlier book, *Through Our Enemies' Eyes,* I wrote with rather too much certainty that bin Laden was heavily influenced by Sayyid Qutb (whom to my everlasting embarrassment I mistakenly identified as Muhammad Qutb, Sayyid's brother). In the decade since writing that book, it has become clear that Sayyid Qutb—to whom common wisdom assigns the role of 'father of modern Islamic fundamentalism'—did not have much, if any impact on bin Laden's thought." So, after making an embarrasingly serious set of mistakes and correcting them parenthetically after nine years, Scheuer sets out to make an even bigger mistake by trying to minimize the importance of the original error by making a much more fundamental error, insisting that Sayyid Qutb was not really important, though bin-Laden "read the works of the Qutb brothers"—a reference that brings to mind a kind of sibling act like the Doobie Brothers and the Pointer Sisters. See Michael Scheuer, *Osama Bin-Laden* (New York: Oxford University Press, 2011), pp. 34, 40–42. Actually, Sayyid Qutb was a soloist, and his younger brother was more of a devotee or disciple than a partner. Scheuer's sloppy work is apparent throughout his work, as when he misspells Sayyid Qutb every time differently from earlier books. Where Sayyid Qutb was "Muhammad" Qutb in first book, "Sayyid" Qutb ever so briefly in the second book, and unmentioned in the third book, he emerges as the frequently noted but not really noteworthy "Sayyed" Qutb in his most recent book. One of the ways Scheuer "proves" Qutb was unimportant is by saying that bin-Laden never quoted from Qutb, although bin-Laden's deputy, Ayman Zawahiri, did quote from Qutb many times. This is really quite illogical. After all, bin-Laden cited Scheuer in one broadcast, and no one would believe that Scheuer was more influential on bin-Laden than Sayyid Qutb. There is a much simpler explanation. Bin-Laden was not a big quoter of others, never an intellectual or a scholar, like Zawahiri. True, bin-Laden liked to pretend once in a while to offer a *fatwa,* or religious edict, but bin-Laden was much more interested in being a charismatic symbol, an inspirer of others. He loved the role of speaking like a pre-Islamic poet on videotape, and he liked having his picture taken firing or holding a gun, like Yasser Arafat and Saddam Hussein. Meanwhile, Zawahiri seemed to fit the part of the thinker, philospher, and planner, more in the background. Scheuer also launches a kind of sterile argument against some of the world's top Islamists, insisting that bin-Laden always influenced Zawahiri, and never the other way around. Here, too (see *Osama Bin-Laden,* pp. 9–10), this is a kind of juvenile approach, reminiscent of boys arguing whose father is stronger or whose football team is better. A more reasoned analytical approach would be to suggest that bin-Laden and Zawahiri influenced each other and complemented each other.

69   Michael Scheuer, *Through Our Enemies' Eyes*, rev. ed. (Washington, DC: Potomac Press, 2006), p. 20.

70   Similar arguments are raised by the isolationist conservatives such as Ron Paul and Patrick Buchanan.

71   For a discussion of this tactic of trying to appear reasonable to a Western audience, see Raymond Ibrahim, ed., *The Al-Qaeda Reader* (New York: Doubleday, 2008), cf. pp. 20, 196–208, where Ibrahim explains bin-Laden's address to the American people in 2002. See Gilles Kepel's explanation of a 2004 bin-Laden video in Gilles Kepel and Jean-Pierre Milelli, eds., *Al-Qaeda in Its Own Words* (Cambridge, MA: Harvard University Press, 2008), pp. 70–77, 292–93.

72   Ibrahim, ed., *The Al-Qaeda Reader*, p. xii.

73   Gilles Kepel, "General Introduction," p. 6, in Kepel and Milelli, eds., *Al Qaeda in Its Own Words*, p. 6.

74   Scheuer, *Imperial Hubris*, p. xiii.

75   James Carville was Bill Clinton's campaign manager during the 1992 presidential election.

76   Scheuer has been a paid consultant for CBS News and Fox News, while his *Through Our Enemies' Eyes* features a foreword by Bruce Hoffman, a noted student of terrorism, who has worked and taught at RAND, Georgetown University, and other institutions. Hoffman refers to Scheuer's writings as "seminal" in his *Inside Terrorism* (New York: Columbia University Press, 2006), p. 274.

77   See Wright, *The Looming Tower*, p. 274.

78   Scheuer credits this absurd line of reasoning to John Esposito, and Esposito, among others, deserves some "credit," but Scheuer really extrapolates and extends the analogy. See Scheuer, *Through Our Enemies' Eyes*, pp. 9–13.

79   Ibid., p. 13.

80   Ibid., p. xxi.

81   For example, in Arabic broadcasts of Hizballah's Al-Manar television, Hamas radio and television, and Palestinian Authority's broadcasts, the broadcasters often say *"ma usamiy al-irhaab"*—what is sometimes called terror—or "what America calls terror" or "what Israel calls terror."

82   Scheuer, *Imperial Hubris*, p. 77.

83   Scheuer, *Through Our Enemies' Eyes*, pp. xxi–xxii. The factual premise behind Fisk's comment and Scheuer's citation is incorrect: both the mosque murderer (Dr. Baruch Goldstein) and Rabin's convicted assassin (Yigal Amir) were unequivocally condemned by Israel's government and an overwhelming majority of Israelis. The Israeli government even passed a

law forbidding memorializing the mosque murderer, while denying even the most basic prison privileges to the convicted assassin, who has been kept in solitary confinement for years. Moreover, the premise that the Western media constantly refer to Arab murderers as terrorists is not correct. Many of the Western media—the *New York Times,* Reuters, and other outlets—prefer to use euphemisms, as is shown in another chapter of this book.

84 Osama bin-Laden, video address to the American people, broadcast September 7, 2007.

85 An English translation of the bin-Laden address is available at http://publicintelligence.net/osama-bin-laden-september-7-2007-video-with-transcript/ or http://en.wikipedia.org/wiki/2007_Osama_bin_Laden_video, and additional analysis of his various speeches and letters is available through Ibrahim, *The Al Qaeda Reader,* and Kepel and Milelli, *Al Qaeda in Its Own Words.* For Scheuer's reaction, see http://www.youtube.com/watch?v=Aqm4XVylLLc.

86 Scheuer, *Imperial Hubris,* p. 3.

87 Scheuer, *Through Our Enemies' Eyes,* p. 272.

88 Scheuer, *Imperial Hubris,* p. 268. His use of the gambling term *trifecta* would really insult Muslims.

89 *CBS Evening News,* September 7, 2007.

90 Scheuer, *Through Our Enemies' Eyes,* p. 261.

91 This analysis is based on interviews with past and present Israeli intelligence officials, including Major General (Res.) Yaakov Amidror, Major General (Res.) Aharon Ze'evi-Farkash, and Brigadier General (Res.) Shalom Harari, among others.

92 See http://original.antiwar.com/scheuer/2009/05/19/obama-steers-toward-endless-war-with-islam/, where Scheuer says that Barack Obama is controlled by Rahm Emanuel (then White House chief of staff), a Jew who, according to Scheuer, chose to serve in Israel's armed forces and not in the American military. See also *National Journal* blog site http://security.nationaljournal.com/2009/03/how-to-talk-about-israel.php#1311539.

93 Chomsky, in various writings, has referred to Israeli leader Shimon Peres as a terrorist—this of a man who made far-reaching concessions to the Palestinian Arabs. He has also called President Ronald Reagan one of the world's biggest terrorists. Meanwhile, he has minimized (along with colleague Edward S. Herman) the genocide committed by Cambodian leader Pol Pot and his Khmer Rouge.

94 See http://security.nationaljournal.com/2009/03/how-to-talk-about-israel.php, filed by Scheuer on the blog site on March 16, 2009.

CHAPTER SIX: COUNTERTERROR INTELLIGENCE: OXYMORONIC OR JUST MORONIC?

1 Pillar served as Middle East intelligence officer, as deputy director of the counterterrorism section, and as executive assistant to CIA director George Tenet.

2 See for example, Paul R. Pillar, *Negotiating Peace: War Termination as a Bargaining Process* (Princeton, NJ: Princeton University Press, 1983).

3 Paul R. Pillar, *Terrorism and U.S. Foreign Policy* (Washington, DC: Brookings Institution Press, 2001), p. 46.

4 Ibid., p. 5.

5 Steve Coll, *Ghost Wars: The Secret History of the CIA, Afghanistan, and Bin Laden, from the Soviet Invasion to September 10, 2001* (New York: Penguin Books, 2004), p. 261.

6 The 2004 NIE on Iraq, which Pillar apparently leaked, predicted the United States would not succeed in establishing a stable government in Iraq. This assessment also proved incorrect.

7 Paul Pillar, "Are We Safe Yet?" *Foreign Affairs* (September 7, 2006), http://www.foreignaffairs.com/discussions/roundtables/are-we-safe-yet.

8 To be fair to Pillar, he was not alone in his analysis, and the United States *did* find evidence of Iraqi WMD programs, but U.S. forces neglected to confiscate at least three large weapons bunkers, which were stripped of whatever was inside. There is also evidence that some WMD may have been moved to Syria or Iran.

9 Paul Pillar interview, National Public Radio, part of Tom Gjelten, "Iran NIE Reopens Intelligence Debate," January 17, 2008, http://www.npr.org/templates/story/story.php?storyId=18177103.

10 Paul R. Pillar, "Intelligence, Policy, and the War in Iraq," *Foreign Affairs* (March/April 2006).

11 Coll, *Ghost Wars*, p. 257.

12 See John Ranelagh, *The Agency: The Rise and Decline of the CIA from Wild Bill Donovan to William Casey* (New York: Simon & Schuster, 1986), pp. 697–700.

13 See Claire Sperling, *The Terror Network: The Secret War of International Terrorism* (New York: Holt, Rinehart & Winston, 1981).

14 Dr. Ray S. Cline, "The Strategic Framework," Benjamin Netanyahu, ed., *International Terrorism—Challenge and Response: Essays and Speeches By Fifty Leading Public Figures on One of the Crucial Problems of Our Time* (Jerusalem: Jonathan Institute, 1981), p. 91.

15 Christopher Andrew and Vasili Mitrokhin, "Middle East Terrorism and the Palestinians," in *The World Was Going Our Way: The KGB and the Battle for the Third World—Newly Revealed Secrets from the Mitrokhin Archive* (New York: Basic Books, 2005), pp. 246–59.

16   Ibid., p. 246.

17   See Isabella Ginor and Gideon Remez, *Foxbats Over Dimona: The Soviets' Nuclear Gamble in the Six-Day War* (New Haven, CT: Yale University Press, 2007). Several historians have shown that the Soviets encouraged Syrian and Egyptian military moves in April and May 1967, but Ginor and Remez actually show that the Soviets had a strategy to try to use the war as a pretext to attack Israel's nuclear reactor in Dimona. The Soviets also took a bellicose posture in the 1973 war, prompting the Nixon administration to heighten America's nuclear alert status to DefCon 3.

18   Andrew and Mitrokhin, *The World Was Going Our Way*, p. 257, show how USSR support for the PLO led to British recognition.

19   The indoctrination center was linked to Patrice Lumumba University, where students ranging from PLO official Mahmoud Abbas to Ilich Ramirez Sanchez ("Carlos the Jackal") got training in techniques ranging from bomb making to disinformation and suborning Western media.

20   Ray S. Cline and Yonah Alexander, *Terrorism: The Soviet Connection* (New York: Crane, Russak, 1984), p. 101.

21   Quoted in Robert D. Kaplan, *The Arabists: The Romance of an American Elite* (New York: Free Press, 1993), p. 7.

22   Anthony Lake, *Six Nightmares: Real Threats in a Dangerous World and How America Can Meet Them* (Boston: Little, Brown, 2000), p. 57.

23   Ibid.

24   Scheuer, *Through Our Enemies' Eyes*, p. 21.

25   Iran's repression of the protests over its rigged 2009 elections probably involved thousands of dead.

26   Paul Pillar, "Iran and North Korea: Can They Be Deterred And Contained?" *National Journal* blog, June 22, 2009, http://security.national journal.com/2009/06/iran-and-north-korea-can-they.php#1337516.

27   Paul R. Pillar, "What Regime Change in Syria Would Mean," *National Interest,* March 29, 2011, at http://nationalinterest.org/blog/paul-pillar /restrain-your-enthusiasm-about-syria-5089. At the time Pillar was writing, there was evidence the Assad regime had gotten help from Iran's Revolutionary Guard and the Hizballah militia to suppress Syrian demonstrations in cities across the country.

28   The author served as a visiting professor in 2007–2008 at Washington University in St. Louis, offering a special course at NGIA.

29   Part of Israel's problem was that it relied too heavily on this one agent, Ashraf Marwan, who many today think was a double-agent. It largely ignored warnings from other sources. In this sense, John Keegan's criticism is valid because it shows that intelligence sources and data alone are not enough. Politicians and generals also need to have the intelligence and the will to use their sources effectively.

30 Henry A. Kissinger, *Diplomacy* (New York: Simon & Schuster, 1994), p. 303.

31 Kissinger himself, and other American officials, were behind a totally politically based decision to hide proof that PLO leader Yasser Arafat ordered the murder of three captured Western diplomats in Khartoum, Sudan, in 1973. Arafat's Black September group—a unit within Arafat's Fatah—took over the U.S. embassy, demanding the release from American jail of Sirhan Sirhan, the Palestinian who had assassinated Senator Robert F. Kennedy in 1968. America's National Security Agency captured a communication in which Arafat commanded the "execution" of U.S. ambassador Cleo Noel, deputy U.S. ambassador George Curtis Moore, and Belgian diplomat Guy Eid.

32 "Shin Bet" is the Hebrew abbreviation for "Sherutei Bitahon," or security services. It is also sometimes known by the Hebrew acrostic SHABAK—Sherutei Bitahon Klali, or General Security Service. The documents were part of a half million documents, tapes, and films seized in February 2002 at Orient House, a complex of homes that the PLO turned into a forward base in Jerusalem, in violation of its treaties with Israel. At the time, Arafat was still head of the PLO, Fatah, and the Palestinian Authority, while Sheikh Ahmad Yassin was still head of Hamas.

33 Israeli leader Shimon Peres has several times made similar comments, most famously: "I don't read history. I make history." Peres, now Israel's president, was the foreign minister who negotiated most of the agreements with the PLO.

34 Rashid Khalidi, *Palestinian Identity: The Construction of Modern National Consciousness* (New York: Columbia University Press, 1997), pp. 183–84.

35 Maimonides was a prolific commentator on religious texts and a physician. He lived in Spain and later served the Fatimid caliph in Cairo, but he was not alone. Don Isaac Abravanel, another religious scholar, served the Spanish and Portuguese royal courts. But some similar sentiments have been made by Christian scholars such as St. Thomas Aquinas and Thomas Becket.

36 It has become fashionable in the United States for senators and representatives to demand punishment for all kinds of "crimes" by intelligence analysts. Those who have repeatedly demonstrated this proclivity range from former House Speaker Nancy Pelosi (D-Calif.) to Senators Carl Levin (D-Mich.) and Patrick Leahy (D-Vt.). They often forget or ignore what they themselves have heard or seen in intelligence briefings. President Barack Obama named former congressman Leon Panetta, who was Clinton's chief of staff, as his CIA director. Not surprisingly, the move did not stem the politicization of the intelligence oversight process.

37 Timothy Naftali, *Blind Spot: The Secret History of American Counterterrorism* (New York: Basic Books, 2005), p. 33.

38   Ibid., pp. 70–72.

39   Ibid., p. 71. The evolution of presidential policy is also discussed by David
     C. Wills, *The First War on Terrorism* (Lanham, MD: Rowman & Littlefield,
     2003). Dr. Harold Saunders went on to become a deputy secretary of state,
     and he was involved in the Egyptian-Israeli peace talks of 1978 and 1979.
     Since retiring, he has directed the International Institute for Sustained
     Dialogue.

40   Ibid., p. 213.

41   Assistant Secretary of State Richard Murphy, a former U.S. ambassador to
     Syria, suggested letting the ship dock in Syria, where, he believed, Syrian
     leader Hafez Assad would surely capture the terrorists. Others in the State
     Department and the CIA consistently opposed the idea that the ship car-
     rying the terrorists or the plane that later took them out of Egypt be forced
     into Israeli territory, where the Israelis would gladly have captured them
     and extradited them to the United States. The CIA even lost track of the
     ship several times, but Secretary of Defense Caspar Weinberger specifically
     forbade asking the Israelis for intelligence help. Eventually, however, the
     Israelis tipped off Reagan aides, and the ship was reacquired by American
     intelligence and SEAL units.

42   Wills gives a blow-by-blow account of Egyptian actions and statements in
     The First War on Terrorism, pp. 147–52.

43   A few of Pillar's public appearances and alleged leaks—some while still
     at CIA—are detailed by Rowan Scarborough and Kenneth Timmerman,
     respectively. See Scarborough, *Sabotage: America's Enemies Within the CIA*
     (Washington, DC: Regnery, 2007), pp. 89–94, and Timmerman, *Shadow
     Warriors: The Untold Story of Traitors, Saboteurs, and the Party of Surrender*
     (New York: Three Rivers Press, 2007), pp. 71, 171–74.

44   Paul R. Pillar, "Enemies of Intelligence: Knowledge and Power in Ameri-
     can National Security," *Foreign Affairs* (March/April 2008), p. 138.

45   He claims the CIA successfully warned the United States of the Vietnam
     Tet Offensive, and that it also provided tremendous prewar intelligence on
     the 1967 Arab-Israeli war. The first claim is apparently not accurate, and
     the second is very stretched. He makes no mention, for example, of the
     CIA botching ballistic missile intelligence in 1998 or not supplying in-
     formation ahead of the India-Pakistan nuclear bomb explosions. There are
     numerous other examples.

46   Amy B. Zegart, *Flawed by Design: The Evolution of the CIA, JCS, and NSC*
     (Stanford, CA: Stanford University Press, 1999), p. 1.

47   The *9/11 Commission Report* is particularly detailed regarding FBI actions
     and procedures.

48   Pillar, "Enemies of Intelligence," p. 141.

49   Ibid., p. 142.

50 Pillar, *Terrorism and U.S. Foreign Policy*, p. 234.
51 Michael A. Sheehan, *Crush the Cell: How to Defeat Terrorism Without Terrorizing Ourselves* (New York: Crown, 2008), p. 82.
52 Ibid.
53 Ibid., pp. 78–88.
54 Pillar, *Terrorism and U.S. Foreign Policy*, p. 5.
55 U.S. Centers for Disease Control and Prevention website.
56 A Web search shows that this holds true for France's wars in Vietnam and Algeria; Britain's wars in the Falklands, Afghanistan, and Iraq; American wars in Vietnam, Korea, Kuwait, and Iraq; and even in Israel—with long-term war and terror—there is generally greater loss of life from road fatalities.
57 Institute for the Analysis of Global Security, "How much did the September 11 terrorist attack cost America?" http://www.iags.org/costof911.html. See also Dean C. Alexander and Yonah Alexander, *Terrorism and Business: The Impact of September 11, 2001* (New York: Transnational, 2002).
58 Pillar, *Terrorism and U.S. Foreign Policy*, p. 9.
59 Ibid., p. 2.
60 Ibid.
61 Oklahoma TV journalist Jayna Davis (KFOR-TV) discovered that McVeigh had contacted Iraqi officials to get bomb-making directions. See Micah Morrison, "The Iraq Connection," *Wall Street Journal*, September 5, 2002. Another intriguing possible connection is the mysterious explosion outside the University of Oklahoma stadium on October 1, 2005, which killed Joel Hinrichs III, who was apparently planning to set off his bomb inside the stadium. Hinrichs's roommates say he was considering converting to Islam and had been attending local mosques.
62 Robert Baer, *Sleeping with the Devil: How Washington Sold Our Soul for Saudi Crude* (New York: Three Rivers Press, 2003), p. 33.
63 U.S. Department of State, Office of the Secretary of State, Office of the Coordinator for Counterterrorism, "Middle East Overview—Saudi Arabia," *Patterns of Global Terrorism, 1999*, Department of State Publication 10687, April 2000, http://www.state.gov/www/global/terrorism/1999report/mideast.html#Arabia.
64 Mughniyeh was murdered in Damascus in 2008, and the Syrians charged the Mossad, Israel's overseas intelligence service, with the attack.
65 Dore Gold, *Hatred's Kingdom: How Saudi Arabia Supports the New Global Terrorism* (Washington, DC: Regnery, 2003), pp. 177–78.
66 The Egyptian record of concealing details of its own terrorists and Islamist violence is extensive. U.S. officials were hampered interviewing Egyptians regarding the mysterious crash of Egypt Air flight 990 in October 1999 off the East Coast of the United States. All 217 people on board died,

including two Egyptian generals and thirty air force officers. The Egyptian response was typical, including media censorship of important details. The state-supported Egyptian media even speculated that American and Israeli actors were responsible. For a good account of the incident, see William Langewiesche, "The Crash of EgyptAir 990," *Atlantic,* November 2001, http://www.theatlantic.com/doc/200111/langewiesche. Foreign officials are not allowed to travel freely in Egypt, especially to areas of Islamist violence such as Asyut in Upper Egypt. A senior U.S. diplomat (who later served as ambassador to Egypt and Israel, respectively) once asked the author, then a student in Egypt, to "let me know if you see anything interesting" when visiting the area as a tourist.

67 Yaroslav Trofimov, *The Siege of Mecca* (New York: Anchor Books, 2008), p. 22, and Gold, *Hatred's Kingdom,* pp. 243, 288, where Trofimov describes receiving the U.S. document—CLASSIFIED "Secret" MORI Doc ID123290—under the Freedom of Information Act. Interestingly, Trofimov notes that the Saudis succeeded in leaving a lasting impression that the attack was driven by extremists from the Iranian-supported Shiite movements in eastern Saudi Arabia. As in the subsequent Khobar Towers attack, the Saudi regime covered up the role of Saudi Sunnis—the backbone of the Kingdom—and then pulled back from the charges of Iranian involvement.

68 Baer, *Sleeping with the Devil,* p. 160. Later statements and interviews by Osama bin-Laden supporting the attack and recalling it along with other attacks for which he had taken credit seem to indicate his involvement in the 1995 Riyadh attack and the 1996 Khobar Towers attack. Bin-Laden bragged about his men leading the force that attacked U.S. soldiers in the Somali capital of Mogadishu in 1993. Three U.S. Black Hawk helicopters were shot down and eighteen U.S. soldiers were killed.

69 Jessica Stern, "Mind Over Martyr," *Foreign Affairs* (January/February 2010).

70 U.S. Department of State, Office of the Coordinator for Counterterrorism, "Overview of State-Sponsored Terrorism," in *Patterns of Global Terrorism, 2000,* April 30, 2001, http://www.state.gov/s/ct/rls/crt/2000/2441.htm.

71 Pillar, *Terrorism and U.S. Foreign Policy,* p. 5.

72 Ibid., p. 176.

73 Ibid.

74 Ibid., p. 177. For other examples of similar CIA sacrificial offerings, one can read the accounts of Baer, Scarborough, and Timmerman, describing how the United States undercut potential allies in Iran and Iraq.

75 The Einstein quotation, said to have been posted in his Princeton office, is sometimes given as "Everything that can be counted does not necessarily count; everything that counts cannot necessarily be counted."

76 "Iran and North Korea: Can They Be Deterred and Contained?" *National Journal* online, Expert Blogs panel, posting by Paul Pillar on June 22, 2009,

http://security.nationaljournal.com/2009/06/iran-and-north-korea-can
-they.php#1337516.

77 See Paul R. Pillar, "The Right Stuff," *National Interest,* September/October 2001, pp. 53–59.

78 "The CIA's Insurgency: The CIA wages an insurgency against President Bush," *Wall Street Journal* (editorial), September 29, 2004, p. A18, also available at http://www.opinionjournal.com/editorial/?id =110005686.

79 See Thomas Powers, *The Man Who Kept the Secrets: Richard Helms and the CIA* (New York: Knopf, 1979), pp. 176–77, and Ranelaugh, *The Agency,* pp. 473–75; p. 781, n. 84. This is probably an example of how the CIA takes credit ex post facto for a prediction it did not really make. CIA sources, some of whose statements were leaked to the public in May 1967, declared that Israel would "hold its own" against Egypt but would be hard-pressed if battling Egypt and Syria. And no CIA prediction—even the one claimed by Helms—predicted the astonishingly successful preemptive Israeli air strike on Arab air forces. Actually, there is documentary evidence that the opposite is true: Helms gave President Johnson a memo that said "Israel might lose up to half its air force" but still gain air superiority. This estimate would have been a closer approximation of what happened in the 1973 war, which most Israelis consider a bloody debacle. See Ginor and Remez, *Foxbats over Dimona,* pp. 118; 246, ns. 20–22.

80 Powers, *Intelligence Wars,* p. xxvi.

81 Morton Halperin, *Bureaucratic Politics and Foreign Policy* (Washington, DC: Brookings Institution, 1974), p. 181.

82 President Barack Obama had the same number of press conferences in four months in office.

83 Cheney gave a long speech on national security policy in May 2009—four months after the inauguration of President Barack Obama.

84 Many of the charges began with or involve Joseph Wilson, a former diplomat and Bush opponent, and his wife, Valerie Plame, a CIA employee.

85 Dave Gaubatz, interview by Jamie Glazov, "The Iraqi WMDs That Slipped Through Our Fingers," *Front Page Magazine,* April 6, 2006, http://archive .frontpagemag.com/readArticle.aspx?ARTID=4942.

86 See Baer, *See No Evil;* Douglas J. Feith, *War and Decision: Inside the Pentagon at the Dawn of the War on Terrorism* (New York: Harper, 2008); Timmerman, *Shadow Warriors;* Scarborough, *Sabotage;* as well as Stephen F. Hayes, *The Connection: How Al-Qaeda's Collaboration with Saddam Hussein Has Endangered America* (New York: HarperCollins, 2004).

87 Zegart, *Flawed By Design,* p. 1.

88 Ibid., p. 236. In essence, Zegart synthesizes the call for the selection of good personnel with Morton Halperin's view of the bureaucratic model.

To paraphrase Halperin, in the bureaucratic setting, "where you sit" (your organizational setting) determines "where you stand" (your policies).

89 Marc Bloch, *Strange Defeat: A Statement of Evidence Written in 1940* (1949; reprint, New York: Octagon Books, 1968), p. 39.

90 Reading some good science fiction and political thrillers, as well as watching some movies like *Black Sunday,* is not a bad place to start.

91 Feith, *War and Decision,* p. 159.

92 Weiner, *Legacy of Ashes,* pp. 600–1. For two completely different perspectives, see Caleb Carr, *The Lessons of Terror: A History of Warfare Against Civilians: Why It Has Always Failed and Why It Will Fail Again* (New York: Random House, 2002); and Rhodri Jeffreys-Jones, *The CIA and American Democracy,* 3rd ed. (New Haven, CT: Yale University Press, 2003). Carr, who paints with broad brushstrokes, says "America would be better off if the Agency were abolished," its functions carried out by other agencies (p. 241). Jeffreys-Jones (p. xvii) doubts whether higher U.S. intelligence budgets—which already dwarf all European countries by five times—would improve the situation.

93 Hanna Arendt, *The Origins of Totalitarianism* (New York: Meridian, 1958), p. 307.

94 Graham E. Fuller, "Islamic Fundamentalism: No Long-Term Threat," *Washington Post,* January 13, 1992, p. A17.

95 Ernest May, *Strange Victory: Hitler's Conquest of France* (New York: Farrar, Straus & Giroux, 2000), p. 453. May pointedly encouraged readers to draw analogies from the Hitler–France/Britain confrontations to other events.

96 Sir John Wheeler-Bennett, *The Nemesis of Power: The German Army in Politics, 1918–1945* (London: Macmillan, 1964), p. 461.

CHAPTER SEVEN: THE IDEOLOGIES, METHODS, AND MOTIVES OF ARAB-ISLAMIC TERROR

1 The Israelis are credited with having a profile for terrorists, and this is usually said to be a 16 to 30-year-old single male, but there have been many, many exceptions to this. Moreover, terror organizations, who know of Israeli profiles, sometimes select people who defy the profile, such as women, older men, and non-Arab-looking men (even non-Arabs who have converted to Islam).

2 I told the questioners that marked changes in behavior (especially in combination) such as frequent trips to mosques by someone who never previously went to prayer, wearing flowing robes rather than pants, growing an Islamic-style beard, and/or the avoidance of contact with women or with non-Muslims, were often signs. And yet there are many exceptions to these observations.

3   See, inter alia, Anat Berko and Edna Erez, "Ordinary People and Death Work: Palestinian Suicide Bombers as Victimizers and Victims," *Violence and Victims* 20, no. 6 (December 2005); Mia Bloom, *Dying to Kill: The Allure of Suicide Terror* (New York: Columbia University Press, 2005); and Barbara Victor, *Army of Roses: Inside the World of Palestinian Women Suicide Bombers* (New York: Rodale, 2003). See also Anat Berko, *Isha Petzatza* (Woman Bomb), translated as *The Smarter Bomb: Women and Children as Suicide Bombers,* http://www.terrorism-info.org.il/malam_multimedia /English/eng_n/html/ipc_e085.htm.

4   Marc Sageman, an ex-CIA analyst, has developed a prescriptive model based on a carefully selected set of data, which he has offered in two books and in congressional testimony. The model, like much CIA analysis, has certain superficial advantages, such as supporting the theory that Arab-Islamic terror will decline on its own and that the West could do itself a favor by not offending Muslims with broad antiterror efforts. The model argues that terrorists are molded by a group experience. The model has many structural and scholarly flaws, such as cherry-picking data, insufficient attention to religious and cultural influences, and politically correct and factually inaccurate historical support. Professor Robert Pape of the University of Chicago has written at length about the strategic logic of suicide bombing, especially in national struggles. Some of his broad conclusions have been called into question by the analysis of Dr. Martin Kramer. See "Suicide Terrorism in the Middle East: Origins and Response," http://www.washingtoninstitute.org/templateC05 .php?CID=2401.

5   Putting water near potassium creates an explosion, and even amateur chemists will recognize that an explosion can be achieved by lighting a combination of fertilizer (ammonium nitrate) and diesel fuel. The multiple-stage approach to explosives is even evident in the first atomic bombs, when one small detonation was required to set off the chain reaction.

6   There are some reports, based on eyewitnesses, that suggest that Idris tried to back out of the bomb attempt at the last moment, but failed to stop the explosion that was either set off accidentally or set off by a handler using a remote control detonator.

7   *Istish-haad* is the reflexive (tenth-form) verbal noun in Arabic for the action of the *shahid*, the martyr. The reflexive form shows that the person martyred herself or himself and was not merely a passive victim. The term *shahid* in Arabic is from the root *SH-H-D*: literally to see or to be a witness. The martyr is a witness to God's greatness.

8   Israeli filmmaker Hila Medalia portrayed the families of two women—a Palestinian suicide bomber and a woman killed by her attack. Medalia

found evidence that the attacking woman was suspected of having an affair, and this was what motivated her.

9 Bloom, *Dying to Kill,* p. 29.

10 Victor, *Army of Roses,* pp. 25, 34, 92–95.

11 Scott Atran, "Genesis of Suicide Terrorism," *Science,* March 7, 2003, p. 1538.

12 See Pierre Rehov, *Suicide Killers,* fifty-minute documentary film, 2006. The film's findings dovetail with my own observations of the Palestinian Authority's use of radio broadcasts and television films and songs to inspire suicide bombings. Similar findings have been made by researchers at MEMRI and at Palestinian Media Watch.

13 Claude Berrebi, "Evidence about the Link Between Education, Poverty and Terrorism among Palestinians," RAND Corporation paper, Santa Monica, CA, 2007, p. 1. Scott Atran's work also supports this finding.

14 Ibid., p. 30, also cited as Claude Berrebi, "Evidence about the Link Between Education, Poverty and Terrorism among Palestinians," *Peace Economics, Peace Science and Public Policy* 13, no. 1, http://www.bepress.com/peps/vol13/iss1/2.

15 Bloom, *Dying to Kill,* pp. x–xi.

16 Ibid., p. x.

17 The formal term in Arabic in the vocative form was *ayoo ha-al-masriyyin.*

18 May 1960 lecture by Abd al-Rahman Azzam, first secretary-general of the Arab League, cited in Nissim Rejwan, *Arabs Face the Modern World: Religious, Cultural, and Political Responses to the West* (Gainesville: University Press of Florida, 1998), p. 85.

19 Egypt's central location and large population were also factors.

20 The Treaty of Versailles, Woodrow Wilson's "Fourteen Points," including self-determination.

21 Abdul-Nasser's name is often rendered simply as "Nasser" or "Nasr" or "Nasir" in English references. This is common, but incorrect. "Nasser," like "Jabbar" or "Rahman," is one of the Arabic epithets for Allah or God. The names Abdul-Nasser or Abdul-Jabbar or Abdul-Rahman are the names of human beings who are, of course, servants of God.

22 Other European powers such as Germany and Russia were not major colonizers of the area. That is one reason many Arab nationalists were drawn to the policies of Nazi Germany and Soviet Russia. Some observers have stressed that Arab nationalists—such the grand mufti of Palestine, Haj Amin al-Husseini; the Baathist pan-Arab nationalists of Syria and Iraq; and even Anwar Sadat—applauded the ideologies of Nazism or communism. However, in most cases this does not seem to be true.

23 Mohamed H. Heikal, *Cutting the Lion's Tail: Suez Through Egyptian Eyes* (London: Andre Deutsch, 1986), p. xii.

24 Malcolm Kerr, *The Arab Cold War: Gamal 'Abd al-Nasir and His Rivals, 1958–1970* (London: Oxford University Press, 1971), p. 7.

25 Ibid., p. 31.

26 Attaturk literally means "father of the Turks."

27 For discussion of Kemal, see Bernard Lewis, *The Emergence of Modern Turkey* (New York: Oxford University Press, 1968), pp. 242–44. For Attaturk's influence on the Iraqi national movement, see also Reeva S. Simon, "The Education of an Iraqi Ottoman Military Officer," esp. pp. 159–63, in Rashid Khalidi et al., eds., *The Origins of Arab Nationalism* (New York: Columbia University Press, 1991). See also Eliezer Be'eri, *Haketzuna Ve-Hashilton Ba-Olam Ha-'Aravi* (The Officer Class in Politics and Society of the Arab East) (Tel Aviv: Sifriat Poalim, 1966).

28 Peter Mandaville, *Global Political Islam* (London: Routledge, 2007), p. 55.

29 C. Ernest Dawn, *From Ottomanism to Arabism: Essays on the Origins of Arab Nationalism* (Urbana: University of Illinois Press, 1973), p. 184.

30 Rejwan, *Arabs Face the Modern World*, p. 2.

31 Azzam lecture, as cited in ibid., p. 85.

32 The secular side of *qawmiyya* became the common basis for Baathist socialism in Syria and Iraq, where Christians and non-Sunni Muslim sects like the 'Alawites could feel comfortable.

33 Sylvia G. Haim, ed., *Arab Nationalism: An Anthology* (Berkeley: University of California Press, 1962), p. xi. The pan-Arab Baathist leaders of Syria and Iraq—Hafez Assad and Saddam Hussein—worked to establish their religious bona fides, even though both leaders were avowed secularists. Assad got Ayatollah Khomeini to issue a ruling that Assad's 'Alawi sect was genuinely Muslim, and Saddam put the Islamic call to prayer and battle—*Allahu Akbar*—on his flag.

34 British and French officials compared Abdul-Nasser's magnetic effect to that of Adolf Hitler.

35 A. I. Dawisha, *Egypt in the Arab World: The Elements of Foreign Policy* (London: Macmillan, 1976), p. 165.

36 Abdul-Nasser himself, in his famous "Three Circles" theory, describes the Islamic circle as the second of three in which Egypt lives. The third is the nonaligned sphere. The three circles (employing Africa instead of "nonaligned") are set forth in Gamal Abdel Nasser, "The Philosophy of the Revolution," in Haim, ed., *Arab Nationalism*, pp. 229–32.

37 On Arafat, see Michael Widlanski, "Palestinian Broadcast Media in the Palestinian State-Building Process: Patterns of Influence and Control" (doctoral thesis, Bar Ilan University, 2004). On Saddam, see Michael Barnett, *Dialogues in Arab Politics* (New York: Columbia University Press, 1998), p. 219.

38 Bruce Maddy-Weitzman, *The Crystallization of the Arab State System, 1945–1954* (Syracuse, NY: Syracuse University Press, 1993), pp. 178–79.

39 Fouad Ajami, *The Arab Predicament*, updated ed. (Cambridge: Cambridge University Press, 1991), pp. 3; 254, nos. 7, 8.

40 The term in Arabic is *Al-qadiyya la-felastiniyya*. *Palestine* itself is a foreign word in Arabic (having come from Greco-Roman sources), and because there is no "p" in Arabic, Palestine is rendered as *Felasteen*. The term also never appears in the Quran.

41 Maddy-Weitzman, *The Crystallization of the Arab State System*, p. 9.

42 The cross-border infiltrators and fighters were called *fedayoun* or *fedayeen*—men of sacrifice—but very few really wanted to sacrifice. There was also the "Arab Salvation Front," but most Arab leaders used the Palestine question to save themselves, to distract their own people from paying too close attention to corruption and policy failures.

43 Barnett, *Dialogues in Arab Politics*, p. 9.

44 The term is from Maddy-Weitzman, *The Crystallization of the Arab State System*, p. 4, describing the internal Arab rivalries. Another fine description is offered in Kerr, *The Arab Cold War*.

45 The Egyptian-Syrian union lasted for four years (1958–62), but the countries kept functioning separately. Tunisia and Libya began a similar endeavor in 1974 and then thought better of it.

46 The Arab defeat of 1948 and Israel's creation are known in Arabic as *Al-Nakba*: the Catastrophe.

47 Abd al-Wahhab's doctrine is sometimes called "puritanical" or "fundamentalist" —both Protestant terms that do not do it justice. It is a doctrine of never-ending jihad that defined itself by being against most Muslims (especially Shiites and Sufi mystics) and almost every reform or compromise ever instituted in Islam, which it regarded as *bida*: heresy. Wahhabism is unalterably hostile to everything Christian and Jewish (two groups that are marked for protection as *dhimmis* under most Islamic teaching), not to mention other "infidels." They are to be killed, if they do not convert. Abd al-Wahhab made so many enemies that he needed the refuge and protection offered by the Saud family.

48 The British finally intervened to stop Saudi expansion that threatened areas that are today Iraq, Kuwait, Qatar, and Oman.

49 The name recalls the Muslim Brotherhood—*Al-Ikhwan al-Muslimoun*—founded in Egypt by Hasan al-Banna some years thereafter. This was no accident. Al-Banna was a disciple of Muhammad Rashid Rida, an Egyptian theologian who was profoundly influenced by Wahhabism.

50 Chronicles of battles describe the barbarity of Wahhabi forces slaughtering everyone in their path. At one site, body parts were hurled over the city walls, and because there was fat on them, it was clear that the gaunt invaders had beaten the urbanized Hashemites.

51 *Shirk* literally means partnership, believing that God has partners such as angels or lesser gods.

52 Yaroslav Trofimov, *The Siege of Mecca* (New York: Anchor Books, 2008), p. 27.

53 Philip K. Hitti, *The Arabs: A Short History,* updated ed. (Washington, DC: Regnery, 1996).

54 Trofimov, *The Siege of Mecca.*

55 Report of Harold Rhode, a Turkish-speaking former U.S. official who surveyed many of the texts.

56 There are about two million people in U.S. jails, and at least one-fifth are believed Muslims. Many criminals have been recruited to Islamic terror in jail, where inmates are pressured to join groups.

57 Dore Gold, *Hatred's Kingdom: How Saudi Arabia Supports the New Global Terrorism* (Washington, DC: Regnery, 2003), pp. 125–26.

58 Robert Baer, *See No Evil: The True Story of a Ground Soldier in the CIA's War on Terrorism* (New York: Three Rivers Press, 2002), p. 10.

59 For example, bin-Laden sent Ramzi Yousef to Mindanao in the Philippines to train the Islamic Abu Sayyaf terror group. He also planned an attempt on President Bill Clinton during a Philippines visit in 1994. He also developed the Bojinka Plot to blow up eleven U.S.-bound commercial jets. He was not the only Al-Qaeda operative active in Southeast Asia. See Simon Reeve, *The New Jackals: Ramzi Yousef, Osama Bin Laden and the Future of Terrorism* (Boston: Northeastern University Press, 1999), esp. pp. 72–91. See also testimony of Jamal Ahmad al-Fadl, U.S. District Court, Southern District of New York, February 6–7, 2001, as cited in Barry Rubin and Judith Colp Rubin, eds., *Anti-American Terrorism and the Middle East: A Documentary Reader* (New York: Oxford University Press, 2002), pp. 169–72.

60 Baer, *See No Evil,* p. xviii. Baer is very critical of U.S. officials who, he says, cover up Saudi failings and later profit from Saudi money themselves.

61 Steven Emerson, *American Jihad: The Terrorists Living Among Us* (New York: Free Press, 2003), p. 160. Also, some money, it should be stressed, was not *official* Saudi state funds, though there is often a mingling of official and unofficial royal funds and charities. Some wealthy Saudis (including princes and cabinet ministers) contribute from their private accounts, though the recruitment of the "charity" was often handled on official Saudi television and newspapers.

62 Hassan al-Banna, *Bayn al-Ams wa-al-Yawm* (Between Yesterday and Today), cited in Richard P. Mitchell, *The Society of the Muslim Brothers* (1969; reprint, New York: Oxford University Press, 1993), p. 30.

63 In the 1980s there were several groups in Egypt that had roots in the Brotherhood—Al-Gema'at al-Islamiyya ("The Islamic Groups"), Takfir

Wa-Hijra, and Egyptian Islamic Jihad. Among those active in these groups were Sheikh Omar Abdul-Rahman (involved in the first World Trade Center attack, in 1993, as well as plots to bomb bridges in New York) and Ayman Zawahiri, later Osama bin-Laden's deputy in Al-Qaeda.

64 Trofimov, *The Siege of Mecca,* p. 22.

65 *Encyclopedia of Islam,* 1st ed., s.v. "Takiyya" (Djumayyil, *Kdmus al-shanca,* pp. xiii, 127–28). Please note the many alternative spellings in English for *taqiyaa.*

66 See Sura 7 for the Islamic version of the story of the golden calf, especially verses 150–51. The account here echoes the biblical text as well as the Jewish Midrash literature and Bible commentaries.

67 See Joseph Schacht, *An Introduction to Islamic Law* (Oxford: Oxford University Press/Clarendon Press, 1982), p. 118. In this limited defensive mode, *taqiyya* is similar to Jewish theology's concept of *pikuah nefesh* (saving a life), which permits transgression of some of God's commandments if a life is in danger. For example, a Jew is allowed—even required—to break the rules of Sabbath in a medical emergency. A Muslim may also feign apostasy, as in the case of 'Ammar, though most Jewish legal authorities prohibit feigning apostasy or committing adultery or violence even when life is threatened.

68 This general concept is also common in Jewish religious thought, though the concept of "persuading a woman" was not part of the Jewish approach, and has been used broadly by some Islamic commentators who cite the fact that Muhammad thus managed his multi-wife household.

69 Hadith Sahih Bukhari (5:369).

70 H. A. R. Gibb and J. H. Kramers, *The Shorter Encyclopedia of Islam* (Ithaca, NY: Cornell University Press, 1953), pp. 272–73. See also Hitti, *The Arabs,* p. 36, as well as Carl Brockelmann, *History of the Islamic Peoples,* rev. ed., trans. Joel Carmichael and Moshe Perlmann (New York: Capricorn Books, 1973), p. 26.

71 Ahmad ibn Naqib al-Misri, *The Reliance of the Traveller: A Classic Manual of Islamic Sacred Law,* trans. Nuh Ha Mim Keller (Beltsville, MD: Amana, 1997), sec. 8.2, p. 745.

72 The Hudaibiya treaty is only one of many incidents of this kind that reflect the sometimes harsh realpolitik exercised by Muhammad against his rivals, usually the local Jews (from the tribes of the Nadir, Qurazah, and Qaynukah) or their allies in Quraysh. For a discussion of Muhammad's tactics against the Arabian Jews and their use as a target of convenience, see Brockelmann, *History of the Islamic Peoples,* pp. 24–28.

73 Ignaz Goldziher, *Introduction to Islamic Theology and Law* (Princeton, NJ: Princeton University Press, 1981), p. 180. This is a translation from the German of Goldziher's original work published in 1910. Goldziher was a

non-Muslim who studied at Al-Azhar in Egypt. See also entry on *takiya* in Gibb and Kramers, *The Shorter Encyclopedia of Islam*, s.v. "takiya," p. 561.

74 Raymond Ibrahim, "War and Peace—and Deceit—in Islam," testimony before U.S. Congress, February 12, 2009, http://www.meforum.org/article /2066, and originally published at http://pajamasmedia.com/blog/war -and-peace-%E2%80%94-and-deceit-%E2%80%94-in-islam-part-1/ and http://pajamasmedia.com/blog/war-and-peace-%E2%80%94-and-deceit -%E2%80%94-in-islam-part-2/.

75 This far exceeds what we call today "Saudi Arabia." "Historian Michael Cook captures some of the vastness of the Arabian Peninsula when he describes it as "a vast rectangle, some 1,300 miles long and 750 wide." In other words, it is quite a bit larger than the land area of Western Europe. It is about one-third the size of the entire continental United States, and far larger than Alaska and Texas combined.

76 Bernard Lewis, *The Political Language of Islam* (Chicago: University of Chicago Press, 1988), p. 73.

77 Brockelmann, *History of the Islamic Peoples*, p. 43.

78 See Joshua Muravchik, "Is Obama's Muslim Outreach Working?" *Wall Street Journal*, December 29, 2010, http://online.wsj.com/article/SB100 01424052748704774604576035640578457696.html, and Pew Research Center surveys from 2006 to 2011 on views of Muslim countries and Muslim Americans: http://pewresearch.org/assets/pdf/muslim-americans.pdf, http://pewglobal.org/files/2010/12/2010-muslim-01-05.png, and http:// pewglobal.org/files/2010/12/2010-muslim-01-13.png.

79 Pew Research Center, "Muslim Americans: Middle Class and Mostly Mainstream," May 22, 2007.

80 Dalia Mogahed, "Muslims and Americans—The Way Forward," Gallup Center for Muslim Studies, http://www.mostresource.org/gallup/gallup_1_ Muslims_and_Americans.pdf. It should be noted that anti-American views, pro–Al-Qaeda views and Islamist views (that is, compulsory Sharia) are not completely synonymous.

81 See Karen Armstrong, *The Battle for God: A History of Fundamentalism* (New York: Ballantine, 2000); *Islam: A Short History* (London: Weidenfeld & Nicolson, 2000); and "Was It Inevitable?" in James F. Hoge Jr. and Gideon Rose, eds., *How Did This Happen? Terrorism and the New War* (New York: PublicAffairs/Council on Foreign Relations, 2001).

82 Marc Sageman, *Leaderless Jihad: Terror Networks in the Twenty-First Century* (Philadelphia: University of Pennsylvania Press, 2008), p. 37.

83 Sageman claims to produce only scientifically validated evidence. A survey of a Quran concordance in Arabic for the words *salaam* (peace), *sulh* (tranquility), *ja-ha-da, yu-ja-hidu* (war, struggle), and *qatala, yuqatilu* (fight, combat) showed Sageman was completely off-base. Of the 114 chapters

(Surahs) and 6,236 verses in the Quran, there are more than 100 direct references to *jihad* alone and hundreds to *jihad* and other forms of violence by context or by slightly different word choice.

84 The author's personal experience in Egypt and other countries. See also M. Piamenta, *Islam in Everyday Arabic Speech* (Leiden: Brill, 1979).

85 Ibid., p. 124, and Lewis, *The Political Language of Islam*, pp. 78–79, citing the Quran, Sura 20:49.

86 Lewis, *The Political Language of Islam*, p. 79.

87 Samuel P. Huntington, *The Clash of Civilizations and the Remaking of World Order* (New York: Simon & Schuster, 1996), p. 209.

88 Philip Carl Salzman, *Culture and Conflict in the Middle East*, pp. 171–74.

89 Huntington, *The Clash of Civilizations*, pp. 256–57.

90 Barry Buzan, "New Patterns of Global Security in the Twenty-First Century," *International Affairs* 67, no. 3 (July 1991), pp. 431–51, http://www.jstor.org/stable/2621945. See esp. pp. 447–48.

91 M. Steven Fish, "Islam and Authoritarianism," *World Politics* 55, no. 1 (October 2002), p. 24.

92 Ibid. See also Montgomery Watt, *Muhammad: Prophet and Statesman* (New York: Oxford University Press, 1976), and H. A. R. Gibb, *Mohammedanism* (New York: Oxford University Press, 1976).

93 Watt, *Muhammad*, p. 109.

94 Only one of Muhammad's battles, the "Battle of the Trench," is considered a defensive battle.

95 Daniel Pipes, *Militant Islam Reaches America* (New York: Norton, 2002), p. 263.

96 The term *fundamentalist* is actually a misnomer when applied to Muslims, because it is a term from Christian Protestant ideology.

97 The English word *caliph* is derived from the Arabic term *khalifa*, which means deputy.

98 These four caliphs came to be known as "the Righteous Caliphs," although their rule was contested from the beginning. They were Abu Bakr, 'Omar (also written 'Umar), 'Othman, and 'Ali. See http://www.princeton.edu/~batke/itl/denise/right.htm.

99 The term *shi'a* is a cognate of the Hebrew term *see'ah*, which is used in modern Hebrew to describe a political faction.

100 This author has seen many reporters refer to Friday, for example, as the Muslim Sabbath, comparing it to Saturday for Jews or Sunday for most Christians. However, there is no Sabbath in Islam. Similarly, there is no separation of mosque and state in Islam; one cannot hear Muhammad or one of his successors speaking about "rendering unto God what is God's and unto Caesar what is Caesar's." See Mark 12:17; Luke 20:25; Matthew 22:21.

101 P. M. Holt, introduction to *The Cambridge History of Islam,* vol. 1 (Cambridge: Cambridge University Press, 1970), pp. xiii–xv. Holt acknowledges that a great deal of *hadith* material is clearly extraneous matter added for social or religious purposes. Still, there is enough solid material for a good picture of Muhammad.

102 Dutch parliamentarian Ayaan Hirsi Ali received death threats after saying Muhammad would be classified today as a pedophile, and she was eventually forced to leave Europe. Geert Wilders, a right-wing Dutch parliamentarian, is under constant protection, and filmmaker Theo Van Gogh was brutally murdered and a threatening note was stuck on his body.

103 See, for example, the book of Exodus, first five chapters, for the continuing efforts of Moses not to get the job leading Israel out of Egypt. As for Jonah, the first chapter in the book of Jonah recounts to what lengths he literally ran to escape the job of prophesying to the city of Nineveh.

104 See, for example, Bernard Lewis, *The Arabs in History* (New York: Harper & Row, 1966), pp. 58 and 94.

105 Barbara Crossette, "Study Warns of Stagnation in Arab Societies," *New York Times,* July 2, 2002, http://www.nytimes.com/2002/07/02/international /middleeast/02ARAB.html.

106 See Charles Issawi, "The Change in the Western Perception of the Orient," in *The Arab World's Legacy* (Princeton, NJ: Darwin Press, 1981), pp. 363–72.

107 For example, Egyptian religious intellectual Muhammad Abduh offered a path integrating Western ideas and techniques with Muslim faith and principles. Turkish secularists such as Mustafa Kemal tried a secular path. Egyptian literati such as Taha Husayn incorporated Western ideas in their writing.

108 See, for example, Fatima Mernissi, *Islam and Democracy: Fear of the Modern World* (Reading, MA: Addison-Wesley, 1992), esp. pp. 14–20, 50–54.

109 Muhammad Abid Al-Jabiri, *Nahnu Wa-al-Turath* (We and Heritage), as cited in Issa J. Boullata, *Trends and Issues in Contemporary Arab Thought* (Albany: State University of New York Press, 1990), p. 47.

110 Daniel Pipes, "Counting Islamists," *Jerusalem Post,* October 8, 2008, http:// www.danielpipes.org/5967/counting-islamists.

111 The term most frequently used in Arabic is *'amaliyat istish-haad,* using the tenth (reflexive) form of *SH-H-D,* to bear witness.

112 Azhar and Qaradhawi quotations are from Yotam Feldman, Middle East Media Research Institute, "Debating the Religious, Political and Moral Legitimacy of Suicide Bombings Part 1: The Debate over Religious Legitimacy," Inquiry & Analysis Series Report, No. 53, May 3, 2001, http://www .memri.org/report/en/0/0/0/0/0/0/248/451.htm#_edn5.

113 No Arab state or Islamic judge would approve "honor killings," but they happen all the time. State authorities often do not intervene or enforce law, even when identity of the perpetrator is not in doubt.

114 Philip Carl Salzman, *Culture and Conflict in the Middle East* (Amherst, NY: Prometheus Books, 2008), p. 12.

115 Ibid., p. 13.

116 Ibid., p. 16.

117 This view is supported by the work of anthropologist Ernest Gellner, *Encounters with Nationalism* (Cambridge, MA: Blackwell, 1994), p. 166.

118 Dawn, *From Ottomanism to Arabism,* p. 184.

119 Albert Hourani, *A History of the Arab Peoples* (New York: Warner Books, 1991), p. 249.

120 Thirteen people were killed and thirty-two wounded in the Fort Hood attack.

121 The report was redacted or censored at the request of the FBI and other agencies, but it is clear that Hasan was in contact with Anwar al-Awlaki, a top recruiter for Al-Qaeda.

122 All remarks from Senator Susan Collins and Senator Joseph Lieberman are from joint U.S. Senate press conference, February 3, 2011, where the Homeland Security Committee released its report "A Ticking Bomb." See http://www.c-span.org/Events/News-Conference-on-Fort-Hood-Shootings/10737419394-1/; http://www.c-span.org/Events/News-Conference-on-Fort-Hood-Shootings/10737419394/; http://www.aolnews.com/2011/02/03/fort-hood-shooter-a-ticking-time-bomb-4-key-conclusions-from/; and http://hsgac.senate.gov/public/_files/Fort_Hood/FortHoodReport.pdf.

123 Dorothy Rabinowitz, "Major Hasan, 'Star Officer,'" *Wall Street Journal,* February 16, 2011, http://online.wsj.com/article/SB10001424052748704409004576146001069880040.html.

124 Prime Minister Tony Blair, Address to Labor Party Conference, July 16, 2005, http://news.bbc.co.uk/2/hi/uk_news/4689363.stm.

CHAPTER EIGHT: COUNTRY CASE STUDIES: OPERATIVE LESSONS

1 David Carlton, *The West's Road to 9/11: Resisting, Appeasing and Encouraging Terrorism Since 1970* (New York: Palgrave Macmillan, 2005), p. 131.

2 Ibid., p. 125.

3 Fidel Sendagorta, "Jihad in Europe: The Wider Context," *Survival* 47, no. 3 (2005), p. 66, http://dx.doi.org/10.1080/00396330500248029.

4 David Keohane, senior researcher, European Union Institute for Security Studies, appearing on *France Vingt-Quatre* (France Twenty-Four), morning television show, December 1, 2010.

5 Bruce Hoffman, "Is Europe Soft on Terrorism?" *Foreign Policy* no. 115 (Summer 1999), pp. 62–76.

6 For governments' first reactions to terrorists taking hostages, see Norman Antakol and Mayer Nudell, *Political Hostage-Taking in the Modern World* (Medina, OH: Alpha, 1990). See also Timothy Naftali, *Blind Spot: The*

Secret History of American Counterterrorism (New York: Basic Books, 2005), p. 71, to contrast Nixon's view with the U.S. State Department view.

7   For years the United States has hidden how its officials spoke to Palestinian terrorists, even covering up—for nearly forty years—the role of Yasser Arafat in the murder of U.S. diplomats in Sudan in 1974. Arafat was demanding the release of Sirhan Sirhan, the convicted murderer of Robert Kennedy.

8   In 1986, for example, Secretary of State George Shultz said he was appalled that the Reagan administration had agreed to send arms to Iran to get the release of Americans held ransom in Lebanon by pro-Iranian terrorists. See Benjamin Netanyahu, *Fighting Terrorism: How Democracies Can Defeat Domestic and International Terrorists* (New York: Farrar, Straus and Giroux, 1995), pp. 72–73.

9   Hoffman, "Is Europe Soft on Terrorism?" p. 63.

10 Ibid.

11 See, inter alia, "Europe Not So Swift—The European Parliament nixes counterterrorism cooperation," *Wall Street Journal–Europe,* February 16, 2010, http://online.wsj.com/article/SB1000142405274870443140457506694 1940401092.html and John Rosenthal, "Terrorist Finance Tracking Program Re-Starts under Anonymous European Oversight," *Weekly Standard,* September 20, 2010, http://www.weeklystandard.com/blogs/terrorist-finance -tracking-program-re-starts-under-anonymous-european-oversight.

12 The commission's official name is the National Commission on Terrorist Attacks Upon the United States; chap. 12, point 12.2, http://govinfo .library.unt.edu/911/report/911Report_Ch12.htm. The report also cited flaccid security in the United States itself.

13 Tony Paterson, "Row over treatment of immigrants reopens Turkey's rift with Europe," *Independent,* February 28, 2011, http://www.independent .co.uk/news/world/europe/row-over-treatment-of-immigrants-reopens-turkeys-rift-with-europe-2227548.html. See also Özlem Gezer and Anna Reimann, "Erdogan Urges Turks Not to Assimilate: 'You Are Part of Germany, But Also Part of Our Great Turkey,'" *Spiegel,* February 28, 2011, http://www.spiegel.de/international/europe/0,1518,748070,00.html.

14 Evan Kohlman, *Al-Qaida's Jihad in Europe: The Afghan-Bosnian Network* (Oxford: Berg, 2004).

15 Choudhry said she was inspired by Anwar al-Awlaki, an Al-Qaeda operative.

16 Michael Seamark, Katherine Faulkner, and Stephen Wright, "Woman Charged With Attempted Murder Over Stabbing of Labour MP Stephen Timms," *Daily Mail,* May 16, 2010, http://www.dailymail.co.uk/news /article-1278459/Woman-charged-stabbing-Labour-MP-Stephen -Timms.html#ixzz18N1xoLyd, and Katherine Faulkner, "Extremist Website That Inspired Stabbing of Stephen Timms Urges Muslims to

'Raise the Knife of Jihad' to Other MPs," http://www.dailymail.co.uk/news /article-1326842/Extremist-website-inspired-Stephen-Timms-stabbing -urges-raise-knife-jihad.html#ixzz18I5nz7tL.

17 Lorenzo Vidino, "The Muslim Brotherhood's Conquest of Europe," *Middle East Quarterly* 12, no. 1 (Winter 2005), p. 25, http://www.meforum .org/687/the-muslim-brotherhoods-conquest-of-europe.

18 For an excellent discussion of the doctrine that is common to Sunni and Shiite Muslims, see *A Shi'ite Encyclopedia* at http://www.al-islam.org/EN CYCLOPEDIA/chapter6b/1.html, as well as Raymond Ibrahim, "War and Peace—and Deceit—in Islam," testimony before U.S. Congress, February 12, 2009, http://www.meforum.org/article/2066.

19 Vidino, "The Muslim Brotherhood's Conquest of Europe," p. 26.

20 The comments are part of prepared text by Bat Yeor (pseudonym for an Egyptian-born author), "From Europe to Eurabia," at an international symposium on "Antisemitism, Multiculturalism, and Ethnic Identity," Hebrew University in Jerusalem, June 15, 2006.

21 Manfred Gerstenfeld, "Israel and Europe: An Expanding Abyss?" Jerusalem Center for Public Affairs, 2005, http://www.jcpa.org/israel-europe /ier-gerstenfeld-05.htm.

22 Bat Yeor and her ideas were classified as conspiracy theory and myth at Wikipedia, for example. See http://en.wikipedia.org/wiki/Eurabia and "Tales from Eurabia," *Economist*, June 22, 2006.

23 Niall Ferguson, "The Way We Live Now: 4-4-04; Eurabia?" *New York Times Magazine*, http://www.nytimes.com/2004/04/04/magazine/the-way -we-live-now-4-4-04-eurabia.html.

24 Raphael Israeli, "The New Demographic Balance in Europe and Its Consequences," *Jerusalem Viewpoints*, no. 552, Jerusalem Center for Public Affairs, March 2007.

25 William Shakespeare, *Richard II*, Act 2, Scene 1.

26 Peter Bergen, "Our Ally, Our Problem," *New York Times*, July 8, 2005, p. 23, http://www.nytimes.com/2005/07/08/opinion/08bergen.html.

27 Melanie Phillips, *Londonistan* (New York: Encounter Books, 2006), p. viii.

28 Bergen, "Our Ally, Our Problem."

29 Muslim Council of Britain profile, http://www.mcb.org.uk/downloads/ MCB_acheivments.pdf.

30 For the threat to Cheryl Cole, see "Cheryl Cole Visits Afghanistan Amidst Rivers of Muslim Blood," http://www.muslimsagainstcrusades.com/ press-releases/cheryl-cole-in-afghanistan. The cynicism of the threat from the Muslim group was shown by the fact that it was also accompanied with a so-called disclaimer that read: "DISCLAIMER: We would like to reiterate that this press release is NOT a 'death threat' to Cheryl Cole as has been espoused by British tabloid newspapers, but rather a strong warning

(to her) to cease from supporting the Nazi British armed forces, who are guilty of severe war crimes in Afghanistan." For the quote from and background material on Prince Charles, see Ronni L. Gordon and David M. Stillman, "Prince Charles of Arabia," *Middle East Quarterly* 4, no. 3 (September 1997), pp. 3–7. Charles's views of Islam Britain have been so strikingly positive that some of his countrymen think he is Muslim, like some Americans do President Barack Obama. Indeed the grand mufti of Cyprus declared that Prince Charles underwent Islamic conversion on a trip to Turkey in the 1990s. The Royal House denies the claim. Prince Charles is correct about the spirituality of his flock, however: church attendance in Britain is about 10 percent or lower, while more than two-thirds of Muslims report regular attendance at mosques.

31 For a typically superficial example of the academic view see Steve Hewitt, *The British War on Terror* (London: Continuum Books, 2008), esp. pp. 6–7, where Hewitt relies on Michael Scheuer and James Fallows for their views on what motivates Arab-Islamic terror.

32 Supplementary Memorandum from Institute for Policy Research & Development (PVE 19A), September 2009, www.publications.parliament.uk/pa /cm200809/cmselect/cmcomloc/memo/previoex/uc19a02.htm.

33 Martin Bright, "When Progressives Treat With Reactionaries—The British State's Flirtation With Radical Islamism," London Policy Exchange Limited, July 2006, p. 11. Bright has been a reporter at the *Observer, New Statesman,* and Channel 4 in Britain.

34 Ibid., p. 12.

35 For reports on Holocaust studies in British schools, see Alexandra Frean, "Schools Drop Holocaust Lessons to Avoid Offence," London *Times,* April 2, 2007, http://www.timesonline.co.uk/tol/news/uk/education/article 1600686.ece; "No Holocaust Lessons," *Daily Telegraph,* April 2, 2007, http://www.telegraph.co.uk/news/uknews/1547369/No-lessons-on-the -Holocaust.html; and Laura Clark, "Teachers Drop the Holocaust to Avoid Offending Muslims," *Daily Mail,* April 2, 2009, http://www.dailymail .co.uk/news/article-445979/Teachers-drop-Holocaust-avoid-offending -Muslims.html.

36 Andy Dolan, "Muslim Bus Drivers Refuse to Let Guide Dogs on Board," *Daily Mail,* July 19, 2010, http://www.dailymail.co.uk/news/article -1295749/Muslim-bus-drivers-refuse-let-guide-dogs-board.html?ito =feeds-newsxml.

37 Soeren Kern, "Creeping Sharia Slides Over Britain," Hudson Institute, November 11, 2010, http://www.hudson-ny.org/1656/creeping-sharia-britain.

38 Dennis Leppard, "Met allows Islamic protesters to throw shoes," *Sunday Times,* April 11, 2010, http://www.timesonline.co.uk/tol/comment/faith /article7094311.ece.

39   The British royal family helped raise more than a million pounds sterling together with King Fahd of Saudi Arabia. Prince Charles himself clearly has a special relationship with Islam.

40   BBC News, "Profile: Abu Qatada," http://news.bbc.co.uk/2/hi/uk_news /4141594.stm, updated February 26, 2007; Daniel McGrory and Richard Ford, "Move to Expel 'Al-Qaeda Cleric' Will Test Britain's Resolve on Law," London *Times*, August 11, 2005, http://www.timesonline.co.uk/tol/news /uk/article554031.ece.

41   Alan Travis, "Abu Qatada: From Refugee to Detainee," *Guardian*, February 19, 2009, http://www.guardian.co.uk/world/2009/feb/19/abu-qatada -profile.

42   Tom Whitehead and Duncan Gardham, "Abu Qatada And Eight Other Terror Detainees Awarded Compensation By European Judges," *Daily Telegraph*, February 20, 2009, http://www.telegraph.co.uk/news/uknews/law -and-order/4699941/Abu-Qatada-and-eight-other-terror-detainees -awarded-compensation-by-European-judges.html.

43   Abu Hamza entered Britain in 1980 on a student visa, married a Muslim convert in 1981, got British citizenship through marriage, and betrayed and divorced his wife in 1984.

44   His name Hamza is also a kind of joke, because the hamza is a hook-shaped diacritical mark in Arabic, usually signifying a glottal stop.

45   Phillips, *Londonistan*, pp ix–16.

46   Rebecca Camber, "Even in Jail, They Can't Get Abu Hamza to Pipe Down," *Daily Mail*, November 17, 2009.

47   BBC Four profile documentary, first broadcast March 17, 2003. See http:// www.bbc.co.uk/bbcfour/documentaries/profile/abu-hamza.shtml.

48   Gilligan's series on British Islam aired in March 2010, and transcripts and clips are available at various sites. See http://blogs.telegraph.co.uk/news /andrewgilligan/100060409/britains-islamic-republic-full-transcript-of -channel-4-dispatches-programme-on-lutfur-rahman-the-ife-and-tower -hamlets-the-full-transcript/ and http://www.channel4.com/programmes /dispatches/episode-guide.

49   Interview by Eliot Spitzer of Anjem Choudary, *Parker-Spitzer*, CNN, October 29, 2010, http://parkerspitzer.blogs.cnn.com/2010/10/29/spitzer -you-are-a-%E2%80%98heinous-terrorist%E2%80%99/ and http://www .youtube.com/watch?v=IaCep_ZEaek&NR=1.

50   Pew Research Center, "Muslim Networks and Movements in Western Europe," September 10, 2010, http://pewforum.org/uploadedFiles/Topics /Religious_Affiliation/Muslim/Muslim-networks-full-report.pdf.

51   Pew Research Center, "The Great Divide: How Westerners and Muslims View Each Other," June 22, 2006, http://pewglobal.org/2006/06/22/the -great-divide-how-westerners-and-muslims-view-each-other/.

52 James Slack, "Almost a quarter of Muslims believe 7/7 was justified," *Daily Mail*, August 7, 2006, http://www.dailymail.co.uk/news/article-399352/Almost-quarter-Muslims-believe-7-7-justified.html#.

53 Nile Gardiner, "Trends in the European Union And Russia," paper at Durrell Colloquium, Hillsdale College, October 28, 2006, p. 7.

54 Peter Bergen, "Our Ally, Our Problem."

55 Alan Cowell, "Britain Sentences 7 in Terror Plot," *New York Times*, June 15, 2007.

56 Peter Taylor, "Terror charge pair unrepentant," BBC News, August 12, 2010, http://news.bbc.co.uk/2/hi/8500782.stm.

57 Claire Cozens, "French TV boss admits censoring riot coverage," *Guardian*, November 10, 2005, http://www.guardian.co.uk/media/2005/nov/10/france.tvnews.

58 "In November 2003, for example, a young French Jewish DJ, Sebastien Selam, was approached by his Muslim neighbor, Adel Boumedienne, in their building's underground garage. Boumedienne slit Selam's throat, gouged out his eyes with a carving fork and then ran upstairs and told his mother, 'I killed my Jew, I will go to paradise.'" See Tom Gross, "The barbarians of Europe," *National Post* (Toronto) and *Jerusalem Post*, February 28, 2006.

59 Joseph Berger, "Israel Sees a Surge in Immigration by French Jews, but Why?" *New York Times*, http://www.nytimes.com/2004/07/04/world/israel-sees-a-surge-in-immigration-by-french-jews-but-why.html.

60 Daniel Pipes, "The 751 No-Go Zones of France," November 14, 2006, updated January 16, 2010, http://www.danielpipes.org/blog/2006/11/the-751-no-go-zones-of-france.

61 The new French law went into effect in April 2011 and bans garments that entirely hide the face.

62 European worry has spurred Europe to reconsider its open-border policy.

63 There are varying estimates of the rapidly growing Muslim population figures in Europe. See Pew Research Center, "Muslim Networks and Movements in Western Europe"; Andreas Goldberg, "Islam in Germany," in Shireen T. Hunter, ed., *Islam, Europe's Second Religion* (Westport, CT: Praeger, 2002), pp. 29–50, esp. pp. 30–33.

64 BBC News, August 19, 2005, http://news.bbc.co.uk/go/pr/fr/-/2/hi/europe/2349195.stm.

65 Bruce Hoffman, *Inside Terrorism* (New York: Columbia University Press, 2006), p. 262.

66 Simon Reeve, *The New Jackals: Ramzi Yousef, Osama Bin-Laden and the Future of Terrorism* (Boston: Northeastern University Press, 1999), p. 231.

67 Vidino, "The Muslim Brotherhood's Conquest of Europe," pp. 26–27.

68   Peter J. Katzenstein, "Same War, Different Views: Germany, Japan, and the War on Terrorism," *Current History* 101, no. 659 (December 2002), p. 427.

69   BBC News, "Merkel says German multicultural society has failed," October 17, 2010, http://www.bbc.co.uk/news/world-europe-11559451.

70   J. N. Westwood, *Russia—1917–1964* (New York: Harper & Row, 1966), p. 29. Over the years other police/intelligence units included the army's GRU and NKVD as well as the KGB.

71   Lenin himself spoke of "exterminating" his opponents, whom he called "vermin." See Richard Pipes, *The Unknown Lenin: From the Secret Archive* (New Haven, CT: Yale University Press, 1998), pp. 10–11. "With the evidence currently available," writes Pipes, "it becomes difficult to deny that Lenin was, not an idealist, but a mass murderer, a man who believed that the best way to solve problems—no matter whether real or imaginary—was to kill off the people who caused them" (p. 181).

72   This is but one of many messages and memoranda cited by Robert Conquest, *The Great Terror: A Reassessment* (New York: Oxford University Press, 1990), pp. 286–87.

73   George F. Kennan, *Russia and the West Under Lenin and Stalin* (Boston: Atlantic Monthly Press, 1960), p. 307. Kennan and Conquest show that some officials were afraid of not showing enough enthusiasm for their murderous tasks, knowing only too well that today's judges could become tomorrow's victims.

74   The anti-Nazi resistance in Europe largely failed. A biographer of Churchill wrote: "those who heeded his call to 'set Europe ablaze' would pay a terrible price for doing so." See John Keegan, *Churchill* (London: Weidenfeld & Nicolson, 2002), p. 128.

75   The comment, apt for the next seventy years, was made by A. Ksiunin in *Vechernye Ogni*, no. 55 (June 22, 1918): "Whatever happens, it is better not to look out the window." Richard Pipes, *The Russian Revolution* (New York: Vintage, 1991), pp. 841–42, note on p. 914.

76   There are well-substantiated charges the Putin regime has assaulted and even murdered troublesome journalists, most notably investigative reporter Anna Politkovskaya in Moscow on October 7, 2006.

77   All forty-one terrorists died, but none of the Russian special forces. Authorities later claimed the victims died of asphyxiation and fatigue. Some doctors said they might have saved more victims had Russian authorities divulged the nature of the poison gas used in the abortive rescue raid.

78   John Dunlop, *The 2002 Dubrovka and 2004 Beslan Hostage Crises: A Critique of Russian Counter-Terrorism* (Stuttgart: Ibidem-Verlag, 2006), p. 22. He and other observers raise the possibility that Russian authorities did not stop some terror attacks because terror solidified Putin's leadership.

79   Stephen Lee Myers, "In Russia, Terror Also Vanishes From the Radar," *New York Times*, August 29, 2004, http://www.nytimes.com/2004/08/29

/weekinreview/the-world-in-the-dark-in-russia-terror-also-vanishes
-from-the-radar.html.

80 The Soviet regimes used their own terror, what Pipes has called "unprec-edented application of largely random terror," against those who resisted their policies: tremendous force, systematic torture, concentration camps, show trials, even mass starvation, to suppress "counterrevolutionary" move-ments of the "White" (anticommunist) forces, as well as "deviators" (for example, socialists, social democrats, and even internal Communist Party ri-vals). See Pipes, *The Russian Revolution,* esp. "The Red Terror," pp. 789–842.

81 Myers, "In Russia, Terror Also Vanishes From the Radar."

82 Donald N. Jensen, foreword to Dunlop, *The 2002 Dubrovka and 2004 Beslan Hostage Crises,* p. 13.

83 Gordon M. Hahn, *Russia's Islamic Threat* (New Haven, CT: Yale University Press, 2007), pp. 217–19.

84 Estimates for 2009 show a 30 percent increase in terror attacks over 2008. Gordon Hahn, *Islam, Islamism, and Politics in Eurasia Report,* nos. 2 and 3, November 20 and 30, 2009, respectively, http://www.miis.edu/academics /faculty/ghahn/report.

85 Ellen Barry, "Russian Envoys Back European Criticism of Kremlin's Cau-casus Policy," *New York Times,* June 23, 2010, p. A4.

86 Richard Boudreaux, "Bombing in North Caucasus Kills 16, in Blow to Kremlin," *Wall Street Journal,* September 10, 2010.

87 Putin's office has actually released publicity photos of him sitting bare-chested on a horse.

88 Putin said that 15 percent of the population of the Russian Federation was Muslim and that most inhabitants of eight of twenty-one autonomous republics were Muslim. Jacques Lévesque, *Le Monde Diplomatique,* English edition, December 5, 2008, http://mondediplo.com/2008/12/05russia.

89 Jamestown Foundation, "Insurgency Related Violence Reported in Dage-stan, Ingushetia and Kabardino-Balkaria," *Eurasia Daily Monitor* 7, no. 221 (December 13, 2010).

90 Hahn, *Russia's Islamic Threat,* p. 1.

91 Ibid., p. ix.

92 Before Putin, Prime Minister Yevgeny Primakov was also an ex-KGB official who specialized in the Mideast and who worked hard for an anti-Western or antihegemonic foreign policy.

93 The USSR and its satellites set up training camps, sent weapons, and offered political training for many terror groups. The KGB's Patrice Lu-mumba School in Moscow taught disinformation methods to many "Third World" leaders, including Mahmoud Abbas, successor to Yasser Arafat.

94 Edward N. Luttwak, "Rewarding Terror in Spain," *New York Times,* March 16, 2004.

95   Fernando Reinares, "The Madrid Bombings and Global Jihadism," *Survival* 52, no. 2 (March 25, 2010), p. 84.

96   Ibid., p. 85.

97   Sergio Kiernan, "Unfinished Business: The AMIA Bombing, Six Years Later," *International Perspectives,* no. 46, American Jewish Committee, July 2000, p. 3.

98   Agence France-Presse, "Argentina: Ex-President Is Charged With Obstructing Bombing Inquiry," *New York Times,* October 2, 2009, http://www .nytimes.com/2009/10/02/world/americas/02briefs-ArgentinaBrf.html. See also BBC News, "Flashback: Argentina Bomb," August 25, 2003, http://news.bbc.co.uk/2/hi/americas/3179861.stm and "Terror Argentina," http://www.jewishvirtuallibrary.org/jsource/Terrorism/argentina.html.

99   Larry Rohter, "Americas: Argentina: Freeze on Ex-President's Assets," *New York Times,* February 25, 2004, http://www.nytimes.com/2004/02/25 /world/world-briefing-americas-argentina-freeze-on-ex-president-s-assets .html.

100   Larry Rohter, "Argentines Criticize Investigation of '94 Attack," *New York Times,* July 19, 2004, http://www.nytimes.com/2004/07/19/world/argentines -criticize-investigation-of-94-attack.html?ref=carlos_saul_menem.

101   Mughniyeh was assassinated in 2009 in Damascus, and it is not clear whether he was killed by Israel, by Syria, or even by fellow members of Hizballah.

102   The missiles include the Iranian Shihab 3 (range 1,300–1,500 kilometers), Scud-B (285–330 km), and Scud-C (300, 500, and 700 km), all giving Venezuela an ability to intimidate many of its neighbors.

103   C. Wergin and H. Stausberg, "Achse Caracas–Tehran: Iran plant Bau einer Raketenstellung in Venezuela" (Caracas-Tehran Axis: Iran sets up rocket base in Venezuela), November 25, 2010, http://www.welt.de/politik /ausland/article11219574/Iran-plant-Bau-einer-Raketenstellung-in -Venezuela.html and Anna Mahjar-Barducci, Hudson Institute, "Iran Helping Bolivia Build Nuclear Power Plant, Bolivia Sending Uranium to Tehran," December 3, 2010, http://www.hudson-ny.org/1692/bolivia-iran.

104   The Sikhs comprise less than 2 percent of the population in India, but they are a majority in the substate of Punjab.

105   Johnston Counter-Terror archives, http://www.johnstonsarchive.net/terror ism/wrjp394.html and http://www.johnstonsarchive.net/terrorism/global terrorism1.html.

106   An Air India Boeing 747 en route from Montreal to London exploded in midair at 7:15 A.M. off the coast of Ireland, killing all 329 aboard. The aircraft was about 110 miles west of Cork, Ireland. About one hour earlier, a suitcase taken off a Canadair flight from Vancouver, Canada, to Tokyo

exploded at the Vancouver airport. Two baggage handlers were killed and four injured. It was concluded that the suitcase bomb exploded prematurely, having been intended for transfer to an Air India flight. Another bomb exploded at Tokyo International Airport before being transferred from a Canadian jetliner to a flight bound for Bombay. The Indian government believed Sikh extremists were responsible.

107 William Maley, "The 'War against Terrorism' in South Asia," *Contemporary South Asia* 12, no. 2 (June 2003), p. 206, http://dx.doi.org /10.1080/0958493020001476.

108 Angel Rabasa et al., *The Lessons of Mumbai* (Santa Monica, CA: RAND, 2009), http://www.rand.org/pubs/occasional_papers/OP249/.

109 "Islamic Extremism in India: The Rise of Homegrown Jihad," *Strategic Comments* 15, no. 3 (April 2009), http://www.informaworld.com/smpp/ti tle~db=all~content=t724921302~tab=issueslist~branches=15-v15, pp. 1–2, http://dx.doi.org/10.1080/13567880902941890.

110 Many other successes are far less dramatic, but they are still closely guarded secrets. Some successes involve merely protecting one's own population effectively by having well-drilled emergency plans. For a good summary of Israel's successes in counterterror organization and civil defense, see Leonard A. Cole, *Terror: How Israel Has Coped and What America Can Learn* (Bloomington: Indiana University Press, 2007).

111 Nadav Shragai, "Releasing Terrorists: New Victims Pay the Price," Jerusalem Center for Public Affairs, *Viewpoints* 8, no. 8 (August 24, 2008). See also report by Almagor Organization—Israeli Victims of Arab Terror—at http://www.al-magor.com/almagor%20investigation.htm.

112 PLO documents confiscated at Orient House in 2002 show Arafat signed off and paid for attacks by Fatah's own Al-Aqsa Martyrs Brigade. The documents were edited by the author.

113 This table was reproduced from the Jewish Virtual Library, based on statistics compiled by Israel Ministry of Foreign Affairs, "Victims of Arab Terror," Israeli media and other sources. See http://www.mfa.gov.il/MFA/MFA Archive/2000_2009/2000/1/Terrorism%20deaths%20in%20Israel%20-%20 1920-1999; http://www.jewishvirtuallibrary.org/jsource/Peace/osloterr.html; and http://www.zionism-israel.com/vic/Terror_statistics.htm.

114 Israel unveiled its "Iron Dome" rocket intercept system in April 2011.

115 Ariel Merari, "Israel's Preparedness for High Consequence Terrorism," in Arnold M. Howitt and Robyn L. Pangi, eds., *Countering Terrorism —Dimensions of Preparedness* (Cambridge, MA: MIT Press, 2003), p. 349.

116 During this post-1973 period, the one bright spot for Israeli counterterror and intelligence was the brilliantly successful Entebbe Airport rescue

mission of July 4, 1976, when Israeli commandos succeeded in releasing passengers hijacked by Palestinian terrorists to Uganda.

117   Ira Sharkansky, *Coping with Terror: An Israeli Perspective* (Lanham, MD: Lexington Books, 2003), p. 162. This view is verified by the author's own interviews with Israeli officers over the years, among them Major General Shlomo Yanai (then a colonel in charge of Jebalya region in Gaza) and Brigadier General Menachem "Mendy" Merom.

118   The captured documents from the PLO operations center in Jerusalem at Orient House include a handwritten letter of cooperation between Arafat and Yassin that was transferred by Palestinian Legislative speaker Salim Za'anoun.

119   Interview by author in 1993 with IDF chief of staff Lieutenant General Ehud Barak, later to become Israeli prime minister.

120   The set of agreements is known as the Oslo Accords, because many of the talks were held secretly in Scandinavia, under the direction of Rabin's foreign minister, Shimon Peres. The formal agreement, known as the Declaration of Principles, was signed on September 13, 1993.

121   The idea was to make it seem as if he died of natural causes, while the agents could escape Jordan.

122   Arafat conducted the deal for the ships via his personal representative, Fuad Shoubaki, to whom he granted personal sanctuary in the Palestinian Authority presidential compound in Ramallah. The largest shipment was aboard the *Karine A,* whose cargo was seized on January 3, 2002, off the coast of Saudi Arabia. Original estimates said fifty tons of weapons and ammunition were confiscated, but subsequent inventories went much higher, and they included 700,000 rounds of small arms ammunition; 735 hand grenades; 311 antipersonnel mines and 211 antitank mines; 345 long- and short-range Katyusha rockets and 10 launchers; 29 mortar tubes and 1,545 shells; six Sagger wire-guided antitank missle launchers and 10 missiles; 51 RPG-7 antitank missiles and 328 rockets; 30 high-powered Dragonov telescopic rifles; 212 Kalashnikov assault rifles; more than 2,000 kilograms of explosives; and two speedboats with powerful Yamaha engines and a range of diving equipment. The arms shipment was a clear violation of treaties between Israel and Arafat's PLO.

123   Norwegian and Swedish politicians and officials have gone out of their way to help Arab-Islamic terrorists. They have sharply criticized and isolated Israel at international forums, and have suggested anti-Israel boycotts, while offering visas to Hamas officials, as well as being the first European officials to make state visits to the Hamas regime in Gaza. Norwegian deputy foreign minister Raymond Johansen visited Hamas prime minister Ismail Haniyeh in 2007. Norway's foreign minister Jonas Gahr Stor said that Israel's military response to Hizballah's attack and abduction of Israeli

soldiers in 2006 was "unacceptable." Swedish politicians, from the late prime minister Olof Palme to onetime foreign minister Anna Lindh and Sten Andersson, have routinely characterized Israeli policies as Nazi-like. See Manfred Gerstenfeld, ed., *Behind the Humanitarian Mask: The Nordic Countries, Israel and the Jews* (Jerusalem: Jerusalem Center for Public Affairs, 2008), pp. 24–27, 31–33.

124 Daniel Byman, "Do Targeted Killings Work?" *Foreign Affairs* 85, no. 2 (March/April 2006), p. 102.

125 Efraim Benmelech and Claude Berrebi, "Attack Assignments in Terror Organizations and the Productivity of Suicide Bombers," National Bureau of Economic Research, Cambridge, MA, Working Paper 12910, February 2007, http://www.nber.org/papers/w12910. See also Yoaz Hendel, "The Lone Terrorist," Bar Ilan University, BESA Center, Perspectives Papers on Current Affairs, no. 86, July 13, 2009, where Handel notes how Hamas was pushed into an almost petulant use of mortars from Gaza to show that it was still active.

126 Byman, "Do Targeted Killings Work?" p. 111.

CHAPTER NINE: SCENARIOS AND SOLUTIONS

1 See John Mueller, "Is There Still a Terrorist Threat? The Myth of the Omnipresent Enemy," *Foreign Affairs* (September/October 2006), and "The Iraq Syndrome," *New York Times*, November 8, 2005.

2 Fawaz Gerges, "A Nuisance, Not a Strategic Threat," *Foreign Affairs* (September 7, 2006), http://www.foreignaffairs.com/discussions/roundtables/are -we-safe-yet.

3 Alan B. Krueger, *What Makes a Terrorist: Economics and the Roots of Terrorism* (Princeton, NJ: Princeton University Press, 2007), p. 132.

4 Jessica Stern, "Muslims in America," *National Interest*, April 19, 2011.

5 The author and his book are generally known in the West as Sun Tsu, *The Art of War*; there have been many translations and editions.

6 Lieutenant General James Clapper, remarks in response to question at House Intelligence Committee hearings, February 10, 2011. See http://abcnews.go.com/Politics/video/james-clapper-muslim-brotherhood -largely-secular-12886575 and http://www.realclearpolitics.com/news/ap /politics/2011/Feb/18/political_headlines___part_1.html.

7 Clapper remarks to Senate Intelligence Committee, a week later, on February 16, 2011.

8 See, for example, former president Jimmy Carter negotiating with Hamas in 2008 and thereafter, as well as Carter statements in 2010 and 2011 claiming that his experience with Iran in 1978–79 proved that he knew best how to deal with Iran.

9 Scott Wilson, "Obama Administration Prepares for Possibility of New Post-Revolt Islamist Regimes," *Washington Post*, March 4, 2011,

http://www.washingtonpost.com/wp-dyn/content/article/2011/03/03/AR2011030305531.html?hpid=topnews.

10   Barry Rubin, "Now We Know: How the Obama Administration is Going to Bring Disaster to the Middle East and U.S. Interests," March 5, 2011, http://www.gloria-center.org/gloria/2011/03/now-we-know-how-obama-administration-brings-disaster.

11   Sami G. Hajjar, "Hizballah: Terrorism, National Liberation, or Menace?" Strategic Studies Institute, U.S. Army War College, August 2002, http://www.au.af.mil/au/awc/awcgate/ssi/hizbala.pdf. Hajjar is currently a visiting professor at National Defense University.

12   Paul Pillar, "What Regime Change in Syria Would Mean," *National Interest*, March 29, 2011, http://nationalinterest.org/blog/paul-pillar/restrain-your-enthusiasm-about-syria-5089.

13   Secretary of State Hillary Clinton called Syrian leader Bashar Assad a reformer in February 2011. She and President Bill Clinton previously had embraced Yasser Arafat and his corrupt wife, Suha. Arafat was the foreign leader most frequently hosted at the Clinton White House. See Tony Karon, "Clinton Saves Last Dance for Arafat," *Time*, January 2, 2001. For a longer look at the tradition of stupidity, see Graham Fuller, "Islamic Fundamentalism: No Long-term Threat," *Washington Post*, January 13, 1992, p. A17. Fuller, a former CIA researcher and a senior analyst at RAND, was writing about an Islamic movement in Algeria that subsequently chopped off the heads of the populations of entire towns and villages (all of them Muslims) in an orgy of death that left between 100,000 and 200,000 dead from the time of Fuller's article until about 2007.

14   John Esposito, *The Islamic Threat—Myth or Reality?* (New York: Oxford University Press, 1992), p. 274.

15   During the 2011 political foment in Egypt, the *New York Times* described Islamist TV preacher Yousef Qaradhawi as a moderate pragmatist, although, speaking to the crowds in Cairo, Sheikh Qaradhawi said he would love to die a warrior's or martyr's death even while sitting in his wheelchair.

16   Ian Shapiro, *Containment: Rebuilding a Strategy Against Global Terror* (Princeton, NJ: Princeton University Press, 2007), p. 5.

17   Ibid., p. 7.

18   Leonid Brezhnev and his comrades unseated Nikita Khrushchev in 1964 because his gambit in Cuba was seen as an unnecessarily dangerous provocation of the United States.

19   Michael Armacost, foreword to Richard N. Haass and Meghan L. O'Sullivan, eds., *Honey and Vinegar: Incentives, Sanctions, and Foreign Policy* (Washington, DC: Brookings Institution, 2000), p. vii.

20   Meghan L. O'Sullivan, *Shrewd Sanctions: Statecraft and State Sponsors of Terrorism* (Washington, DC: Brookings Institution, 2003), p. 284.

21   Thomas C. Schelling, *Arms and Influence* (New Haven, CT: Yale University Press, 1966), p. 2.

22   Popular resentment of the war caused Hizballah's leader Hassan Nasserallah to say that he would not have attacked Israel had he known it would strike back so hard. After time passed and he rearmed, his public position toughened again.

23   An example of this was when Ayman Zawahiri hosted an Internet forum to explain Al-Qaeda actions. Similarly, Hizballah leader Nasserallah felt compelled to say in 2006 that he would not have killed and kidnapped Israeli soldiers had he known it would bring such massive Israeli responses that hurt so many Lebanese. See Mitchell D. Silber and Arvin Bhatt, "Radicalization in the West: The Homegrown Threat," New York City Police Department, 2007. See also Olivier Roy, "Radicalisation and Deradicalisation," in International Centre for the Study of Radicalisation, "Perspectives on Radicalisation and Political Violence: Papers from the First International Conference on Radicalisation and Political Violence," London, January 17–18, 2008, p. 12.

24   In Mexico, at Chichén Itzá, and in other Latin American locales, ancient tribes like the Maya used to have "football games" where the winners were glad to be sacrificed as part of a human sacrifice cult.

25   For example, an Israeli countermissile is 50 to 100 times more expensive than a Katyusha, Scud rocket, or mortar shell, while an armed U.S. or Israeli drone or fighter jet strike is even more expensive.

26   The United States has fought a noble and inspiring effort both in Afghanistan and in Iraq, especially the 2006 surge, but a range of local forces and local conditions conspire against America maintaining its costly presence so far from the States. Israel, too, had great immediate success in liberating Lebanon in 1982 from the PLO, even supporting elections that produced a pro-Israeli Lebanese president and a 1983 Lebanese-Israeli treaty witnessed by the United States. All of this went down the drain as local Shiite forces backed by Syria and Iran exacted a price that Israel—used to short wars—could not pay.

27   Marc Sageman, *Leaderless Jihad: Terror Networks in the Twenty-First Century* (Philadelphia: University of Pennsylvania Press, 2008).

28   For example, Jessica Stern referred to Louis Beam's use of the term "leaderless resistance" five years earlier. See Jessica Stern "The Protean Enemy," *Foreign Affairs* (July/August 2003).

29   Jessica Stern, "Muslims in America," *National Interest*, May–June 2011, http://nationalinterest.org/article/muslims-america-5167. Stern contradicts

herself by using trite descriptions like "fad" while still allowing that "things will likely get worse before they get better."

30 Fernando Reinares, director, Program on Global Terrorism at the Elcano Royal Institute in Madrid, remarks at a Terrorism and Homeland Security Forum on the 3/11 Madrid bombings cosponsored by the Woodrow Wilson Center and Georgetown University's Center for Security and Peace Studies, April 6, 2009. Reinares shows the wide variation in attacks: the twenty-seven Madrid terrorists carried out the attacks, though several were under surveillance. The Madrid attacks were led by Moroccans recruited by Al-Qaeda while the London bombings were led by men who grew up in Britain. Video of session at http://legacy.wilsoncenter.org/ondemand /index.cfm?fuseaction=home.play&mediaid=873BC330-9523-4E6A -C91368AFFD9D6F02.

31 Merari, "Israel's Preparedness for High Consequence Terrorism," pp. 354– 55.

32 Philip Bobbitt, *Terror and Consent: The War for the Twenty-First Century* (London: Penguin, 2008), pp. 534, 541, where Bobbitt says that some of the post-Watergate restrictions on U.S. intelligence agencies should not be seen as sacrosanct.

33 Ibid., p. 543.

34 See this option discussed by Gal Luft and Anne Korin, "Provide for U.S. Energy Security," and Chris Holton, "Stop Investing in Terror," in Frank Gaffney, ed., *War Footing: 10 Steps America Must Take to Prevail in the War for the Free World* (Annapolis, MD: Naval Institute Press, 2006), pp. 39–72.

35 Yonah Alexander, ed., *Counterterrorism Strategies: Successes and Failures of Six Nations* (Washington, DC: Potomac Books, 2006), p. 190.

36 Robert Satloff, *The Battle of Ideas in the War on Terror* (Washington, DC: Washington Institute for Near East Policy, 2004), pp. 3–4.

37 Ibid., p. 60, citing Adam Garfinkle, ed., *A Practical Guide to Winning the War on Terrorism* (Stanford, CA: Hoover Institution Press, 2004).

38 Bin-Laden quoted in Lee Smith, *The Strong Horse: Power, Politics and the Clash of Arab Civilizations* (New York: Doubleday, 2010), p. vii. Nasserallah frequently referred to Israel as a spider whose web was weakening, before his attacks on Israel in 2008.

39 Helena K. Finn, "The Case for Cultural Diplomacy: Engaging Foreign Audiences," *Foreign Affairs* 82 (November/December 2003), p. 15.

40 Margaret Thatcher, *Statecraft: Strategies for a Changing World* (New York: HarperCollins, 2002), p. 220.

41 In 1993 and 1996, Samuel Huntington cited figures showing the predominant role of Muslims, particularly Arabs, in five of six major wars. Huntington used three different sets of statistics drawn by Ted Robert Gurr, the

New York Times, and Ruth Leger Sivard. See Samuel P. Huntington, *The Clash of Civilizations and the Remaking of World Order* (New York: Simon & Schuster, 1996), pp. 210–11, 256–58.

42 Thatcher, *Statecraft,* pp. 221–22.

43 Steven Emerson, *American Jihad: The Terrorists Living Among Us* (New York: Free Press, 2003), p. 160. A similar point is made by William Boykin et al., *Shariah: The Threat to America: An Exercise in Competitive Analysis: Report of Team B II* (Washington, DC: Center for Security Policy, 2010).

44 Philip B. Heymann, *Terrorism and America: A Commonsense Strategy for a Democratic Society* (Cambridge, MA: MIT Press, 1998), p. 155.

45 The Clinton Justice Department's rules and views on these matters were articulated by Attorney General Janet Reno and her assistant Jamie Gore-lick. See also 9/11 Commission questioning and testimony, cited earlier, by John Lehman of former national security advisor and later secretary of state Condoleezza Rice.

46 Heymann, *Terrorism and America,* p. 156.

47 Shamir was one of the leaders of the LEHI organization in British-controlled Palestine, and he had a price on his head for several acts of terror, including the assassination of Swedish mediator Folke Bernadotte, who offered a plan for dividing Jerusalem, even after Israel had won independence. Shamir did not belittle Palestinian Arab motivations, but he made clear that he believed that the Palestinian Intifada—usually low-grade ter-ror—and subsequent terror waves subsided when met with the kind of determination that made the attacks a wasted effort. Interview with Michael Widlanski, 1991.

INDEX